CHERNENKO

The Last Bolshevik

Chernenko

The Last Bolshevik

The Soviet Union on the Eve of Perestroika

Ilya Zemtsov

Transaction Publishers
New Brunswick (U.S.A.) and Oxford (U.K.)

Library of Congress Catalog Number: 88-19993
ISBN: 0-88738-260-6
Printed in the United States of America

Library of Congress Cataloging-in-Publication Data

Zemtsov, Ilya.
    Chernenko : the last Bolshevik : the Soviet Union on the eve of
Perestroika / Ilya Zemtsov.
        p.   cm.
    Bibliography: p.
    Includes index.
    ISBN 0-88738-260-6
    1. Chernenko, K. U. (Konstantin Ustinovich), 1911–   . 2. Soviet
Union — Politics and government — 1982–   3. Heads of state — Soviet
Union — Biography.   I. Title.
DK275.C45Z46   1988
947.085′092′4 — dc19
[B]   88-19993
                                                                    CIP

Contents

Preface

The quirks and caprices of history are often surprising. They often turn mediocre personalities into famous statesmen, or contrariwise, deliver outstanding and original figures to undeserved oblivion.

Chance and circumstance combined to create the image of Chernenko as a mediocre, even pitiable figure. In actuality this image was merely a disguise that enabled him to ascend unnoticed the sharp and slippery slopes of power to the very apex of the Soviet pyramid. He remained in power very briefly, barely more than a year. Nevertheless, without an understanding of the qualities of his personality and the course of his career, modern Soviet history would be incomplete and the nature of the political changes being urged on the Soviet Union by his successor, Gorbachev, less comprehensible.

It was not a simple matter to get rid of the half-truths and misconceptions that had built up around Chernenko's person. Platitudes and superficialities usually prove resistant to the truth. I must admit that in trying to rectify them, I have often relied on evidence that is not public. First, I have relied on my own impressions of the man derived from the few occasions on which I met him. Second, I have made much use of hearsay, of reminiscences and impressions of people who knew Chernenko and worked with him. This does not mean, of course, that I just repeated what I received from such sources. Not at all. Well aware that much about Chernenko that has reached my ears could not be true, I have treated it as a point of departure for indirect inferences rather than as evidence that could be relied upon directly. In drawing such inferences, my familiarity with Soviet history and, in particular, with subcultural peculiarities of the Soviet power elites was of much help. More important by far, however, was public evidence at my disposal: primarily Chernenko's own writings. Not without a certain initial surprise, I found that

Chernenko's political views and principles were revealed in them more fully than in his political life-history.

On the whole my purpose has been not to stick doggedly to evidence in search of a rather spurious certitude but to extract from it maximum knowledge, even if hypothetical in character. To explain the process of extracting relatively rich knowledge from relatively poor evidence, let me consider for a while any closed institution — be it a prison or army barracks or a ship or a boarding school — as a situational model. The stricter the institution's regimen, the lesser the likelihood of its regulations' being violated, which means that once we know the regulations, we are in a position to predict the location and the behavior of any single "inmate" at any particular time. True, the possiblity of error remains; to the sorrow of professional managers and administrators, there is no such thing in this world as perfect rule enforcement. But under a very strict regimen, the probability of deviation from the rules becomes so small that for practical purposes it can be disregarded. It is exactly the standardization of conduct and the suppression of conflict in closed institutions that leave wide room for the prognostication of individual behavior.

What is true of microsystems, such as closed institutions, is true of macrosystems, such as, for example, totalitarian societies. The USSR is a land of uniformities caused by a variety of factors: indoctrination, regimentation, police terror and resultant intimidation, absence of opportunities for display of individual initiative, and even the imponderable but very tangible mood of all-pervasive grayness of life and boredom. All these factors conspire to obliterate personal differences, whether in attitudes or in behavior, in daily schedules, in interests pursued, and even in human characters and personalities. The only major differentiating factor is that of social roles: entirely different sets of proscriptions and prescriptions regulate, for example, the behavior of high-ranking Communist Party members and of ordinary Soviet citizens. But in either case, the regulations, however different, are highly standardized, covering the minutest details.

In achieving a uniformizing effect, written laws, statutes and regulations are not alone. There are many unwritten rules whose content and modes of enforcement are understood by everyone without verbalization. Furthermore, the cultural gap between the USSR and the rest of the world has resulted in a high degree of cultural uniformity. Meanings attached to human interactions, although tacit, are typically shared across the nation. Likewise, every Soviet citizen is from early days of life exposed to insistent, obtrusive, and strident indoctrination. The contents of this indoctrination may somewhat vary from one level of political "initiation" to another, but at each level, beginning with the Politburo and ending with some forsaken village lost in the expanses of Siberia, it produces individuals strikingly similar to one another in attitudes and behavior.

And finally, there is intimidation by police terror, always present even if varying in intensity from one period of Soviet history to another. Not without significance for the present book is the fact that police terror was at its ghastly peak during Stalin's rule, i.e. in the early days of Chernenko's political career, recounted here in chapter 1. Although direct evidence pertaining to this period of Chernenko's life has been the poorest, the assumption that in those days he behaved in exactly the same manner as all others at his level of political hierarchy has been the surest.

The reader will be perhaps surprised by my frequent use of *verba sentiendi* in relation to Chernenko, i.e. by my speaking about what Chernenko thought, felt, experienced, understood, desired, hoped for, or feared. Certainly, such phrases are not to be interpreted as mind reading on my part but merely as expressions of my virtual certainty that under given sets of circumstances Chernenko's mental life was hardly distinguishable from that of others of his social station. Needless to say, the same holds true for my use of *verba sentiendi* in relation to other figures in this book, as well as for some trivial details of Chernenko's and his *apparatchik* confreres' behavior, for which I may not have had direct evidence.

My methodology of reconstructing mental features or behavior of single individuals on the basis of general knowledge of reigning uniformities, their causation, and their enforcement has one aspect that is curious, even paradoxical. It is the fact that a methodological procedure is in this instance dictated by substantive considerations. Had my story unfolded in some other land, not as thoroughly uniformized as the USSR, the choice of this particular procedure would not have been valid. It is precisely the empirical fact of the uniformization of all walks of life in the Soviet Union that can be turned into a heuristic device and become a source of a relatively rich and firm knowledge. Contrary to Churchill, the USSR is very far from being "a riddle wrapped up in an enigma," no matter how paranoiac government secrecy in that country may be. The Communist Party leadership, while using all its power to jealously guard its secrets from foreign inspection, at the same time reveals the very same secrets to inquisitive eyes of outside researchers by its urge to keep everything in the USSR under its control, regulated, and predictable. A paradox? Perhaps, but also an incentive for us to attempt and, through hard work, to penetrate Soviet official secrets further and further, by peeling off layer after layer of mendacity and fakery that protect these secrets from exposure.

Prologue: In Retrospect

Power is a dramatic spectacle that depends on the stage set.

Time obliterates memories. Years fade, emotions die, impressions are eclipsed, but images of people generally remain in one's memory, refusing to vanish. When chance causes a memory of an encounter from the distant past to reappear in one's mind, the image may at first be pale, but suddenly it may acquire clarity, as if the encounter had happened only recently.

It was February 1984. In the chill above the cobblestones of Red Square in a gray fog engulfing Lenin's mausoleum, Chernenko was freezing, bent, emaciated, weak, and somewhat absentminded. Inhaling the chilled air and breathing heavily, with difficulty, the Soviet leader delivered the eulogy for Andropov.

On this same rostrum had stood Leonid Brezhnev when reviewing the parade on the anniversary of the Revolution for the last time on November 7, 1982. Barely a few days later Andropov ascended the same steps to eulogize the already-dead Brezhnev. Now Chernenko stood on the mausoleum, flanked by all the gray and motionless Politburo members, braving the cold. No joy could be seen on his puffy simple face with a heavy chin. If anything, he appeared a distracted, spiritually broken, devastated man. There was fear in his eyes, as if the ambition and greed for power, which had consumed his whole life, had temporarily receded. After all the humiliations he had suffered from Andropov, he had good reason to feel triumphant. Although he had not succeeded in defeating Andropov, he had outlived him. And now, no matter what his rule would bring, whether it would be long or short, prosperous or disastrous, he would leave his mark in history as the sixth leader of the Soviet Union.

Yet, far from feeling triumphant, Chernenko felt pain and sorrow, not because of Andropov, whom he had feared and whom he now could only despise. He pitied himself, acknowledging his own age and infirmity. And he was afraid, for he could foresee himself stiff with rigor mortis, lowered into the earth, and covered with a heavy marble slab in the not too distant future. Glancing up from the sheet of paper in front of the microphone, flanked by associates arrayed as if posing for a souvenir photograph in their identical dark overcoats and deerskin hats, he could not help wondering *who* would be the one to deliver his eulogy. Watching the funeral on a television screen, and seeing how Chernenko's hand trembled, I suddenly recalled a different Chernenko, the one I had met thirteen years earlier: imposing and radiating the self-confidence that goes with authority.

I had seen Chernenko twice before, and that was enough to get an impression of what he was like. Yet, when I was planning to meet him a third time, I was quite apprehensive. It was one thing to have met him in an informal setting — at the birthday party of General Ivan Khalipov, and for several minutes at the dacha of Fedor Konstantinov. It was quite another to have to meet him in an office of the Central Committee, as had been suggested to me by Gennadi Osipov.[1]

At that time Osipov paused surprisingly in the midst of our conversation, stared out the window of his apartment on Leninsky Prospekt, beyond which the Moscow morning was shrouded in a silver wrap of mist, then continued: "Tomorrow you will be received at 11 A.M. by Konstantin Ustinovich . . . " — his voice and his whole bent, slight figure radiated tension; he straightened up, rubbed his freezing hands, and continued, "Chernenko." His delicate, sharply defined lips parted in a smile.

"But remember the condition: not a single word about me. He must be persuaded that sociology is too important a matter to be handed over to the philosophers — whether Kovalchik, Rutkevich, or anyone else. The Institute of Sociology should be headed by a sociologist, and I am the most suitable candidate."

Thus, fate brought me to encounter for the third and last time the person who was destined later to become head of the Soviet state. But then, in the spring of 1971, Chernenko in no way looked like a future general secretary of the CPSU. He did not seem to be of the stuff of which leaders are made.

At that time my understanding of what a general secretaryship involves was far from perfect. The image of a general secretary I then had was a composite of what I concluded about various Communist leaders known to me personally, or heard about from others, and to a lesser extent, read about in written sources. On this basis I was convinced that a general secretary had to be arrogant, arbitrary in his decisions, and coarse toward others. These features—which I then interpreted as conscious imitations of the general secretary's style—I observed in almost every regional Party secretary I ever met. I could see their penchant for relying on clichés and handy formulae, and this led me to believe that the general secretary personified the narrow-mindedness and intellectual sterility I observed in provincial Party functionaries.

Chernenko in no way confirmed these notions of mine. When I entered his office, he was sitting in his deep armchair, looking as if he were a collective-farm accountant. His red, immobile face was impassive, reflecting neither emotion nor thought, nor even an interest in the person he was about to talk to. His lower lip drooped listlessly while the bloodless upper lip scarcely moved when he spoke. His watery eyes, which turned deep blue when he became angry, lacked eyelashes. His well-groomed hands lay still on a polished desk on which no papers, notes, or books were seen. Chernenko was dressed not at all in the usual Party style. Although he was not a fashion plate, he was quite presentable. He wore a modest brown suit with matching tie, and a gray shirt. The effect was a bit spoiled by the clumsy, thick knot of the tie.

"Permit me, Konstantin Ustinovich," I began, "in the name of the Presidium of the Soviet Sociological Association to present you with a certificate of honorary membership in the association." This was the sentence I had rehearsed a number of times and had also used in meetings with other Party figures.

Chernenko pretended not to have heard and asked quietly, "Would you like some tea?" There was a touch of irony in his voice. He was relishing the opportunity to size me up.

"Thank you, with pleasure," I said, looking away for a moment at the heavy door covered with padding and dark leather to regain my composure, and I continued, "Essentially Party work is also sociological work." I paused and looked at Chernenko, expecting him to approve this formula in the same way other Party functionaries had done. Chernenko's reaction was quite different.

"But sociological work is not Party work," he said sharply. Then he abruptly asked, "Are you a Party member?" in a tone that revealed his displeasure. "To equate scholarly activity with Party activity is a mistake. An impermissible mistake!"

Carefully (I then thought somewhat squeamishly), Chernenko took from my hands the association membership certificate I held out. He opened the small leather booklet embossed with gold.

"Are you trying to compare your certificate to those issued by the

Central Committee? Why is it red? Only a Party card can be red. Are you trying to shield yourself under the authority of the Party?"

I became ill at ease. The conversation was going nowhere, and together with it the hopes of eliciting Chernenko's support for the idea of equating sociological research with Party work. It had been hoped that Chernenko's support could save the capital's sociologists from their condemnation by the Central Committee, which shortly before had been instrumental in crushing the Institute of Concrete Social Research.[2]

In desperation I then mumbled, quite stupidly, "Of course you are undoubtedly right." If he were right, if the sociologists were indeed equating themselves with the Party, nothing remained for me but to apologize; certainly not to seek his support for the appointment of Osipov as director of the institute. I should have never expressed my agreement with him, but instead have tactfully and gently tried to point out his misunderstanding.

Trying to divert the conversation to a less dangerous topic and to avoid speaking for myself, I said, "We believe that Party work" (I frantically searched for suitable formulas) "has qualities closely resembling scholarly research. The same aspirations, the same underlying spirit."

"Nonsense!" Chernenko exclaimed even more angrily. "We do not need useless sociological surveys. Without them we know everything we need to know. The Party has a sizable army of volunteer informants. We have a complete picture about everyone. You are trying to outsmart us by distorting social phenomena to make them fit your imaginary categories. One has to confront reality in a Party-like manner, to distinguish facticity from real living truth. Time and again, you sociologists lose sight of goals, ignore ideals, calumniate our people."

"But objective information can help the Party make correct decisions," I ventured.

"What? Correct decisions!" Chernenko straightened up in the armchair and raised his voice: "The only information that the Party needs is that which proves that its decisions are correct."

Chernenko was right: since after Lenin, Party leaders have lived in an insulated social environment. The defects of their education (and culture) were both compounded and eased by their lack of contact with real life, with the world beyond their huge offices and luxurious government dachas. Of course, they had their advisers and experts who submitted reports, but they tended to choose aides who were no better than themselves. Such a selection of Party cadres guaranteed a compliant attitude toward orders received and mindless execution of them. The effects were socially calamitous in that information reaching the authorities from lower administrative echelons conformed to what they wanted to hear, not to what they needed to know. Thus, the feedback was bound to be distorted. On the one hand, information passed to lower administrative ranks was ridden with falsehoods; on the other hand, reporting to higher authorities did not correspond to reality either. A surrealistic situation ensued: the people did not know the state of mind of its rulers and the rulers were cut off from popular concerns.

Dispirited, I left Chernenko. Gradually, I found reason to cheer myself up a little. I knew that decisions concerning major social problems were not made on *his* level of administrative structure.

As could be expected, Osipov listened to my report nervously and distractedly. He concluded, "One should never talk to petty Party bureaucrats. They have their masters' conceit without their masters' powers."

Neither Osipov nor I had the slightest inkling that one day Chernenko would become the master of the Soviet Union.

Notes

1. In 1970 the recently established Institute of Concrete Social Research affiliated with the Academy of Sciences of the USSR (Institut konkretnykh sotsial'nykh issledovaniy AN SSSR) faced the threat of being closed. An inspection commission (chaired by the head of a sector of the Central Committee of the CPSU, Nikolay Pilipenko) asserted that there was a lack of Party spirit in the institute's research. It seemed that certain conclusions and generalizations of sociological studies on public opinion, the causes of crime, the motivation of workers, and so on did not fully coincide with the directives and positions of the Central Committee of the CPSU. As a result, four members of the institute were arrested; they were accused of various crimes, e.g. spreading rumors derogating the Soviet government and political system, and anti-Soviet activity. Twenty members were subjected to Party chastisement or removed from their work in the institute.

   The director of the institute, academician Aleksey Rumyantsev, and the chairman of the national Soviet Sociological Association (SSA), Professor Gennadiy Osipov, attempted to pacify the Party bureaucracy. On their initiative a series of meetings was arranged and held with influential Party officials, i.e. heads of key departments of the Central Committee, with first secretaries of a number of republic and provincial Party committees, and with political functionaries of the Ministry of Defense and state security. Participating in these meetings were members of the presidium and executive of the SSA, including the author of this book.

2. In the 1970s Kebin was first secretary of the Central Committee of the Communist Party of Estonia; Gorbachev headed the Party organization of Novosibirsk; and Eshtokin and Loshchenkov, those of Kemerovo and Yaroslavl, respectively.

1

Rising over the Abyss

*A legless man following the right path will in the
end overtake a racehorse galloping off course.*
— *Folk proverb*

It is impossible to say which of the faces of Chernenko history will preserve: that of a diligent, hardworking lad from Siberia who made it to the very top from the practically inescapable lower depths of deprived and poverty-ridden rural society, or that of a mediocrity whom the muddy waters of the Party happened to cast up to the very heights of the Kremlin.

Who was the real Chernenko: an accomplished master of intrigue who carefully avoided the spotlight of history and remained in the shadow of his patrons, or a bureaucrat whose gestures of prostration reflected the degradation of the regime he served, a man at times so lifeless that the only image people retained of him was his impaired motions and breathing?

His Politburo associates referred to him by a number of derogatory terms, such as "towel rack," "coat hanger," and "paper pusher." Other associates were more circumspect; for some, Chernenko was "an enigma capable of surprising," and "a scheming politician endowed with common sense and even a sense of humor." Still others were more blunt and referred to him simply as "stupid," or a "mediocrity on wheels."[1]

A different image seems more appropriate and correct: Chernenko as a symbol and likeness of the Soviet system that produced him, that he faithfully served, and that he incarnated. Before Chernenko all Soviet leaders were, in one way or another, more or less out of step with the social realities surrounding them. Lenin lived outside reality, superimposing ill-fitting Marxist schemes upon it. Stalin refused to be bound by

1

reality; he constructed it himself to suit his own manic hunger for power. Khrushchev was ahead of his time;[2] his schemes did not fit the social framework of a totalitarian structure. Brezhnev lagged far behind his time; he just plodded through his long term of office without making any significant change. Andropov did not live long enough to measure up to his time. Only Chernenko adapted himself to the social context of his time perfectly. Herein lies the key to understanding him. It follows that his personality is to be deciphered through insight into the peculiarities of Soviet society, which at this particular stage of its growth, or decline, conferred the top leadership position on a leader who was quite different from all his predecessors, a nondescript character, a personification of the Party line. The Soviet state was apparently stable enough to afford a physically and intellectually feeble leader. The weakness of the ruler's personality can be taken as proof of the continued strength of the system.

Chernenko's personality should therefore be looked upon as formed by the interaction between his personal weakness and the immense power of the regime. This, however, only begs the question of what compelled a timid peasant boy to throw himself into the whirlpool of Party activity. Was it overarching ambition, or did peasant shrewdness also play a role? The seeds for the future were planted when the young Chernenko discovered for himself that the Bolshevik Revolution had not raised the standard of well-being but merely reallocated benefits, using violence to take from some in order to give to others, those willing to serve the revolutionary regime.

Under the impact of social cataclysms engendered by the Revolution, traditional peasant values, such as attachment to one's family, household, and soil, were destroyed. Yet, these were the values to which Chernenko was exposed as a young boy in his parents' home, and they were the values he absorbed, perhaps under the impact of tender loving care, perhaps under the impact of the whip. The dearth of information about Chernenko's childhood and adolescence raises the suspicion that official Party biographies intentionally absconded with whole periods of his life. The facts are reduced almost to the zero point: all we learn is that Chernenko was born in 1911 in the Siberian village of Bolshoy Tes, went to work in 1923, and joined the Komsomol in 1926.[3]

What actually happened between 1923 and 1926? The Bolshevik Revolution could have left only dim memories in Chernenko's mind, but they were likely to have been ones of pillage and arson, when grain was burned to the root along with the whole estates of wealthier peasants, which initiated the class warfare in the country; in Siberia, however, this warfare ended right after it began, in November 1917.

The new Bolshevik authorities issued their two decrees: "On Peace" and "On Land." The Siberian peasants, weary of war, found much to like in the former but were rather indifferent toward the latter because they had owned land in abundance without the Revolution. As for bread, they had no desire to supply it free of charge to those who had seized power. The peasants wanted neither to starve nor to put up with harsh and arbitrary measures of the commissars from the city. They refused to have their rights trampled. Peasant resistance in Siberia fired its first shots in Cossack settlements such as Chernenko's birthplace, Bolshoy Tes.

Thirty years earlier, toward the end of the nineteenth century, Chernenko's parents had resettled in Bolshoy Tes from the Ukraine. Chernenko was always to remember his family homestead: spacious, one corner of the house dug snugly into the earth, while another corner, covered with grass and moss, abutted on a rivulet that was shallow in the summer but abounding in water—and fish—in spring and fall. Although the family owned seventy-five *desyatinas* of land (1 desyatina=2.7 acres), which meant fifteen per capita, Chernenko's father did not like farming. He preferred to hire himself out for seasonal work, first in copper mines, and then at gold diggings in the hope of striking it rich quick. His wife worked in the fields; she was tall, strong, and efficient, capable of lifting and carrying sacks weighing three *poods* (1 pood=36 pounds).

The Chernenko's son Konstantin (Kostya) was puny and sickly. This is why, upon his completion of primary school, rather than be put to work he was sent off to a boarding school in the town. There he did not distinguish himself by diligence or accomplishments. Soon after matriculating he dropped out to enlist as a soldier in one of the *prodotryady* units set up to enforce mandatory deliveries of farm produce. The soldiers of these units behaved toward the peasants like soldiers at war toward the enemy: they conducted searches for bread as if it were enemy weapons caches. They drove holes in walls with ramrods, they broke into cellars with grenades, they plowed up kitchen gardens with bayonets. And they took hostages to be shot if the unit did not succeed in requisitioning the amount of grain envisaged by the plan.

The peasants attempted to resist: they slaughtered livestock, refused to harvest their crops, and occasionally killed an overzealous Soviet requisitioner or two. The reprisals increased in cruelty. The Party declared war on the countryside: from a policy of social discrimination against the peasantry, it shifted to a policy of liquidation of the peasantry as a class. The way of life and economic basis of the livelihood of dozens of millions of peasant families were ruined. Their property was confiscated when they were forced to join the collective farms (*kolkhozy*). The process of "remolding" (*pereplavka*—Stalin's term) the peasant into a collective farmer (*kolkhoznik*) involved the physical annihilation of the kulak class.

The term *kulak class* had never been really defined. The semantic indeterminacy allowed the Communists, whenever they found it convenient, to broaden the scope of this concept at will. Thus, they included within it various categories of peasants: those who relied on hired labor (in 1918–20), well-off peasants who owned a nice house and some livestock (1920–28), and in the end, poor peasants, if they resisted collectivization, were conveniently referred to by the specially coined term *podkulachnik*, or protokulak.[4]

The norms of dekulakization (i.e. peasant household liquidation) were precise: 5 to 7 percent. In absolute figures the targets would be passed from provincial authorities to the regions, and then local Party authorities would break them down by village soviet jurisdictions. Village soviets (councils) would compile lists of prospective victims, using the occasion to settle old scores, to satisfy envy, and to collect bribes. The operation proceeded by several stages. At first wealthy peasants were taxed. Exorbitant as these taxes were, they kindled the victims' hopes that by impoverishing them the state would get what it wanted and spare them. Then the arrests began. Peasants who had resisted collectivization were shot in prison, and the rest, after several months' confinement, were exiled to "special settlements," with all their property being taken away, ostensibly to be returned to them later. The prisoners were dispatched to their destinations in sealed freight cars on a journey that often lasted several months. Then they were unloaded, right onto the snow in the taiga. The sick, the children, and the elderly did not survive for long. The able-bodied and strong pulled down trees and with their bare hands dragged or rolled them to suitable sites, and there built themselves shelters and workshops under the watchful eyes of the commanders and team bosses. They were on their own in regard to finding themselves food.

Trains transporting kulaks began to arrive in the Krasnoyarsk Territory in 1929. There were not enough KGB personnel (chekists) to meet, unload, and resettle the exiles, so Komsomol members were mobilized for the purpose. Chernenko was one of these. He was not one who had private scores to settle with these unfortunates, nor was he a thoroughly indoctrinated activist, but he did hold Stalin sacred. His attitude was that of unquestioning obedience to, and total prostration before, the all-powerful Party. In addition, this frail adolescent harbored an instinctive hostility toward the independent and resourceful peasants he was to deal with. Yelling, intimidating Party instructors warned: if you show any compassion, if you prove indecisive or weak-kneed, you yourself, though young and innocent, will not escape becoming transformed into a class enemy.

Chernenko had no doubts: the kulaks were betraying the Revolution, burning grain, raping women, killing children. They were parasites and everything about them was repulsive, including their views. Chernenko believed that the kulaks were responsible for all the misfortunes, all the hardships, all the disarray, and above all the hunger. The only remedy was to destroy them; this would automatically guarantee happiness, serenity, and abundance.[5] In this state of mind Chernenko performed his duties. He guarded the kulaks at work, and those who were sick and dying on their barracks bunks. He also chased emaciated and frightened kulak children away from the railway stations, where after having made their way through fields and woods so as to circumvent police roadblocks, they congregated to beg for alms.

Chernenko was earning something of higher value than the gold his father dreamt of: the trust of the Party. He realized that the favor of the Party meant more than riches, that this was where power and prestige originated. He believed that violence and cruelty ultimately served compassion and justice. He perceived life through the prism of the ideology or philosophy of the class struggle. By granting to the higher-ups unquestioning compliance, Chernenko discovered a path to power.

On the tide of the first massive purge of Soviet institutions in Siberia Chernenko advanced into the Party *nomenklatura*. (The *nomenklatura* is a group of official positions that can be filled only by decisions of Party organizations; included are all positions of any significance, whether political, public, state, economic, or scientific. For a fuller discussion of this concept see *Lexicon of Soviet Political Terms* by Ilya Zemtsov.) In 1929 he was appointed the head of the Department of Agitation and Propaganda (Agitprop) the Komsomol organization in Novoselovo. At that time the town was small; it had 14,000 inhabitants, one flour mill, one distillery, and several artisan workshops. And only 800 Komsomol members. One of Chernenko's first assignments was to check the biographies of the local functionaries. Some fell into a first category, which meant that they were arrested and shot. Others fell into a second category, which meant that they were dismissed from their posts and exiled to polar regions. Those who fell into a third category were merely demoted and evicted from their apartments.[6]

Chernenko was one of the organizers of the "light cavalry" units of the Komsomol. The task of these units was to discover (but not punish, because punishment was a prerogative of the GPU, forerunner of the KGB) the saboteurs of production, negligent and lazy workers. The fear that gripped the entire nation of being "discovered" as belonging to some type of enemy was for Chernenko a blessing. He enjoyed the trust of the Party and he repaid it with devotion. He volunteered for tasks without waiting to be ordered. If denunciations were needed, he would write them; if a trial witness was sought, he was ready to oblige; if workers had to be found for a *subbotnik* (an extra day of "voluntary" labor) he would find them. He demonstrated a zeal to serve: to indoctrinate, organize, do whatever he was called for. He did not like to read, hated music, and had no particular attraction to nature. Komsomol work meant everything to him.

Then suddenly a snag occurred in Chernenko's career. Its progress was halted for three years. The fall of 1930 found Chernenko serving as border guard in Kazakhstan. How had he ended up there? Had he been overzealous in persecuting the miserable peasants and failed to respond in time to new ideological trends? In fact, in the spring of 1930 the authorities chose to announce that the excessively speedy collectivization was an error. The new tenet was that agriculture should not be collectivized by force.[7] Like houses of cards, collective farms in Siberia began to fall apart and the blame fell on those who had set them up. Chernenko was one of these. However, one also cannot exclude another possibility, even if a rather unlikely one, that at a certain point Chernenko got fed up, that having been nurtured on traditions of peasant common sense and tolerance, he might have found himself too repelled by the methods required of him and decided to leave the whole bloody mess. When in 1930 he reached draft age, he had such an opportunity.

There exists still another possibility: Chernenko fell victim to a mystification; that the widely propagandized myth of the chekists as fearless and untainted "knights" of the Revolution succeeded in winning Chernenko's heart and mind. Or more pragmatically, Chernenko may have believed that service in state security bodies (which included the border guard units) could bring him more rapid advancement and higher rewards than service in the Party.

Chernenko himself suggested the romantic explanation of the military episode in his biography when he wrote:

> You know that for the Soviet country the early 1930s was not an easy time, but there was pathos in making socialist construction advance in all directions: in administration, economy and culture. The whole country was seized by enthusiasm for labor. . . . Serving on the border was the most cherished dream of Komsomol members of that time.[8]

However, this version raises suspicions precisely because it is included in an official biography and therefore intended as an "educational" example to raise people's "consciousness." Particularly suspect is Chernenko's assertion that he volunteered to serve in the border guards.[9] Volunteering in the USSR is never totally voluntary; an element of coercion is always present. Most likely, his decision was influenced by the unfortunate turn his Komsomol career had taken, and possibly also by a degree of dissatisfaction with that career. Certainly his inner deliberations about what to do were affected by ideological stereotypes.[10]

Military service could hardly have lived up to Chernenko's expectations. For days the border guards did not dismount from their steeds. Exposed to malaria and burning heat, they lacked water and food. They survived by hunting. There were constant states of alert — a day did not pass without their having to pursue those seeking to escape the bounds of Soviet life. They would constantly patrol the border, often receiving the order "to arms." In exhaustion, they tied themselves to their saddles in order not to fall to the ground. The miserable fugitives they had to face at dagger point were hardly more exhausted than they were.[11]

The deprivation and mindlessness of such a life were the antithesis of the secure existence Chernenko had experienced in Novoselovo. There he not only had had a large bright room in a shared apartment and a warm cozy office in the Komsomol Regional Department in the same building where the regional Party functionaries officiated but also had received handsome rations and had had access to a comfortable dining room for important officials. Still, Chernenko soon got used to the military uniform and even to the constraints of its high stiff collar. But he found it much harder to adapt both to the mountain snows, which under the icy wind could become as solid as stone, and to the blasting sun of the desert. He had to sleep in his riding breeches without loosening his belt so he could jump to his feet and take his place in formation in the prescribed sixty seconds after the alarm was sounded.

Mess was in the barracks: a long hall smelling of slops and filled with tables made from rough boards. The men sat according to rank: first the head of the post, next the commissar, the commanders of units, and then junior officers. They would observe the orderly closely as he apportioned the food, although whatever he dished out was not enough, whether a hunk of bread, a bowl of oat soup, or rotten herring, which fell apart at a touch and left a foul taste in one's mouth. On major holidays a smelly slab of butter and some sugar were added to their portions. By the end of the meal the unhealthy food would bloat the stomachs of the fighters, and an hour later its digestion would give them abdominal pains.

Fifty years later a sycophantic biographer would write the following about Chernenko's border guard service: "In skirmishes with the bandits the young fighter showed uncommon valor and courage. He fired accurately from the rifle and hand machine-gun and hurled grenades right on target. He was also considered an excellent horseman and was always assigned as group commander in border defense assignments."[12]

In all probability Chernenko was less than enthusiastic about this service. Amid severe deprivation and sleepless nights, whatever patriotism he might have felt could only be dissipated in the very first months of service. His memory must have recalled fragments of his comfortable past life and stirred his desire to return to it.

Then opportunity knocked. Since his border post was undermanned and few of the men were literate, Chernenko was charged with responsibility for an educational program for new recruits. Owing to his Komsomol experience, he was good at lecturing. Consequently, he was entrusted with conducting regular political instruction sessions, a responsibility that entailed his being recommended for Party membership. Chernenko conducted the propaganda work with such enthusiasm and zeal that he soon found himself being returned to a familiar sphere of activity: he was chosen Party secretary of the post and sent as delegate to a conference of border guard Party members.

When his compulsory service was about to end, Chernenko declined the offer to extend it, although this would have meant a promotion to officer rank, and thereafter studies at a military school. Instead he returned to Novoselovo, where he regained his niche in the *nomenklatura* "paradise" he had lost three years earlier. He found a sinecure in the regional Party committee (*raykom*), where he was put in charge of the propaganda department.

At that time the country was already leaving behind the realm of reality, and Chernenko followed suit. The world he was living in was the one of total fiction: imaginary plans, doctored statistics, nonexistent achievements. It seemed to him — and to millions of others — that socialism was just around the corner. Just one more sacrifice, one final effort and the reign of rationality and justice would be attained.

The Party stressed that to achieve this leap into utopia it was imperative to abolish illiteracy. By threat and intimidation, in accordance with Moscow's dictate, Chernenko demanded, and received, from the local authorities the quotas and deadlines he needed. The resulting directive required that by 1935 there remain not a single factory employee who could not read and write, that by 1936 all young children be enrolled in school, and that during 1937 a network of literary programs encompass every single factory and plant in the region.[13]

Education naturally desired by the people was no longer sufficient. The acquisition of literacy became a legal obligation; failure made one liable to criminal prosecution.[14] But Chernenko was satisfied with these conditions. With force and violence he was determined to bring his region into the society of the future. And the Party leadership of the territory was satisfied with his performance, to the point that it charged him with the task of improving the life of another region. He was appointed head of the Propaganda Department of the Uyarsk Party *raykom*. There Chernenko discovered that the workers were lazy, so he decided to expose them to some physical education to make them fit for heroic labor and the defense of the country. "Exposure" meant sending them via Komsomol "travel assignments" to work in Siberia, where in the absence of living accommodations, they had to dig bunkers in the earth as their home. At that time Chernenko got, and implemented, the bright idea of constructing a 20,000-seat stadium in a regional center with a total population of 13,000. Still, he was in line with ideological demand for giant constructions supposed to reflect the greatness of the era lived through. The stadium naturally soon fell into disrepair as a result of disuse, at first being put into service for garbage disposal and then being converted into a detention center. Yet, such a monumental white elephant propelled him to territorial prominence.

In 1938 Chernenko was appointed director of the Krasnoyarsk House of Party Enlightenment, and a year later, deputy head of the Agitprop Department of the Territorial Party Committee (*kraykom*). Here Chernenko faced the challenge of molding ideologically a territory equal in size to Western Europe, comprising one province, two national districts, forty-three regions, fourteen towns, dozens of urban settlements, and more than a thousand collective and state farms.[15]

In this vast expanse Chernenko had no trouble finding fertile territory for his propaganda work. Diverse peoples had lived for centuries in the boundless spaces of the North along the Yenisey River as well as in the southern fringes of Krasnoyarsk territory. The Khakass, the Nganasan, and the Evenki people had until then managed to create and preserve their original cultures. But the Party decided to destroy their ethnic identities by assimilating them all into the Russian culture. Socialist concepts and values were imposed on the mental world of these peoples so as to destroy their traditional values. Their traditional life-styles began to fall apart. Native skin-tents (*chumy, yurty*) covered with warm reindeer or walrus skin began to vanish. In the midst of the taiga there rose apartment houses with board roofs quite unsuitable to northern skies. Even heavy sheepskin (*tulupy*) and fur coats were "evicted" from their traditional habitats by poor-quality clothing that was uncomfortable and offered little protection from the cold.

Clubs were speedily set up to carry out mass indoctrination. In 1937 there were only 700 such clubs; by 1940 there were 1,763. A broadcasting network was established to disseminate Communist ideas and mold minds.[16] With pride, Chernenko reported to the Central Committee the results of his work: "230,000 workers, employees and collective farmers were regularly subscribing to newspapers."[17] Moscow was favorably impressed with the ardent and energetic activist, and named the thirty-year-old Chernenko secretary of the Party *kraykom* for propaganda. Thus, he became one of the top leaders of the territory, with considerable powers concentrated in his hands. This happened in early 1941.

On June 22, 1941, war broke out, putting an end to his governance in Krasnoyarsk. But in the months just before people did not yet think the war being fought in faraway places would reach them. There were rumors to the effect that an attack on the Soviet Union by Germany was imminent, but the Party explained that they were falsehoods, spread with provocative intent.[18] In conformity with instructions, Chernenko dispatched to enterprises and offices of the territory his team of more than 1,500 propagandists to explain the "unwavering and indestructible" alliance between Moscow and Berlin. All the manpower under his authority was used for that purpose. Chernenko himself was getting ready for an inspection tour of his fiefdom. He planned to visit dozens of towns and regions scattered for 2,000 to 3,000 km along the Yenisey Valley, from the foothills and mountains of southern Siberia to the shores of the Arctic Ocean. He planned to survey his subjects and to confirm himself in his new position. From now on for him there would be neither fawning nor comradely hobnobbing. His behavior would be strict, businesslike, demanding, and if necessary stern and merciless, as befits a representative of the Party. It would be inappropriate now to be polite, sociable, readily responsive, as in the past, when he sought the favor of superiors or the good graces of colleagues.

It seemed a good idea to rearrange his work schedule. Meetings would be held at nighttime, to produce the impression that he was a hardworking type who spared no effort. (Stalin himself set such a schedule, and it was aped throughout the country.) He would receive people only by previous appointment. With his two chauffeurs, he would be courteous but reserved: he would preserve a dignified distance, exchange a few words about their families and health, and then withdraw, as behooves a busy person who knows how to plan his work and make the best use of his time.

Getting used to others' servility came easily, especially because it boosted his self-esteem. But it was another thing to get used to the telephones in his office, of which there were six: a government *vertushka* for contact with local high officials; the *VCh*, high-frequency for long-distance direct calls to Moscow; two intercoms; and two for regular local calls. Chernenko found himself constantly getting mixed up; to answer his secretary, for instance, he would reach for a long-distance phone. He was also uncomfortable about having a room (with a bath) adjacent to his office. After all, what time did a dedicated official have to rest on the job?

What was important was not to get ruffled, not to let others see how confused, upset, and apprehensive he was about his ability to meet his responsibilities. For a thirty-year-old it was no joke to be put in the position of a boss over the entire territory. True, he was not the top boss; there were two others. But he was the youngest of the three, and hence would probably go farthest. In the very near future he could reasonably expect to become a member of the Supreme Soviet and attend the next Party Congress. The previous, 18th Congress had been held in 1939, and it was reasonable to expect that the next one would be held in 1942 or 1943. With a little bit of luck, he could even become a member of the Central Committee, as had his neighbor, Nikolay Pegov, secretary of the Far East *kraykom*, or at least a candidate member. Given the fact that his current position was secretary for ideology in a territory that was the largest and richest in the entire country, Chernenko had reason to hope for full Central Committee membership. After all, Krasnoyarsk Territory had tremendous resources. There was coal, oil, and precious metals. The diversity of its soils and climates pointed to a vast potential for the development of agriculture, for cultivating grain and breeding livestock. And the ocean in the North beckoned with the promise of intensive fishing industry.

Forced industrialization was in full swing, spelling ruin for the rural areas. In 1940 industrial production output grew by a factor of 20.8 in comparison with 1913 (the year Soviet statisticians are fond of using as a comparison base). Huge enterprises were constructed, including plants for building heavy machinery and combines, and shipyards. Coal mines and strip-mining areas proliferated.

The Krasnoyarsk Territory was also distinguished as an important part of the Gulag archipelago. Dozens of "corrective labor" (i.e. concentration) camps were located there.[19] The mass terror of the 1930s is usually explained by Stalin's desire to get rid of the revolutionary generation of Old Bolsheviks in order to replace them with Party functionaries totally subservient to him. This can at best be only a partial explanation of Stalin's motives. There was another, no less important reason: the need to create vast manpower reserves to be assigned to the new constructions of socialism. The conveyer belt designed to supply that manpower was a model of simplicity and efficiency. Each province received arrest quotas: so many "enemies of the people" had to be delivered by a specified date.

The arrest quotas explain how 3 million prisoners (or 1.5 times the resident population of the territory) found themselves in Krasnoyarsk.[20] The GULAG (Gosudarstvennoe upravlenie lagerey), or State Directorate of Camps, under the authority of the NKVD, performed a major role in running the economy. The prisoners labored in lumbering, in the woodworking industry, in copper mines and diamond mines. Included also in this system were prisoner-staffed laboratories that worked for military industry. Chernenko believed that it would be a good idea to get on the good side of NKVD chief Lavrenty Beria. And apparently he succeeded because in 1941, when terror in the country was already on the wane, in the Krasnoyarsk Territory the frenzied campaign of exposures of "wreckers and saboteurs"[21] was still raging.

Chernenko had to be wary in the choice of persons he associated with. He would endanger himself if he consorted with tainted family members of "enemies of the people." The same applied to the women he pursued, in view of the interest the Party was taking in the private life of its members. Given these circumstances, Chernenko apparently felt it would be safer not to tempt fate by taking his summer vacation of 1941 at one of the coastal resorts on the Black or Azov Sea. It was preferable to rest at the local resort, Shira. Of course, it would have been more fun at Sochi, at the "Riviera of the Caucasus"[22], where there were no Party stalwarts.

In the end Chernenko did not manage to have any vacation in the summer of 1941, either on the Black Sea or at a local Siberian resort. War broke out, shattering his dreams of an easy path to success.

At the beginning of July a defense committee was established in Krasnoyarsk, with Chernenko as a member. He became head of a special division that supervised all departments of the *kraykom* in all matters related to supplies sent to the front.[23] Chernenko had to learn to cope with his new duties, and the learning took some time. Because no instructions were arriving from Moscow, he had to proceed by intuition. This frightened him.

Chernenko first decided to stick to methods he was familiar with: to issue appeals and resolutions that he believed would arouse patriotic sentiments in the population of the territory and revitalize commitment to the fatherland. The following is the text of one such resolution that he submitted to a team of the Yenisey River Steamship workers: "All of us unanimously, support our Soviet government, our glorious Communist Party. . . . We will not spare our labor or our lives for victory over the enemy. At our workposts or in the ranks of the Red Army we will defend our country, its honor and freedom.[24]

Chernenko determined that his contribution to the war effort would be to increase the effectiveness of ideological work. Because he perceived this as a task of great importance, he founded six regional newspapers and recruited 15,000 new "propagandists" to raise the morale and ideological consciousness of the people. He set up 573 posts for public listening to broadcasts, busied himself with the printing of slogans and appeals to the populace, and authorized the printing of 200,000 placards. Also, he initiated a variety of meetings: "antifascist" meetings, meetings of wives of frontline soldiers, and meetings at train stations and movie houses featuring lectures delivered by soldiers.[25]

The army draft officer of the city received many applications to volunteer. During the first three months of the war, a fourth of all Party members of the territory (7,140 out of 24,000, including 153 of the 280 local Party secretaries) were enlisted and sent to the front.[26] Chernenko, however, apparently had no intention of volunteering for army service. Long experience with Party work had taught him to play it safe. Common sense dictated to him that during wartime the rear, in addition to being safer, offered more opportunity for advancement.

A flood of refugees was streaming into Krasnoyarsk. By the winter of 1941–42 a million had arrived, half the number of the native residents of the territory. Then there began to arrive plants and factories evacuated from the European part of the country. Their staffs had to be rapidly accommodated in their new location and set to work at full capacity. On the successful performance of this task depended Chernenko's future. He could not make head or tails of the technical aspects of the task and left these matters to subordinates. They oversaw the equipping of the new factory buildings and work schedules while he was busy with drafting instructions concerning work discipline. In accordance with these instructions, the employees were attached to places of their employment, with no right to leave or change them. If they tried to do so, they were liable to the same penalties as deserters from the army. Mandatory overtime could be imposed, without upper limits; vacations and days off were annulled.[27]

Chernenko did not bother unduly about housing for the evacuees; they could be housed, often three or four families together, in bunkers dug into the earth or hastily built barracks. Rationing of foodstuffs fell short of satisfying even elementary needs: 500–600 grams of bread daily for the employed (300–400 grams for their dependents), a maximum of 2 kg of meat or fish, 500 grams of fat, and a maximum of 1.5 kg of groats or macaroni per month. Anything in excess of that had to be obtained for exorbitant sums or barter on the black market.

At one end of the social ladder, therefore, glaring poverty reigned in Siberia. Most of the ordinary workers were soon driven to exhaustion by hunger and the scarcity of all essentials. They were at the limit of their physical endurance. At the other end of the social ladder, however, there was considerable wealth amassed by speculators, many of them family members of leading Party and government functionaries. Chernenko decided to requisition some of this "black" property for defense needs and thus to bolster his own political reputation. In 1942 he issued an instruction to collect from the population (i.e. the speculators) of the territory enough assets to set up a tank column in Stalin's honor.[28] When money and valuables expropriated in the towns turned out to be insufficient for the purpose, Chernenko dispatched propaganda activists to the countryside to collect a tax in kind from the peasants (i.e. from women, the elderly, and children, for the men were at the front). The collective farmers were "encouraged" to contribute 190,000 pood of grain from their private stocks to the army stores.[29]

Stalin acknowledged these efforts by sending a telegram with thanks to the Krasnoyarsk *kraykom*. In the course of the following several weeks Party officials of the territory managed to extract from the population a further 30 million rubles and 110,000 pood of grain.[30] Although hardly expected to contribute to Chernenko's popularity in the territory, these steps, as soon became clear, did not earn him the favor of Moscow either.

In the fall of 1942 the idea occurred to Chernenko to celebrate the twenty-fifth anniversary of the Revolution by collecting gifts for the defenders of Leningrad. No fewer than fifty freight cars of food and warm clothing were "donated" by the people of Krasnoyarsk Territory. Chernenko's enterprising imagination produced such propaganda feats one after another. Krasnoyarsk assumed "sponsorship" or "patronage" (*shefstvo*) over the Karelo-Finnish front. A delegation of Party activists (without Chernenko of course, for he continued to maintain his distance from the battlefields) was dispatched to the front. Krasnoyarsk industrial enterprises sponsored the hospitals. The territory's kolkhozes registered frontline soldiers as honorary members of their agricultural teams, with promises of benefits, such as a house or a garden plot with a cow and geese. The fulfillment of these promises was set for the end of the war.[31] Perhaps the most original of Chernenko's innovations was to include a fully equipped "red corner" propaganda wagon in the makeup of "bath and laundry trains" destined for the front.

Chernenko's innovations in propaganda did not meet with any objections from the Central Committee but, to his surprise, they won no plaudits either. The Kremlin adopted a relatively pragmatic attitude toward Party work, evaluating it in terms of its practical effects on strengthening the regime and bringing the country closer to victory. For a time, ideological considerations became secondary. Thus, when it came to light that dozens of Krasnoyarsk enterprises had failed to meet their plan targets, that the construction of crucial defense installations in the territory had been delayed, and that compulsory supplies of grain from kolkhozes to the state had fallen below the norm, Moscow hit the ceiling.

The whole Party apparatus of the territory was roundly criticized, but particularly harsh treatment was reserved for Chernenko. The Central Committee resolution asserted that as a secretary of a territory, he had been personally responsible for supplying the front but failed to meet his responsibilities due to an excessive concentration on lesser affairs to the point of losing sight of the main goal. Specifically, the resolution said that "while making correct decisions, he did not succeed in converting them into practice," that he had "lost touch with the masses," and so on.[32]

Chernenko abjectly admitted the error of his ways, but evidently without the degree of conviction and resolve to mend his ways that was expected. He was severely reprimanded and dismissed from all Party posts: as secretary of the Territorial Committee (*kraykom*), as head of the department responsible for supplying the front, and as a member of the Party bureau.[33]

The threat of being drafted now hung over Chernenko: the problem was, in what capacity? He lacked officer training or any other vocational education. Precisely this factor, however, ultimately proved to work in his favor. The Party had no qualms about casting thousands of its members from the Party heights to suffer along with the plebes, and this included top leadership members, but it stopped short of undermining its own prestige. It did not want to weaken its authority by making an ousted Party secretary serve as a frontline private, or even as a political instructor of a platoon or a company. There was a dilemma of sorts, because a disgraced Party functionary certainly could not be awarded a higher rank either. The Party found a way out of this dilemma. In the spring of 1943 Chernenko was ordered to Moscow, to enroll at the Higher School for Party Organizers.

The Party school to which Chernenko was sent had two programs of instruction: the regular three-year program for low-ranking Party workers, and an elite one-year program for higher-ranking officials.[34] Chernenko lacked any higher education and therefore was not admitted to the one-year course but enrolled in the three-year program. However, either because the Central Committee bureaucracy felt sorry for the unsuccessful former *kraykom* secretary or because Chernenko, on his own devices, succeeded in gaining the favor of the school's director, he was granted one year's credit and allowed to begin at the second-year level. His study period was thus reduced to two years, but for Chernenko these were two extremely painful years, filled with the suffering of a student who does not know how to study. Lacking a systematic education, he could capitalize on nothing except bits and pieces of information that he had absorbed during his ten years of activity in the capacity of Party propagandist. All he knew were various resolutions of the Central Committee, decisions of Party Congresses and Plenums, and random quotations from the classics of Marxism, mostly from Stalin. For weeks on end he had to break his head over political economy, philosophy, law, and "the building of Soviet society" (which was included in the curriculum as a separate subject). He also had to memorize the entire "Short History of the Communist Party of the Soviet Union [Bolsheviks]" by heart. His untrained memory did not assimilate and retain information. It was hard for him to compete with his peers and pass the tests. His ego obviously suffered.

The student population at the Higher Party School during the war years was unusual. It mostly consisted of middle-aged men, either too old or too infirm to serve in the army, of war invalids, of former political functionaries (commissars) of battalion rank, and of women just beginning Party careers. The latter were miserable because they were largely recent war widows or were separated from husbands serving at the front. Under such conditions there was little femininity left in them.

Chernenko was not impressed by the pompous "socialist-realist" pseudoclassical architecture of the building in which the Party school was located. His Krasnoyarsk *kraykom* building (it seemed so long since he had worked there) was no less imposing, and the red carpeting resembled that which had silenced footsteps in the corridor leading to his office. Nor was he impressed by the Party school's huge reading room with shelves filled by thousands of books. Books were the problem in that he hardly enjoyed the hours he had to spend poring over them.

Moscow was unrecognizable. It was not the city that had greeted him in a friendly manner before the war. Now it appeared grim, with its windows covered with dark paper, and cold. He had either to walk or be squeezed like a sardine in overcrowded buses or streetcars. The contrast with the shiny black Zil limousines he had at his disposal as a *kraykom* secretary was a constant source of mental discomfort. The city was hungry, its angry inhabitants scoured stores for groats, potatoes, jam. Chernenko himself did not experience hunger. In the Party school dining-room meals were served three times a day, and food was bountiful. In addition, the students had special ration cards, entitling them to purchase powdered eggs, canned stew, or smoked meat in special distribution centers.

Compared to most Muscovites, Chernenko lived quite comfortably. The room he shared in the dormitory with a classmate was warm and cozy. Still, he felt deprived and lonely compared with the earlier period in his life when he had a five-room apartment opposite the Party *kraykom* together with his wife and son, from whom he was now separated. His brother was not serving at the front but was still far away working in distant Tomsk Province. Chernenko no longer had a complaisant aide always at hand to fulfill his orders. Now he himself felt like an errand boy vis-à-vis the professors at the school. He was alone in the big city. Hardly any of his old buddies were around the Central Committee anymore. Many had fallen prey to the purges, some had been called up for army service. Those few who succeeded in staying in the capital were now climbing fast toward the top. Chernenko did not want, for the present at least, to remind these people of his existence. He knew he could count on their help only once. This is why it made sense to wait to turn to them for assistance later, when postgraduation work assignments would be distributed.

Cultural activities were held by the school once a week at picture galleries, concert halls, museums. (The school management was trying to elevate the artistic tastes of the students.) On such occasions Chernenko felt quite uncomfortable; painting bored him, and neither history nor music interested him. Only in the theater was he capable of responding, responding to the life of beauty on the stage that contrasted starkly with the gloomy, despair-filled, drab life of the real world by which he felt so depressed. The high plaster ceilings, the sparkling chandeliers, the lively audiences reminded him of the better days of his past life. And those women who thought of coming to the theater to get warm were not like the ones who could be seen on the street in dirty quilted jackets, dragging heavy girders on sleds at construction sites. These women were young and good-looking. With some of them friendly relations might be established. Chernenko often had extra tickets to share with them, which they might appreciate.

During intermissions he heard officers on leave from the front discussing military communiques. Their comments were a far cry from the confident and uplifting reports of victory that could be heard over the radio; they were indicative of the misfortunes of soldiers ineptly and thoughtlessly commanded by their superiors. But toward the end of 1944 other types of comments could already be heard: the war was finally approaching an end. Another sign was the artillery salvos: first they were heard once a month; then once a week, as cities were recaptured or battles won; finally they could be heard almost daily, and even several times a day.

The day of victory was imminent, and to prepare for this event many of Chernenko's compatriots, including lawyers, railway workers, diplomats, and schoolchildren, donned uniforms. A rumor made the rounds of the Party school that uniforms would also be devised for Party officials, with a bronze insignia for *raykom* secretaries, silver for *gorkom* secretaries, and gold for *obkom* secretaries. Had they introduced such uniforms for Party functionaries, then Chernenko would have deserved one with gold insignia because after graduation he was appointed (apparently Malenkov had remembered him) Party secretary for ideology of the Penza Provincial Committee (*obkom*). To be sure, this was a demotion of sorts; Penza Province was hardly the equivalent of the Krasnoyarsk Territory, which was ten times larger.

Established shortly before the war, Penza Province was practically the poorest and most undeveloped Soviet province. It had few enterprises, few institutions of higher learning, a museum of local social and natural history, and an art museum. Furthermore, Chernenko was informed, unofficially of course, that the province's agriculture had been disrupted by the war and hence in particularly bad shape. Nevertheless, Chernenko was glad to get out of Moscow, for Moscow was a place where after having been cast down from the Party Olympus, Chernenko experienced the degradations of a less privileged existence. In 1945 he could scarcely imagine that forty years later Moscow would be the place of his ultimate, albeit brief, triumph, of his attainment of absolute power.

What Chernenko found in Penza was most depressing. Wooden sidewalks, unpaved streets, dirt, squalor, incorrigible drunkenness. The poverty was terrible. Apartments were subdivided by plywood partitions and thus shared by several families: local residents, refugees, and families of frontline soldiers. There was unemployment, for during the war the population had doubled, and the major industrial enterprises had been evacuated to the East.

The rural areas of the province were in a state of decay; villages were deserted, some of them entirely so. Touring the countryside, Chernenko encountered many cripples and mental retardates, for whoever was in good health had fled to the city. The forests had been felled or burned down. Only the steppe was left, but now denuded of berries and mushrooms. This province, once known for its willow forests, had wilted, its landscape barren and desiccated.

But Chernenko was still young and ambitious, and he proceeded to assume the role of ideological mentor of the province. Moscow had decided to turn Penza into a center of development of the country's fledgling chemical industry. In 1946 foundations were laid for the construction of a paper-cellulose industrial enterprise. Chernenko addressed the builders with an appeal: "In this shock-work year at a shock-work construction there are not 365 days, but 365 days and nights."[35] Chernenko's proposal was approved by the *obkom*. Work in three shifts around the clock became the norm.

Chernenko did not try—he did not know how—to get along with people, to familiarize himself with their viewpoints, to understand their problems. He preferred to deal with people from the distance of his office, using numerous assistants as his conduits. On those rare occasions when he was in the presence of workers, he continued to speak and think in clichés. It once happened that in the process of being assembled, a crane toppled to the ground, and was thus put out of commission. Engineers proposed to replace it by a system of blocks, but Chernenko vetoed the idea. He demanded an inquiry that would elucidate the political aspects of the accident. He reasoned: "Without viewing the problem politically, one cannot find the correct solution, and without the correct solution, one cannot make progress."[36] And indeed, the appropriate conclusion was drawn: "saboteurs" were found at the site.

Penza Province did not fulfill its grain targets for 1946. It could not have been otherwise. It had been devastated by the mandatory supplying of grain during wartime. The crops had been requisitioned even prior to harvest, and the small amount that remained was seized by the machine-tractor stations in payment for their harvesting services. Thus, all the peasants received for their work was a check mark in their workbooks. The barns of the collective farms were empty. Furthermore, the farmers were still in debt to their kolkhozes for the hay they fed their stock, and for the water they used for irrigation of their private plots. From these tiny 0.4-hectare plots they somehow managed to squeeze their subsistence: in the fall from various vegetables, and in the winter from potatoes that they baked or made into soup. As supplements there were only eggs and milk; there was no fruit and no meat, except on holidays when a pig might be slaughtered.

The life of the peasants was monotonous drudgery: they rose at five o'clock, milked the cows, then trudged out to the kolkhoz fields to sow or reap. After the day of work there, they had barely any strength left to weed or water their own plots. At night they fell into bed in utter exhaustion. Their homes were miserable clay-daubed huts made from bricks of manure and sand. In one corner was the livestock; in another, the chickens; in a third, close to the stove, the human beings slept and washed; and in the fourth, they ate and their children did their homework. Theirs was an existence of unrelieved sadness, bitterness, and boredom.

The hardest toilers were the women, who weeded and cleaned beets while sitting on the wet ground, sowed rice, loaded grain, and gathered straw. The lowliest and most downtrodden social class in Soviet villages, they were without rights and had no choice but to take up whatever jobs the men refused to do. The men were slightly better off in social standing. They worked on horseback transporting fodder and grain, or in stables and workshops. The "rural technocracy," i.e. the machine operators, enjoyed a somewhat higher standing because they received their wages from the machine-tractor stations and were not dependent on the kolkhoz.

At the top of the kolkhoz hierarchy stood the chairmen of the kolkhoz and of the village council, the Party secretary, and the work-team leaders. They lived in solid houses and ate to their satisfaction from the collective farm stores. Their private harvests were used for black market speculation.[37]

Such, then, was the social makeup of the decaying countryside in Penza Province when Chernenko arrived there. Had the Party leadership been interested in (or capable of) encouraging collective farmers to take their work seriously, it would have based its accounting not on acreage but on harvest yield, and it would have paid at least a minimal (no matter how meager) wage. It might also have refrained from passing resolutions as harshly critical as the Central Committee resolution of 1947. The resolution noted that in Penza Province "the reconstruction and development of the grain industry is not proceeding satisfactorily, and cultivation and harvesting is proceeding particularly slowly." The resolution further noted that on many collective farms one could hardly find eight cows.[38] But how could there be more? Like the human beings, the cows of the province had nothing to eat. Yet, Chernenko managed to find an appropriate response to the criticism from Moscow. He drafted a letter to Stalin, to be signed by the collective farmers of the province. The signatories promised "their dear father and friend . . . that the resolution of the February Plenum would become the battle plan for the laborers of the village who would spare no effort to fulfill future targets."[39]

The letter did not convince Stalin. Chernenko was demoted and transferred to Moldavia. Moscow apparently believed that Chernenko's propagandistic activity would be less damaging there (for Moldavia was too rich to be easily ruined) and at the same time more useful. In these early years of Soviet rule, Moldavia was a virgin area as yet uncultivated by ideology. A heavy infusion of propaganda was considered desirable. Thus, in 1948 Chernenko was appointed head of the Agitprop Department of the Moldavian Central Committee.

This event marked the second *nomenklatura* demotion of Chernenko in five years. The first time he was removed as *kraykom* secretary and went to study at the Party school, upon graduating from which he was assigned to the post of *obkom* secretary. From the latter post he was now being demoted to head of a department of the central committee of a secondary and problem-ridden Soviet republic. There Chernenko would see familiar sights, for in Moldavia scenes from earlier Soviet history were now being reenacted, and waves of deportations, agrarian reforms, dekulakization, and collectivization unfolded according to the already familiar pattern.

During the first three postwar years, 80,000 Moldavians (8 percent of the total population of the republic) were branded as "alien-class" or "unreliable" elements, and either sentenced to prison terms of varying length or exiled permanently to Siberia. By 1948 the waves of mass deportations were receding, so that Chernenko's role in them was limited to the last stage, when the primary target was the local intelligentsia. But collectivization soon got under way, and Chernenko had plenty to busy himself with in creating the appropriate psychological atmosphere by manipulating public opinion and reeducating the masses in the spirit of Communism.

Despite all Chernenko's zeal, the rural population of Moldavia continued to resist forced collectivization. At that time the Communists conducted their onslaught on the Moldavians according to the scenario they had worked out in the 1920s. Famine was deliberately created to break the peasants spiritually, and riots were provoked to identify and exterminate the ringleaders of peasant resistance. These measures were followed by the settlement of substantial numbers of ethnic Russians and Ukrainians in the Moldavian countryside. As the social structure of the Moldavian village was being destroyed, the preconditions for peasant resistance were liquidated. Even so, collectivization in Moldavia did not proceed as successfully and efficiently as Moscow had expected. Thus, when Chernenko entered his office in the Central Committee building on Leninsky Prospekt in Kishinev, the capital of Moldavia in 1948, over 40 percent of the peasant households were still privately owned rather than collectivized. However, dekulakization carried out in the usual form of violent harassment and dispossession of wealthy peasants failed to arouse any revolutionary élan in Moldavia. Pondering the reasons for this failure, Chernenko came to the conclusion that Party propaganda had apparently not been effective enough. Hence, he would have to do his utmost to deepen class consciousness in the republic.

Chernenko set to work in earnest. His point of departure was "criticism." Apparently the forms of propaganda in Moldavia practiced thus far were too abstract, insufficiently related to the needs of the moment. The instruction of officials in charge of ideology also must have been lacking. Therefore, in the newspapers of the republic a new regular column, "Na agitatsionnom punkte" (At the propaganda post), made its appearance. The first target of the column's "criticism" was the *raykom* of Rezina, which was scored for its failures to establish lecture facilities, organize a propagandizing team, and recruit the local intelligentsia for propaganda work. Predictably, the operative conclusion was to fire the *raykom*'s secretary. This event would have been routine except that the criticism originated not with the Central Committee but with the Propaganda Department. In terms of standard Soviet operating procedures Chernenko exceeded his authority. It is thus reasonable to conclude that he must have felt quite confident about the solidity of his position in the Party bureaucracy and that his personal ambitions ran far ahead of his relatively modest position.

Symptomatic of Chernenko's ambitions was the first article he published (anonymously), on February 4, 1949, in the form of an editorial in the newspaper *Sovetskaya Moldaviya*. Its basic idea was that with Stalin guiding the Soviet people securely and inexorably toward Communism, Lenin already belonged in the past. Thus, the press of the Moldavian Republic blazed a new trail: the idea of relegating Lenin to the past had not yet been mooted elsewhere in the USSR.

Chernenko worked hectically. He presided over countless meetings, conferences, and discussions convened on flimsy pretexts, such as to exchange views or to encourage the practice of criticism and self-criticism. Chernenko was fond of quoting Zhdanov to the effect that "where there is no criticism, there develops stuffiness and stagnation, which precludes forward movement."[40] All this feverish activity was clearly subordinated to a single purpose: gaining attention and establishing his reputation as a strongman. As for the style of his work, it remained essentially unchanged from his days in Krasnoyarsk and in Penza. It was as dogmatic and as out of touch with reality as it had been then. All the penalties and demotions he had suffered failed to produce corrective change. He seemed genuinely incapable of adapting, and oblivious to the fact that he was no longer a *kraykom* secretary or even an *obkom* secretary but merely head of a department in a provincial central committee.

Chernenko tried his best to convey the impression that he was Moscow's man in the republic rather than a demoted Party functionary. He hoped that the coming second Party Congress of Moldavia (1949) would elevate him to the post of CC secretary for propaganda, but the Congress turned out to be a disaster for him. He was bypassed in elections to the credentials committee and to the post of the Congress secretary, and his main rival, N. G. Kvasov, the head of the CC agricultural department, was elected a member of the Congress presidium. Chernenko had to content himself with the inconsequential position of member of the Congress editorial commission.

An even worse humiliation was in store for Chernenko. In his summary report to the Congress, First CC Secretary N. G. Koval did not even deign to mention ideological work. He ignored it as too inconsequential to merit attention. While devoting considerable attention to industrialization, he

discussed in detail the "Socialist reconstruction of the countryside," ritu-
alistically calling for a struggle against remnants of underground resistance, then equated with the kulaks. And he completely ignored propaganda, which for Chernenko was the key element of both collectivization
and dekulakization.

Chernenko genuinely believed that collectivization was unthinkable
except as the culmination of large-scale indoctrination, whereas the constant playing up of the "kulak threat" was an indispensable way of de-
flecting responsibility for failures of agricultural production onto convenient scapegoats. Chernenko knew, of course, that the peasants were
selling off their livestock before entering the collective farms, that they
were arranging fake land distributions, and concealing agricultural inven-
tory to prevent it from becoming communal property. What he could not
understand was how these common practices—and the concomitant failure of Party vigilance—could be "explained" to the masses and prevented
from reappearing in the future without a sustained propaganda effort.
He knew that in rural areas CC propagandists were few in numbers and
worked poorly. This was for him the root cause of all the malpractices
and disasters of collectivization.

Chernenko wondered how the class enemy was waging its struggle. The
answer he came up with (which had not occurred to Koval) was that the
class enemy heavily relied on nationalistic propaganda. This was how
Chernenko accounted for the floating of provocative rumors (about famine, for example), for slander against Party propaganda activists (for
example, that they coerced peasants to join the kolkhozes), and for intimidation of poor and moderately well-off peasants (with such threats as
that they would be deprived of their identity cards, and permanently
attached to village soviets without the right to move elsewhere in the
country). And, on top of that, the class enemy (among whom Chernenko
included all well-off peasants) was acting by stealth and deception. Dis-
guising themselves as poor peasants, kulaks were infiltrating the collective farms in order to subvert them from within and wreck the socialist
economy. They would disrupt labor discipline, mess up accounts, pilfer
common property, destroy tools, and see to it that state-set production
targets were not met. Chernenko knew this from his experience in Siberia,
but others somehow failed to realize this. Most disconcertingly and un-
fathomably the Party leadership of the republic also failed to realize this.

Of course, part of the explanation for unsatisfactory agricultural production lay in local conditions. (Chernenko had learned in Moscow that
local conditions need always to be taken into account.) The republic's
population—or at least a significant part of it—was, after all, still
trapped in a cocoon of bourgeois prejudices and biases. However, class

struggle is "merciless" (Stalin's description), and it required steadfast resistance to nationalism. Also not enough was being done, by Chernenko's standards, to restrain the kulaks on their own farms, by taxation, denial of rights, and so on.

According to Chernenko, the Party also failed to respond with sufficient severity to incidents of sabotage. By not punishing the perpetrators of such acts exemplarily the republic Party leadership implicitly allowed them to continue. To Chernenko's chagrin, the campaign against cosmopolitanism (i.e. Jews) was being waged without sufficient zeal as well. For example, the Yiddish Theater was in 1949 (!) still performing, and announcements of its performances appeared openly and regularly in the newspapers of the republic![41]

Chernenko found fault not only with the policies of the republic's leadership but also with its Party work. He believed that the Party organization of Moldavia was just marking time. It had no more than some 20,000 members, of whom almost a fifth were candidate members. In defiance of its solemn declarations to the contrary, the Central Committee was not exercising effective day-by-day control over primary organizations. Some of its decisions were inexplicable, and other decisions were not implemented because control over Party functionaries was usually slack.[42] What disturbed Chernenko most was that the regional committees had a total of only 239 propagandists on their payrolls. He decided to make a special effort to raise the theoretical level of the leading cadres. To provide an example, he enrolled in a teachers college. At the same time under the sponsorship of the Central Committee of the republic he initiated a nine-month-long upgrading program for top Party officials, in addition to the already operating two-year Party school. In 1949, 314 persons (of whom only 138 were Moldavian) were already attending the program. In the large cities of Bel'tsy and Tiraspol, Chernenko set up evening schools for the study of Marxism-Leninism, for which purpose 878 activists were selected. For officials of the local central committee, he established a permanent seminar to study the works of Stalin. To raise the ideological competence of the secretaries of primary organizations, he projected sixty-six evening correspondence schools, with the aim of making 10 percent (i.e. 2,200) of all the Communist Party members of Moldavia attend.[43] In this way during the first two years of his work Chernenko succeeded in involving 92.3 percent of the republic's Party membership in instructional programs. Still, 7.7 percent (or over 1,500) comrades escaped all exposure to ideological conditioning.

There were other unsolved problems. For example, no single work of Lenin had as yet been translated into Moldavian; as far as Stalin was concerned, only his *On The Great Patriotic War* was available plus a short biography about him. The entire library of Marxism then available in Moldavian consisted of little more than *The Communist Manifesto*. Determined to overcome these difficulties, Chernenko undertook to improve Party instruction. In 1949 alone he organized more than 45,000 propaganda meetings (with compulsory attendance), reportedly attended by a total of more than 9 million people (which amounts to nine meetings per capita, infants included). In addition to that, the republic was treated to 35,000 lectures compulsorily attended by 6 million people.[44]

While ensuring quantity, so that the republic should show amazing successes, Chernenko did not neglect qualitative aspects. In this regard, to his chagrin, he discovered that propaganda functions in the villages had assumed the character of "friendly gatherings." This description was Chernenko's own, but it subsequently was taken up by the press. Chernenko was concerned that propaganda had limited effectiveness because it was being conducted perfunctorily, with insufficient enthusiasm. In particular, he worried that in urban areas it was totally failing to involve the intelligentsia, which meant that more than 40,000 people remained beyond its reach.[45]

It came to Chernenko's attention that Moldavian literature apparently had somehow retained certain universal (i.e. non-Party) themes and that "objectivism" had found its way into Moldavian history and Moldavian journalism. Such harmful and dangerous phenomena needed to be urgently rectified. But how? Chernenko could not rely on local associates of his; neither CC First Secretary N. G. Koval nor the chairman of the Republic's Council of Ministers, G. Rud, had any sympathy for him or his ideas. This is why Chernenko decided to appeal to Moscow, specifically to the chairman of the Central Committee bureau in charge of Moldavia, V. A. Ivanov, and his deputy, V. E. Efremov. From them he eventually received some understanding and support, but not immediately. In the meantime his pet column, "In The Propaganda Department," disappeared for several months from the republic's newspapers. This was the way the republic's leadership signaled its dissatisfaction with Chernenko until the central authorities expressed support for him. In the republic, however, Chernenko was never popular, either then or later.

Chernenko revealed his true colors at a republic conference of propaganda activists at which he finally gave vent to his great Russian chauvinism. As a chief target of "criticism" he chose the writers. He had loathed these "clever scoundrels" for a long time but had concealed his feelings. Barely one month after his posting to the republic, Chernenko had already managed to be the moving spirit behind the decree of the Moldavian Central Committee of November 22, 1948, which vilified Moldavian writers, many of whom were, not coincidentally, Jewish. The charges against them were borrowed from the vocabulary of the campaign against the "rootless cosmopolitans" (Jews) waged a year earlier in Moscow. Their sins were idealizing the past, ignoring the laws of class struggle, indulging in formalism, liberalism, estheticism, and departing from the principles of socialist realism. Chernenko also followed the Moscow example in revealing the original names of certain writers who used pen names so there should be no doubt about their Jewish origin. He was responsible, too, for specific accusations, tailored to the local situation, for example, that there was a failure to recognize the exploitative nature of Rumanian nationalism, or to sufficiently appreciate the civilizing mission of the Russian tsars (who had conquered and subjugated Moldavia). In all probability, he can also be credited for inventing the epithet that characterized the writers as "Jesuits of the ideological front." He charged them as well with "a lack of principle, reflecting their devotion to their own interests and those of their friends." The mention of the writers' "friends" in this context can probably be seen as an obscure echo of the "friendly-gatherings" charge mentioned earlier.[46]

After the decree of the Moldavian CC on literature (which was formally directed against the journal *Oktyabr*) but before Chernenko's speech at the republic conference of propaganda activists, an article appeared in the newspaper *Sovetskaya Moldaviya* purporting to analyze the ideological features of literary criticism in the republic. It accused a number of well-known literary critics of "having confused ideas about artistic creation." (This fault, being merely aesthetic, entailed only an administrative measure: their expulsion from the Union of Writers. But for the additional charge of "incitement of readers against our spiritual values," which is a political crime, they were liable to receive long prison terms.)

Significantly, the *Sovetskaya Moldaviya* article appeared without a signature. This fact can be interpreted in two ways: either the article was written by Chernenko himself or it was "inspired" by him. It could not have been written by someone from the newspaper's staff for two reasons: first, it contained harsh criticism of the paper itself; and second, it could not have been an instance of "self-criticism" by a staff member because in such cases protocol would have required a signature.[47]

A salient feature of Chernenko's activity at the time — perhaps its only distinctive characteristic — was his constant search for evils to combat and causes to become involved in. In the spring and summer of 1949 the "evil" he took up arms against was Moldavian literature — whatever he could not understand, he loathed intensely. He considered it not only a threat to his self-esteem but a social danger as well. The latter point is revealed in the phraseology he used when he charged that someone "presumed to teach the Party" or that others "thought they could deceive the working class."

Still, Chernenko preferred to keep in the wings and have others do his dirty work for him. For example, he instructed his deputy, Nikolay Il- yashenko, to convene and chair a special meeting of the Union of Writers of Moldavia.[48] The agenda of that meeting corresponded closely to the contents of the above-mentioned article in *Sovetskaya Moldaviya*, fur- ther evidence that it had been Chernenko who bore responsibility for the latter.

Like the article, the meeting dealt with the "antipatriotic" tendencies of a group of writers from the journal *Oktyabr*. The personalities attacked by name were the same as in the article but with three additions: Kolpan, Borzhansky, and Altman (the second and third names are Jewish). The avowed purpose of the meeting was to "defend" Moldavian literature from being "degraded" by the named writers. The Party, acting through Chernenko's department, would not allow such "degradation." The anti- Semitic element in these slurs was readily recognizable in constant refer- ences to the victimized writers' alleged disrespect for things "patriotic," "national," or "Moldavian." Thus, they were said to be "antipatriotic," "seeking to hinder the development of young national talents," and "arti- ficially exaggerating the faults of Moldavian literature," and also "push- ing decadent theories." The anti-Semitism was officially inspired, having spread from the center of the provinces, from Moscow to Kishinev.

Mass dismissals and transferrals of Jews from authority positions in Moldavia began in 1949. Chernenko's ideological bureaucracy was among the first to be purged of Jews.[49] In due time in 1952–53, he would return to the issue of "cosmopolitanism" once again, in connection with the affair of the "murderers in white coats." (In 1952, the "Doctors' Plot" was fabricated on Stalin's orders. Well-known physicians, mostly Jews, were accused of plotting to kill top Party and government leaders. In 1953 after Stalin's death, the arrested doctors were released.) In the mean- time, however, Chernenko concerned himself primarily with rural issues. The Second Party Congress of Moldavia was approaching, and Moscow was resolved to implement full collectivization. A thousand Party mem- bers and a thousand tractors were dispatched to the countryside for the purpose, but the one-to-one man-to-machine ratio proved unsuccessful: by the end of the year 25 percent of peasant households were still uncol- lectivized. The situation stirred Chernenko to try an ingenious remedy: to organize Party propaganda in the countryside on a round-the-clock basis "to match the goal of round-the-clock work of the tractors."[50] His depart- ment published suitable recommendations in the newspapers and dis- patched its representatives to the machine-tractor stations.

Still, the intended transformations in agriculture failed to ensue. More- over, the republic failed to meet its targets for grain and fruit delivery to the state. Political consequences followed: two Central Committee secretaries of Moldavia, I. Zykov and M. Radul, were dismissed. No wonder that Chernenko assessed the position of Koval, the first secretary, as also precarious, and therefore had no hesitation about trying to get rid of his rival. He did so by informing Moscow that the republic leadership was underrating ideology and negligent in carrying out educational functions.

Having come from the Russian Republic, the heartland of Great Russian chauvinism, Chernenko was disturbed by the persistence of traditional ties between Moldavia and Rumania. He blamed the local leadership for its complacency on this score. He was further disturbed by the fact that the Moldavian language had a Latin script, which seemed incomprehensible to him and therefore dangerous. When the Cyrillic script was substituted for the Latin one, Chernenko had reason to feel relieved.

At that time Chernenko could derive some real satisfaction from his work. He had succeeded in recruiting 100,000 people for Party educational assignments: instilling Communist consciousness and creating Party-committee-sponsored atheist councils, with the aim of uprooting religious attitudes. A further development in his activity was the founding of "parents' clubs" intended to strengthen Party influence on the way parents raise their children.[51]

The Kremlim appeared pleased with Chernenko's work. He was awarded the Labor Order of the Red Banner, normally awarded to officials more senior than he. This is why criticism directed at him by the CC Plenum of the republic in February 1950 took him by complete surprise. The criticism was Koval's revenge. Koval had escaped being sacked (although, as it later turned out, only temporarily until the anniversary of the founding of the Moldavian Soviet Republic was celebrated). At the 1950 Plenum Chernenko was castigated for the unsatisfactory work of his department and held responsible for propaganda activities' being out of touch with economic realities. There were also other reproaches more routine in character, similar to the ones he himself had made against local organizations.

Thus, Chernenko was said to have committed errors in the selection of cadres and to be responsible for their inexperience and ineffectuality, as well as for their high turnover rates. The attack against Chernenko was waged on several fronts: references were made to the unsatisfactory work of clubs, theaters, and groups for dissemination of political and scientific knowledge. Finally, there was a charge directly related to Chernenko's personal sphere of responsibility: the instruction of Party propagandists had fallen below required standards.[52]

Confident of the support of Moscow, Chernenko had no intention of caving in to the criticism. Realizing that the charges against him were not serious enough to warrant his dismissal, he responded by attacking Koval. He was responsible for publication of an article in *Pravda* ostensibly directed against the newspaper *Sovetskaya Moldaviya* (for having lost touch with reality) but really directed against Koval. In the article the leading officials of the republic were implicitly criticized for not having paid sufficient attention to establishing collective farms, for concealing the backwardness of industry from public knowledge, for failing to organize socialist competition, for avoiding criticism and self-criticism, and in general for failing to be aware of, and respond to, realities. The implication ran that the Moldavian leaders were lacking in Party-mindedness and incapable of appreciating the changing aspects of Soviet life.[53]

Not content with this, Chernenko dealt a further blow to Koval. The latter had an old buddy, Tsonchev, then the director of the republic publishing house,[54] whom Chernenko accused of illiteracy and pilfering, and of being a dyed-in-the-wool bureaucrat. When Koval was finally dismissed in July 1950, Chernenko felt a new burst of energy. With a passion and intensity quite atypical of him, he lashed out in public at "persisting nationalist elements," and "hostile influences seeking to revive remnants of capitalism in the consciousness of the Soviet people."

Then Chernenko appealed to incoming Moldavian First Secretary Leonid Brezhnev to establish the proper atmosphere in the Party apparatus: to stamp out petty intrigue, to strengthen discipline, and to staff positions with dynamic, innovative, and ideologically motivated people.[55] Needless to say, Chernenko had himself in mind as an exemplar of these qualities. He was already approaching the problematic age of forty. He had suffered from his political fiascos and his falls from the Party grace. It was now or never: his last chance for doing something decisive to regain his lost eminence as a secretary of ideology. By turning his hard-won experience to good use and by reestablishing old contacts he might — if he were careful — succeed in advancing to become first secretary of some important province by the age of fifty and spend the rest of his career in assured comfort. Chernenko was determined to avoid repeating his past mistakes; to avoid any clashes with his new first secretary, and to become his confidant; to avoid bragging about his Party experience or his past merits; to keep a low profile but prove indispensable. It was not that Brezhnev attracted him by his urbanity or consideration; on the contrary, he oppressed him by his strictness and authoritarianism. It was simply that Brezhnev differed from the Party characters familiar to Chernenko. He belonged to the generation of young Soviet leaders who rose to political prominence after the war. He did not care to delve into the details of work, had no patience to prepare speeches, relied on intuition, and would not study reports prepared for him but demanded instead brief, half-page summaries. He radiated strength and independence. Chernenko realized that Brezhnev must have support in Moscow and correctly identified his patron there as Khrushchev.

Brezhnev proved to be a risk-taker. Soon after assuming his position in Moldavia, he reported to Stalin the overfulfillment of the grain delivery target by 2.9 percent,[56] notwithstanding the fact that barely weeks previously the underfulfillment of the triennial agricultural produce delivery had been reported and Koval blamed for this failure.

Chernenko knew that Brezhnev's figures were fictitious; he himself helped the Moldavian first secretary to falsify the reports. For example, the indicators of ideological work were raised and the number of religious believers in the republic conveniently underreported. For a while Chernenko may have felt some discomfort, even embarrassment, at such falsehoods, but if so, he got over his misgivings fast enough, for he was soon initiating "whitewashing" (ochkovtiratel'stvo) practices as a regular element of the official reporting system. He suggested that Brezhnev encourage such practices at low levels of officialdom, which was less risky than doctoring reports at the top before presentation to the Central Committee. The suggestion was received favorably. Soon Brezhnev was able to report to Stalin that targets for delivery of grain, wool, and grapes had all been met before their deadlines.[57]

Brezhnev's audacity and self-confidence did not faze his subordinate because Chernenko was party to the transformation of Moldavian agriculture on paper. He in fact helped Brezhnev draft reports (in 1951) about how in the course of two years the grape harvest had sextupled, the beet harvest had quadrupled, the tobacco yield had increased by 150 percent, and the economic situation of the collective farms had improved to the point of every fourth collective's becoming a "millionaire."[58]

Later, when Brezhnev was ruler of the country, the doctoring of production output reports would be referred to as "write-ups" (pripiski) and their perpetrators, if prosecuted, would be subject to serious punishment. However, in the early 1950s, the practice was still in its infancy; Brezhnev was one of the first who used it to advance himself. By winning over, or bribing, the right people in Moscow, Brezhnev succeeded in achieving recognition of the "development" of agriculture in Moldavia as a model for all other republics to follow.[59] He also succeeded in extracting from the national State Planning Committee (Gosplan) extra funds for the construction of power plants and of textile, sugar, and jam factories in Moldavia. The allocations were made at the expense of other republics.

The secret of Brezhnev's popularity in Moscow was known to a few, but those few, of course, included his trusted aide. Brezhnev quickly grasped the fact that as an outsider in Moldavia, Chernenko had no local ties that might conflict with his personal loyalty. Consequently, he began to entrust Chernenko with sensitive assignments. One of them was the organization of special flights to Moscow with cargoes of choice fruits and flowers to which notes were attached, such as "To the Great Leader from the Moldavian Workers." Similar shipments contained lamb fur, the pride of Moldavian peasants of Gagauzi origin, delicious Moldavian wines, and fine aged cognac.

At this time, while many Soviet cities were still lying in ruins, Kishinev had priority in reconstruction effort. With the sanction of Moscow, parks were laid out, skyscrapers were constructed, and broad boulevards crossed the city. Chernenko oversaw the work, ensuring that the reconstruction conformed to Brezhnev's tastes.

Chernenko also knew how to cater to his boss's weaknesses. At the republic's opera or Russian dramatic theater he would often appear alongside the elegant Brezhnev dressed in an unironed shirt, rumpled jacket, and baggy trousers. As if by magic, tables would then be arranged, beverages and hors d'oeuvres would be served. The atmosphere of noisy revelry that Brezhnev enjoyed would be created. There would be drinking and singing, and Brezhnev would be surrounded by a bevy of young singers and actresses.

All the boss had to do was to single out one with a nod and Chernenko would get the message. His assignment was to approach the young woman and inquire about any difficulties she might have in regard to working conditions, salary, apartment, living conditions, or whatever. Then he would suggest that she should speak to Brezhnev about her problems in his limousine, which would be taking him home to his luxurious dacha. This is how Nina Mirsal'skaya, Sofya Skulberdina, and other actresses and singers became soloists and received titles of honor. Moldavia with its five theaters and six music and dance groups offered Brezhnev considerable opportunities to help attractive women in need and, hence, for Chernenko to help the first secretary help them.

Brezhnev also liked to make surprise 6:00 P.M. visits in Chernenko's company to the Party school located right next to the Central Committee building. He would tour the offices and visit classrooms. On one of his visits there he met Klava Bodyul, the secretary to the director, a tall dark-eyed beauty who was the wife of the secretary of the Kishinev *raykom*. For a long while thereafter, Brezhnev ceased attending the theater because he was fully occupied with Klava. The arrangement had benefits even for those not directly involved, for Klava's husband found new career paths open to him and Chernenko was free of the obligation to attend theater premieres, which bored him.[60]

Chernenko's colleagues treated him with scorn for pandering to the private whims of his boss. Few realized how Chernenko was also using Brezhnev to further his own interests. For example, Chernenko drafted for Brezhnev an article for *Pravda* into which he slipped praise for the achievements of the Chernenko-headed Prcpaganda Department, for example, in publishing works of Stalin, Lenin, and Marx in Moldavian.[61] Chernenko found numerous opportunities to broach to Brezhnev suitable ideas, for example, to launch a republic-wide campaign to increase vigilance. Taking the cue, Brezhnev placed on the republic's bureau agenda the issue of the insufficient vigilance at industrial enterprises, quoting Stalin to the effect that in the interstices of the Soviet state, bourgeois countries were planting huge numbers of wreckers, spies, and saboteurs.[62]

At the very beginning of Brezhnev's term of office in Moldavia, it appeared that the new first secretary was handling the repٰublic with kid gloves, but in 1951 he suddenly began to act decisively against the *neugodnye* (the undesirables), as he termed them. He dismissed several ministers, pensioned off the chairman of the republic's presidium of the Supreme Soviet, and reshuffled the Party apparatus. He even put Chernenko's loyalty to the test. This happened at the Fourth Congress of the Communist Party of Moldavia when, for the first time, Chernenko failed to be selected as a member of the Congress's editorial commission. At the same time his Propaganda Department was harshly criticized for errors in local newspapers, for ideological deviations in lectures, for the primitive level of propaganda work, for failures in Marxist education, for unsatisfactory work in educating the intelligentsia, and the like.[63]

Chernenko gave no sign of resentment. In fact, he hastened to congratulate Brezhnev on the occasion of the latter's transfer to Moscow following his appointment to the Secretariat of the Central Committee at the 19th Congress of the CPSU. Probably Brezhnev then determined to take Chernenko along with him, but fate ruled otherwise, dooming Chernenko to remain in Moldavia from October 1952 until 1956. During that time Chernenko witnessed the fall of his patron, and then his subsequent spectacular rise.

Right after the death of Stalin in March 1953, following a brief stay in Moscow, Brezhnev was sent to the political backwoods as deputy head of the Main Political Administration of the Soviet armed forces. Then he was demoted even further, to a Party secretaryship in distant Kazakhstan. There his zealous activity in campaigning for "virgin-land" (i.e. previously uncultivated soil) development earned him the first secretaryship in the Kazakhstan republic. Subsequently, at the 20th Congress of the CPSU in February 1956, he was recalled to Moscow to become again, after a three-year lapse, a secretary of the Central Committee and a candidate member of the CC Presidium (now Politburo). Within slightly more than a year, Brezhnev would rise further, to become a full member of the Presidium.

Before his last promotion, in the late fall of 1956, Brezhnev summoned Chernenko to the capital to ensconce him there as the first and, as it eventually turned out, the key link in the ranks of a Moldavian "mafia," which was to provide Brezhnev with a number of faithful colleagues in the years to come.

But before Chernenko would go to Moscow, his personality would undergo a rather substantial change. He would find it necessary to depart from his habitual forms of behavior that had served him well at the early stages of his career but later turned out to be a hindrance to further advancement. The first time his habits and routines betrayed him occurred in Krasnoyarsk, after his initial unproblematic successes in ascending the rungs of the Party hierarchy from the district to the city level and then to leadership of one of the largest Soviet territories. This early rise to prominence Chernenko owed to his meticulous abiding by Party directives without any attempt to display his own initiative. His forte appeared to be an ability to organize the subordinates and mobilize the masses to carry out the will of the Party leadership.

The situation altered when World War II, the so-called Great Patriotic War, caught the Soviet Union and its infallibly wise leader by complete surprise. Seized by panic over the prospect of losing his empire, Stalin changed. Instead of demanding blind compliance, he began to demand that his subordinates and aides show some initiative and even risk their own skins in order to stave off the disaster that threatened the country. His associates proceeded to impose similar expectations upon the rest of the population. Chernenko, however, was not able to adapt: he could not rid himself of mental stereotypes and working routines that he had learned and developed into habits in earlier years. This explains his first failure, in Krasnoyarsk.

His second failure came in Penza province. There, too, he had proved unable to adapt to expectations from the above. Trying to learn from his bitter experience in Krasnoyarsk, he continued to display a modicum of initiative, but it turned out that this was not what was wanted at a new "dialectical" stage. With the enemy defeated and peace restored, Stalin reverted to his earlier self, demanding from his *apparatchiki* blind obedience to the point of complete self-effacement of their personalities and individual characteristics.

In Moldavia Chernenko for the third time failed to comprehend the spirit of the time. After his failure in Penza, he was determined to follow blindly the directives of the central authorities and to impose a strict regimen that would please the Kremlin. However, the terrain on which he operated had unique features resistant to Chernenko's best efforts. The Moldavian Republic had been only recently (in 1940) incorporated into the Soviet Union and had not yet been integrated either socially or psychologically. To succeed there, insight was needed and flexibility in action, but Chernenko acted rigidly. As a result, he found himself on the brink of his third failure within a decade.

What rescued Chernenko from likely downfall was the arrival of Brezhnev in the Moldavian Republic. Only at this point did Chernenko apparently fully realize how complex, if not downright impossible, it was to adapt oneself in time to the perpetually changing expectations of the Moscow leadership. Only then did he finally comprehend that success in the Party would require more than a willingness to follow blindly each turn of the changing party line. The first prerequisite of success in the Party apparatus was to find an influential patron under whose protective wings personal careers could be furthered.

Chernenko was a determined, goal-oriented person. As soon as he discovered the prerequisite for success, there was no stopping him. He would not only win and keep Brezhnev's favor but also transform himself so profoundly that there are grounds to speak of him in his subsequent Moscow career as a new Chernenko with different values and a different self-concept. Under Brezhnev's patronage Chernenko gained sufficient security and self-confidence to bring to fruition a previously latent talent of his, that of a social scientist.

Notes

1. I had the opportunity to become acquainted with some details of Chernenko's personal life via Professor K., an outstanding Soviet scholar who from 1965 to 1975 lived in the same building as the future general secretary. Professor K. and his wife, also a professor and head of a department at Moscow State University, often visited Chernenko and hosted him in their home. The professor was evidently also to some degree involved in Chernenko's first theoretical research and in the writing of the latter's books and articles.

   It was Professor K. who in 1968 introduced Professor Osipov to Chernenko, and the next year introduced Osipov to Gorbachev. Because Osipov did not have a high opinion of Gorbachev, he was unpleasantly surprised when the latter became first secretary of the Stavropol Party *kraykom*. In amazement, Osipov retorted, "Who would have thought that contrary to the rules of the Party game the second secretary of a *kraykom* would become the first secretary?" Nevertheless, Osipov was sufficiently farsighted to agree to become the dissertation adviser of Raisa Gorbachev, at her husband's request. Gorbachev did not forget Osipov's consideration; when he became general secretary, he rescued the sociologist from the disgrace that had been his lot since 1972 after his removal from the post of deputy director of the Institute of Sociological Research (then IKSI).

Osipov unexpectedly appeared at the International Sociological Congress in New Delhi in the summer of 1986. As a Soviet representative, he was selected to be a member of the executive of the International Sociological Association, in other words, after a twelve-year hiatus, he returned to this impressive public position. However, he did not attain the position of chairperson of the Soviet Sociological Association, which fell to Tatyana Zaslavskaya, who took part in the elaboration of Andropov's economic reforms. Nevertheless, Osipov exuded confidence to the extent of not concealing his ambition of becoming a member of the Academy of Sciences.

2. See Ilya Zemtsov, *Policy Dilemmas and the Struggle for Power in the Kremlin: The Andropov Period* (Fairfax, Va.: Hero Books, 1985).
3. K. U. Chernenko, *Speeches and Writings*, 2d enlarged ed. (Oxford: Pergamon Press, 1984), pp. ix–xiii.
4. Mikhail Geller and Aleksandr Nekrich, *Utopia u vlasti* (Utopia in power), (London:.Overseas Publications Interchange, 1982), pt. 1, pp. 246–55.
5. A. M. Anfimov, *Rossiyskaya derevnya v gody pervoy mirovoy voyny* (The Russian village during the First World War) (Moscow, 1961), pp. 290–91.
6. Krasnoyarsky kray (Krasnoyarsk territory) Partarkhiv (Party archives), f.96, op.5, d.22, 1.1–2. (The foregoing abbreviations are those used by Soviet archivists to designate the following: *fond*=f.; *opis*=op.; *delo*=d.; *list*=1.; and *khranilishche*=khr.)
7. *Sovetskaya Sibir*, June 9, 1930.
8. B. Sopelnyak, "Na dal'ney zastave" (On the distant frontier post), *Ogonek*, no. 22 (May 1984): 7.
9. Ibid., p. 6.
10. *Slavnoe sorokaletie. Iz istorii Krasnoyarskoy partiynoy organizatsii (1917–1957)* (Glorious fortieth anniversary. From the history of the Krasnoyarsk Party organization, 1917–1957) (Krasnoyarsk, 1957), pp. 365–68, 371–74, 375.
11. Sopelnyak, "Na dal'ney zastave," p. 6.
12. Ibid., pp. 6–7.
13. *Slavnoe sorokaletie*, pp. 437–40.
14. *Narodnoe obrazovanie v SSR* (National education in the USSR), collection of documents, 1917–73 (Moscow: Izd-vo Pedagogicheskikh Nauk, 1974), p. 337.
15. See "Krasnoyarsky kray" (Krasnoyarsk territory), in *Bol'shaya Sovetskaya Entsiklopedia*, 2d ed. (Moscow: Gosudarstvennoe Nauchnoe Izd-vo BSE, 1953), 23: 267–72.
16. *Slavnoe sorokaletie*, p. 445.
17. Ibid., pp. 445–46.
18. TASS communiqué, *Pravda*, June 1941.
19. B. Yakovlev, *Kontsentrastsionnye lagerya v SSR* (Concentration camps in the USSR) (Munich, 1955), pp. 137–38.
20. Ibid.
21. Krasnoyarsky kray Partarkhiv, f.25, op.2, d.I, I.317–324, 333.
22. Kavkazskaya rivyera (Riviera of the Caucasus), a popular medical-health sanatorium located in the city of Sochi that was in fashion in the 1930s with Party functionaries.

23. *Krasnoyarsky rabochy*, July 18, 1941; *Slavnoe sorokaletie*, pp. 451–52.
24. *Krasnoyarsky rabochy*, July 25, 1941.
25. *Slavnoe sorokaletie*, pp. 450–51.
26. Ibid., pp. 449–52.
27. Krasnoyarsky kray Partarkhiv, f.26, op.9, d.I, 11.144–148; *Slavnoe sorokaletie*, pp. 484–85.
28. *Slavnoe sorokaletie*, pp. 455–63.
29. Ibid., p. 460.
30. Ibid., p. 461.
31. Ibid., pp. 464–70.
32. Krasnoyarsky kray Partarkhiv, f.1319, op.3, d.21, 1.1–3; *Slavnoe sorokaletie*, pp. 484–85.
33. Krasnoyarksy kray Partarkhiv, f.1319, op.3, d.21, 1.4.
34. See "Vysshaya partiynaya shkola pri TsK VKP (b)" (Higher Party School under the Central Committee of the All-Union Communist Party [Bolsheviks], in *Bolshaya Sovetskaya Entsiklopedia*, 2d ed. (Moscow: Gosudarstvennoe Nauchnoe Izd-vo BSE, 1953), 9: 507–8; "O podgotovke i perepodgotovke rukovodyashchikh partiynykh i sovetskikh rabotnikov" (On training and upgrading top party and state functionaries), resolution of the CC, All-Union Communist Party (Bolsheviks), *Partiynaya zhizn* no. 1, (1946).
35. *Penzenskiy oblpartarkhiv* (The archives of Penza Province), f.11, op.2, d.3, 1.72.
36. Ibid., f.8, op.4, d.2, 1.13.
37. For a description of the mores and life in rural Penza Province, see Petr Abovin-Egides, "Filosof v kolhoze. Fragmenty iz knigi" (Philosopher on a kolzhoz. Fragments from a book), *Kontinent*, no. 42 (1984): 199–239.
38. *KPSS v rezolyutsiyakh i resheniyakh syezdov, konferentsiy i plenumov CC* (The CPSU in the resolutions and decisions of the congresses, conferences and plenums of the Central Committee), vol. 6 (1941–1954) (Moscow, 1976), p. 215.
39. "Neustanno vospitivat' kadry v dukhe bolshevistskoy kritiki i samokritiki," (To unfailingly educate cadres in the spirit of Bolshevik criticism and self-criticism), *Sovetskaya Moldaviya*, February 4, 1949.
40. Lead article in *Sovetskaya Moldaviya*, February 4, 1949.
41. "Kosmopoliticheskie prikhvostni" (Cosmopolitan Parasites), *Sovetskaya Moldaviya*, May 19, 1949.
42. Report of N. G. Koval, the secretary of the Central Committee of the Communist Party (Bolsheviks) of Moldavia, at the second Congress of the CP (B) of Moldavia, as printed in *Sovetskaya Moldaviya*, February 7, 1949, p. 3.
43. Ibid.
44. Ibid.
45. Partarkhiv Instituta Istorii Partii pri TsK KP(b) Moldavii (Party archives of the Institute of Party History of the Central Committee of the Communist Party [Bolsheviks] of Moldavia), f. 298, op. 14, khr.3.
46. *Sovetskaya Moldaviya*, February 19, 1949, Lead article.
47. *Op. cit*, V. Porfirev, "Ob odnoy kritike-Kosmopolita" (About a Criticism of a Cosmopolite), April 3, 1949.
48. Ibid., March 22, 1949.
49. Partarkhiv Instituta Istorii Partii pri TsK KP(B) Moldavii, f. 311, op.2, khr.4, 1.6.

50. "Organizovat' kruglosutochnuyu rabotu traktorov" (To organize twenty-four-hour tractor work), *Sovetskaya Moldaviya*, March 26, 1949.
51. *Slavnoe sorokaletie, 1924–1964* (Glorious fortieth anniversary, 1924–1964) (Kishinev: Izdatelstvo TsK KP Moldavii, 1964), pp. 22–44.
52. *Sovetskaya Moldaviya*, February 26, 1950.
53. *Pravda*, July 3, 1950.
54. *Sovetskaya Moldaviya*, June 11, 1950.
55. Ibid., August 3, 1950.
56. Tsentralny Partiyny arkhiv Instituta marksizma-leninizma pri TsK KPSS (Central Party Archives of the Institute of Marxism-Leninism under the Central Committee of the CPSU), f. 46, op.42, d. 2116, 1.17.
57. *Sovetskaya Moldaviya*, August 4, 10, October 13, 1950.
58. *Leonid Ilich Brezhnev* (Moscow: Izd-vo politicheskoy literatury, 1981), p. 43.
59. Ibid., p. 47.
60. Details of the life of Chernenko in Moldavia are based on the oral accounts of two scholars now in the West who formerly taught at University of Moldavia, Dr. Mikhail Volodarsky and Dr. Mikhail Brukhis.
61. "Pod znamenem druzhby narodov" (Under the banner of friendship of the peoples), *Pravda*, February 14, 1951.
62. "Povyshat beditelnost i politicheskuyu zorkost sovetskikh lyudey" (To increase the vigilance and political perception of Soviet people), *Sovetskaya Moldaviya*, September 24, 1950.
63. See reports of the Fourth Congress of the Communist Party of Moldavia in *Sovetskaya Moldaviya*, September 19, 1952.

2

In Moscow: "Ever Ready"

By just marking time in place one can advance;
You just need to know the right place to do it.

In 1957 Moscow was the intersection where the paths of four future rulers of the Soviet Union crossed. The four were Nikita Khrushchev, then presiding over the Central Committee of the Party; Khrushchev's favorite, Leonid Brezhnev, who a few years later would send his patron into the political wilderness; Brezhnev's unintended heir, Yury Andropov, who had just been called back to Moscow from diplomatic service in Budapest in appreciation of his role in crushing the uprising in Hungary; and Konstantin Chernenko, who was fated to be the last of the quartet, the one who would bring to a close the era in which the USSR was ruled by Stalin's heirs.

The four men's respective points of departure in the race for absolute power were anything but equal. Khrushchev was first off the starting blocks, and by 1957 he had attained the first prize. Taking adroit advantage of bureaucratic procedures, he got rid of his rivals. He began by squeezing out of the Party apparatus Georgy Malenkov, who had failed in his bid for dictatorship. In September 1953 Khrushchev succeeded in having himself appointed first secretary of the Central Committee, and he proceeded to use this position subsequently to relieve Malenkov of his responsibilities as head of the government on the grounds of "lack of experience and adequate training." In 1955 Khrushchev installed in the premier's chair his old buddy, the narrow-minded but obliging Nikolay Bulganin.

Khrushchev used an outlandish pretext (the need to prevent the restoration of capitalism) to dump the clever and dangerous master of intrigue, Lavrenty Beria, minister of the state security and internal affairs. Beria was accused of being a British spy and executed. Khrushchev also succeeded in compromising Vyacheslav Molotov, the minister of foreign affairs, who was considered one of the Party's leading thinkers. Molotov was forced to recant publicly his "false views," to admit his "theoretical errors," and to express contrition for the "harm" these caused.[1] Further, Khrushchev cast doubt on the revolutionary record of the "founder of the Red Army" (an appellation once reserved for Trotsky), "the very talented commander and strategist," the chairman of the Presidium of the Supreme Soviet, Kliment Voroshilov. Then Khrushchev squeezed out of key administrative posts Lazar Kaganovich, who had claims on being the most experienced of the leaders of the Communist old guard. The final blow dealt to these Bolshevik stalwarts was Khrushchev's revelation of Stalin's crimes ("the cult of personality"), which implicated them as criminals responsible for the annihilation of millions of people (at this point Khrushchev included only Party members and activists among the victims).

The associates of Stalin who had survived both physically and politically were consequently in no position to stand in Khrushchev's way. However, it does not follow that Khrushchev was thereby able to do what he wished without their agreement and support. They after all jointly constituted a majority of the Politburo, especially when, in the course of a dramatic power struggle, their ranks were augmented by "turncoats" like Dmitry Shepilov, whom Khrushchev had cultivated and promoted to the post of minister of foreign affairs only to demote him to a lowly position in the Party apparatus a half year later, and like Bulganin, who could no longer stand the first secretary's arbitrariness and tactlessness. Thus, power was shared temporarily. But the situation was irreconcilable with the intrinsic nature of the Communist regime, which operates according to the classical Leninist formula of *kto-kogo*, "who will get the upper hand over whom."

Without wasting any time, Khrushchev went on the offensive. He announced a plan for the decentralization of the government apparatus and, in passing, offered the public the alluring prospect of catching up to the United States within a couple of years in the production of meat, milk, and butter.

The reorganization of the governmental apparatus led to the ouster not only of Khrushchev's enemies like Molotov, Malenkov, and Kaganovich but also of some of his allies, like Bulganin, M. G. Pervukhin, and M. Z. Saburov. At one point it turned out that those who were supposed to be on their way out actually formed a majority in the Presidium of the Central Committee. Unexpectedly (for Khrushchev), they took the logical course of action and united to depose Khrushchev at one of the Presidium sessions.

Khrushchev's position was saved by his appointees in the Secretariat of the Central Committee, who, albeit a minority in the Presidium, were able to mobilize the support of the armed forces by asserting that the matter at stake involved the security of the state. With that support, they succeeded in convening the Central Committee Plenum. In the course of the debate at the longest Plenum meeting in Soviet history (lasting from June 22 to June 29, 1957), Khrushchev emerged triumphant, thus thwarting the Presidium majority. He was saved by his supporters: Georgy Zhukov, Ekaterina Furtseva, Mikhail Suslov, Aleksey Kirichenko, Anastas Mikoyan, and Leonid Brezhnev.

One should not assume, however, that Soviet politics leaves any room for gratitude; the contrary is illustrated both by Khrushchev's rise and his fall. Soon after this victory at the Plenum, Khrushchev hastened to get rid of his most reliable ally, Marshal Zhukov, because the latter's popularity overshadowed his own—this Khrushchev could not tolerate. Subsequently, Khrushchev himself was ejected from the Kremlin by his protégé, Brezhnev.[2]

Still, in 1957 Brezhnev could hardly yet imagine that he would ever be in a position to bid for supreme power over the country. At that time Khrushchev was surrounded by a constellation of far brighter stars: A. B. Aristov, Otto Kuusinen, Mikoyan, and Suslov. Brezhnev could only be pleased at being allowed to join these luminaries in the Central Committee Presidium, the top authority in the country. (From 1952 to 1966 the Central Committee *Politburo* was referred to as the *Presidium*.)

As far as Andropov was concerned, he had not the faintest premonition of ever becoming head of state. The peak of his aspirations at that time was the post of Central Committee secretary, a promotion he could reasonably expect from the post he held as head of the CC Department for Socialist Countries. Assuming that he would thereafter ascend the steep gradient of the Party bureaucratic heights, he might eventually reach the Presidium, although being tripped up en route by intrigue must have appeared to him as at least as likely an outcome. Appointment to the Presidium would open his way into the Foreign Ministry and a career quite in keeping with his preferences and experience. At that time Andropov's ambitions certainly reached no further. He was quite preoccupied with the dilemma of choosing between possible patrons in the Central Committee: the elderly Kuusinen, with his revolutionary credentials, or the fast-ascending Suslov. In the end Andropov chose the latter, correctly estimating the promising prospect of Suslov's patronage for his own future career.

Chernenko did not face such a dilemma. His choice of patron was a foregone conclusion based on his experience in Moldavia. Brezhnev enjoyed the favor of Khrushchev; therefore, by serving Brezhnev, Chernenko indirectly served Khrushchev. In Moscow, however, Chernenko did have a dilemma: where to begin, when at least temporarily he was distant from Brezhnev? The latter served in a series of supervisory positions: in charge of heavy industry, of major construction projects, of space programs, and finally of arms production. All that time Chernenko was stuck with ideology, as head of the agitation section in the Department of Propaganda and Agitation.

Chernenko's instinct told him to try to get on good terms with the head of the department, but he could not. Fedor Konstantinov was an intellectual, a scholar in philosophy. He treated Chernenko with contempt. Although he was not about to cause problems for one of Brezhnev's minions as long as Brezhnev was a favorite of Khrushchev's, he would not help him either. No less indifferent to Chernenko's sycophancy was the arrogant Central Committee secretary for ideology, Petr Pospelov, the real author of the famous *Short Course of the History of the All-Union Communist Party (Bolsheviks)*, which had purportedly been penned by Stalin.

It is therefore quite doubtful that in 1957 Chernenko could have expected to ever attain the top Party post himself. This does not mean that it was beyond the scope of his imagination to aim at one day becoming an *eminence grise*. Under Brezhnev's sponsorship, Chernenko hoped to become the head of the Propaganda and Agitation Department of the CC or, because he was not too particular, of any other department, for that matter. Yet, he realized that the path from head of a CC section to the directorship of a department was difficult and full of pitfalls. Direct promotion to the top was out of the question; this way it was possible to rise only to the level of deputy head of the department. The only way to advance from there was by moving horizontally to first secretaryship of a province or through a transfer to high-level work on the state administration level. Without attaining this requisite, he could not be raised by the *nomenklatura* to the level of department head.

Chernenko coveted the directorship of an influential department in the hope of eventually becoming eligible for appointment as one of the nine to eleven secretaries of the CC. But even if that hope did not materialize, Chernenko would not be particularly disappointed because even as a CC department head he would be boss over several ministries, have a sumptuous office, numerous aides, a car, and a government-owned dacha at his disposal, in addition to being entitled to the special Kremlin rations (*payek*). Moreover, in retirement he would receive a handsome pension and after his death his name would be immortalized by an obituary in *Pravda* with a photograph, and a grave in the Novo-Devichye Cemetery, where only celebrities are entombed. In 1957 such thoughts still had the quality of unrealistic daydreams for Chernenko. In any case, his first order of business was not to make long-range plans but to find a place for himself and consolidate his position in the central Party apparatus.

Chernenko began with small steps. His aim was to win the favor of his colleagues by showing himself to be responsible, dedicated, and industrious. Thus, he was among the first to report to work at the Central Committee each morning, along with the typists and secretaries. He would be there even before eight o'clock in order to scan newspapers and decipher their encoded messages, searching for indications of the latest changes in policy so that he could pass them on to his subordinates at appropriate occasions. He would also remain at work after hours so that the higher-ups would notice the lone light shining in his office.

During the initial period of his work there, as earlier in Krasnoyarsk, he sought to convey the image of a decent fellow, easily accessible to ordinary people. However, he soon realized that in Moscow such qualities were not appreciated. Thereupon he became more reserved and stern, although still preserving an image of benevolence.

In the circles of those who worked for the Central Committee it was considered a mark of good taste to have a hobby. Tennis was very popular, along with fishing and hunting. Chernenko's hobby was the card game *preferans* (preference; a card game popular among the Soviet intelligentsia and with governmental officials), which, not coincidentally, was favored by Brezhnev. There was something original about the manner in which he furnished the apartment allotted to him in a new house on Kutuzov Prospekt opposite the just-completed tall structure of the Ukraina Hotel. In a display of simplicity of taste, and of patriotism (by virtue of buying Soviet rather than imported products), Chernenko rejected Rumanian goods, which Party dignitaries tended to favor, for simple and solid quality furniture from Riga.

With his typical devotion and efficiency Chernenko immersed himself in his work. His job was to organize and direct propaganda throughout the country. Here, he experienced certain conflicts and uncertainties. His penchant for approaching matters systematically suggested that before undertaking his new responsibilities, he should carefully consider his options and their implications. At the same time both common sense and bureaucratic experience dictated that he should not appear to be hesitant or diffident. In the end Chernenko overcame his innate caution and resolutely began to improve the operations of the propaganda apparatus by upgrading and improving various aspects of its operations.

It soon became clear that Chernenko's agitation section was expected to produce impressive results that could be reported in figures. Khrushchev, frustrated by his failures to make the economy viable, knowing that real productivity would be achieved only under private ownership, but not yet daring to change the system of the totally unprofitable collective agriculture, resolved to rely on propaganda to make whatever progress in agriculture might be made. His avowed goal was the rapid transition of the Soviet Union to an era of general prosperity by rapidly catching up to and then surpassing the volume of agricultural production of the United States. This was his vision of Communism. Because this leap from poverty to abundance was envisioned in Party offices in complete detachment from reality, the quantitative targets were quite fantastic.

The forecasts were that in seven years' time (from 1958 to 1965) the gross productivity in agriculture would increase from 8 to 16 million tons, the production of milk would rise from 58 to 105 million tons, and that of wool from 300 to 548 million tons, and the annual grain harvest would grow from 8 to 11 billion pood.[3] Khrushchev's ardor proved contagious. Local leaders, eager for awards and promotions, promised to fulfill their seven-year plan targets in six, five, or even four years, or to reach the levels of labor productivity envisaged for 1965 by 1961!

As in the Gospels, in the beginning was the word; deplorably, deeds did not follow. Instead, fakery, mendacity, and deception were rampant throughout the country, especially in Party committees.

The Russian Republic announced that it had harvested hundreds of millions of pood of marketable grain more than envisaged by the state plan, and the Kazakh Republic reported millions of acres of virgin land prepared for cultivation. The Ukraine reported a vastly expanded harvest of corn, and Uzbekistan, the harvest of millions of tons of cotton above the target. The whole people, Khrushchev included, was impressed by the initiative of Ryazan, where regional leaders undertook to quadruple or quintuple the production of meat within a few years.[4] The delighted first secretary decided to reward Comrade Larionov, the chief of the province, with the title of Hero of Socialist Labor for this initiative. However, it soon became apparent that the Ryazan "miracle," like many other similar undertakings, was a plain fraud. When this was revealed, Larionov was given the "opportunity" to commit suicide. The true scale of the CC-inspired fabrication of data was revealed only after Khrushchev's ouster. As long as he was in charge, the government and the press were inundated with reports of wondrous achievements.

Chernenko, willy-nilly, like other officials, was caught up in the flood of disinformation. He had to produce "miracles" in his propaganda work. His first reports had to impress the Party functionaries. Consequently, in articles appearing in *Agitator*, for which he, as a member of the editorial board and as the journal's supervisor, was responsible, it was reported that in 1957, 50 million people were engaged in Communist educational undertakings, and that 12 million propaganda workers (*agi-*

tatory) were devoting their best efforts to improving the educational system even further. The latter figure was 50 percent higher than the one for the previous year,[5] thereby implying that the credit for this achievement was due to Chernenko.

In the following year, on the occasion of the elections to the national Supreme Soviet, Chernenko advanced the slogan "Every Communist Party member a propagandist," but, evidently, this did not seem to reflect suitably the significance of this great "historical moment." Therefore, to magnify the impact, he added a phrase, "every Komsomol member — to the polling station." Anyone who cared to translate these slogans of Chernenko into figures would discover with surprise (most gratifying for the Central Committee) that they increased the ranks of propaganda workers in the USSR (Communists plus Komsomol members) to most impressive levels, indeed to 40 million, which amounted to one-fifth of the country's population, infants included.

To Chernenko's chagrin it turned out that in many voting districts there was a shortage of qualified (i.e. ideologically dependable) lecturers, that appropriate visual-educational propaganda material was not displayed, and that propaganda discussions were not being held as required. He immediately demanded reports from each republic about the situation. Predictably, the reports were quite rosy. The system of official "whitewashing" had been so perfected that it invariably provided the functionaries with the kind of information they wanted to receive. All reported data testified to achievements; other data were simply not passed on to the higher-ups. In this instance, however, Chernenko needed to obtain an objective view of the state of affairs of the electoral campaign in connection with the national Supreme Soviet. After all, these were the first elections for which he was ideologically responsible. Chernenko was totally averse to assessing the situation of propaganda work on location. The Soviet Union was not Moldavia; it had thousands of cities and towns, hundreds of provinces and regions. He could not possibly inspect them all, and his staff of five instructors was hardly sufficient for this purpose.

It would have been both tempting and convenient to check out the Party organizations of the capital, which operated right under his very nose and where he could rely on the assistance of the well-oiled and exemplarily functioning supervisory bureaucracy. However, this would involve great personal risk because Moscow was a special case. Chernenko understood that in Moscow every *raykom* secretary had a patron, either in the Secretariat or in the Politburo itself, with whom he had a give-and-take relationship. One district of the city was the location of institutions of higher learning. In this district someone's hand jotted down lists for admission (of the children of the *nomenklatura*) to university. The same hand obtained (from university scientific councils) academic degrees and honors for its protégés to enhance their prestige and power positions. Another district was filled with theaters, furnished with comfortable VIP boxes kept in reserve for the huge retinues of those with eager hands. Still another district had warehouses where goods in short supply in the country were stored. In their greed, pampered hands also reached out there when not satisfied with what they could obtain in closed distribution shops that served them alone.

Chernenko realized that it was also too risky to interfere in districts where industrial enterprises were located. Out of these enterprises, after all, originated black capital, which would be circulated in ways calculated to benefit hundreds of eager hands from the Party apparatus. The stakes were high for both sides: while Party hands were helping themselves to property worth millions of rubles, the directors of plants and shops were earning positions of honor as representatives in various official bodies, or were proclaimed Heroes of Socialist Labor. Public criticism of such mutual back-scratching networks could hardly originate from a level lower than a secretary of the Central Committee. If such criticism were voiced, it was usually intended to indicate that the hands were not satisfied with their take.

Chernenko also knew enough to avoid inspections in those districts of the city that housed KGB institutions, which represented a danger zone where rival camarillas of hands waged bitter "socialist competitions" for power and spoil.

As a consequence of his fear of trespassing on others' preserves, Chernenko was not included either among the speakers or among the guests of honor at the convocation of the 10,000 propagandists of Moscow convened by the Moscow *gorkom* (City Party Committee). This spectacle, at which Chernenko had to content himself with the role of a nonparticipant observer, was conducted by its organizers in a manner that lacked all sense of proportion. As the secretary of the *gorkom* reported, the number of propaganda points (*agitpunkty*) established in the capital amounted to 1,700, and the number of mobilized propagandists to 300,000. Chernenko considered that these figures could safely be doubled in the report. He thought that Moscow should be an example, a model for the rest of the country. Other figures might have had to be treated with care because they could be easily disproved. For example, an additional 4,130,000 square meters of living quarters were promised to be ready for use within two years' time. This would mean an increase of almost 15 percent over what had been available in Moscow. This was ridiculous, as Chernenko or any other thinking person knew, because two years would never suffice to construct what had been impossible to build in the capital during the preceding forty years of Soviet rule. And that was not the only promise that was bound to raise doubts. The promise to double urban transport capacity within a very short time was likewise utopian. Buses and streetcars were not balloons — hot air would not expand them to double or triple their size!

Chernenko understood that although propaganda was aimed at producing immediate impact, its long-range effects were of at least equal importance. Secretary of the Moscow Party Committee, S. Orlov, had evidently lost sight of the latter consideration. He failed to recognize that declaring that only one (!) of 430 industrial enterprises in the capital had failed to meet its plan targets[6] would weaken the propagandists' case for reproaching workers for the low level of their productivity, ideological immaturity, or poor discipline.

Chernenko understood, too, that the art of manipulating peoples' minds depended on the selection for publication of information that was either unverifiable or at least difficult to verify. In that case the propagandist need not be limited by facts because there is no danger of challenge to his statements. So, when Chernenko himself published wholly imaginary figures about the (ostensibly nationwide) debate on the agricultural reforms proposed by Khrushchev, he knew there was no way that his figures could be either verified or challenged. Thus, he had no qualms in saying that there had been 576,000 discussion meetings with 49 million people present, all in the course of three weeks' time![7]

Chernenko gave free rein to his imagination: he reported that the discussants made 3 million proposals, of which more than 100,000 found their way into print.[8] All was reported in detail, including the exact locations of the meetings, the contents of the "workers' councils" proposals, and even the sequence of publication of the proposals. Such details were intended to convey the notion of the triumph and the grandeur of Soviet democracy, under which millions of citizens purportedly participate in the formation of government policy. But this report was also intended to please the vainglorious Khrushchev and allow him to boast that the people understood his goals and supported his efforts. However, one small detail escaped the attention of Chernenko's advisers in their mendacity. They overlooked the fact that issue No. 7 of *Agitator*, sent to press on March 23 (!), reported the number of meetings held (hundreds of thousands of them, with breakdowns by various categories), as well as the number of motions presented (running into the tens of millions) between March 1 and March 25 (!), 1958. The slip passed unnoticed.

Chernenko heavily relied on the customary management method of criticizing his subordinates in such a way as to highlight the failures of their work and thereby present himself as an example. Cautiously and cleverly steering clear of what was happening in the capital, he directed all his criticisms at the provinces, which he inundated with numerous directives and instructions. In the process Chernenko punctiliously calculated the right doses of criticism: the more distant a territory or province was from Moscow, the safer he was from any adverse feedback. In cases of distant locations, such as the cities of Tomsk or Irkutsk, his observations could be harshly critical (e.g. that the local Party organization was doing a poor job in propagandizing the achievements of science and advanced technology, that it was not doing enough to involve the intelligentsia in public activities, or that it was not providing adequate opportunities for people to spend their leisure time in cultural pursuits). In the case of Vladivostok, located on the far eastern border of the USSR, there was no need for kid gloves. Chernenko therefore suggested that the celebration of religious holidays there be curtailed because they interfered with sowing and harvesting schedules, and because large quantities of sugar, used for brewing homemade alcoholic beverages, were consumed as a result of such celebrations.

Criticism of Lvov province, which was closer to the capital but still several thousand kilometers away, was somewhat milder but still fairly severe. There the provincial Party committee was reproached for an insufficient level of propaganda, not on a par with what "life" required; for the poor quality of its "explanations" of policy to the masses; and for failure to utilize the local activist ranks for these purposes.

Saratov and Stalingrad were criticized according to entirely different criteria because they were located relatively close by. In regard to these locations any criticism had to be carefully calibrated in its expression. They could be faulted for such minor matters as the lack of appropriate placards or for poorly organized displays. As for the remedies suggested, they had to be low-keyed, for example, the publication of small-format propaganda brochures for distribution in rural areas and workers' settlements.[9]

Chernenko was constantly on the lookout for innovative ways to disseminate Communist ideology. He called for political information sessions to be conducted at factories before the beginning of the workday, and for propaganda exhibits to be set up in kolkhoz fields in mobile vans. He also advocated setting up propagandists' schools attached to Party organizations, and recommended that propaganda lectures be delivered at railroad stations.

Believing that change originated with ideas, Chernenko proceeded to offer new ideas. For example, in reference to the activist ranks involved in propaganda work, he coined the term *kultarmeytsy* (culture troopers) to make it sound analogous to the revolutionary term *krasnoarmeytsy* (Red Army troopers). Another of his innovations was organizing question-and-answer evenings for the purpose of indoctrinating people with prescribed beliefs. He also lent his support to the establishment of clubs for young women in urban areas. Intended as social work facilities to facilitate control over young women's mores and the inculcation of official Communist values, the clubs soon turned into dens of vice.[10] Recognizing this, Chernenko was left no alternative but to close them. It was not that Chernenko did not appreciate female charms; he simply considered the corruption of Communist educational activities impermissible. He shortly also had to abandon the question-and-answer evenings. Without a clearly set agenda and jammed with unmanageable crowds, such meetings too often deviated from the Party line.

The antireligious campaign that raged through the country during the late 1950s provided Chernenko with a further opportunity to show off his inventiveness. He "discovered" a new "fundamental contradiction" between Communist philosophy and religious thought. He maintained that Marxism teaches people to be active and involved, but religion calls for an otherworldly detachment from life, a more passive waiting for eternal life. In the process Chernenko was so eager to expose the evil inherent in religion that he revealed his own ignorance. At a conference of the Central Committee of heads of permanent propaganda points, he called for elaboration of a universal program of antireligious propaganda without bothering about the fact that different religions imply radically different spiritual values. Chernenko soon had an occasion to correct this oversimplification. Recommendations for atheist education published under his direction in *Agitator* recognized the necessity for individual work with religious believers. In this regard Chernenko again offered an original suggestion of his own. He proposed to assign to each religious family (in 1958 there were 20 to 30 million such families in the USSR) at least one atheist propagandist, or better still, to settle such propagandists in close proximity to the believers.[11]

Despite such achievements, Chernenko felt dissatisfied. He felt he was somewhat peripheral to the mainstream of Party life. The country was continuing to be overtaken by new efforts to implement Khrushchev's numerous projects. In 1954 there began the attempt to cultivate the "virgin lands"; in 1955 there began the massive cultivation of corn as the solution to the country's food crisis; in 1957 the idea was proclaimed of catching up with and eventually surpassing the United States in economic development; this was followed by reorganization of the machine-tractor stations (MTS), school reform, and finally a further agricultural reform consisting of the amalgamation of collective farms.

In the whirlwind of such endeavors, no one seemed to have any patience for ideology. Propaganda departments continued to function in all Party committees. They continued to draft and circulate endless directives and instructions, which were routinely followed because no one in the country dared ignore the will of the Party. But propaganda work was no longer held in esteem. This prompted Chernenko to try to restore propaganda to its previous position of prominence. His idea was to exploit the same mechanism that had led to its decline, to attempt to transform Khrushchev's reformist zeal from a factor detrimental to the status of propaganda work into a factor enhancing its importance.

Khrushchev himself inspired and organized all major government initiatives. He castigated and pardoned, encouraged or banned, issued directives and delivered reports. It was only natural for Chernenko to turn to Khrushchev with arguments about how productivity in industry and agriculture would grow if Party organizations and heads of industries themselves would conduct uninterrupted propaganda efforts, if they would consistently supervise its contents and concern themselves with its effectiveness.[12]

Khrushchev showed an interest in Chernenko's proposals, for he found them attuned to changes then taking place within the Party bureaucracy. The arrogant Konstantinov was replaced as head of the CC Propaganda and Agitation Department by the ambitious L. Ilichev, and the new CC secretary, N. A. Mukhitdinov, who temporarily replaced Pospelov, was eager to win popularity and recognition. These two newcomers saw Chernenko's proposals as possible means of their own self-advancement. By pushing propaganda into the ideological limelight, they hoped to push themselves into the political limelight. Mukhitdinov, however, soon fell into disfavor, but within several years Ilichev became a CC secretary and a member of the Academy of Sciences. Chernenko also advanced. Probably with Brezhnev's help, he became one of the inner circle with access to Khrushchev.

From this moment onward Chernenko's activity began to have nationwide repercussions. New CC instructions dealing with propaganda work and based on drafts prepared by Chernenko were issued in March 1959.[13] This marked the first time that a CC *section*, rather than a department of the secretariat, had dared to criticize the Party organization of an entire province, that of Stalino (in the Ukraine). The hierarchical system operating within the Party permitted Chernenko to investigate matters in any province, but only and exclusively matters pertaining to the strictly defined scope of Chernenko's concern, i.e. political propaganda for the masses. However, the new CC directives encompassed the totality of problems related to ideology, and their conclusions were binding on all Party committees.

The new arrangement was clear proof that Chernenko had succeeded in winning the support of the first secretary and the Department of Organization of Party Work, which was responsible for the provincial *nomenklatura*. A further indication of the same could be found in the tone of the resolution, which was stern and called for drawing "personal conclusions," evidently in regard to the first secretary of Stalino province, who was in fact subsequently dismissed. The CC resolution served as a strict warning to administrators of other provinces, who from then on began to shower the CC with promises to improve their propaganda performance. It was then that Chernenko's name became widely known in Party circles. At long last he could sign the articles he wrote for *Agitator* rather than leave them anonymous. However, he was still not ready for a solo performance. He had not yet learned how to express his ideas with clarity and conviction and with the requisite citations from the canonical Marxist sources. This is why he solicited help of one of his associates, P. Rodionov, a history instructor, to draft an article. Chernenko even allowed Rodionov to appear as co-author.

Chernenko and Rodionov's cooperation worked as follows: Rodionov wrote while Chernenko provided him with the records of the investigation pursued in Stalino province. This explains why the phrasing in the article and the phrasing in the CC resolution were nearly identical. In all probability Chernenko had made use of Rodionov's talents in drafting the resolution as well. After all, as a head of a CC sector, he could not afford to reveal the poverty of his self-expression to the Party elite. True, he did, on occasion, speak at meetings and conferences, but speaking was one thing and writing another. Almost all Party officials spoke in the same style: laconic and unemotional. In contrast, this particular CC resolution was intended to capture (and it did actually capture) attention by its expressiveness, its use of imagery and elements of novelty. This was essential because one of its points was that events in the country were not being explained with clarity or effectiveness, and that the declarative and stilted style of public lectures needed to be replaced.[14]

For Chernenko, the Stalino province resolution was a medium to advance a new program for organizing propaganda work, a new program that contained many of his old ideas, such as a differentiated approach to political propaganda for the masses that would take into consideration the mood and needs of people, their employment, the level of their ideological maturity, and their ethnic background. He called for lectures to be given during night shifts at enterprises, for newspapers and magazines to be available to workers in field camps, for leisure time to be enlivened with lectures, reports, and amateur artistic performances. He recommended that propagandists be assigned to clubs, houses of culture, and "red corners." ("Red corners" are educational-propaganda units, similar to clubs, that operate in workplaces, dormitories, large apartment houses, and so on under the direction of Party and labor-union officials.) He demanded that adequately briefed Party members conduct propaganda work in worker and student dormitories, and he stressed the need for indoctrinating the youth in Communist traditions and principles.

The CC resolution allowed Chernenko to issue directives that exceeded the authority inherent in his rank. Thus, he instructed the State Committee on Radio and Television Broadcasting to prepare a series of lectures and discussions explaining Party documents. Likewise, he instructed the Ministry of Culture to encourage the production of popular-science films; newspaper editors, to bring to public attention the results of propaganda work; publishing houses, to issue books dealing with theoretical aspects of propaganda dissemination; the Znanie (knowledge) association, to improve its lecturing services.

But what exceeded everything else in importance was the instruction for all ranking Party officials to participate in propaganda activities. In this way even officials ranking higher than Chernenko were placed in a position of direct dependence on him because it was now his responsibility to report to the CC Secretariat about their delivery of political reports and lectures. Consequently, Chernenko's favor began to be sought by powerful heads of territorial and provincial committees. He became a feared visitor in the union republics, where the first secretaries themselves catered to his needs.

In the resolution Chernenko did not neglect to make obeisances to Khrushchev. Studying and explaining the speeches and writings of the first secretary of the Central Committee were therein defined as an important task of all Party and Komsomol organizations. Yet, Chernenko did not miss the occasion to toot his own horn either. The CC resolution instructed the CC Propaganda and Agitation Department (i.e. Chernenko's own department) to proceed with the publication of popular brochures in the series Bibliotechka agitatora (The propagandist's little library).[15] The first brochure to appear in this series, "Guidelines for a Propagandist," was a compilation of writings by M. Kalinin, the former chairman of the Supreme Soviet who had compliantly served Stalin for more than a quarter of a century, until his death in 1946.

The second brochure, "Toward a New Upsurge of Political Work among the Masses," could have been expected to have been written by Khrushchev or at least one of the CC secretaries. Instead, the author turned out to be Chernenko. This represented his first step toward joining the ranks of certified interpreters of the Marxist classics. At this point he already had the requisite authority to call for the Central Committee to convene a special conference to discuss issues of political work with the masses. The conference took place in October 1959 and was attended not by the rank-and-file propagandists or heads of propaganda points (*agit-punkty*) but by leading functionaries of republic and provincial Party organizations, top officials of central ideological institutions, and representatives of radio and television. As a token of approval from the very top, the key speech at the conference was delivered by Ekaterina Furtseva, a CC secretary and member of the CC Presidium, *and* Khrushchev's latest companion.[16]

From then on, Chernenko no longer had any reason to avoid the limelight. His next piece for *Agitator* was therefore signed by him alone, although the precise and professional style of the article indicates that he might well have been helped in preparing it by his subordinates. The ideas, however, were undoubtedly his own and were expressed with the condescension and self-confidence of a successful Party functionary. Scornfully, Chernenko asked what kinds of contact with the masses can leaders have if they rarely visit enterprises and institutions. He even went so far as to poke fun at a republic CC secretary who "rented" a ready-made report to read as his own at a meeting.[17]

But time was already running out for Chernenko as head of the CC Propaganda and Agitation Department. His instinct told him not to switch patrons. Although he probably had a fairly good chance to gain the patronage of the flighty Furtseva or even to push his way into the good graces of the dour Suslov, the Kremlin's chief ideologist, he remained loyal to Brezhnev. As soon as his own office work was completed, he would drop by Brezhnev's office, ready to sit late into the night in order to look through and file Brezhnev's papers. Loathing clerical work, Brezhnev welcomed Chernenko's assistance in reviewing and revising the drafts of his speeches and in preparing required reference material. And on weekends Chernenko would obligingly show up at Brezhnev's dacha to issue instructions to the service personnel, to cook fish soup (*ukha*) or the Siberian *pelmeni* of which Brezhnev was fond, and to play with Brezhnev's children.

Twice a year, at the end of summer and at New Year, he would go on holiday with Brezhnev to the Crimea or the environs of Moscow. His task there was to procure female company for Brezhnev. He sought women who would please Brezhnev, became acquainted with them, learned what their tastes and weaknesses were, screened their backgrounds from the point of security, and duly forewarned them not to gossip about the private life of the CC secretary. When Brezhnev lost interest in a current consort, she would be quietly and tactfully dismissed.

In May 1960 Brezhnev was appointed chairman of the Presidium of the Supreme Soviet of the USSR. Immediately afterward Chernenko's career took a sharp turn. He relinquished his job in the Party apparatus to become director of his patron's new office. By standards of the Soviet "vanity fair," the Supreme Soviet chairmanship was not a particularly impressive position. For Chernenko, who had just turned forty-nine, his new post entailed a certain risk. A Party functionary who by that age fails to ascend to a top position (such as that of a CC department head, chief editor of a central newspaper, or first secretary of an *obkom*) starts to lose political momentum and within a few years will descend to research work or a position in the state administration. There he will be tolerated for a while and then honorably pensioned off, and thus relegated to oblivion.

Four years of work in Moscow did not satisfy Chernenko's ambition. He had not succeeded in winning a top post in the Party apparatus. Above him there were too many levels of the hierarchic ladder. Newspapers referred to heads of CC sections like Chernenko anonymously as "high Party functionaries." Not granted any real policy decision-making powers, he had merely been the eager and compliant executor of the will of others, such as the CC department heads and their deputies. Nor was Chernenko a member of any elected body, like the Central Committee or the Supreme Soviet, which are devoid of real authority yet still endow their members with some power standing of their own.

Materially, he was not faring very well either, to the point that his means hampered his advancement. He received a relatively modest salary of several hundred rubles per month, his "Kremlin rations" were below those to which the top elite were entitled, and he did not have his own car with a chauffeur but had to order one from the car pool whenever he needed it.

His feeling of insecurity was constant. Like everyone else in the Central Committee, he did not know whose support he could rely on. Khrushchev was ceaselessly shuffling the Party deck and discarding former aces who, like Mukhitdinov, could fall from CC secretaryship to a mere ambassadorship in Syria. At the same time Khrushchev would suddenly and inexplicably pick up some "small card" and cash him in for big political stakes. This was the good fortune of, for instance, N. I. Belyaev, whom Khrushchev rapidly advanced to the Presidium of the CC.

There were hardly any features in Chernenko's personality that would make him stand out in the crowd of Party careerists. In particular, he did not have leadership qualities, such as decisiveness or the willingness to take risks. Instead, he had in abundance qualities that those above him could use: servility, self-effacement, industriousness, and a sense of dedication. This willingness to subordinate himself to his superiors partly explains why Chernenko agreed to the, at least apparently, unpromising move from the Central Committee apparatus to the Secretariat of the Presidium of the Supreme Soviet. Although the latter position situated him far from the corridors of power, he was close to Brezhnev, with whose help he could hope to reverse his fortunes and further his Party career. He had been diminished in terms of the scope of his political authority, but he hoped yet to rise on the coattails of his patron, and to skip some intermediate career plateaus in the process.

Eventually Chernenko would succeed in doing just that. Meanwhile, everything indicated that he had chosen badly. The Soviet system is run by the CPSU Central Committee; it is this body that sets policy and exercises power over the nation. The Moscow Party Committee enjoys high prestige; major Soviet leaders tend to begin their careers there. The Leningrad Party organization is also highly prestigious; with time its leaders tend to become Politburo members. Apart from these two, several *obkoms* are also considered to be suitable power bases, especially those of Sverdlovsk, Gorky, Stavropol, Chelyabinsk, and Krasnoyarsk. A number of CC secretaries formerly served in these *obkoms*.

A shift from Party to state work, even on the highest level, is generally considered undesirable because it forecloses the avenues of upward mobility within the *nomenklatura*. As a rule, a minister is not promoted to head of a CC department, and even a deputy chairman of the Council of Ministers, unless he has been first deputy, rarely becomes a CC secretary.

The Supreme Soviet has little inherent importance or authority. It represents state authority without political substance. Formally it is a legislative body; in reality it merely makes legislative acts public. It does not provide its members with access to either the CC or the Council of Ministers. It is not a good point of departure for one's career. It is even worse as a place where a career can be advanced. In fact, it is the refuge for failures, especially for Party functionaries who, for one reason or another, have been found unsuitable and removed from active politics.

Chernenko himself perceived his transfer from the CC to the Supreme Soviet as far from being a disaster. In forging his political career Chernenko tended to count less on position and more on the influence of a single patron. In the early 1960s Brezhnev, after all, proved to be second only to Khrushchev. Because the latter combined the posts of first secretary of the CC and chairman of the Council of Ministers, the Supreme Soviet chairman emerged as the natural second in the ranking order. By tying himself to Brezhnev, Chernenko was thereby joining the person who had a good chance to emerge as victorious in the succession race after Khrushchev.

Under Khrushchev it was no simple matter to make a successful career. It was not sufficient to submit to his unbounded will; one also had to adapt to the rapid reversals in his moods and personal sympathies, to his impulsiveness, vanity, and iconoclastic tendencies. He could totally reverse his views or interests overnight. He was restless, never satisfied with anything or anyone, himself included. Nevertheless, Brezhnev had the knack of maintaining himself in his boss's good graces, with the result that he was elevated above his colleagues in the Politburo to the second-ranking position in the state.

Chernenko did not need to be told that he had to involve himself wholeheartedly in his new responsibilities. After all, Brezhnev had no intention of devoting himself seriously to the presidency. As previously, he would concentrate all his attention on the Politburo.

Chernenko had no reason to feel disappointed. It soon turned out that his duties as head of the Secretariat of the Presidium of the Supreme Soviet provided him with an unexpected opportunity to exert influence and power. In addition to its decorative function as an empty shell of socialist democracy, the Supreme Soviet Presidium has one prerogative of real power: the right to pardon criminals. There are no strict juridical criteria for granting pardon in the USSR. Decisions in regard to pardons are left entirely to the discretion of the Presidium chairman. Consequently, many attempt to influence him. These people range from high *nomenklatura* functionaries who have displeased their higher-ups to the point of getting themselves embroiled in criminal show trials, to big operators in the "second economy" who were caught "redhanded" when they failed to remain on good terms with everyone who counted. Both the former and the latter were ready to pay huge sums of money amounting to hundreds of thousands or even millions of rubles to receive pardons. Chernenko sounded out Brezhnev about taking advantage of this opportunity. Brezhnev was willing not for the money's sake (in a country in which everything was in short supply, Brezhnev had everything he could dream of, including a government dacha, a private airplane, and an unlimited bank account) but because he was a far-sighted father who knew that neither fame nor power was inheritable. The case of Stalin's children provided an instructive example. One of Stalin's two sons (Vasily), a heavy drinker, had fallen out of a window in an act that might have been a suicide or a homicide; and Stalin's daughter had been both corrupted by her father's power and spiritually crushed by it and also tormented by guilt to the point of fleeing the country. Although Brezhnev knew that material well-being was no guarantee of happiness, it was clear to him that money could insulate his children from need and help them succeed in life.

Still, Brezhnev preferred to be kept in the dark about Chernenko's deals. Brezhnev was concerned that the reputation of the president's office remained untarnished. Thus, he never became involved in the specifics of such cases when he signed a decree granting someone pardon. He merely checked to see if the matter had the approval of the Central Committee and the procurator (attorney) general.

Brezhnev did not even care to know whether out of the huge sums that passed through Chernenko's hands, some stuck to them. The evidence, though, seemed to point against this because Chernenko's wife never sported expensive jewelry or fine clothes but dressed in modest dresses made in government workshops. Nor did Chernenko act like an arrogant nouveau riche; he appeared to be as obliging and eager to please as he had always been.

Chernenko's new responsibilities, however, exposed him to elegantly dressed foreigners. No wonder that his image began to mirror theirs. Suddenly he felt awkward in his thick-toed, heavy clodhoppers, wide trousers, and poorly tailored jackets. He decided to change his appearance and began buying imported suits, shaving carefully, and concerning himself with his hairstyle. Nevertheless, he did not enjoy meeting with foreign delegations, and derived more satisfaction from paperwork, preparing protocols of meetings, and issuing reports and directives.

Following his inclinations, Chernenko restructured the bureaucracy of the Supreme Soviet. He amalgamated the office of the Presidium and the Secretariat. For diplomatic contacts, he created the Department of International Relations and appointed one of his deputies, Vladimir Vysyatin, its director. From then on it was Vysyatin's duty to receive ambassadors when they came to present their credentials. Chernenko was free to occupy himself with other matters. Practically every week the Supreme Soviet approved alterations in the administrative structure of the country. Districts were abolished, new towns and settlements established. Pertinent committees of the Supreme Soviet began to work more efficiently when, on orders of Chernenko, representatives of the Council of Ministers, Gosplan (State Planning Committee), and consultants from the Academy of Sciences attended their working meetings. Chernenko particularly relished reviewing the lists of people nominated for honors. Although the Central Committee drafted the lists, it was within his power to hold them up and this tickled his vanity.

Chernenko was involved in the drafting of the decrees about the institution of the death penalty for currency speculators. He punctiliously worked out their phrasing because additional details of these decrees could provide his patron with additional income and himself with wider powers and influence.

Thus, the years of Chernenko's work in the Supreme Soviet passed auspiciously, without major disturbances or nasty surprises—until 1964.

In that year there occurred an event of great significance for him. Khrushchev fell, whereupon Chernenko's boss was unexpectedly propelled by the waves of intricate political intrigues into the post of the first secretary of the Party.

Notes

1. *Pravda*, July 7, 1957; *Plenum Tsentralnogo Komiteta Kommunisticheskoy Partii Sovetskogo Soyuza, 15-19 dekabrya 1958g* (Plenum of the Central Committee of the Communist Party of the Soviet Union, December 15-19, 1958) (Moscow: 1958); Mark Frankland, *Khrushchev* (New York: Stein & Day, 1967); Alexander Dallin and Thomas Lanson, eds., *Soviet Politics since Khrushchev* (Englewood Cliffs, N.J.: Prentice-Hall, 1968).
2. *Pravda*, July 12, 1957; *Kommunist*, no. 10 (1957): 66-72.
3. *Agitator*, no. 5 (1958): 35-37.
4. *Agitator* (1958): no. 1: 1-3; no. 2: 2; no. 12: 6-7; no. 19: 14-19.
5. "For Active Agitation in the Electoral Campaign," *Agitator*, no. 2 (1958): 3-6.
6. "Instructing Moscow's Agitators and Propagandists," *Agitator*, no. 4 (1958): 6-13.
7. "A New Major Step on the Path to Communism," *Agitator*, no. 7 (1958): 3-4.
8. Ibid.
9. *Agitator*, no. 7 (1958): 38-43; no. 11 (1958): 47-78; no. 16 (1958): 51-52; no. 2 (1959): 50-57; no. 7 (1959): 29-34.
10. "For Discussion," *Agitator* (1958): nos. 9, 14, 15, 16, 17.
11. *Agitator*, no. 9 (1958): 53-56.
12. "In the CC of the CPSU: About the State of Mass-Political Work among Workers of Stalino Region and Measures to Improve It," *Agitator*, no. 5 (1959): 3-12.
13. Ibid.
14. Ibid.
15. Ibid.
16. *Agitator*, no. 21 (1959): 7-11.
17. K. Chernenko, "Agitate Concretely, with Your Goal in Mind," *Agitator*, no. 1 (1960): 55-60.

3

Lessons of Political Maneuvering

The Soviet system perpetuates itself—by successive dictatorships.

One peculiarity of political crises is that they are easy to understand in hindsight. Thus, until May 1, 1960, when the United States U-2 intelligence plane was shot down over the USSR,[1] no one would have suspected that a new anti-Khrushchev opposition was coalescing in the Kremlin for the first time since the rout of the anti-Party group.[2] Least of all did Khrushchev himself suspect this. Actually, this challenge to his rule had been crystallizing for a long time but became apparent only gradually. Khrushchev's authority was first undermined by opposition of the General Staff to his plan to demobilize the army, then by dissatisfaction within the Central Committee Secretariat over his rift with China. Much opposition to the general secretary, particularly in the provinces, was aroused by his organizational reforms, which were resented for their unseemly haste and patchiness.

On top of all that, the conservative wing of the Party was far from pleased with Khrushchev's rapprochement with Washington, which did not fit its members' ideological preconceptions. Meanwhile, however, an appearance of unanimity in support for Khrushchev's policies was maintained in the Central Committee and the Party apparat.

First cracks in the unanimity appeared when the downing of the U-2 aircraft and the capture of its pilot, Gary Powers, exposed the brittleness of friendship with a U.S. president who would sanction the flight of a spy plane over Soviet territory. As soon as this happened, Khrushchev had to confront criticism in the Presidium, with the effect that his grip on power, which had previously seemed incontestable, immediately became precarious. It happened not only that Khrushchev could be stopped in his tracks

59

but that he could even be made to retreat. In fact, he was compelled to admit the failure of his policy in regard to the United States.

At the May Central Committee Plenum two Party functionaries—Alexey Kosygin and Dmitri Polyansky—neither in any way indebted to Khrushchev, were raised to full membership in the Presidium. Their advancement strengthened the budding opposition, which, however, still refrained from aiming at the removal of the first secretary. It was too weak, too inexperienced, and too disorganized to think in terms of such a goal. But it did challenge Khrushchev's policies and thereby raised a storm within the Party, which for reasons to be shown later, ultimately resulted in Brezhnev's being "kicked upstairs" to the honorific presidency of the state, thus effectively distancing him from the real levers of power.

But Brezhnev possessed unusual skills of political survival, which he had demonstrated earlier. After Stalin's death in 1953 a major purge flushed the entire Soviet leadership. As a result of this purge, Brezhnev wound up in an insignificant post in the Ministry of Defense.[3] In 1960 he found himself again in a position of relative disadvantage in the race for power only to ascend eventually to the very top with aplomb. (In a country where the Party is proclaimed to be the "leading and guiding" force of society, the presidency does not entail real power. It is a kind of political cold storage for past-their-prime political figures before they are pensioned off. Such was the fate of Brezhnev's predecessor (as chairman) in the Presidium of the Supreme Soviet, Kliment Voroshilov, and such was to be the fate of his successors in this post, Anastas Mikoyan and Nikolai Podgorny.) Yet, the reason for Brezhnev's 1960 misfortune had nothing to do with his performance; rather, it reflected the balance of forces in the Kremlin that propelled him to the position of central importance within the body of Central Committee secretaries. This alarmed the ever-vigilant Khrushchev, who did not wish to see any generally acknowledged heir apparent emerge. Hence, in haste, in a manner that spelled inadvertent risks to both his prestige and power, he tried to elevate another CC secretary for the purpose of counterbalancing Brezhnev.

The unemotional, stern, and callous Mikhail Suslov did not suit Khrushchev; his asceticism and unflappability were not congenial to the impulsive, vain, and mercurial first secretary. Futhermore, Suslov evinced no desire to become the leader of the Party eventually. He appeared quite satisfied with the role of recognized chief Party ideologist. Otto Kuusinen was unqualified to become first secretary because he was too intelligent, too soft, and too mild-mannered, as well as too old. Nuriddin Mukhitdinov was too young and inexperienced, and additionally handicapped by his Central Asian extraction. A. B. Aristov, Ekaterina Furtseva, N. G. Ignatov, and Petr Pospelov were proving too independent-minded, i.e. failing to show Khrushchev due respect. Consequently, he was already seeking ways to drop them from the Central Committee Secretariat.

Nor did Khrushchev have confidence in Aleksey Kirichenko. The latter, like Khrushchev himself, was curt and even coarse with government ministers. He managed to antagonize the military and proved incapable of cooperating with the security organs as well. The main point against him, however, was that he was too sure of himself in his bid for top power. To Khrushchev's distaste, Kirichenko took it for granted that his second secretaryship naturally entitled him to reach the first at some point. Khrushchev, of Ukrainian or at least partly Ukrainian background himself, was suspicious of Party functionaries with roots in the Ukraine. He believed, not without reason, that conspiracies were being hatched by them. Thus, Khrushchev removed Kirichenko from his post in the Central Committee and Brezhnev from his in the Party apparat in an attempt to nip the leadership of the unruly and unmanageable Ukrainian group, which then consisted of four members of the CC Presidium: full members Kirichenko and Brezhnev, and candidate members Podgorny and Andrey Kirilenko.

To counterbalance this group, Khrushchev began promoting Leningraders. This is how the star of Frol Kozlov came to rise in the Party firmament. Khrushchev trusted him because Kozlov, then secretary of the Leningrad Party *obkom*, had supported him at the critical juncture in 1957. (In June that year a majority of the CC Presidium members had demanded the resignation of the first secretary, but Kozlov used his authority as Party leader of Leningrad to help Khrushchev remain in power.) Kozlov also vindicated his patron's trust when he became deputy premier. He learned how to navigate successfully the corridors of power in Moscow, and soon made the appropriate contacts with provincial leaders to the advantage of both his boss and himself.

The fall of Kirichenko secured for Kozlov second place in the Party hierarchy. However, contrary to Khrushchev's expectations, the reshuffle had the effect of strengthening the position of Brezhnev, to whom the former factional supporters of Kirichenko shifted their allegiance. Brezhnev, who simultaneously held two posts, the prestigious chairmanship of the Presidium of the Supreme Soviet and a real power-commanding Central Committee secretaryship (until June 1960), was in a position to attract supporters and knew how to use his extensive powers to maximum advantage. He removed N. I. Belyaev from Kazakhstan party leadership and installed in his stead D. A. Kunaev. Likewise, Brezhnev managed to appoint a number of his men in the Ukraine and in Moldavia before Khrushchev forced him out of the CC Secretariat. From the moment Kozlov became second secretary, he enjoyed a monopoly of power over the Party bureaucracy. However, the balance of power in the Kremlin had been upset; Khrushchev began gradually to lose control over events. In alarm and even in panic, he watched the struggle of the two candidates for succession and switched his support back and forth from one to the other.

Khrushchev's uncertainty over the succession issue, as well as his growing concern about his capability to survive in power, affected the political life of the country for three years: from June 1960 to 1963.

Kozlov needed less than a year to install dozens of his supporters in the Party apparat. He followed the same strategy that Brezhnev had used before him. To get rid of opponents, he would utilize plenums and conferences of Party committees to denounce failures in administration or in fulfillment of economic plans. This method targeted officials for dismissal and thus made room for the advancement of one's own appointees. As a means of establishing one's political base, this procedure is common in the USSR.

Initially, Kozlov cut the number of CC secretaries and appointed as one of them his flunky, Ivan Spiridonov. The secretaryship of the Leningrad *obkom* that Spiridonov vacated was awarded to another henchman of Kozlov's, Vasili Tolstikov. Then Kozlov proceeded to launch his attack against Brezhnev's supporters.

The first to fall was Kirilenko, who lost his influential place in the CC Presidium. Kirilenko was an old friend of Brezhnev's; during the war both had served as political commissars, and after the war they had been bosses of adjacent provinces in the Ukraine. Kozlov pursued the attack by undermining Brezhnev's influence in the republics: in Kazahkstan he removed D. A. Kunaev from the first secretaryship of the Central Committee, and in Moldavia he demoted first deputy chairman of the Council of Ministers, Nikolay Shchelokov, to the post of deputy chairman.

The political crosscurrents in Moscow proved tricky, however. Somehow Kozlov unexpectedly became involved in disputes with Khrushchev over the issue of the rapprochement with Yugoslavia, which Kozlov opposed, and over funds earmarked for agricultural development, which Kozlov considered excessive. As a result of these disputes, Kozlov lost the first secretary's support. From that moment on, Kozlov's career began to wane.

Brezhnev's career meanwhile took a different turn. An ambitious achiever, Brezhnev was not one to acquiesce in a role (e.g. that of chairman of the Presidium of the Supreme Soviet) that commanded high honors but little power. He was determined to squeeze out of it the maximum political advantage and succeeded in doing so. He made many more public appearances at festive occasions and formal state receptions than did his predecessor. He also endeavored to appear as often as possible on the nation's television screens.

Eagerly and with relish, Brezhnev sought occasions to travel abroad, visiting India, Afghanistan, Iran, Finland, China, Western Europe, and Syria and other Arab countries, making fifteen trips in three years. He took advantage of the journeys to gain a polish and charm that his rival Kozlov, encapsulated as he was in the Party bureaucracy cocoon, totally lacked. Brezhnev's tastes became more refined, his worldview broader, and his opinions better informed than those of Khrushchev.

Yet, Brezhnev refrained from open attacks against Kozlov and from expressing any disagreement with Khrushchev. For this he was rewarded: first with an Order of Lenin; then, for "distinguished service," with the order of Hero of Socialist Labor, the highest honor, for which only the most trustworthy citizens of the state qualify. This flattered his vanity, which chafed at the lack of a real political role. The capricious first secretary, miffed at Kozlov's ingratitude, and probably alarmed by the growth of his influence, decided to play favorites once again — this time in favor of Brezhnev.

As a sign of special favor, Khrushchev began taking Brezhnev along on vacations to the Crimea and the Caucasus, in the course of which Brezhnev became involved in sensitive matters and in important negotiations. Most important of all, Khrushchev allowed Brezhnev once again to build up a power base by following the latter's recommendations for filling vacant Party and government posts. At the same time Brezhnev hastened to bring from the Central Committee to the Supreme Soviet his former aides, Georgi Tsukanov, a cadres (manpower) specialist, and Andrey Aleksandrov-Agentov, an adviser on foreign affairs.

Aleksandrov-Agentov acted under the instructions of Chernenko, who was active behind the scenes. The two men formed a brain trust for Brezhnev that eventually enabled him to undertake a campaign to win the succession. They served as recruiters of administrative talent for Brezhnev's team while at the same time seeking ways of undermining Kozlov's authority. Brezhnev succeeded very rapidly in finding replacements for the depleted ranks of his supporters. Helped by Khrushchev, who wished to readjust the balance of forces between the contending rivals at the 22d Congress of the CPSU in October 1961, Brezhnev succeeded in bringing into the Central Committee Marshal A. A. Grechko and Admiral S. G. Gorshkov, Vladimir Shcherbitsky, Ignati Novikov, Venyamin Dymshits, Nikolay Tikhonov, Lev Smirnov, and the Dnepropetrovsk and Tula *obkom* secretaries, Nikita Tolubeev and Ivan Yunak. Without exception, all of them were Brezhnev's old cronies, factional allies, or at least dependable potential supporters. Moreover, in April 1962 Brezhnev succeeded in rehabilitating Kirilenko and even promoting him to full membership of the Presidium and deputy chairmanship of the newly established office of the Presidium dealing with the RSFR (the Russian Republic). For Kozlov, this was a blow, for it involved treading on his turf (as second secretary) in the most important Soviet republic.

During his years out of the mainstream of active politics, Brezhnev came to understand that filling positions with his men was not enough and that success in making it to the very top was contingent on ousting his rival Kozlov's men from their posts. By exploiting every opportunity to the utmost, in particular by capitalizing on his close ties with the security bodies, he succeeded in removing Spiridonov. This was relatively easy because Spiridonov exposed himself by making a number of errors. First, in his function as Central Committee secretary, he was responsible for supervising the Ministry of Defense, and the way he fulfilled this responsibility hardly endeared him to the army brass. Second, he rashly proposed that the corpse of Stalin be removed from the mausoleum. Of course, the idea was Khrushchev's and Spiridonov was merely carrying out his orders. Nevertheless, in the event of settling accounts over this profanation of the once "holy" remains, Spiridonov rather than Khrushchev would be first in line to be scapegoated.

Because Stalin-worshippers did not dare attack the first secretary directly, they eventually vented their wrath on Spiridonov until he was scorned as a pariah. Given this background, Brezhnev had only to hint to Nikolay Mironov, head of the important Administrative Department of the Central Committee, that it might be worthwhile to delve into Spiridonov's past. When Spiridonov began to be investigated in Leningrad, it indeed turned out that this Central Committee secretary had some skeletons in his closet, that he was rash in acting and in expressing his views and had a weakness for women to boot. It is impossible today to determine whether Spiridonov's misconduct was indeed opprobrious enough to warrant his unceremonious dismissal, contrasting with the norm of the Party's leniency toward minor transgressions of its major dignitaries, or whether Mironov, to please Brezhnev (his superior from the time he was head of the Leningrad secret police), fabricated a case against Spiridonov. Whichever was the case, the Presidium was compelled to accept Spiridonov's "resignation."

Even without Spiridonov, Kozlov still retained a strong power base in Moscow, comprising dozens of people whom he had brought from the provinces and continued to advance upward. One of these, Vitali Titov, a holder of a key post in the Central Committee, had become the director of the Organizational Division. Nevertheless, the influence of Kozlov in the Party apparatus was irretrievably declining as he became more and more deeply involved in the opposition to Khrushchev. His career ended in a quite unexpected manner. In the spring of 1963 he had a stroke that left him a bedridden invalid. Owing to this, Khrushchev gained the opportunity (as it turned out, his last) to restore his shaken monopoly on power. He could have done so by placing his trust either in Brezhnev or in another political figure as dependent on him as Brezhnev was but possibly somewhat less ambitious. But Khrushchev did something else. Trying to avoid repeating the mistakes of his predecessors Lenin and Stalin, who had risked precipitating their own downfall by choosing an heir designate (Stalin and Malenkov, respectively) during their lifetimes, he chose not one but two heirs designate, hoping that their rivalry would enable him to keep his own authority intact.

The CC Plenum of June 1963 announced the return of Brezhnev to the CC Secretariat and simultaneously the appointment of Nikolay Podgorny as CC secretary. The balance of power in the Kremlin was again upset. The precipitous rise of Podgorny surprised everyone except Khrushchev.

As a new arrival in Moscow from the Ukraine, where he had headed the local party organization, Podgorny could not help being totally dependent on Khrushchev. By using him to counterbalance Brezhnev, Khrushchev planned both to control his activity and to derail any potential opposition that might emerge. And indeed, Khrushchev's ploy seemed to work: Podgorny was assigned control over Party cadres and gradually began to place his henchmen in important positions. He began with the central administration in the Ukraine, where he succeeded in appointing his own protégé as first CC secretary instead of Brezhnev's protégé, Vladimir Shcherbitsky, who was chairman of the republic Council of Ministers and an aspirant to the same post.

The influence of Podgorny rose even more when in early 1964 he gained responsibility for relations with Communist countries. Suslov, who had been in charge of ideology (and thus relations with Communist countries) from the time of Stalin, could not forgive Khrushchev this insult. Although previously disinterested in power struggles, Suslov then began to contemplate joining a conspiracy. At this point Khrushchev made two mistakes, one right after the other. In April 1964 he appointed Podgorny chairman of the government commission to elaborate measures for the reorganization of agriculture. This antagonized the six members of the commission, all members of the CC Presidium: Brezhnev, Gennadiy Voronov, Kirilenko, Kosygin, Polyansky, and Suslov. Khrushchev's second mistake was in pursuing too far his scheme of playing two contending heirs apparent against each other. Khrushchev decided to relieve

Brezhnev of his post as chairman of the Presidium of the Supreme Soviet because it was an obstacle to his potential utility as CC secretary.

The return of Brezhnev to active politics was announced as follows: "The Central Committee considers it necessary that L. I. Brezhnev concentrate his efforts on carrying out his duties in the Secretariat of the Central Committee." Such a formula had been used once before, in March 1953, when it foreshadowed by three months the seizure of power in the Kremlin by Khrushchev himself. Khrushchev apparently underestimated the prospect of history's repeating itself, for in exactly three months' time Brezhnev would become head of the Party, driving Khrushchev, his benefactor and patron, into political oblivion.

In the opinion of many scholars, the selection of Brezhnev as Khrushchev's successor was a last-minute decision of the conspirators for want of a more appropriate or acceptable candidate. This hypothesis assumes that the initiators and planners of the coup were A. N. Shelepin and Suslov, and according to some, Kosygin as well.

This version of the plot assumes more or less the following pattern of events.[4] The members of the Presidium of the Central Committee came to prefer the cautious and savvy Brezhnev to the ambitious and impulsive Shelepin, at this time head of the KGB. Furthermore, they were appalled by the plot worked out by Shelepin, which to the prudent *nomenklatura* oligarchs appeared too reckless and which by ordinary Soviet standards was reckless indeed. Essentially, the plot consisted of assigning precise roles to all actors involved: the CC secretaries, ministers, and the operation sectors, i.e. the army and secret police. Shelepin prepared matters much more thoroughly than had his unsuccessful predecessors, Vyacheslav Molotov and Georgy Malenkov, in 1957 when the Politburo decision to oust Khrushchev (by a vote of 8 to 2) encountered opposition on the part of the Secretariat and Plenum of the Central Committee. For his attempt Shelepin succeeded in winning over the CC Secretariat to his side. His success was due to the timely death of one pro-Khrushchev CC secretary, Otto Kuusinen, and the no less timely illness of another, Frol Kozlov. According to the commonly accepted view of these events, Brezhnev was practically brought into the plot by chance, due to Khrushchev's blundering in relieving him of the Supreme Soviet chairmanship (on July 15, 1964).[5] Until then Brezhnev had maintained a respectful attitude toward his patron; thereafter detestation allegedly began to dominate. Insult was added to injury when the Supreme Soviet chairmanship was taken over by the ever-obliging Anastas Mikoyan. Fear also played a role: removal from one's post by Khrushchev often foreshadowed ensuing disgrace. Khrushchev was quick to rid himself of subordinates. Like Stalin, he operated on the well-tested principle of resolutely firing associates no longer needed. The difference was that Stalin's style could be compared to the behavior of a dynasty or regime founder who after cruel battles usurps power while trampling law underfoot but at the same time attempts to project a dignified image to the public. Khrushchev, however, acted tactlessly and in an unseemly fashion, like an heir to a throne that he subsequently dishonors.

During the last years of his rule, perhaps as a result of age and illness, Khrushchev no longer cared about what his associates thought. It was not enough for them to unconditionally submit to his unbridled will; they were also expected to adapt to his constantly shifting moods. He was capricious, irritable, and restless, always on the lookout for some new ventures to get involved in. His speeches were dictated by his moods and emotions rather than by reason and cold political calculation. At times his popularity rose, at others it fell. Unlike Stalin, he lacked charisma. Popular attitudes toward him were never admiring (as was the case with Stalin), always tainted by an element of irony, which was sometimes good-natured but often malicious.

On the basis of such a generally correct view of Khrushchev as a person, a number of scholars have concluded that Shelepin's plot was motivated only or at least primarily by the personal failings of Khrushchev. Shelepin is understood to have won over such guardians of orthodoxy as Suslov and Boris Ponomarev by pointing to the opportunistic and dilettantish manner in which Khrushchev handled ideology and sullied its purity. In regard to technocrats like Kosygin, Kirill Mazurov, and Polyansky, he is supposed to have aroused their resistance to the importunate efforts of Khrushchev to force reforms on them by playing on their predispositions to bureaucratic order. In regard to the professional apparatchiks like V. V. Grishin, Sh. R. Rashidov, Yury Andropov, and P. N. Demichev, Shelepin is supposed to have used a different argument, frightening them by the possible consequences of Khrushchev's plan of restructuring Party committees.

Two CC secretaries (Titov and V. I. Polyakov) remained loyal to Khrushchev, and the position of three Presidium members (Mikoyan, Voronov, and Podgorny) was unclear. In order not to jeopardize the chances of the coup, Shelepin is supposed to have agreed, under pressure from Suslov and Kirilenko, that during the transitional period after the coup Brezhnev would serve as first secretary. Such a decision could be described as farsighted on Shelepin's part; it was supposed to give him a chance to establish a base in the Politburo, to become a Politburo member himself, and then, with the help of the KGB, to advance his claim to power over the country. The choice of Brezhnev was also supposed to create the impression of continuity, and to make the change engineered more acceptable to the masses. Indeed, it could only appear natural that the CC second secretary (Brezhnev) succeeded the first secretary (Khrushchev).

With numerous variations, the described scenario of political developments in Moscow in the fall of 1964 has almost gained canonical status. The scenario has turned up in various books written over the years. It is surprising that their authors do not realize that in the USSR power is not granted to secondary participants who willy-nilly become involved in a conspiracy but only to primary conspirators, i.e. the leaders.[6]

Brezhnev was never a bystander in the power struggle. He was always in the thick of things. Through the long years of his Party career he learned how to survive bloody purges. He emerged safe from the fires of World War II, quickly learned how to make the best of the situation under the unpredictable Stalin, and finally, by deploying the requisite hypocrisy and complaisance, he proved able to obtain what he wanted from Khrushchev.

It is nevertheless possible, even likely, that being cautious by nature, Brezhnev did not join the plot right from its inception. There might well have been other plots conceived in the minds of the humiliated members of the CC Presidium and subsequently aborted. But the fact is that only when Brezhnev joined a plot, did it gain a good chance of success. In any event, Brezhnev was aiming at the top spot from the moment he became a CC secretary. He proceeded methodically and single-mindedly, first by establishing and expanding his political base through placing and advancing his supporters in the Party machine. In the Soviet system the loyalty of subordinates is the most dependable foundation of personal power. Brezhnev rewarded loyalty generously, by bestowing high posts, honors, and prestigious decorations.

Thus, as soon as the idea of this plot was conceived, it turned out that of all the members of the CC Presidium, only Brezhnev had the requisite resource: dependable and experienced men, tested by years of Party intrigue and willing to take a political risk for the sake of their patron and for themselves as well. Brezhnev's men, many of whom were friends and like-minded buddies from his student days, provided the most convincing arguments for Brezhnev's taking the lead of the conspiracy.

Without Brezhnev's help, his men would not have had a chance to make brilliant careers. But it worked the other way too: without their support, Brezhnev would not have reached the pinnacle of power. Brezhnev played a simultaneous game on several "chessboards" and on each he had an advantage over the other players. The Ukrainian Party organization was the most important and complex. There he had important and properly groomed allies, the most influential of them being

Vladimir Shcherbitsky. In 1955 Brezhnev promoted him to first secretary of Dnepropetrovsk Province in place of Kirilenko, whom he had made head of Sverdlovsk Province. Two years later, when Brezhnev became a member of the CC Presidium, he advanced Shcherbitsky to Kiev, where he became CC secretary of the republic and two years later its premier.

Brezhnev's next move in the Ukraine was less successful: in 1963 he attempted to make Shcherbitsky Party boss of the republic to replace Podgorny, who had moved on to Moscow. In this Brezhnev failed. Podgorny managed to put his man, Petr Shelest, in as first secretary of the Ukrainian CC, as a result of which Shcherbitsky had to return to his original post in Dnepropetrovsk.

Having suffered a defeat in his frontal attempt to capture the central authority in the Ukraine, Brezhnev attacked from the flank. He moved Nikolay Drozdenko, another proven supporter from the Dnepropetrovsk Party organization, to secretary of the Kiev city Party committee, and Yuriy Tursuev, a Komsomol activist also from Dnepropetrovsk, to secretary of the Central Committee of the Ukrainian Komsomol.

Two more of Brezhnev's buddies from Dnepropetrovsk were installed in the republic Party bureaucracy. In 1961 Leonid Lunich became chairman of the Dnepropetrovsk Sovnarkhoz (Council of National Economy) and Aleksey Gaevoy became secretary for cadres of the Ukrainian Central Committee. The following year still another man from Dnepropetrovsk, Ivan Grushnitsky, was appointed chairman of the republic Party-Government Control Commission.

In his struggle with Podgorny over Ukrainian Party appointments Brezhnev achieved only limited success. Although the contest between the two rival Ukrainian *nomenklatura* groups subsequently continued openly for many years, in Moldavia Brezhnev attained clear superiority from the very beginning. As early as 1961, he was already a virtual kingmaker when he installed his ally, Ivan Bodyula, as Moldavian first secretary.

In the Russian Republic (RSFSR), too, Brezhnev had considerable room for political maneuvering. From 1958 to 1960 he was a member of the CC CPSU bureau for administering the RSFSR, and in 1962 he succeeded in getting appointed as first deputy chairman of this bureau Andrey Kirilenko, who in 1950 had taken over from Brezhnev Dnepropetrovsk Province, i.e. the customary recruitment pool for Brezhnev's supporters. Georgi Enyutin, who became the chairman of the Party-Government Control Commission of the Russian Republic, also originally came from Dnepropetrovsk.

Brezhnev's Dnepropetrovsk clique also operated successfully on the provincial level. In 1962 Ivan Yunak was appointed secretary of the Tula Party *obkom*, and Georgi Pavlov secretary of the Mari *obkom*. Between

1960 and 1964 Brezhnev brought a considerable number of his Dnepropetrovsk men to key posts in Moscow. One of these, Vinyamin Dymshits,
became chairman of the Sovnarkhoz of the USSR, the economic administrative body established by Khrushchev, and another, Ignati Novikov,
became deputy chairman of the Council of Ministers. Likewise, the
chairman of the Dnepropetrovsk Sovnarkhoz, Nikolay Tikhonov, was
first placed by Brezhnev in the post of chairman of the Government
Scientific Council attached to the Council of Ministers, and then promoted to deputy chairmanship of Gosplan, which ranked as a ministerial
position in the government.

Furthermore, many of Brezhnev's protégés were elected to the Central
Committee. The number grew from five in 1961 to sixteen in 1963. Their
authority and connections proved a valuable contributing factor in the
plot to overthrow Khrushchev.

There is no doubt that the security services and the armed forces played
an important role. That role, however, should not be exaggerated. It was
not Shelepin who recruited Brezhnev to the coup, but vice versa. It was
Brezhnev, who supervised both the armed forces and KGB, who recruited
Shelepin.

The extent of Shelepin's participation in the upcoming coup was strictly overseen by Brezhnev. Shelepin was responsible for technical arrange-
ments, such as bringing Central Committee members to Moscow for a
special Plenum. Of course, Brezhnev did rely on Shelepin's connections
within the KGB, which the latter had headed for a number of years, and
on his closeness to the current KGB chairman V. E. Semichastny. But
Brezhnev was well aware that Shelepin's influence in the KGB was limited
for a number of both external and internal reasons.

External control over the KGB was maintained by the administrative
division of the Central Committee, which since 1959 had been headed by
Nikolay Mironov, whose career had been shaped by Brezhnev in his usual
manner. Mironov came from Dnepropetrovsk and owed his promotion to
the personal support of Brezhnev. He first received an important post in
the KGB with the rank of lieutenant general and then, his connections
still working, was promoted to the Central Committee of the CPSU.
Within the KGB apparatus itself the ability to maneuver of both Semichastny and Shelepin was restricted by Semen Tsvigun, a relative of
Brezhnev's who headed the KGB in Tadzhikistan, and by Georgiy Tsinev,
also a native of Dnepropetrovsk, who with Brezhnev's help became head
of the KGB cadres administration.

Yet, the degree of involvement of Shelepin in the preparation and
execution of the plot should not be underestimated. Shelepin was the
youngest CC secretary and had made a brilliant career. He joined the

Party at the age of twenty-two. After graduating from the prestigious Institute of History, Philosophy, and Literature, he plunged into sociopolitical activity. While Stalin was still alive, Shelepin headed the Komsomol and, in 1952, became a member of the Central Committee. To all appearances, he was quite successful in mobilizing Soviet youth for work on Khrushchev's virgin lands project, the best proof being that in 1958 Khrushchev rewarded him by appointing him head of the KGB. This post offered him wide scope for the exercise of his enterprising spirit and propensity for recklessness.

Under his aegis the Soviet secret services committed a number of assassinations of opponents of the Soviet regime in Europe. The world was shocked and perturbed, but Khrushchev was gratified by Shelepin's boldness. He was mistaken though in his appreciation, for despite being indeed bold, Shelepin had no intention of being a reliable executor of Khrushchev's will. Khrushchev heaped favors on him (CC secretaryship, then deputy chairmanship of the Council of Ministers and directorship of the powerful Party-Government Control Committee), but Shelepin neither trusted nor respected Khrushchev. Shelepin constantly compared himself with the other CC secretaries and with members of the Council of Ministers and the CC Presidium. He noted, with justification, his superiority. He had a sharp mind, broad knowledge, and an iron will. Accordingly, he believed that he deserved even more power than he had. Nevertheless, he knew that, for the time being, there was no chance for him to become head of the Party. For that, he first needed to enter the Areopagus of power, the Central Committee Presidium, where in time he might become the equal of its leading and lording members. Only then might he vie in prestige with Brezhnev, in influence with Suslov, and in authority with Kosygin. The highest price Shelepin could exact for participation in the plot was membership in the CC Presidium, not general secretaryship. In other words, he would have to share power with others. The size of Shelepin's "lobby," comprising his loyal clique of Komsomol buddies, of numerous KGB supporters, and most important, of the Party-Government Control Committee, which he headed, corresponded to his expectations.

The events that took place in the summer and fall of 1964 decisively affected the nature of the conspiracy. Nothing augured the imminent fall of Khrushchev. Not long previously, in April, his seventieth birthday had been celebrated with exceptional pomp and circumstance. Yet, at times, it appeared as if Khrushchev were absentmindedly heading into a swamp. By committing one political mistake after another, he was bringing on his own downfall. The best example was the announcement of his intention to convoke, before the end of 1964, an international conference of Communist parties to formalize the rift with China. The CC Presidium, anxious to avoid an irreparable schism in the world Communist movement, opposed the idea. It preferred a more refined ideological contest with China.

Then, as inexplicably, without providing a convincing ideological justification, Khrushchev encouraged rapprochement with West Germany. This innovation upset the more orthodox members of the Presidium, who were concerned about the adverse impact upon relations with East German leader Walter Ulbricht and upon the viability of his Communist regime.

Furthermore, Khrushchev recognized Yugoslavia as a Communist state over the objections of Suslov, who opined that such recognition could lead only to encouragement of nationalist sentiments in Eastern Europe and, hence, to jeopardizing the security of the USSR. In contrast to the first secretary, Brezhnev immediately hastened to distance himself from the "pseudorevolutionaries" in Belgrade and to refer to them as the schismatics.

In September Khrushchev aggravated the already simmering conflict with the armed forces by emphasizing the importance of the development of the consumer sector of the economy. He also tried to exploit the need for reorganization of agriculture as a pretext for reshuffling the leadership.

Khrushchev's reorganization proposal was expected to be brought up (and automatically approved) at the upcoming November party Plenum. In the press there appeared scarcely veiled hints of another purge that would sweep the top leadership. The CC secretaries could avert it only by deposing Khrushchev. The choice was plain: either the members of the Presidium would go *at* the Plenum or Khrushchev would go *before* it.

The imminent purge made the fall of Khrushchev inevitable. Once the latter was decided on, the choice of Brezhnev as a successor was just as inevitable. Brezhnev was the unassailable heir apparent. No member of the Presidium could match him in experience (he was the sole CC secretary with almost thirty years of service in both the Party and state bureaucracy), in mastery of political infighting (he survived all the turmoil in the Kremlin after Stalin's death), and in popularity (he had the reputation of being considerate, tolerant, and sincere in dealing with people).

Also in purely formal terms (and forms have significance in a system as hierarchical as the Soviet one), Brezhnev had no rivals. All previous first secretaries had come from among CC secretaries who were also full members of the Presidium and who, in addition, had considerable government experience. This is why Kosygin, Mikoyan, Voronov, Kirilenko, Polyansky, and N. M. Shvernik had no chance for the top post: in 1964 they were *not* CC secretaries, though they were members of the Presidium. Suslov and Podgorny were simultaneously CC secretaries and members of the Presidium with considerable experience in Party work, but they lacked experience in government work. Furthermore, Suslov, with his interests confined to ideology, did not view himself as a pretender. As for Podgorny, in his mere year and a half of service in Moscow he had not yet struck roots in the Central Committee bureaucracy.

Having all the qualifications, Brezhnev turned out to be the sole real pretender to the post of first secretary. He was the natural candidate to translate the simmering dissatisfaction with the rule and the policies of Khrushchev into political action.

As in a work of drama, in the ensuing events one can distinguish the phases of presentation, culmination, and denouement. Also in a way reminiscent of some dramas, the chain of events contained an element of suspense about the characters. As in a detective story or play, there was a question of "whodunit." Was Brezhnev the inspirator of the coup, the one who set the plot in motion? This is quite likely, but one should not preclude the possibility that the plot was collectively hatched by Suslov and Kosygin jointly with Brezhnev. This does not mean that on a given day the three met and decided that there would be a coup. In totalitarian regimes the conception and planning of a political plot is an intricate matter abounding in contradictions. The potential allies are beset by mutual distrust and doubts, not about whether they are right or wrong but about whether their participation in the coup is in their own interest. In the event of the coup's failure, repressions are certain. Public denunciation is to be expected and, together with it, loss of prestige and attendant privileges. A plotter is recurrently tempted to withdraw from the plot, rein in his ambitions, and put up with insults and humiliations dealt him in order to avoid the risk of downfall from a position of power and high privilege.

Treachery and betrayal are perfectly compatible with the standards of Communist morality. Consequently, potential plotters spend considerable time cautiously sizing one another up, each reassessing the nature and depth of his grudges against the first secretary and weighing present dissatisfaction against the risk of openly making the first move, until one of them dares to propose that his potential confreres unite and proceed to action.

Launching of a conspiracy does not come easily. Given the fact that Soviet society is one of hierarchical subordination, the initiative for such a move must come not from the most respected or the boldest but from the most senior-ranking figure. Otherwise, the other members of the Presidium would not accept his leadership, would not follow him. Only

Brezhnev was such a figure. It is quite possible that Brezhnev was activated by Khrushchev's appointment of Podgorny as his successor. Brezhnev must have felt betrayed. At the same time Suslov and Kosygin probably realized that the first secretary's new favorite owed them nothing and would seek and find others to form his power base either within the Presidium or outside it. Thus, in late 1963 or early 1964 the nucleus of the conspiracy was formed, with Brezhnev as its leader, Suslov as its ideological sponsor, and Kosygin, Polyansky, and Shelepin as coconspirators.

The culmination took place in the summer of 1964 when Khrushchev visited Bonn. The conspirators then decided to openly discredit the first secretary by blocking his proposed rapprochement with the West. The KGB received the order (possibly from Brezhnev via his subordinate Mironov or possibly, via several links, i.e. Brezhnev, Shelepin, and Semichastny, to conceal its origin) to carry out a number of provocations to undermine the proposed detente. The provocations included the gas poisoning of a diplomat from West Germany (the "Schwinermann affair"), the break-in by KGB agents into a hotel where English and U.S. officers were staying (the "Khabarovsk incident"), and the arrest in Moscow of a distinguished American scholar (the "Barghoorn affair").

The denouement of the conspiracy began on September 30 when Khrushchev went off to rest at his residence on the Black Sea coast. Preparing an alibi for himself in the event that the plot was uncovered, Brezhnev flew to Berlin on October 5, the pretext being the fifteenth anniversary of the German Democratic Republic. Thereupon the machinery of the plot went into action. High-ranking officers who supported Khrushchev were dispatched to Warsaw for the commemoration of Polish Army Day. Suslov, accompanied by top KGB officials, visited republic capitals and provincial centers. Their dual task there, prior to the beginning of the coup, was to "prepare" members of the Central Committee before they would be summoned to a Plenum in Moscow and to prevent from attending the Plenum those who could not be won over to the side of the plotters.

The plot was developing successfully. At the behest of Mironov and Shelepin, KGB agents succeeded in preventing premature exposure to the extent that Khrushchev's own son-in-law, who was both a Central Committee member and the editor in chief of *Izvestiya*, did not have the slightest suspicion of unfolding developments even though he was in Moscow the entire time. Evidently Podgorny also suspected nothing, for he calmly left Moscow on October 10. It was then decided that the coup would take place on October 12–13, no earlier because Brezhnev had first to return, and no later because the government delegation with the army officers would by then be back from Poland. When Brezhnev landed at Moscow's Vnukovo airport, he was met by quite different people than those who saw him off. As head of the Party, he was met by members of the Presidium headed by Suslov. Because it was only a matter of hours before the coup was scheduled to take place, the plotters no longer had a reason to keep out of the public eye. Khrushchev, still suspecting nothing, continued his vacation. When he was joined at his villa in Sochi by Mikoyan, it was clear that the existence of the plot had not come to Khrushchev's notice. To the plotters, this was a good portent of the plot's ultimate success.

On Monday, October 12, Khrushchev made his last television appearance as first secretary. Just before the launching of the Soviet spaceship *Voskhod*, Khrushchev phoned the space center from Sochi to wish the astronauts a safe journey and promise them a triumphant welcome on their return. But the promise was not to be kept, for upon their return Khrushchev would no longer be in command. As the spaceship was completing its first orbits around the earth the Central Committee Presidium convened in Moscow.

The time of convening the Presidium session on the night of October 12–13 was selected purposely because only seven of the eleven Presidium members were then present in Moscow. Brezhnev, who opened the session, calculated that those seven would unanimously vote for the immediate removal of Khrushchev. Thereafter the vacationing Podgorny and Mikoyan would be offered a choice: either to support the Presidium decision or share the fate of Khrushchev.

The Presidium session began exactly as the conspirators planned. Suslov delivered a resounding denunciation in which he accused Khrushchev of arbitrariness and incompetence, adventurism and abuse of authority. Kosygin blamed Khrushchev for economic failures, and Polyansky attributed to him responsibility for the crisis in agriculture. They were seconded by Kirilenko. Nevertheless, something unexpected happened toward the end of the session: Voronov and Shvernik, without defending Khrushchev overtly, proposed waiting until the remaining members of the Presidium returned to Moscow. A complicated and risk-laden situation ensued. There was a danger that the 1957 scenario, when the plotters against Khrushchev were completely routed, would be repeated. This time, however, Khrushchev was not able to overrule the Presidium. A majority of CC members had already arrived in the capital and Brezhnev and Suslov had reason to be assured of their support. Khrushchev was isolated. The KGB cut off the telephones of his supporters in the Party bureaucracy. Unlike 1957, the army had neither the opportunity nor the desire to become involved in intra-Party conflict. Khrushchev had squandered whatever political support he once had had in military circles, and Brezhnev had powerful allies in the General Staff among the so-called Ukrainian marshals, his old buddies like Grechko and K. S. Moskalenko. Owing to their support, Brezhnev could afford to convene an extraordinary Presidium without Khrushchev. It opened at noon on October 13 as soon as Mikoyan and Podgorny arrived in Moscow.

An airplane was sent for Khrushchev, with the regular crew replaced by KGB agents. It was dispatched only when it was already certain that Brezhnev had a firm and stable majority in the Presidium. Voronov, now satisfied that protocol had been scrupulously observed, joined the conspirators. Podgorny, too, preferred to betray his benefactor rather than accept the consequences of loyalty to him.

Shvernik abstained in voting and only Mikoyan, confused and flustered, for the first time in his life made a real political blunder by motioning that Khrushchev's retirement be reconsidered at the Plenum. The CC Plenum met on October 14 and rubber-stamped Khrushchev's ouster. No more than half of the CC members attended the session. Still, there must have been some hitch in the conspirators' plan. Two days passed, and only on October 16 did *Pravda* finally report Khrushchev's retirement, marking the moment when the former first secretary became a political has-been. His name disappeared from Soviet history and faded from the memory of the Soviet citizenry as the new leader became the focus of public attention. Into Brezhnev's "magnetic field" dozens of completely new Party figures would now be drawn. One of these, to all appearances a rather insignificant one, Chernenko, would himself become general secretary exactly twenty years after the coup that brought Brezhnev to power.

Notes

1. On May 1, 1960, in the airspace of the USSR in the vicinity of Sverdlovsk a U.S. U-2 intelligence aircraft, piloted by Francis Gary Powers, was shot down. The incident occurred only two weeks before a scheduled summit conference in Paris between President Dwight Eisenhower and Nikita Khrushchev, leader of the Soviet Union. In Washington there were expectations that it would be possible to reach agreement with the Soviet Union on banning nuclear testing in the atmosphere, in space, and under water. Moscow utilized the blunder of the president in sanctioning Powers's flight at such a time to call off the summit. In August the Soviets staged the most raucous show trial of the Cold War, starring the ill-fated spy-pilot in the Hall of Columns of the Palace of the Unions in the Kremlin.
2. The June Plenum of the CC CPSU of 1957 dropped from the Presidium and from the ranks of the Central Committee Molotov, Kaganovich, Malenkov, and Shepilov. This was the group that had planned the removal of Khrushchev from his post as first secretary of the CC and demanded the convocation of the Presidium (in the absence of several members who were supporters of Khrush-

chev) on the ostensible grounds of purely regular business, to discuss the texts of Soviet leaders to be delivered at the upcoming two-hundredth anniversary of the founding of the city of Leningrad (Petrograd/Petersburg). However, when the Presidium convened, they instead called for the removal of Khruschchev. The supporters of the first secretary succeeded in having the vote postponed until the convocation of the Central Committee Plenum. There the conspirators did not receive the support they required, and it was they who were removed from their central Party positions.

3. In March 1953, immediately upon the death of Stalin, Brezhnev was removed from his post as secretary of the Central Committee and named deputy head of the Main Political Directorate of the Soviet Army and Navy. He remained in this post until February 1954, when he was made second secretary of the Central Committee of the Communist Party of Kazakhstan.

4. *Leonid Ilyich Brezhnev. Kratkiy biograficheskiy ocherk* (Leonid Ilyich Brezhnev. Short biographical sketch) (Moscow: Izd–vo politicheskoy literatury, 1961), pp. 54–57.

5. *Pravda*, July 16–17, 1964.

6. A. Avtorkhanov, *Tekhnologiya vlasti* (The mechanism of power) (Frankfurt am Main: Posev, 1978), pp. 715–21; Leonard Schapiro, *The Communist Party of the Soviet Union* (New York: Random House, Vintage Books, 1960); J. Murphy, *Brezhnev: Soviet Politician* (Jefferson, N.C.: McFarland, 1981); George W. Breslauer, *Khrushchev and Brezhnev as Leaders: Building Authority in Soviet Politics* (London: Allen & Unwin, 1982); John Dornberg, *Brezhnev: The Masks of Power* (London: Andre Deutsch, 1974).

4

The Party Boss

In such a regime both truth and lie disappear.
What remains is their simulacrums.

After he took over Khrushchev's place, Brezhnev did not immediately become a second Khrushchev. To perform as Khrushchev number two, he had to build up a Khrushchev-style personality cult, but he proceeded toward that goal cautiously.

The fundamentals of power in the Soviet Union can be reduced to two elements: the government bureaucratic system and the Party. In advancing within the former, Brezhnev was hampered by the new ethos of collective leadership that precluded the first secretary of the Central Committee from simultaneously holding the post of chairman of the Council of Ministers. Joint incumbency of both posts by both Stalin and Khrushchev had provided them with the opportunity to develop the cult of their personalities. The new oligarchy resented this and, accordingly, imposed restrictions. This is why Brezhnev had to cede the chairmanship of the Council of Ministers to Kosygin.

Nevertheless, ways to get around this restriction still remained, and Brezhnev proved adept at taking advantage of them. First, he engineered his appointment as head of the committee to draft a new constitution, notwithstanding the agreed-upon rules of "collective leadership," which would have seemed to confer this position on the chairman of the Presidium of the Supreme Soviet. Subsequently, Brezhnev was named chairman of the Defense Council and in this capacity was responsible for decisions relating to armaments and military command although by tradition this post should rather have been assigned to the minister of defense or the chairman of the Council of Ministers. Thus, by raising the power of the Party at the expense of that of the government bureaucracy,

Brezhnev was simultaneously raising himself as the Party leader above the leadership of the government. However, in order to make this situation permanent, he had first to consolidate his own position within the Party.

In the USSR there is really not one but two parties: the outer one, which at that time had 12 million members, and the inner one, comprising several hundred thousand professional functionaries.[1] The outer Party members are only somewhat less deprived of rights than the rest of the Soviet population, and they function as the appendages to the real actors of the inner Party where actual, unlimited power is located. It was the inner Party whose favors Brezhnev sought. He did *not* have to win over to his side many thousands of Party secretaries of various ranks from various regions, provinces, and republics because their power, irrespective of their varying personal influence, was ultimately limited by the hierarchical principle of "democratic centralism," i.e. by their subordination to the Party higher-ups. Thus, over the *raykoms* (the regional committees) stood the *gorkoms* (the city committees); over the *gorkoms*, the *obkoms* (provincial committees) and *kraykoms* (territorial committees). And over all of these stood the Central Committee and over the Central Committee stood the Politburo (under Khrushchev known as the Presidium), which alone was not subordinated to any authority higher than itself. Democratic centralism is therefore to be understood as follows: democracy for the Politburo and centralism, stringent, at times even brutally so, for all other Party bodies.

Whoever dominates the Politburo dominates the Party and, hence, the government. However, it was not a simple matter for the general secretary (known as the first secretary between 1952 and 1966) of the Central Committee to make the Politburo comply with his will. In 1964 the first secretary's authority had been parceled among the members of the Politburo, and Brezhnev had to find a way to win it back. The Politburo adopts its resolutions, which give direction to the political and social life of the country, by simple majority vote. This is one of the paradoxes of the Soviet system, which is autocratic and totalitarian on all levels except for one-man, one-vote suffrage at the very top.

On the lower rungs of the Party hierarchy the arbitrariness of the first secretaries is in no way limited by the views or will of members of Party bureaus. These secretaries are accountable only to higher-ranking first secretaries. However, in the Politburo the general secretary has to make a show of personal power while actually following the dictatorial will of the Politburo until (if at all) he succeeds in imposing on it his personal will. This complicated and long process has never, at least since the death of Stalin, been carried to its ultimate conclusion. The general secretary proceeds toward this end in stages, following a strategy gradually elaborated and tested over the many years of the existence of the regime. At first he attempts to detect and expose the differences of opinion between the various members of the Politburo; then, by playing on their vanity, to split them into contending camps; and finally to support the faction that will prove the stronger and more influential. This method enables him to remove from the Politburo the "troublemakers" and replace them by newly co-opted conformists. No matter how loyal to him personally, the conformists eventually gain growing influence. To avoid becoming dependent on them, the general secretary carries out major reshuffles, thus expanding the number of his supporters in the Central Committee Secretariat and the Politburo.

In other words, the general secretary consolidates his power at the expense of the power of the Politburo, but never to the end. The general secretary is never able to stymie completely the activity of the Politburo and totally block the danger it poses to him. The new members he co-opted into the Politburo can never be taken for granted as being loyal to him because they might always develop their own ambitions to the point of seeking to replace him.

Within the system reigning in the Party the boss is often betrayed first by his own henchmen, just those whom he had promoted. Brezhnev's predecessors were well aware of this. Therefore, Stalin began with purging his supporters while arriving at temporary accommodations with his opponents, whom he then tried to cow into submission. This process was characterized by certain regularities. Thus, as could be observed again in Khrushchev's time, a period of one to five years was needed for the newly co-opted members of the Politburo to find themselves in a position to challenge the general secretary. Until they had been integrated into the Politburo, and gained some authority in the Party apparat and a nation-wide reputation, they would remain compliant executors of the general secretary's will. The looser their connections with the Central Committee were, the more durable would be their dependence on him. This is why all general secretaries tend to keep to a minimum (two or three perhaps) the number of members of the Politburo who also are secretaries of the Central Committee. The more veteran politicians the Politburo comprised, the more limited the power of the general secretary would be, and contrariwise, an increase of the number of new Politburo members would stabilize and strengthen his position.

One excellent means of fostering his monopoly of power is for the general secretary to introduce into the Politburo a person whose background is quite unsuitable in terms of education, work experience, lack of Party seniority, and age (too young or too old), and who lacks deep and firm roots in the capital or in the Party bureaucracy.

Most ideal would be a situation that would allow the general secretary constantly to reshuffle the membership by injecting new blood into the Politburo. To Brezhnev, this way was not open: the resolution of the Plenum of the Central Committee that had appointed him general secretary had mandated the policy of "stability of cadres." Yet, Brezhnev managed to find a way to impose his will on the Politburo, or rather the way was found for Brezhnev by Chernenko.

What Chernenko did was to create mechanisms by which he could manipulate the resolutions (and occasionally even the policy) of the Politburo. This became possible in 1965, when Chernenko returned to the Central Committee to be named head of the General Department. At first sight it might have seemed that this department was no more than a technical appendage of the Party machine charged with preparing drafts of decrees and setting the Politburo agenda. But precisely such tasks of the General Department offered great (although before Chernenko untapped) potential for consolidating and strengthening the authority, and eventually the dictatorship of the general secretary.

As a rule, the Politburo agenda consists of dozens, at times even hundreds, of items of varying degrees of importance, ranging from major state problems to quite insignificant matters that are debated there only because the highest body of the Party does not wish to relinquish oversight over anything. Furthermore, the numerous ministries and state committees (of which there are more than 100) above all else wish to shield themselves from criticism, and hence submit matters of their sectorial concern for the approval of the top Party authority. The idea of collective responsibility is interpreted in the Soviet Union as a kind of insurance policy against the top leadership's wrath. This fact enabled the head of the General Department to select certain matters for immediate consideration by the Politburo while delaying others for subsequent sessions.

The role of Chernenko was to select for the Politburo agenda matters of interest to the general secretary, with an eye on the chances to win approval for Brezhnev's views. When discussion became prolonged, voting (which in the Politburo is by simple majority) would be deferred until the next day, Friday, when the opinion of each member would have been elicited by Chernenko and decisions made only when the majority backed Brezhnev. In preparing items for Politburo consideration, Chernenko was privy to the views and inclinations of each Politburo member. He was thus in the position to assure the passage, or conversely, the defeat of particular resolutions.

Not all of this was easy sailing. Chernenko's role, after all, was no more than to prepare the draft agenda. The draft had to be approved on

Wednesday, the day before the session, by the first among the equals in the "collective leadership," which initially meant Brezhnev, Kosygin, Suslov, and Shelepin and later (after Shelepin was ousted from the Party apparat to head the trade unions) the remaining three. It sometimes happened that as a result of their confidential deliberations a Politburo session agenda would be significantly altered to Brezhnev's dissatisfaction. But even then, Chernenko still had a way to affect the contents of the resolutions adopted. If opinion at the Politburo session was divided (as was always the case when the general secretary was in the minority), then Chernenko in his capacity of technical secretary could stall the proceedings by inviting the testimony of experts or consultants, for example, so that the matter would be carried over to the next session. In such cases the duty of Chernenko was to prepare, jointly with the Central Committee secretaries, a draft of the resolutions on which there had been disagreement: the CC secretaries smoothed out the various versions of the resolutions and Chernenko, as head of the General Department, would edit their final draft. This function provided him with the opportunity to suppress anything that might be embarrassing to the general secretary, especially any criticism of his performance. The CC secretaries were always Party functionaries who represented the interests of specific "constituencies," such as industry, agriculture, the armed forces, state security, and so on. Chernenko could submit for the consideration of the Politburo any matter of importance to a given secretary's ministerial "fief" merely by altering the preset agenda. For this reason, the secretaries were not inclined to oppose the editorial versions of resolutions that Chernenko proposed.

To a certain degree the fate of Central Committee and Politburo resolutions was in the hands of the General Department even after their adoption. The Department had the duty of bringing the contents of such resolutions to the attention of the Central Committee (without disclosing the details of the preceding deliberations). Chernenko, however, could delay this procedure until the resolution might either be outdated or adjusted to the interests of the general secretary. This was possible because the members of the Politburo would be busy preparing for upcoming sessions and would not bother to concern themselves with following up on matters already settled. This was particularly the case because the top four in the Kremlin in the first years after Brezhnev's appointment as general secretary, Kosygin, Suslov, Podgorny, and Shelepin, paid little attention to Chernenko, whom they considered a nondescript serviceable bureaucrat.

They would have preferred in the post of head of the General Department someone more independent than Chernenko. They perceived him as just a functionary in the literal sense of representing nothing more than his function, and in a quite mediocre fashion at that, without any interest in domains other than his Party responsibilities. In addition, his very appearance suggested submissiveness and the desire to please anyone in the Politburo. In regard to Brezhnev such servility became his obsession.

With time, Brezhnev developed the need to see Chernenko constantly in order to be reassured by his fawning words and his total loyalty. Brezhnev needed such gratification and no one excelled Chernenko in pleasing the general secretary, anticipating his wishes, and courting his favor. One could scarcely imagine Chernenko without a notepad in hand ready to jot down whatever Brezhnev wished. Chernenko assessed people solely from the point of view of their utility to Brezhnev. If he found them useful, he paid particular attention to them; if not, he ignored them.

It is possible that it was not easy for Chernenko to reconcile his private feelings with his role, that the latter made him feel ashamed of himself on occasion and always concerned about his future. The prospect of ending up on the sidelines of political life certainly did not appeal to him. While encouraging the boundless vanity of his boss, Chernenko had the good sense to channel it into directions advantageous to himself as well. While helping the general secretary advance to autocracy, he himself rose to power on Brezhnev's coattails. While kowtowing to his boss's authority, he taught him to demand that everyone else kowtow likewise—and they did. In this way Brezhnev became convinced of his own irreplaceability. In such a situation it was not difficult for Chernenko also to convince Brezhnev that it was appropriate to reward his loyal servant by some crumbs from the table of real power. The general secretary could find no reason to object. Why not allow Chernenko into the inner circle as a candidate member of the Central Committee and deputy of the Supreme Soviet? Such privileges sufficed to gratify Chernenko, at least for the moment. Brezhnev had his own reasons to be satisfied. He had promoted to a high Party post a flunky whose role was to cater to him! This was something even Stalin would not have dared! Both Brezhnev and Chernenko knew that they were playing with power and they enjoyed the game.

At first glance it did not appear that Chernenko possessed the qualities needed by a Party leader. He particularly lacked the verbal capacity for empty phrasemongering that Party leaders constantly require. However, he did possess in abundance such career-advancing qualities as goal-centeredness, diligence, lack of principle, and scorn for public opinion.

When he joined the Central Committee, the first task Chernenko set himself was to transfer maximum authority from the Politburo to the bureaucracy of the general secretary's office. He began by providing either incomplete or obsolete information to those members of the Politburo who worked outside the Party bureaucracy or did not live in Moscow. Next, together with the advisers whom he brought into Brezhnev's entourage, Georgiy Tsukanov, Andrey Aleksandrov-Agentov, and Anatoliy Blatov, he proceeded to elaborate a strategy aimed at undermining the collective leadership principle.

The period of relative peace in the Politburo came to an end before it could yield constructive results. The exhortations of the new Soviet leadership against the "voluntarism" and "subjectivism" of the previous leader died out. The situation resembled that of 1953 when Malenkov and Khrushchev clashed in their struggle for leadership of the government and hegemony in the Party. As then, the honeymoon period was bound to end because in politics, as in marriage, conflicts that are temporarily ignored are bound to emerge abruptly later. However, in one respect the 1964 crisis in the Politburo significantly differed from the one that shook the Soviet authority system ten years earlier: the former portended an important theoretical innovation.

Several months after the fall of Khrushchev Brezhnev proposed an expensive program of agricultural development. The policy was provided with suitable ideological grounding by asserting that the improvement of agriculture was vital for the successful building of Communism. Kosygin, however, stood up for a different social policy, that of assigning priority to the production of consumer goods. His policy was provided with ideological justification by contending that investment in industry was, on cost-efficiency grounds, preferable to investment in collectivized agriculture. The dispute between Brezhnev and Kosygin on the direction of development of the Soviet economy, did not mean that Brezhnev's attitude was antiurban or Kosygin's antipeasant. While arguing economy, both meant power. They were competing for dominance in the Politburo and, for that purpose, sought to offer economic programs that would appeal to the masses. Playing to the public in the Soviet Union takes place only during transitional periods of succession struggles at the top. This is when increased resources are allocated to the consumer sector, salaries go up, and the like.

Brezhnev needed to discredit the policy proposed by Kosygin, and here there was a role for Chernenko. Kosygin was a strong opponent, a master of political intrigue whose undeniable skills had brought him at age thirty-six to deputy chairmanship of the Council of Ministers (then referred to as the Council of Peoples' Commissars) and at forty-two to membership in the Politburo. Determined and intelligent, an outstanding administrator, he distinguished himself by his incisive mind and extraordinary capacity for work. He was shy and felt uncomfortable about making public appearances. The last attribute was taken advantage of by Brezhnev's supporters, whose arguments had greater effect due to Kosygin's lack of skill at defending himself against demagoguery.

The opening of the clash occurred in October 1964, when at a ceremony in honor of Soviet astronauts, Brezhnev stated: "We shall heighten the responsibility of the Party and its leading organizational role in Soviet Society." This set the tone for an anti-Kosygin campaign in the newspapers. In *Pravda, Kommunist, Partiynaya zhizn,* and *Agitator,* dozens of articles criticized the government (and therefore Kosygin as its head) for a lack of "realism" in planning and for relying on "past experience."[2] The implications ran that the reforms that Kosygin had proposed were inimical to the building of socialism. The press urged that no efforts be spared to combat "voluntarism" and "subjectivism," terms previously used for condemning Khrushchev and now revived to suggest Kosygin's affinity with Khrushchev's views or methods. Another demagogic device to which Brezhnev resorted was to contrast Kosygin with Lenin. Thus, Brezhnev argued that improvement of agriculture (not the development of light industry) was considered by Lenin to be the most vital aspect of the economic policy of the Party because it affected the base of the Soviet state: the relations between the working class and the peasantry.[3]

We do not know Chernenko's exact role in the anti-Kosygin struggle: all we do know is that Chernenko was by then an accomplished master of affixing damaging political labels on opponents. Similarly, there is good reason to believe that Chernenko helped in portraying the West as a capitalist hell with its inflation, crime, and unemployment: this propaganda line was featured in 1965–66 in the polemics of Brezhnev against Kosygin in which the social and political decline of bourgeois society was constantly invoked as a scare tactic. The purpose of this imagery was to convince the public of the undesirability of political reforms, especially in the direction of creating a mad run after consumer goods "as in the West."

It is debatable how sincere Brezhnev was in expressing such views. But Chernenko and his aides were not bothered by any such consideration; they knew that Brezhnev's rhetoric was in line with the ideological traditions of the regime and promised to win for him the support of the conservative Party apparatus. They were proved right by the 23d Party Congress in 1966, which, in support of Brezhnev, approved heavy investment in agriculture and defense. From then on Kosygin's star was on the wane. This could be seen in the press, where Kosygin's speeches were reported as having been met merely with "applause," and Brezhnev's as having evoked "thunderous applause."

Something else of significance occurred at this Congress that bore clear marks of planning by Chernenko's office: the title of general secretary of the Central Committee was revived to honor Brezhnev. The bestowal of this title on him immediately raised his prestige and influence because it implied that he was no longer first among equals but a boss over subordinates. Likewise, the Presidium was at the same Congress renamed the Politburo, the motion to this effect having come from Brezhnev himself, who justified the renaming in terms of popular demand voiced in "letters of workers" addressed to the central authorities.

Thus in 1966 Brezhnev appeared on the political stage as the autocratic leader of the Party. But prior to this, much effort on the part of his team was required. Right after the anti-Khrushchev coup that brought Brezhnev to power, it became obvious that not only the Politburo but also the Central Committee Secretariat blocked his aspirations. The fall of Khrushchev led to the appointment of Podgorny as second secretary. In this capacity, the latter directed the work of the Organizational Division, which he could easily transform into his own independent power base.

Another CC secretary who posed a potential threat to Brezhnev's drive to monopolize power was Shelepin, who became a member of the Presidium at the November 1964 Plenum. Deputy chairman of the Council of Ministers and a CC secretary, Shelepin had an extensive political base. The vastly powerful Party Control Committee that he headed from Khrushchev's time afforded him control over both Party and government. Podgorny, however, posed the greater threat as he began to follow Kosygin in advocating the development of light industry. Podgorny and Kosygin appeared as potential allies seeking to reorient the economy in favor of consumer interests and to continue Khrushchev's moderate foreign policy.

To this challenge Brezhnev could respond with an alliance with Shelepin, a conservative whose views in regard to international relations coincided with his own. Shelepin was willing to oppose the Kosygin-Podgorny alliance also because he himself was hoping to make a bid for top authority in the Party or, at least, in the government. The Moscow rumor factory (with Shelepin himself perhaps spreading the rumors via the KGB) suggested that Brezhnev was only a transitional ruler who would soon be replaced by a younger, more dynamic figure fast rising to the heights of power. Who could this be if not Shelepin?

The likelihood of such a development was not great. But the very fact that these rumors circulated proved that the rivalry among the Soviet leadership was intense. Another indication of this was the debate in the Party press evidently inspired by Brezhnev's supporters. In *Ekonomicheskaya gazeta* of February 1965 an article appeared that criticized the

Party organizations of Kharkov, the old fiefdom of Podgorny, for inept economic management.[4] By implicitly referring to past mistakes of Podgorny, the article raised doubts about his qualifications as a government administrator. Subsequently, the transition was made from the past directly to the present: an article in *Pravda* noted that "certain Party leaders" — only Podgorny could have been meant — were advocating the priority of light industry without taking objective reality into account.[5] (Kosygin could not have been meant because as *government* chief he had no right to criticize Party policies. Advocacy of priority for light industry would have amounted to a criticism of Party policy.)

Podgorny, however, was still sufficiently powerful to launch a counterattack against Brezhnev. He did so in May 1965 during a visit to Baku. He said, "There was a time when the Soviet people were willing to face material hardships in order to develop heavy industry . . . but now . . . our national wealth is growing and the necessary conditions are being created for the satisfaction of increasing material and cultural demands."[6] This was a mistake on Podgorny's part; it offended not only Brezhnev and Shelepin but also the entire conservative wing in the Politburo, which viewed the priority of heavy industry as the cornerstone of the military sector of the Soviet economy and, hence, the military strength of the state.

Suslov, who had until this point maintained neutrality in the conflict between Brezhnev and Podgorny, could no longer remain on the sidelines. He attacked the "revisionist" views of the CC second secretary less out of solidarity with Brezhnev than in defense of the purity of doctrine that was sacrosanct for him. The entry of Suslov into the Brezhnev camp settled Podgorny's fate. His position in the Politburo became precarious and on December 9, 1965, he was "kicked upstairs" by being named chairman of the Presidium of the Supreme Soviet. (From experience Brezhnev knew well that this strictly ceremonial function entailed no real power.) Within several months Podgorny was also stripped of his CC secretaryship.

The fall of Podgorny marked the beginning of the political end of the man who had done his utmost to bring the fall about: Shelepin. Shelepin's decline was planned ahead of time by Brezhnev and effected when the threatening presence of Shelepin no longer served any purpose. Thus, at the same Plenum at which Podgorny was dispatched to the Supreme Soviet, Shelepin lost the post of chairman of the Party-Government Control Committee, which was abolished. Subsequently, he also ceased to be an important figure in the government hierarchy when he was removed from deputy chairmanship of the Council of Ministers. However, in contrast to the way matters were handled with Podgorny, Shelepin was not attacked directly but offered instead the opportunity to continue in Party work, though not in the second CC secretaryship, as he had hoped. Brezhnev had no intention of having a powerful and ambitious politician installed as his deputy.

Thus ended the first stage of Brezhnev's march toward absolute power in the Kremlin. It had been planned, prepared for, and masterly executed by Chernenko. As soon as Brezhnev became the recognized boss of the Party, Chernenko began his own long way to the Party Olympus, where he would become an influential Party leader, a member of the top clique.

Perhaps nothing reflects the nature of Soviet society as accurately as does the image of its leaders. They differ in personal characteristics and in the strategies they embark upon to reach the top, but for all their differences, their careers follow a similar pattern. During the first decade of the existence of the Soviet regime the "passport" to power was proletarian origin (real or fabricated) and participation in the Revolution. When the generation of the "fathers" (the engineers of and participants in the October coup) died off, the credential of revolutionary activity was replaced by the credential of participation (in one or another capacity) in the Civil War. Later, success in reaching the top was preconditioned by a fixed career sequence: Party activity, study at an institute (either by correspondence or in an accelerated program), headship of a provincial Party committee or a republic, then political work in the regular army, and — after the war — a high *nomenklatura* post in the capital, which opened the way to the Central Committee Secretariat and Politburo. (Minor variations were possible, e.g. in place of army service there could be important work in the rear in a ministry, the Komsomol, or industry.) Party etiquette requires that a secretary of the Central Committee be honored by the publication of his writings. Of course, not everyone could be a Party theoretician of Suslov's standing, but everyone (particularly upon joining the Politburo) was expected to make his own theoretical pronouncements and, if he did not have an original contribution to make, then at least to contribute a collection of his speeches and thereby to reaffirm the monopoly of the Party as the sole legitimate interpreter of Marxism-Leninism.

Chernenko, however, was an exception all the way through. He did not participate in the Revolution or the Civil War (he was too young for both), he did not have the opportunity to administer a province or a republic, nor did he participate in the war (preferring to take advantage of an exemption). His presence in Moscow was due not to any accomplishment of his own but solely to the whim of Brezhnev. But it was precisely because Chernenko had missed out on so much, whether as a result of his lack of ability or daring, that he desperately wanted to achieve everything: always more power than he had, as well as recognition, honors, and finally respect, which he was never destined to win. This is why he decided to erect his own personal power base not from the bottom, but, as it were, from the top. He began the way other powerful Party figures would end their careers, by writing (with the help of his aides) and publishing a theoretical contribution "of his own."

Why did Chernenko issue such a publication? To overcome his inferiority complex (partly due to the unsystematic character of his education)? To compensate for previous career failures (the career descent from Krasnoyarsk to Moldavia)? Or was his frustrated energy, long contained by his subservience, seeking a way to impress people? The Politburo was surprised by Chernenko's efforts at theorizing. Without sufficient prestige (a mere member of the Central Committee and at that only from the time of the 24th Congress) or authoritative position (he did not head a major department), he should not have been making authoritative pronouncements on ideology. Nevertheless, apparently acceding to the whim of Brezhnev to have a "learned" servant, the Politburo raised no objection to having one of its executives appear as a "man of science."

Brezhnev actually had no particular interest in the theoretical endeavors of his assistant: he was too concerned about himself and his own success for that. But he did care about the career of his loyal aide. The rise of Chernenko up the Party ladder clearly reveals the nature of the general secretary's attitude toward Chernenko and what Brezhnev was able to do for him. At the opening of the 23d CPSU Congress in March 1966 Chernenko was listed among the secretariat of the Congress; at its closing he was already listed among the candidate (nonvoting) members of the Central Committee. Just a short while later, on April 15, *Pravda* listed him as a candidate for deputy to the Supreme Soviet of the USSR. In this same year the name of Chernenko appeared on the list of top Party officials who signed the obituary of a secretary of the Central Committee (A. N. Rudakov). Although his name was obscured by its location at the end of the list in forty-third place, this marked the beginning of Chernenko's public renown. Soon thereafter he appeared as a member of the Mandate Commission of the first session of the seventh convocation of the Supreme Soviet. Then he began to appear constantly in the retinue officially greeting or accompanying the general secretary, at first in the middle of the list, then higher, until he regularly appeared close to the top, always a bit higher than Party protocol required. At the 24th Party Congress in 1971 he was again listed as a member of the Congress secretariat, and after the Congress he emerged as full member of the Central Committee.

In recognition of his newly elevated status, the name of Chernenko appeared in second place, directly after that of CC secretary and candidate member of the Politburo M. Demichev on the obituary of M. A. Sivolyubov, the director of Gospolitizdat (State Political Publishing House). Several years later, in 1974, Chernenko's name again appeared second (after that of CC secretary and Politburo candidate member D. Ustinov) on the list of those who greeted Brezhnev on his return from his meeting with President Nixon in the Crimea. Long before that, however, in 1971, an article by Chernenko appeared in the academic journal *Voprosy istorii* (Issues of history), in which Chernenko was authorized to comment on the recently concluded 24th Party Congress. This first theoretical work published by Chernenko provides an interesting confirmation of the fact that in the Central Committee bureaucracy Chernenko dealt not only with protocol matters but also with organizational work, which at that time was supervised by Central Committee Secretary (and Politburo member) Kirilenko.

Chernenko was allowed to exceed the narrow bounds of his authority, which indicates that his special position in the Party milieu derived not from his formal function (as is generally the case in the Soviet Union) but from his informal ties to Brezhnev. This explains why in the run-up to the Congress Chernenko rather than Kirilenko was entrusted with drafting the part of Brezhnev's report dealing with intra-Party work. This circumstance enabled him to return to this subject after the Congress and again consider (and, in some aspects, reconsider) it.[7]

In his *Voprosy istorii* article, Chernenko came up with an original idea: in Soviet society the leading role of the Party (a bow to Brezhnev) could be combined with the expansion ("the continual development" as he put it) of democracy (a bow to Kosygin). Chernenko presented this idea dialectically, using the formula of the growth of the leading role of the Party (a foregone conclusion) as inevitably leading to an increase in the role of Communists in society. It would have been more correct to say that the result would be an increase in the role of the *Party bureaucracy* in society, but such a substitution of concepts (the reference to Communists in place of Communist bureaucracy) was likely to escape the notice of largely uncritical Soviet readers. This was not the case, however, with the completely unfounded conclusion that followed: that millions of non-Party members were following the example of the Communist Party members. If this were indeed the case or even if this were a possibility, the dictatorial ("leading" according to Chernenko) role of the Party would scarcely be needed, and consequently Chernenko's initial hypothesis (an increase in the leading role of the Party) would be refuted, along with its corollary, that the participation of the masses in the social process was expanding.[8]

In an effort to escape from this contradiction Chernenko turned to traditional dogmas. He asserted that the leading role of the Party implied the need to check everything the Communists were doing with Marxist teachings, as Chernenko put it, with "the compass of Leninism." But as Soviet history has shown, this compass invariably points in the direction of totalitarian rule, exercised without the participation of the people and at the expense of the people.

Thus, Chernenko's concept of increasing the leading role of the Party not only did not augur any liberalization in the USSR but, on the contrary, pointed in the opposite direction: an increase of Party involvement in and control of the few remaining institutions that retained some residual democratic elements.

The thesis of Chernenko reflected his lack of theoretical sophistication. Nevertheless, his idea was adopted as a resolution of the Congress, thus assuming the status of an authoritative "truth" that no one had the right to question. This meant also that no one had the right to doubt the qualifications of Chernenko for dealing with theoretical issues.

However, there were occasions when Chernenko departed from such stereotyped thinking. In this same speech there were some interesting ideas of his (even if they were formulated by his assistants, the distinction is not important because Chernenko identified himself with them both by signing his name to them and by defending them publicly). A case in point is his thesis that the plans of contemporary social construction do not necessarily need to follow Marxist teachings but may rely instead on "the experience and opinions of millions of Party members and non-Party members."[9] By standards of Brezhnev's time, such a statement was extraordinary. Chernenko could not have made it without guarantee of immunity to criticism. In any case, the idea was bold enough to make up for all the deficiencies of his speech: its weak structure, endless generalities, and repeated (above the usual norm) references to resolutions of the Congress. A single article could not yet raise Chernenko to the status of a Party theoretician, but it did expand the scope of his authority in regard to the organization of Party work.

Chernenko directly oversaw the process of mass recruitment into the Party that occurred in the period between the 23rd and 24th Party Congresses (1966–71) and that swelled the Party ranks by 2.2 million, almost 25 percent. The new members were likely to perceive Brezhnev as the undisputed leader of the country. Simultaneously, on the initiative of Chernenko's General Department the Party was purged of those who did not muster sufficient appreciation for the new leadership. This purge was camouflaged as an exchange of Party cards. Yet, that it was a purge rather than a routine bureaucratic operation was confirmed by Chernenko himself when he said that "the imminent exchange of Party cards set by the

24th Party Congress is to be carried out as an important organizational and political measure that will facilitate a further strengthening of the Party, an increase of activism, and a tightening of discipline of Party members."[10]

Chernenko set not only the tone but also the pace of Party work: between 1966 and 1971 sixteen Central Committee Plenums took place. He prepared their agendas even when the topics pertained to areas (e.g. in industry, agriculture, social construction, the international Communist movement, and domestic policy) distant from his interests at that time. The fact that so many plenums could be held was possible due only to the extraordinary efficiency of the department Chernenko headed. The department proved its ability to deal with tons of incoming and outgoing (to and from the Central Committee) documents.

One of the issues raised at a 1970 CC Plenum must have been not only prepared in general but actually elaborated in detail by Chernenko: the practical work of the Politburo. Chernenko was a recognized authority on the organization of this highest Party entity. He insisted on punctuality, determining that the Politburo sessions would begin promptly at 9:00 A.M. on Thursdays. By the next day the protocols of the Politburo together with its resolutions would be typed up and distributed for the perusal of the members of the Central Committee, and a special folder would contain an abridged version of the minutes of the Politburo meeting.

Chernenko's skill lay in his ability to foresee the resolutions of the Politburo. Because of that, he could prepare ahead of time concise and precise descriptions of them, contrasting with the long-winded versions of resolutions prepared by the CC Secretariat. Perhaps this was less due to Chernenko's ability than to his inside knowledge and to his personal closeness to Brezhnev. In any case, working under constant stress in the Politburo and adroitly navigating between the views of Shelepin, Podgorny, and Shelest on the one side and Brezhnev and his supporters on the other, Chernenko managed to find a way to present the contents of the Politburo deliberations in such a way that the Central Committee members had good reason to trust the soundness and reliability of the positions taken by the general secretary.

Chernenko succeeded in gaining control over the Central Committee Letters Department. He justified this "necessity" by the need to provide the Politburo with maximum information from within the Party "as an instrument of leadership, education and control." In fact, the flood of letters directed to the Central Committee is an important, perhaps the most important, channel of information not distorted by fake reporting and telling the higher-ups what they want to hear. Chernenko began to exploit his access to this channel as a tool of subtle blackmail. He gained access to fairly reliable evidence concerning the life and activities of the multimillion-strong Party bureaucracy, with its corruption, chauvinism, unprincipledness, and cynicism.

Letters to the Central Committee are, as a rule, cries of desperation or screams for help; they disclose crimes involving either individual Party members or whole Party organizations from regional to republic level and higher, including top functionaries of the central bureaucracy. And it was up to Chernenko to decide which part of this evidence was to be concealed for the subsequent use in some intrigue and which part disclosed, whether immediately or with some delay, to the Politburo, the CC Secretariat, or the Council of Ministers, depending on Chernenko's selection. In this way he became an *eminence grise*, with enormous personal power. No wonder that secretaries of the Central Committee and ministers began to court his favor.

Nevertheless, even in the late 1960s Chernenko remained a functionary little known to the public at large. He was still one of those whom the press habitually refers to anonymously as a "high Party official." But in inner Party circles, it was quite different. Yet, even there Chernenko's influence was less direct than indirect, stemming from his recognized closeness to Brezhnev. It was Brezhnev's authority and power that bestowed on Chernenko a large measure of leeway at Politburo meetings and afforded him the opportunity to manipulate the flow of information.

By the beginning of 1970 all important sectors of Party administration appeared to be in the hands of the various CC secretaries: Andrey Kirilenko and Ivan Kapitonov supervised cadres; Fedor Kulakov, agriculture; Vladimir Dolgikh, industry; Mikhail Suslov, ideology; Dmitri Ustinov, the armed forces; Petr Demichev, culture; Boris Ponomarev, relations with Communist countries; and Konstantin Katushev, the international Communist movement.

That is how it appeared to others, but not to Chernenko. He discovered or rather invented a sector of administration not yet administered: the building of the Party. It probably seemed to others that nothing worthwhile could emerge from this sector, but Chernenko knew better. Why should he not be an ideologue of banality? Was that any worse than endlessly repeating the empty verities of Marxist philosophy? He began to reiterate banalities as if they were great discoveries. He attempted to link his name to Party clichés, hoping to gain renown as their propagator. In this he succeeded: the association of the man with the idea eventually became so ineluctable that they were inseparable.

This is how he began. He stressed the idea of the Party bureaucracy as the chief and irreplaceable executor of Party policies. He waxed emotional about it, stating that the Party bureaucracy created, executed, ex-

pressed in a timely manner, fundamentally evaluated, approved, determined, set direction, and so on. From the Party point of view this was
unchallengeable; hence its value for Chernenko. It aroused no opposition
from the apparatchiks and no objections from the explainers and defenders of the purity of Marxism in the Kremlin.

Meanwhile Chernenko reiterated this thesis with great import at various Party forums, adorning it with examples: positive, to serve as models
to emulate; or negative, to serve as warnings for any skeptics. He hoped
that ultimately the view would come to prevail in Party circles that all
defects and inefficiency in ideological work were due to the faulty structure of the Party apparatus. Then, when the Central Committee realized
the necessity of repairing that structure, the name of Chernenko would
naturally occur to everyone concerned as the ideal person to take charge
of that important matter. Who but he was a recognized expert in the
building of the Party, the new Marxist-Leninist discipline of which he
happened to be the founder?

In this capacity of founder of the theory of Party building Chernenko
took part in the late 1960s in the organization of new Party committees:
of 9 *obkoms*, 21 *gorkoms*, and 291 rural *raykoms*.[11] The opponents of
Brezhnev in the Politburo did not attribute particular importance to these
efforts but, rather, viewed them as an internal Party matter of a limited
local significance that did not affect their basic interests. Eventually, they
would pay dearly for their mistake when the newly created Party committees began to funnel into the Central Committee of the CPSU dozens of
new members who were potential allies of the general secretary.

Another achievement of Chernenko's was the creation of railway junc-
tion Party committees. Rather than strengthen Party control over rail
transportation, as was avowed, the intention was to promote Brezhnev's
personal interests by creating one more branch of the *nomenklatura* subservient to the general secretary.

In the guise of concern about raising the quality of Party work,
Chernenko influenced the Central Committee to pass a resolution about
special courses for improving the qualifications of high officials. Their
purpose was defined as the advanced education of "mature" and "competent" Party workers. (In practice this meant "mature" and "competent"
enough to recognize the general secretary as the sovereign boss over the
Party and to serve him unquestioningly.)

Chernenko also launched a slogan that outlived him and has become a
catchword of the Gorbachev period: "To strengthen Party responsibility
and discipline." He proposed as well a means of implementing this lofty
principle: checking whether resolutions passed by higher authority were
in fact carried out. The Central Committee charged Chernenko's depart-

ment with carrying out such checks, a task that entailed risks and inconvenience. Links that local leadership has with the center are not always easy to investigate. Beginning at the lowest levels, they often extend to the Politburo itself. Chernenko, however, was not cowed. He was well enough informed to know that whoever evaluates the work of Party organizations subordinates them to himself.

Much effort and energy were devoted by Chernenko to putting the organization of work in the Party apparatus on a scientific basis. This was a fashionable idea in the 1970s. Various American theories about the social and psychological aspects of production were then penetrating the Soviet Union. However, the criteria of "scientificity" of work organization as proposed by Chernenko had little in common with American theories; his ideas were general and vague. He mentioned rational use of cadres without making clear what such rationality was supposed to consist of. He advocated the combination of revolutionary zeal with practicality, pragmatism, the struggle against bureaucratism, and similar traditional Soviet exhortations devoid of definite content. However, their lack of content was intentional. Such rhetoric allowed Chernenko to attach to them varied meanings, depending on his goals and political imperatives of the moment.

Chernenko also came out in favor of the use of computer technology in Party work. Although this was quite a startling innovation in the Soviet Union of the 1960s, he succeeded in implementing it: his department was equipped with computers that allowed him to process paperwork speedily and to make efficient use of stored information. Moreover, while espousing advanced communication gadgetry, Chernenko did not confine himself to the Central Committee. Indirectly, via Brezhnev, he proposed improvement of the administration of the government bureaucracy—the Council of Ministers and the Gosplan—thus trespassing into Kosygin's fiefdom. Suggestions were made for improvements in their structure, delimitations of their functions, and streamlining of their organization. Preconditions were thereby created for Brezhnev and for Chernenko to expand their influence in the local *soviet* organizations, i.e. in the fiefdom of Podgorny. In Chernenko's view, as executive councils, the *soviets* needed to be restructured at all levels. In other words, their reform was envisaged as encompassing a broad range of issues in order to have a pretext for involvement in all conceivable sectors: in economic development, culture, social conditions, the health care system, and labor relations.

Podgorny was satisfied. His hierarchy of councils (soviets) was gaining in status at the expense of the government hierarchy under Kosygin. He attributed little significance to the fact that the initiative for reforming the soviets did not come from him and did not dream that he would not be in charge of carrying it out. It was difficult for him, a member of the Politburo, to be suspicious of Chernenko, a mere middle-level Party functionary. He failed to see Brezhnev's shadow behind Chernenko. But it was Chernenko who first broached to Brezhnev the idea of subordinating the soviets to himself. Chernenko even provided a theoretical justification for this. In 1971, with Chernenko's participation, a CC resolution was drafted that provided a rationale for expanding Party control over the soviets.[12] Six years later the Central Committee, pursuing the same idea of "increasing the leading and directing role of the Party," would find it imperative that the general secretary hold the post of chairman of the Presidium of the Supreme Soviet as well. For Podgorny, this would mean total political eclipse.

Between 1971 and 1977 Chernenko used the power of Brezhnev to undermine the power and authority of the Council of Ministers.[13] The Politburo proposed expanding the prerogatives of district and city soviets and granting them larger budgets (at the expense of the ministries), thus enhancing the prestige of the deputies of the Supreme Soviet (at the expense of the prerogatives of the members of the government).

Chernenko encouraged Brezhnev to make Moscow into a "model Communist city." In the spring of 1970 at the health resort suburb of Barvikha an impressive conference of urban planners and sociologists was convened to discuss the development of the capital, its architecture, its transportation network, and its quality of life. Not surprisingly, the conference was chaired by Chernenko, the acknowledged expert not in building but in Party building.

To confirm his expertise, Chernenko produced an interpretation of Lenin's views on administration in an article published in the November 1973 issue of *Voprosy istorii*, the same journal that had published his first work. The publication dealt with "documents setting out the basic principles of government structure." Chernenko's article dealt with the history of the Soviet constitution, including a historical survey of no great interest. More noteworthy was the way the topic was formulated: as a question about the essential nature of the basic Soviet law. Chernenko turned his attention to this matter when Brezhnev was pushing for the promulgation of a new constitution. The latter was driven not by vanity or by the wish to leave a mark on history but by a more pragmatic motive. He wanted to use the new constitution to curtail Kosygin. Again, Chernenko found himself in the forefront of the anti-Kosygin attack.

In his commentary on the new constitution Chernenko's point of departure was the putative perspective of Lenin. Chernenko wrote: "In terms of its significance, one of the most important documents of the contemporary epoch . . . is the Soviet constitution, whose drafting bears the mark of Lenin's genius."[14] It is noteworthy that Chernenko links with Lenin not only the constitution authored under Lenin's guidance but also all subsequent constitutions of the Soviet Union, and hence that of Brezhnev. Thus, Lenin's blessing is conferred on Chernenko's patron, whose ninety-seven-man-strong constitutional commission increased the general secretary's power at the expense of those in the Party apparatus with whom he had previously been supposed to share it.

Chernenko traced in detail the process by which the Stalin constitution was ratified, along the way rehabilitating a number of Stalin's satraps, including Andrey Vyshinsky, one of the organizers of the "Great Terror" of the 1930s. The rehabilitation was not incidental. Far from merely providing a historical backdrop, it suggested to Brezhnev a *modus operandi*. Chernenko discussed not only the desirable contents of the new constitution but also ways of presenting it to the people. With this purpose in mind, he had no qualms about invoking Stalin's spirit or searching the archives for forgotten letters of Lenin's wife, Krupskaya—all this in order to find a model for Brezhnev to emulate. Gradually his scenario became clear. The first stage would be publication and discussion of the draft of the constitution in the press and the radio; this would be followed by explanation of its contents to the masses in lectures, reports, discussions, and study groups organized for this purpose by Party committees.

Chernenko urged Brezhnev to arrange for the dispatch to the Central Committee of millions of "letters of appreciation." Nor did he neglect purely procedural matters: he advised that an extraordinary session of the Supreme Soviet be convoked to consider the proposals, revisions, suggestions, and amendments to the draft. He also argued in favor of establishing a commission to edit the final draft, to be then approved unanimously. All his proposals were presented tactfully. At first glance they seemed no more than an attempt to defer to history by learning from the experience of Stalin's constitutional "debate" of 1936, yet in 1977, when the Brezhnev constitution would finally be enacted, the manner of its enactment would closely follow Chernenko's recommendations.[15]

Years ahead of time Chernenko formulated the arguments that Brezhnev would use to justify the need for a new constitution for "changing the visage of Soviet society," effecting a "rapprochement of classes," and "establishing a state of all the people." Subsequently, these concepts would become ideological clichés and few would remember that Chernenko was one of the first to formulate them.

The fertile imagination of Chernenko devised an appellation for the new constitution: "the constitution of a developed socialist society." He did not dare, however, to call it the "Brezhnev Constitution" by analogy to the 1936 "Stalin Constitution" because the prestige of his boss had not yet reached a level comparable to that of Stalin in the 1930s.

His preoccupation with the new constitution had high but not the very highest priority in Chernenko's life. The highest priority was reserved for his Party responsibilities until it became clear that the latter did not provide him with the satisfaction that only scientific concerns could afford. He no longer was content to confine his narrow "expertise" to Party matters but felt he was compelled to elaborate theories of government. The ideas he expressed often had some originality. At first he expressed them as Soviet tradition prescribed, i.e. by framing them with quotations from Lenin or Brezhnev. Subsequently, however, he relied more on his own words supplemented with references either to sociological research or simply to his own experience.

In a series of articles that appeared in the 1970s Chernenko described the structure of the government bureaucracy and analyzed the methods of its operation. Of interest here was his idea that civil service requires a scientific grounding (he used the term "scientific justification" (*nauchnoe opravdanie*).[16] No less bold, and clearly ahead of its time in the midst of the Brezhnev era, was his view about the utility of accurate and comprehensive information for government use. These views, however, were presented in traditional Marxist jargon and within a Marxist conceptual framework. The result was that sound ideas, like the idea of a managerial approach to government performance, at first glance seemed devoid of real content.

In fact, ideological clichés were used by Chernenko to justify his demand for accountability of both leaders and managers who otherwise would persist in their arrogant self-assured ways. For Chernenko the key to the reorganization of administration lay in direct involvement in the thick of things. Such a down-to-earth approach was bound to clash with the orthodox viewpoint of Suslov, for whom ideology was a panacea for understanding and controlling social processes.[17]

The differences of views between Suslov and Chernenko, which with time would intensify, were not accidental. Chernenko sought, at that time without much success, the image (one of his many images) of a liberal and modernizing leader. He was not then successful because the identification of his person with Brezhnev dissuaded readers from paying attention to what he was saying and prevented them from believing that these ideas, undoubtedly advanced for the time, were really his own. Brezhnev's lack of originality was projected onto Chernenko to the extent that everything that came from his pen was in advance considered clichéd and trivial. And yet Chernenko was perhaps the sole person in the Central Committee in the early 1970s who would dare to criticize the organizational structure of the government apparatus in the USSR openly, even if not consistently. He condemned the style of administration wherein fixed political form prevailed over economic content, he deplored the inability of economic decision makers to make decisions within their sphere of competence without waiting for instructions from above, and he called for increasing the powers of directors of enterprises and decreasing their dependence on planning bodies. Fifteen years later such ideas would be propounded by Gorbachev and treated as a sensation. In the 1970s, however, they were premature and escaped attention, especially because their author lacked the authority to implement them.

Chernenko was among the first (possibly the very first) in the Central Committee to call for learning from the experience of the anticorruption campaigns in Georgia and in Azerbaijan.[18] But such appeals were again premature and thus went unheeded. They would find a response only a decade later on the eve of Gorbachev's ascent to power. But then, paradoxically, Chernenko himself would oppose their realization.

Chernenko proposed the replacement of the multitiered structure of management (ministry-main committee-trust-management-production) by a three-level (ministry-management-production) or even two-level (ministry-production) system. He hoped this would make industrial ministries function better. The proposal also anticipated reforms put into practice when not only Brezhnev but also Chernenko were no longer alive.

What can one conclude about the importance of these ideas? Soviet reformers of the succeeding Party generation (typified by the transient Andropov and the more durable Gorbachev) were essentially following the trail blazed in theory by Chernenko without practical result, and without even the conditions for it. Undoubtedly, the idea is one thing and its realization another. The true nature of a Soviet political figure emerges only when he becomes leader without any superiors. Until then he lives and acts in the shadow of others: he avoids revealing any independent views, and concerns himself not with the merits of ideas but with their potential utility for his career. All Soviet leaders have acted in this manner until reaching the pinnacle of power. Stalin identified himself with Lenin, Khrushchev with Stalin, Brezhnev with Khrushchev, Andropov with Brezhnev, and so on. They suppressed their individuality, their tastes, and views to reveal or assert them only when they became general (or first) secretaries of the Central Committee. Only then did the differences between them and their predecessors come to the surface. Chernenko, however, reached that point of his career too late and for too brief a period—on the very threshold of death, when it was already time for him to think about the obituary he would receive rather than about the policies he would pursue.

Thus, Chernenko's individuality did not have the occasion to manifest itself. His groping liberalism in the Brezhnev period might have been transformed into conservatism if he had lived long enough to rule his country for a significant period. Or—who knows?—he might have attempted, rather, to pursue radical reforms. In any case, one thing is undeniable: although he did not exude brilliance (and which Soviet leader after Lenin did?), Chernenko was sufficiently clever to understand that he could not make it to the top solely by fawning on Brezhnev. This is why he began to seek to make himself useful, indeed, indispensable to the boss. Still, it was still not enough. The general secretary could at best promote him to the CC Secretariat, but he would have to make it into the Politburo on his own steam. For that he needed a modicum of renown. He was able to gain it relatively fast, using his General Department headship as a lever, but outside the Party bureaucracy he continued to be unknown.

Chernenko's relative obscurity may have been what made him try so hard to publish; over the years he turned out dozens of problem-oriented articles. It may also have caused him to run the risk of expressing deviant-sounding views and ideas in order to attract attention. But the risk was well calculated. Thus, Chernenko made the surprising proposal to introduce some order into the activity of government bodies. The suggestions he made in this regard were characterized by a boldness that later became a Gorbachev trademark. Chernenko wanted to lower the enormous costs of the administrative apparatus by cutting unproductive budget allocations, and raising the productivity of administrative performance by tying it directly to the process of production. He proposed increasing the personal responsibility of directors, and introducing a new approach involving continuous review of the actual situation informed by scientific theory. He noted the vital importance of considering public opinion preferences in decision making, and because there were no open outlets (and hence reliable sources) for their expression, he urged that attention be paid to the letters received by Party entities. This proposal reflected his understanding that letters were the only channel available to the masses for voicing their grievances, and as such, the only authentic and undistorted expression of their sentiments.[19]

Chernenko was also critical of the duplication of functions by Party and government organs, which he quite ingeniously tried to remedy by setting a government standard (GOST) for administrative work patterned after the standards existing in production. He even supported *glasnost* (openness, frankness, criticism) in Party leadership in a broad sense more than ten years before the term became a slogan of Gorbachev's.

Chernenko was also original in the way he outlined the profile of a first-rate (in his vocabulary "advanced") leader-manager, whom he described as one who has sufficient general education and specialized knowledge to grasp the meaning of the realities he has to deal with. A further feature of his ideal leader-manager was the ability to distinguish between the essential and the less important, the general and the particular. He should also have broad political horizons, which for Chernenko meant not ideological "maturity" but the ability to handle interpersonal relations.[20]

Of course, the originality of Chernenko's thoughts and views must be qualified as being quite relative. By Western standards most of his ideas can be described only as simplistic or banal. In their Soviet context in Brezhnev's time, however, especially when juxtaposed to the orthodoxy of Suslov's ideas, they stand out as being quite bold and original.

In contrast to his contemporaries in the Party, Chernenko never ceased seeking ways to bridge the gap between theory and practice. In April 1974 he convened in Moscow a conference of the top echelon of the general departments of Party committees and there attempted to implement some of his ideas. The reports and motions he presented for discussion clearly exceeded the bounds of his authority. His presentations reviewed and analyzed the performance of the government bureaucracy in terms of a wide array of aspects: discipline, the nature of decision making, remedies for red tape and bureaucratism. His emphasis on supervision was not a matter of chance. He proposed to transform general departments (from the Central Committee down to the republic Party organizations) into bodies supervising and evaluating the performance of the Party apparat.[21] To all appearances, this proposal was supported by the Politburo; otherwise it would be difficult to explain the direct involvement of Chernenko in the subsequent personnel reshuffles carried out by Brezhnev.

Behind the facade of collective leadership a hidden struggle for power had been going on from the time Khrushchev was overthrown and pensioned off. Its first stage was marked by the purge of the supporters of the ousted first secretary from the Party apparatus. The country was then actually ruled by three men: Brezhnev, Kosygin, and Podgorny. Brezhnev did not control a majority in the Politburo: of eleven members chosen at the 23d Party Congress only four—Kirilenko, A. Ya. Pelshe, Suslov, and Polyansky—were on his side. Furthermore, one of them, Suslov, was an "errant" ally who always endeavored to preserve the balance of forces in the Politburo. When the balance swung in favor of Brezhnev, he went over to the side of Kosygin; when Kosygin was in the ascendant, he did the opposite. As for Shelepin, he was a sort of Brezhnev "fellow traveler." He allowed Brezhnev to use him against Podgorny, but when a clash occurred between the general secretary and Kosygin, Shelepin remained on the sidelines, letting the two big boys fight it out between them and, he hoped, exhaust themselves.

Nor was there any harmony between the Kosygin and Podgorny factions. The two men were permanently at odds in their rivalry for the second spot. Voronov and Shelest were close to Podgorny, and Kirill Mazurov leaned toward the side of Kosygin. But when Kosygin and Podgorny agreed on some issue, Brezhnev would find himself in the minority in the Politburo, especially because the ambitious and ever-wavering Shelepin could never be relied on. This is why Brezhnev's main concern at this time was to sow discord between Kosygin and Podgorny.

A different balance of forces obtained among the eight candidate (non-voting) members of the Politburo. Seven of them sided with Brezhnev: Kunaev, V. V. Kuznetsov, Shcherbitsky, and Ustinov were his personal friends; and P. M. Masherov, Demichev, and Rashidov owed their positions to him. Only one candidate member, V. P. Mzhavanadze, a Khrushchev holdover, could not decide which faction to affiliate with. With his former patron gone, he feared the risks factional affiliation could entail. His respect for power urged him to support the general secretary, but his caution advised him not to antagonize the premier.

Brezhnev also had a majority in the Central Committee Secretariat. There he could unconditionally rely on Kirilenko, Kapitonov, Kulakov, and Ponomarev and partly on Suslov and Andropov, who believed supporting the general secretary was the best bet to advance their own interests.[22]

Lacking the possibility of imposing his will on the Politburo, Brezhnev pushed most of his decisions through the CC Secretariat while relying also on the Central Committee bureaucracy, where he could effect suitable personnel changes with relative ease. Initially, he utilized former victims of Khrushchev. (This method of resurrecting political has-beens would also be widely employed by Brezhnev's successors.) He recalled Fedor Kulakov from political oblivion to head the Agriculture Department, and he brought back from Ivanovo Province Ivan Kapitonov, the former secretary of the Moscow *gorkom* (city Party committee), who had fallen into disfavor in the early 1960s, to appoint him head of the Department of Party Organs for the RSFSR. But three CC department heads in 1965–66 were newcomers: Georgy Pavlov, Administration of Affairs; Mikhail Solomentsev, Heavy Industry; and Sergey Trapeznikov of Science. The last (director of the Higher Party School in Moldavia) had been recommended by Chernenko as someone who deserved to be raised from provincial obscurity.

Trapeznikov was the first among those who later became known as the "Moldavian mafia" in Moscow. The next entrant into this clique was Nikolay Shchelokov, the deputy chairman of the Council of Ministers of Moldavia, who in 1966 was made minister of internal affairs. Among the dozens of others subsequently brought by Brezhnev from Moldavia to join the central authorities in Moscow was Semen Tsvigun, the head of the KGB in Kishinev, who was promoted to the post of first deputy chairman of the central KGB. Thus was established the rule by clans, which became a pronounced feature of the Soviet political system. There would be two such clans: alongside the "Moldavian mafia" there would gradually develop, expand, and gather its forces the "Dnepropetrovsk mafia," comprising functionaries and directors of enterprises who had once been buddies, fellow students, or fellow workers of Brezhnev in Dnepropetrovsk. Subsequently these clans would grow, collecting many (even outside Moldavia or Dnepropetrovsk Province) who had happened to meet Brezhnev on the long and tortuous path of his Party career and had succeeded in winning his attention or favor. This political machine, which was animated by principles of mafia psychology and tribal solidarity, was coordinated by Chernenko. Ultimately, it would enable Brezhnev to crush all his rivals.

In early 1971 came the fall of Vasily Mzhavanadze, the Party boss of Georgia who was accused of corruption. The Politburo was shaken, for this was the general secretary's first move against the top Party body. Previously, Brezhnev had not dared to oust a single member of the Politburo, having no option but to defer to the collective leadership principle. Between 1964 and 1971 only three men had left the Politburo: Frol Kozlov, due to illness, and Anastas Mikoyan and Nikolay Shvernik, due to advanced age. Then at one blow, at the April 1973 CC Plenum, Petr Shelest and Gennadiy Voronov were removed, to be replaced by three supporters of Brezhnev: Yuriy Andropov, chairman of the KGB, Andrey Gromyko, minister of foreign affairs, and Andrey Grechko, minister of defense. Shelest and Voronov apparently fell victim to the rivalry between Brezhnev and Kosygin.

Brezhnev engaged in considerable maneuvering before he resolved to move against the Politburo. As long as he was unable to subvert it from the outside, he tried to shake it up from within. His method was to increase its members from eleven to fifteen so as to assure for himself a majority. In this he emulated Stalin's tactics. Next, he proceeded to intrigue. By appearing to favor Shelepin, Brezhnev induced him to clash with Shelest; and by tolerating the rivalry between Kosygin and Podgorny, he isolated Voronov. Shelest was accused of nationalism and demoted from his post of first secretary of the Ukrainian Communist Party. He was named one of the numerous deputy chairmen of the Council of Ministers. However, deprived of his political base in the Ukraine, he could without difficulty be ousted from the Politburo.

Voronov lost out when, together with Kosygin, he criticized Brezhnev's agricultural plan. He was punished publicly by being denied the award of a decoration on the occasion of his sixtieth birthday (as a member of the Politburo he qualified for the star of Hero of Socialist Labor) and then by being downgraded in rank, with the listing of his name at receptions and gala events being dropped from fifth or sixth place to fourteenth.

Brezhnev could possibly have gotten rid of Voronov earlier, in 1970. At about that time factional ties that had previously carried weight in the Politburo began to be less binding. Losing influence, Kosygin also began to lose allies: first Suslov, then Mazurov. Meanwhile Podgorny acquiesced to his own ouster from the Party apparat, reconciled himself to his honorific place in the Presidium of the Supreme Soviet, and no longer sought to challenge the general secretary. Still, Brezhnev did not exploit the opportunity to get rid of Voronov. We can only speculate that he did not wish to weaken the pro-detente faction while Shelest opposed detente.

The fall of Voronov and Shelest followed the rise of G. V. Romanov. The latter promotion was a clever step on Brezhnev's part because, for the first time in a decade (after the departure of Kozlov), a first secretary of the Leningrad *obkom* was made a full member of the Politburo.

The more Brezhnev succeeded in consolidating his position, the lower fell the prestige and influence of Kosygin. From late 1970 until mid-1971 he was often absent from his office in the Council of Ministers, where he was replaced by Mazurov. He was frequently hospitalized or recuperating at his dacha. Although Kosygin was the main stumbling block preventing Brezhnev from attaining undisputed power, he was not the only one. Another rival was Polyansky, who could not forgive Brezhnev for breaking the promise to make him premier. But Brezhnev soon found a way to deal with Polyansky. Blamed for the poor state of Soviet agriculture, he was removed from the Politburo at the 24th Party Congress in 1971.

The fall of Shelepin proceeded gradually through several stages. His career began to decline as early as 1965, but his fall was complete only in 1975. During this period his power base dissipated first in the Komsomol, then in the KGB, the Party bureaucracy, and finally in the trade unions.

Not a single star in the Kremlin political firmament rose so brilliantly or waned so pitiably as Shelepin's. He became a member of the Central Committee under Stalin. Khrushchev made him head of the security services. Then several years later, in reward for his help in denouncing

Stalin, Khrushchev made him a CC secretary and deputy chairman of the Council of Ministers, as well as watchdog over the government and Party by appointing him chairman of the Party-Government Control Committee. However, Shelepin showed himself as ungrateful to Khrushchev as he did to Stalin (posthumously) and joined the plotters conspiring to overthrow Khrushchev.

The year 1965 marked the apogee of Shelepin's career and the beginning of its end. First he lost the Control Committee when the office was liquidated. Then he was removed from his position as deputy chairman of the Council of Ministers. Yet, he still had too much authority and had played too important a role in the plot against Khrushchev to be pushed into oblivion. So in 1966 Brezhnev awarded him the gold star of the Hero of Socialist Labor in honor of his fiftieth birthday and then promptly removed him from Party work by making him head of the trade unions. Thus, Shelepin lost power in spite of continuing to be a Politburo member. He attempted to use his Politburo membership to regain a power base, and in the process switched from one side to the other. Supporting the opponents of the general secretary, at one moment he endeavored to appear to be a flaming liberal, courting Kosygin's favor by criticizing Brezhnev for his conduct of domestic policy. Then just as suddenly, he became an ardent Brezhnevite when Brezhnev sought support for detente. But it was too late; Brezhnev could not forgive his double-dealing. In 1975 Shelepin was dispatched as head of a labor-union delegation to England. This turned out to be his journey into political oblivion. Using the wave of protests in Europe (perhaps even stirred up by Moscow) against Shelepin as a pretext, at the CC Plenum in April 1975 Brezhnev succeeded in having him dismissed "on his own request." The thus-phrased resolution was his political coup de grâce. It would have been hard to imagine a more refined humiliation for this vainglorious man.

Thus, apart from Kosygin (whom he would dispose of later in a different way), on the eve of the 25th Party Congress Brezhnev no longer had any rivals. He was finally in a position to quietly proceed to the stage of self-glorification. More than enough people were willing to pay homage, but in order to create a cult, a priest was needed. A suitable candidate was at hand: Chernenko. All that was necessary was to elevate him above others, to make him a big Party boss. Then his tributes to the general secretary's honor and glory would command awe and respect. Hence, Brezhnev began to upgrade Chernenko.

Contrary to all the rules of the Party game, in 1975 Chernenko appeared as a member of the government delegation to the Helsinki Conference on Security and Cooperation in Europe. (This was his second trip abroad with Brezhnev; the first had taken place in 1961. On February 9 that year their airplane had been strafed by French fighter-planes 130 km from the city of Algiers. Chernenko responded with admirable coolness and self-control, as Brezhnev would later recall on many occasions.) He was not just a member of the retinue (which consisted of a good hundred advisers, translators, journalists, security guards, and others) but a member of the official delegation comprising Brezhnev, the chairman; Gromyko, the deputy chairman; Chernenko himself; and A. Kovalev of the Ministry of Foreign Affairs.

Brezhnev's performance in Helsinki was impressive. He dominated the conference and was the center of attention. Chernenko, by contrast, kept a low profile. He lacked experience in international meetings and in order to avoid gaffes did his best to evade the questions of obtrusive newsmen. Yet, upon his return home, he was promptly given the opportunity to express himself on the pages of the journal *Mezhdunarodnaya zhizn* (International life), as one of the first to produce an authoritative commentary on the results of the conference. The way Chernenko did so proves that he was no dilettante. He began by surveying the problem of international security from the 1960s, then emphasized the contribution of the Communist parties to the negotiations (reporting just the facts rather than his own views), and finally proceeded to a detailed presentation of the Soviet standpoint in a way that clearly implied that without Brezhnev there would have been no detente and no Helsinki agreements.

Chernenko's ill-wishers in the Party apparat, who had been surprised that he had been selected to go to Finland, soon began to suspect that he was being groomed for a new political function. They were not mistaken. In March 1976 Chernenko was decorated as a Hero of Socialist Labor. This high Soviet award is normally reserved for outstanding Party functionaries on such occasions as a sixtieth or seventieth birthday. Normally, its recipients are members or candidate members of the Politburo or, under special circumstances, first secretaries of a republic central committee, but certainly not heads of a central committee department. Furthermore, it was not Chernenko's birthday; his sixty-fifth birthday would come in September 1976, and the award came in March. The award was followed by his appointment as a CC secretary. On this occasion *Pravda* (on March 5) for the first time carried a separate photograph of Chernenko (included along with photographs of his fellow CC secretaries chosen at the 25th Congress).

Until that moment Chernenko had remained a highly enigmatic figure. Now for the first time together with his photo his brief biography appeared in the press. It was quite laconic: "was born . . . studied . . . worked. . . . " In the photograph his broad cheek bones and slightly narrowed eyes suggested Mongol ancestry. To conceal wrinkles, traces of aging in his face were airbrushed out. One also noted his crop of gray hair and raised shoulders (which suggested a lung ailment). His serious expression may have indicated to some Soviet citizens his capacity for working hard. (He had survived Stalin's rule, when he had to develop his ability to work whole nights through and force his subordinates to do the same.) This was what the average Soviet newspaper reader could see or surmise from the newspaper photo. In any case, from that time onward photographs of Chernenko — alone or in the company of others — would continue to appear in the newspapers with frequency.

On April 2, 1976, Chernenko was seated in the box of the leadership of the Party and government during the commemorative ceremony in honor of Lenin; and on April 29 he appeared for the first time atop the Lenin mausoleum for the funeral of Marshal Grechko. Both then and during the traditional May Day parade two days later Chernenko occupied the position of last on the right.[23] With time, however, he would occupy locations closer to Brezhnev at the center of the row. For example, during the ceremony of bestowing on Brezhnev the rank of marshal of the Soviet army, Chernenko was already closer to the center, having passed three CC secretaries: M. V. Zimyanin, Katushev, and Kapitonov. This was a clear indication of his rise in prominence.

The next stage of his rise brought him to equal footing with Suslov and Kirilenko. The occasion was the signing of the Soviet-U.S. agreement on May 29, 1976.[24] Subsequently, dozens of photographs including Chernenko appeared in the newspapers, each of them revealing something pertinent to his rapid elevation. For example, *Pravda* of June 12 featured the ceremony of the signing of the treaty of cooperation between India and the USSR, with Chernenko standing right next to Suslov, Kirilenko, and Demichev. Two weeks later, on June 28, *Pravda* covered the departure of a Soviet delegation to Berlin for a conference of Communist parties; a photograph on this occasion showed Chernenko in the company of the CC secretaries who were Politburo members, i.e. Kirilenko, Pelshe, and Kulakov. On the return of Brezhnev from Alma-Ata, a photo in *Pravda* of October 6 showed Chernenko right next to the general secretary, and on October 23 *Pravda* reported the participation of Chernenko in the government delegation to the Consultative Council Conference in Bucharest.

A further press item of significance appeared on October 5, 1977, reporting Chernenko's inclusion in the commission charged with drafting the new constitution. The commission was headed by Brezhnev. From this time on, whenever the general secretary appeared in public, on a trip abroad, on travels around the country, or on vacation in the Crimea, he would invariably be accompanied by Chernenko.[25] It is noteworthy that at the general secretary's summer residence Brezhnev and Chernenko alone received and conversed with the leaders of Romania, Poland, and Bulgaria.

Chernenko accompanied Brezhnev to soccer matches, which the latter enjoyed watching. He was also the general secretary's faithful hunting companion, in the forest of Zavidovo and in the steppes of Kazakhstan, where special game preserves were kept for Brezhnev's exclusive use as hunting grounds. Chernenko would see to it that Brezhnev's favorite soccer team, Kiev Dynamo, did not lose. Likewise, he saw to it that every hunt would be successful so that Brezhnev could boast of having brought down a dozen ducks, a wild boar or two, or a dozen rabbits.

For his part, Brezhnev saw to it that the prominence accorded to Chernenko was in proportion to the closeness of their relationship. Because it did not befit the general secretary to consort with someone who was formally no more than one of ten CC secretaries, at the October 1977 CC Plenum, only a year after he had become a CC secretary, Chernenko was co-opted as a candidate member to the Politburo. A year later the death of Kulakov provided the opportunity for Chernenko to be promoted to full membership in the Politburo. He then moved from Kachalov Street, on which the members of the Central Committee lived, to one of the apartments for Politburo members on Kutuzov Prospekt. There Chernenko had six rooms: three bedrooms, a living room, a music room, and an office, plus wide halls, high ceilings, and exquisite furniture. And he gained another exclusive privilege of Politburo members, a California-style bungalow, with swimming pool and patio. Chernenko also traded the Chayka automobile he scarcely had had time to become used to in his two years as CC secretary for the more imposing ZIM-114 limousine. From this time on, as with the other Politburo members, his vehicle would be protected fore and aft by security service cars that would stop oncoming traffic to allow him to make his way unimpeded to the CC building on Staraya Ploshchad (Old Square) along the middle lane of the Moscow boulevards, which is reserved for vehicles of the top Soviet elite and the KGB.

Most important of all, Chernenko was now the holder of the two posts — full Politburo membership and a CC secretaryship — which put him in the running for succession to Brezhnev. Besides Chernenko, only Suslov and Kirilenko held both functions and the status accruing to their joint incumbency. However, Suslov's importance had diminished; he was no longer needed by Brezhnev after the general secretary gained a clear majority in the Politburo at the December 1978 CC Plenum, at which Kosygin's last ally, Kirill Mazurov, was removed and replaced by Nikolay Tikhonov (as a candidate member). Simultaneously in the CC Secretariat, Kulakov's place was inherited by Mikhail Gorbachev, an as yet completely unknown entity in Moscow.

Chernenko succeeded in tripping up Kirilenko on a matter of protocol. When Chernenko was elected to the Supreme Soviet in 1978 (for the first time not from Moldavia but from Penza, which was an additional token of recognition; thus Chernenko's Penza period was not then considered a failure), he was described as an "important Party and government figure," and Kirilenko, formally the second secretary of the Central Committee, was referred to only as an "important Party figure." The first to sense the reshuffling of rank at the top was not someone from Moscow but Todor Zhivkov, the experienced and intrigue-wise head of Bulgaria, who met Chernenko in the company of Brezhnev on the latter's visit to Sofia. Zhivkov was quick to realize that Chernenko was already "number two" in the Kremlin. "And why not?" Chernenko might have well asked himself. Had he not labored hard in Party work? Had he not had the daring and foresight to make the right gamble? Almost thirty years before, in far off Kishinev, Chernenko had bet on Brezhnev. He had won. Now in Moscow the time had come to claim his due.

Notes

1. "The CPSU in Figures," *Partiynaya zhin'*, no. 14 (1981): 5.
2. *Pravda*, November 7, December 10, 1964; March 27, 1965; *Planovoye khozyaystvo*, no. 4 (1965): 8–14.
3. *Pravda*, May 28, July 11, 1965.
4. *Ekonomicheskaya gazeta*, no. 8 (February 1965): 2, 4.
5. *Pravda*, May 22, 1965.
6. *Pravda*, June 5, 1965.
7. "XXIV S"esd o razvitii vnutripartiynoy i sovetskoy demokratii, sovershenstvovanii partiynogo i gosudarstvennogo apparata" (The 24th Congress on the development of intra-Party and Soviet democracy, [and] the improvement of the Party and state apparat), in K. U. Chernenko, *Izbrannye rechi i statyi* (Selected speeches and articles) (Moscow: Izd-vo politicheskoy literatury, 1984), pp. 23–43.
8. Ibid., pp. 24–26.
9. Ibid., p. 25.
10. Ibid., pp. 29–30.
11. Ibid., p. 41.
12. Ibid.
13. Ibid., pp. 40–43.
14. "Rukovodyashchaya rol' V.I. Lenina i KPSS v razrabotke osnovopolagayushchikh dokumentov gosudarstvennogo stroitel'stva" (The leading role of V. I. Lenin and the CPSU in elaborating the basic documents of state-building), in K. U. Chernenko, *Izbrannye rechi i statyi* (Selected speeches and articles) (Moscow: Izd-vo politicheskoy literatury, 1984), p. 44.
15. Ibid., pp. 44–64.

16. "Nekotorye voprosy sovershenstvovaniya partiynogo i gosudarstvennogo apparata" (Some questions relating to the improvement of the Party and state apparatus), in K. U. Chernenko, *Izbrannye rechi i statyi* (Selected speeches and articles) (Moscow: Izdatelstvo politicheskoy literatury, 1984), pp. 65–83.
17. Ibid., pp. 76–77.
18. Ibid., p. 78.
19. Ibid., pp. 79–80.
20. Ibid., pp. 80–81.
21. Ibid., pp. 78–79.
22. See *Sovetskaya Rossiya*, August 4, 1965, lead article; *Pravda*, August 20, 1965, lead article; *Pravda*, December 7, 1965.
23. *Pravda*, May 2, 1976.
24. Ibid., May 30, 1976.
25. Ibid., October 5, 1976.

5

The Struggle for Succession

*Soviet Russia dies with each new leader, and
with each new leader is reborn again.*

The Soviet people often wondered who Chernenko really was. Party
propaganda made a great fuss about him; he headed official delegations
abroad and was a frequent visitor to East European countries. During
one such visit he was awarded the highest decoration Bulgaria could
bestow. He was also allowed to award decorations, e.g. to cities and,
rather surprisingly, to the border unit in which he had performed his
military service in his youth. This was an unheard of honor, both for the
unit and for Chernenko. His portraits began to appear more and more
frequently in the hands of marchers at celebrations in Red Square. At
first their number was kept within limits, to match the numbers of photographs of the other members of the Politburo, but gradually the proportions were altered. With each additional portrait the anonymity that had
surrounded Chernenko for so many years gave way to increasing renown.
Party stalwarts began to speak of the great impression Chernenko made,
about his erudition, brilliant mind, good manners, and consideration for
others.

Chernenko's image as a leader of a new type was confirmed at the all-
union conference of Party workers in Moscow in 1980, at which he delivered a quite unusual speech about the style and method of Party work.
The speech was studded with surprises. Chernenko criticized the office-
bound style of leadership (although the Party knew no other style), endless Party meetings, and collegiality used for the purpose of diffusing the
accountability of officials. Noticeable at this conference was the innovative style, particularly the lack of vague, generalized formulas so charac-

teristic of Central Committee resolutions in past years. This was a contribution of Chernenko's; it was he who came up with the idea of naming specific individuals as guilty of specific offenses regardless of the offender's position, including that of influential minister or director of an enterprise. Chernenko's speech scored bribe taking, drunkenness, amorality, abuse of office, and the like. The Party functionaries who heard this stern attack concluded—correctly—that Chernenko had thrown his hat into the race for the succession to Brezhnev and was a contender to reckon with.

In contrast to the sociable and joke-cracking Brezhnev, Chernenko was much more reserved. He was preoccupied with work to the point of avoiding any distractions. Each morning he would be in his office in the Central Committee building on Staraya Ploshchad several minutes ahead of the prescribed time. His wood-paneled office was furnished simply and modestly, and was graced with a portrait of Brezhnev. Chernenko was fussy about order: the books were neatly arranged on the shelves, the armchairs set symmetrically around the magazine table. On his writing desk everything was always neatly arranged: a tear-off calendar in the middle and carefully clipped bunches of papers on the sides, an ashtray near the inkwell, and an amber cigarette mouthpiece, which Chernenko used in imitation of Brezhnev.

Unless summoned by Brezhnev, Chernenko would as a rule leave his office later than the other CC secretaries, i.e. at about 8 or 9 o'clock in the evening, often taking papers with him to look over at home. Indeed, the problems he faced were quite complex and he sometimes suggested nonconventional solutions that often surprised his rivals. As a pragmatic politician, Chernenko realized that Brezhnev was very unlikely to live more than four years. This left him with very little time, compared to the twenty and ten years Khrushchev and Brezhnev had had for preparing their respective bids to reach the pinnacle of power. He had to "accelerate" things in order to emerge from being just one of the potential claimants to the Party throne to becoming the main claimant. This prospect seemed unlikely; it was hard to imagine the cautious, reserved Chernenko, with his apparently limited interests, in the role of heir apparent.

The other Politburo members considered the general secretary's habit of seeking Chernenko's company as a quirk, which they attributed to senility. They put up with this weakness of Brezhnev's on the assumption that Chernenko himself did not believe in this game and played it only to humor his boss. The CC secretaries were convinced that Brezhnev's favoring of Chernenko was a transient matter, but they were wrong. Brezhnev was exhausted and frustrated by his illness and frightened by the sudden onslaught of old age and infirmity. He was reluctant to think about succession, and he feared that any designated successor would betray him exactly as he had betrayed Khrushchev. But he trusted Chernenko and believed he could rely on him. After all, Chernenko was an unpopular outsider in the Politburo without a power base of his own. Brezhnev could behave with Chernenko as with no one else: without assuming the pose of the Great Man, without the masks that he had to wear and frequently change. And in one of their private moments, Brezhnev must have intimated to Chernenko his decision to designate him as his successor — on condition that Chernenko would assure his hold on power until his death and would protect his posthumous reputation and his place in history.

However, Chernenko understood that promises, the realm of the "ought," are one thing and that politics, the realm of the "is," is another. Although he lacked Brezhnev's ability, he surpassed his boss in political maneuvering. By nature Chernenko was a conservative, but in order to set himself apart from the conservatives surrounding Brezhnev, he became an advocate of reforms. He tried to project the image of a Party leader with experience and energy, who would not shirk from innovation if it were required to make the administrative system more dynamic and effective.

By 1980 Chernenko had already written or edited ten books, more than all the other members of the Politburo (excluding Brezhnev) taken together. In each of the books, despite the mass of clichés, he succeeded in expressing some unorthodox views. In this regard 1980 turned out to be an especially fruitful year, for it was marked by publication of *V. I. Lenin, the CPSU and Work with Cadres* under Chernenko's editorship and of two books of his own: *Issues Concerning the Work of the Party and Government Apparats* and *The CPSU and Human Rights.*[1]

The range of topics in Chernenko's books is impressive; this suggests that Chernenko was helped by a whole team of ghostwriters. Of course, he was not the only one in the Party bureaucracy who used ghostwriters. In Brezhnev's time a scientific degree was already viewed as an appropriate ornament for a high official; thus, ghostwriters were sought and rewarded generously with apartments, privileges, and positions for providing written works which fulfilled part of the requirement towards receiving academic degrees. Chernenko, however, did not seek degrees or membership in the Academy of Sciences; he sought recognition as a theoretician of the Party but, in contrast to Suslov, in regard to a broad range of interests. He first laid claim to expertise in philosophy. This was not difficult in the absence of competition; the other Politburo members were interested in hardly anything but politics. His search for acclaim as an expert in Party affairs followed.[2]

In the anthology *V. I. Lenin, the CPSU and Work with Cadres*, Chernenko arranged the material by suitably elaborating upon familiar articles and speeches of Lenin in order to provide support for his own political strategies. He was critical of Brezhnev's tenet of "consolidation of cadres," which by that time obstructed his efforts to purge from the Party apparat anyone not fully loyal to him. And he attacked leaders responsible "for failures in the economy, for stasis in administration, for organizational malfunctions."[3]

Chernenko's theory always conformed to practice and served it. Soon after he completed the Lenin compilation, he was recognized as an expert on personnel matters and, in this capacity, he drafted a special CC resolution on selection and assignment of leading cadres. Thus, the ideas presented in his books could not be said to lack applications.

The next move of Chernenko from theory to practice occurred when he was preparing materials about cadre policies for the forthcoming (in early 1981) 26th Party Congress. There, he again returned to his favorite topic, namely, to the style of Party leadership. However, the ideas he offered were quite out of step with the Brezhnev period and therefore found hardly any expression in the general secretary's report to this Congress. Chernenko believed that cadres improve when their performance is controlled not only from above but also from below. (This idea would be taken up by Gorbachev five to six years later.) Chernenko also called for the creation of a cadre pool for promotions. Such cadres would work under a superordinate official and provide his replacement when the time came.[4]

The latter idea has not been followed up by the Kremlin to this very day despite the fact that Chernenko qualified it as a systemic imperative. He noted that the existence of competent replacement cadres would allow the rapid removal of incompetent personnel in high positions while at the same time guaranteeing that under no circumstances would production be left without qualified management. However, the Party bureaucracy would not accept (either then or subsequently) Chernenko's demand that criticism of offending rankholders be allowed in primary Party organizations. The standard practice remains unchanged: to maintain the authority of the "good" manager of a collective enterprise his failures can be evaluated only at hierarchical levels higher than the "collective" itself.

Chernenko again returned to the issue of cadres in his next book, *Issues Concerning the Work of Party and Government Apparats*, but this time he viewed the problem in the context of "scientific grounding" of Party work, which was his pet idea. The book did not present new ideas; it essentially amounted to a compilation of articles written earlier. Collected, however, the articles offered the author the opportunity to review once more topical themes related to principles of leadership, collegial power-sharing, accountability of high officials, and control over perfor-mance.[5] The themes were topical not just for Chernenko but for the entire Party bureaucracy as well.

Chernenko's third book, *The CPSU and Human Rights*, is another story. It deals with a completely new world of juridical and social prob-lems. Conceived of as a response to Western accusations of Soviet viola-tions of human rights, Chernenko's book did not entail any great risk on his part because he was offering no new views or solutions. His ideas conformed to the usual Communist line of argumentation, consisting of a composite of references to the Soviet constitution and the Party pro-gram and of banal attacks against the capitalist countries. Chernenko could not avoid quoting the Western press, and such quotations were the sole feature animating the otherwise dry contents.[6] For this effort Chernenko received a political windfall that exceeded all his expectations. In conjunction with Chernenko's other works, the book was awarded the Lenin Prize. This immediately elevated Chernenko above the other mem-bers of the Politburo, who had not been accorded that honor.

In the wake of this award it was only natural that Chernenko receive his second star of Hero of Socialist Labor on his seventieth birthday, where-upon he rose again in the Party hierarchy. He was granted the honor of delivering a report at the commemorative session in Moscow dedicated to the 111th anniversary of the birth of Lenin. This was an honor reserved only for the most renowned of Party leaders, but there was more to it. Official press reported the applause greeting Chernenko's speech as being "thunderous and prolonged,"[7] not merely "prolonged," as is the standard in regard to the speeches of Politburo members. The adjective "thunder-ous" had been strictly reserved for the general secretary's speeches, and not always used even then. (For example, one of the first speeches of Andropov as general secretary, at the November CC Plenum in 1982, was reported to have been met only with "prolonged applause."[8])

How did it happen that Chernenko succeeded in beating out the other Politburo members to become second after Brezhnev? Chernenko had an uncanny ability to grasp the significance of personality as well as politics and to be ready to use the opportunities of the moment. By skillfully taking advantage of the inordinate vanity of Brezhnev, Chernenko was able to engender friction first between the general secretary and Podgorny and then between Brezhnev and Kosygin, until their relations were aggravated to the point of a complete rift.

By the second half of the 1970s neither Podgorny nor Kosygin any longer posed a threat to Brezhnev. Already advanced in years and ex-hausted by Party intrigues, both in the end ceased competing with Brezhnev and acquiesced in the continued buildup of the latter's power and authority. Both had long ago renounced their goals: Podgorny, his ambition of eventually becoming general secretary; Kosygin, the liberalization of the economy. All they wanted was to live out their lives in luxury and tranquility.

Although they were no hindrance to Brezhnev, the premier and the president still stood in Chernenko's way. As long as they were in office, they blocked him from reaching third and second rank in the Party hierarchy, for despite being humiliated and even downtrodden by Brezhnev, Podgorny and Kosygin remained his nominal peers by virtue of incumbency of their posts. It was they who presided at Politburo meetings when the general secretary was absent due to ill health (a frequent occurrence) or travel.

Not even after having been made CC secretary through Brezhnev's favor could Chernenko hope to penetrate the inner circle of Politburo veterans who had participated in the plot against Khrushchev. This circle would be more likely to admit a political rival who could be considered their equal, e.g. Kirilenko or Suslov, than an upstart or Ivan-come-lately like Chernenko. For them, Chernenko was a "mediocrity" who occupied himself with maintaining the structural foundations of the Party and who would never dare to emerge from Brezhnev's shadow. Unwilling to tolerate their condescension, Chernenko began to weave a complex net of intrigue against Podgorny and Kosygin.

One after another Brezhnev's rivals were removed from the political arena, but only gradually, so as to enable the general secretary to protect the system from sudden tremors. They suffered failures and defeats long before they were removed from the Politburo. Podgorny's case was different. Podgorny was not pushed down from the Party Olympus. On the contrary, he ascended it with the full consent and encouragement of Brezhnev, who needed him to undercut the influence and authority of Kosygin. Podgorny was assigned some of the latter's functions as premier and accordingly was raised from third to second rank in the Party hierarchy. Not resting content with this success, Brezhnev resolved to effect the subordination of the Council of Ministers to the Presidium of the Supreme Soviet by establishing the legal basis for this in the new constitution. Podgorny, who was quite happy to gain policy-formulation and execution powers, cooperated fully. At this point, however, Brezhnev had something to be concerned about. It would be most unwelcome if the Presidium of the Supreme Soviet would thus find itself in a position to compete with the Party apparat. Consequently, he instructed Chernenko to delve into the old constitution to find ways to limit the powers of Podgorny.

It turned out that there was no way, the crucial reason being that

Podgorny, as chairman of the subcommittee for government administration, could block any efforts of Brezhnev to circumscribe his power. Chernenko thereupon made the only logical suggestion: the top authority holder in the Party should also be the top authority holder in the government, i.e. the general secretary should also be president.

As could be expected, Podgorny was opposed. On May 24, 1977, the constitutional commission was convoked. Podgorny was removed from chairmanship of the subcommission. This was the first step toward his ouster from the Politburo. On the following day, at the CC Plenum at which the draft of the new constitution was accepted, the political career of Podgorny came to an end. The section of the constitution draft dealing with the leading role of the Party in the government was approved. The approval confirmed Brezhnev's status as top ruler and removed another of Chernenko's opponents to his bid for succession.

The next in line to fall was Kosygin. He began to lose power with the 24th Party Congress in 1971, which for the first time publicized the formula "the Politburo led by Brezhnev." At the following Party Congress, in 1976, Kosygin was forced to approve Brezhnev's economic plan, which sounded the death knell of the hopes for reforms that he had been nurturing for twelve years. Brezhnev steadily expanded Party domination and, along with it, his own authority over government affairs. This process was theoretically justified by recourse to the formula that "administration is a political problem."

Then rumors began circulating to the effect that Kosygin was about to retire due to ill health. Possibly the rumors themselves contributed to his declining health. But one way or another, Brezhnev took advantage of Kosygin's illness to obtain the Politburo's consent to the appointment of Tikhonov as first deputy chairman of the Council of Ministers. Tikhonov was one of the "Dnepropetrovsk mafia" brought to the center of power. Once he took over the administration of the economy via the Council of Ministers, Kosygin was reduced to a standby figure.

The power of the premier continued to decline to the point of his being forced to defer to the general secretary in all matters, whether of Party or government. Brezhnev would have been willing to wait for another heart attack to carry off Kosygin if it had not been for the steady pressures on the part of Chernenko. The latter stoked the general secretary's envy of the popularity of Kosygin until Brezhnev had had enough. Kosygin's name still figured at the June CC Plenum in 1980. He was scheduled to read a report at the upcoming 26th Party Congress; however, at the Congress itself economic developments were outlined not by Kosygin but by the new premier, Tikhonov, who was ready to do Brezhnev's bidding and serve Chernenko.

Kosygin was ousted just a few months before his death. Yet, two of the original founders of Brezhnev's rule, Suslov and Kirilenko, still remained in the Politburo. However, Chernenko had an idea how to bypass them. He would help elevate Brezhnev above the other members of the Politburo, transform him into unchallenged *leader* (*vozhd*); then the Party would have to bow before whoever would receive power from his hands.

Since his installation as head of the General Department, Chernenko had remained in charge of agenda fixing and record keeping for all Party meetings. He consistently used this position to promote the cult of Brezhnev. At the 1971 Party Congress every second CC secretary and every second member or candidate member of the Politburo (to be precise, eight out of sixteen) considered it *de rigeur* to laud Brezhnev and to quote him. At the following Party Congress five years later, the speeches of all sixteen of the CC secretaries and Politburo members acclaimed Brezhnev; some of them devoted whole sections to singing his praises, but Eduard Shevardnadze outdid everyone else. At the 26th Congress in 1981 passionate hosannahs to the general secretary of at least a hundred words reverberated in the speeches of *all* delegates, Party leaders, ministers, and the selected "representatives" of the people. The handiwork of Chernenko could be sensed in these paeans, for he was accomplished not only in Party building but also in sycophancy.

All the praise of Brezhnev echoed the same clichés. Grishin, the first secretary of the Moscow *gorkom* linked Brezhnev with the "successes of domestic and foreign policy," referred to the general secretary as an "ardent fighter for peace and Communism," and credited him with the "elaboration and execution of major measures to further essential causes." Shcherbitsky, the first secretary of the Central Committee of the Ukrainian Communist Party, noted that "Brezhnev has earned the sincere appreciation of true revolutionaries, [and] considerable respect in government and business circles in the entire world." Kunaev, the first secretary of the Central Committee of Kazakhstan, asserted that "Brezhnev's word is listened to attentively and hopefully by all of progressive humanity," which views Brezhnev as the "true continuer of the immortal work of Lenin," and that what further distinguishes Brezhnev is his "inexhaustible talent . . . enthusiasm and penetrating mind, constant concern for the working people, [and] profound sensitivity." Romanov, the first secretary of the Leningrad Party *obkom*, characterized Brezhnev as the "most outstanding political and government leader of our time."[9]

Chernenko viewed such extravagant exultation of Brezhnev as an important indicator of the degree to which the general secretary had succeeded in consolidating his power, but he also believed that verbal praise was not enough, i.e. that Brezhnev's formal status should rise accordingly. Brezhnev already held all conceivable posts, more than either Stalin or Khrushchev. He was general secretary of the Central Committee, chairman of the Presidium of the Supreme Soviet, and chairman of the Defense Council (which made him commander in chief of the armed forces). This is why Chernenko had to come up with something new. Hence, in the winter of 1978 Brezhnev was awarded the title Marshal of the Soviet Union and (in peacetime) awarded the highest military decoration that existed: the Order of Victory. Additionally, he received a weapon of honor emblazoned with the emblem of the Soviet Union in gold.

Although the idea for the awards originated with Chernenko, it was executed by Kuznetsov who, after twenty years in the Ministry of Foreign Affairs, had been brought into the Politburo as a candidate member barely a year before — just in time to sign the decree concerning the decorations of Brezhnev. Until this time there had been no precedent for one ministry to be represented in the Politburo by two officials, the minister and his deputy. It later appeared that this expediency was temporary, a precondition of Kuznetsov's appointment to the revived post of first deputy chairman of the Presidium of the Supreme Soviet, in which position his real role would be to free Brezhnev, the chairman, from boring and burdensome formal responsibilities. This appointment explains why it was Kuznetsov who was charged with emceeing the "coronation" of Brezhnev as supposed military leader of the first magnitude.

The purpose of the ceremony puzzled many, and speculation on the subject abounded. The conjectures ranged from a presumed increase in Brezhnev's actual power to a presumed attempt to subordinate the armed forces more tightly to his will. What escaped the conjecturers' attention was the fact that what lurked behind the event was not a thing, a particular function, but rather a person, namely, Chernenko. While Brezhnev was basking in the fabricated glory, Chernenko was adding new touches to it. A six-volume collection of Brezhnev's speeches and articles was issued, Brezhnev was awarded the Lenin Peace Prize, phonographic records of his speeches appeared, along with stamps depicting his visit to Cuba, and thousands of photographs of him bedecked the streets.

A further stage came with the bestowal on Brezhnev of the title of *vozhd*, the leader. After being discredited by Stalin, the term fell into disuse in the Party, but it was reintroduced into ideological circulation for the sake of Brezhnev's glorification. To apply it directly was the task of others while Chernenko acted in the wings, working out the scenario and assigning roles. He entrusted the person then closest to the general secretary, Kirilenko, to utter the power-endowed and endowing word first,[10] but he then encouraged others, Kunaev, Geidar Aliev, Shevardnadze, and Shcherbitsky, soon to follow suit.

This adulation, the well-rehearsed raptures, and preprogrammed applause, "prolonged, thunderous, and swelling into an ovation," were intended to indicate that Brezhnev was the sole ruler of Party and government. Yet, the attempt to transform Brezhnev into the *vozhd* was essentially abortive. Brezhnev lacked qualities befitting Soviet dictators: the unprincipledness and political acuity of Lenin, the ruthlessness of Stalin, or the recklessness of Khrushchev. The adulation of Brezhnev could be sensed to be mere formality, a sham designed by Chernenko to cover the fact that in his last years as general secretary Brezhnev was unable to become the sole ruler and merely played at being such. The situation in this regard changed in 1981 and the change became evident to all in 1982.

The year 1981 marked the apogee of the cult of Brezhnev, of his proclaimed infallibility and unchallenged leadership, but at the same time it marked the moment at which his actual power began to dwindle. Although the 26th Party Congress hailed the performance of Brezhnev as "epochal" (Shevardnadze) and "brilliant" (S. F. Medunov), it also revealed the fragility of the equilibrium between the general secretary and the rest of the Politburo. The very fact that no Politburo members lost their positions, that there were no personnel reshufflings, clearly indicated that Brezhnev could no longer do whatever he wanted. He was bestrewn with awards and honors, but his prestige was declining, initially precisely because of the contrived manner by which it was being enhanced and then because of the afflictions that befell him. Rumors about the latter circulated openly: that he had not really recovered from his heart attack, that he lacked energy and tired quickly, that his arrhythmia and breathing difficulty prevented him from working more than a couple of hours a day, that at meetings he could be seen staring absentmindedly into space, and so on. Then radio and television ceased live broadcasting of the full text of his speeches but limited transmission to their beginnings and endings. This measure was evidently designed to conceal the extent of his sickness and weakness from the public.

The elderly Politburo members tried to protect their elderly peer. The Politburo also attempted to preserve the status quo, which it considered a prerequisite for maintaining power. Therein lay the weakness of the Politburo and the relative strength of Brezhnev.

Yet, not all members of the Politburo were willing to put up with the status quo and ensuing stagnation until Brezhnev's death would eventually put an end to them. Chernenko, for one, cautiously but persistently began to outmaneuver his more experienced rivals in the Politburo, one after another, by taking over their domains of authority and bases of power. First he shunted Suslov aside from international affairs, replacing this traditional guardian of Communist ideology in representing the Soviet government at the conventions of the Communist parties of Greece, Denmark, Cuba, and France. Next Chernenko impinged on the turf of Kirilenko. By gaining control over cadres, he rapidly began to select and advance people of his choice to power positions in the Party. Because he himself and his recruits were Brezhnevite ultraloyalists, his cadre policy could in no way arouse Brezhnev's suspicion. At the same time he used his personal closeness to Brezhnev to control the access of others to him. Chernenko also helped his boss physically as well as politically: he not only coordinated Politburo proceedings (he began chairing its sessions in Brezhnev's absence) but also helped Brezhnev sit and stand, accompanied him at meetings, and intervened whenever Brezhnev's partial deafness might have led to misunderstandings or embarrassment.

The other members of the Politburo were willing to tolerate Chernenko's hovering around Brezhnev but were not willing to countenance the idea of Chernenko in power as Brezhnev's substitute. The Soviet Party establishment may have been patient, but it bore grudges. It never forgave Chernenko his precipitous political ascent. It might have been prepared to put up with his intrigues but not with his breaches of hierarchical order. This is why the unwritten pact between the Party apparat and the general secretary to let Brezhnev live out his life in peace and quiet and the other members of the Politburo enjoy their comforts and privileges in peace and quiet was finally undermined. It was Chernenko who undermined it with his ambition.

On the eve of 1982 the country experienced a shock as the Politburo underwent the throes of a severe conflict. The bid for succession was opened not by Chernenko but by Andropov. Andropov found an unusual way of unexpectedly expressing his deep but previously concealed displeasure with Chernenko:[11] he attacked Brezhnev while really aiming at Chernenko. Although he did not have wide support in the Party apparat, Andropov did have the state security services at his disposal. He decided to use their methods to compromise Brezhnev and thus demonstrate that the latter's choice of heir was open to question.

One might have thought that attacking Chernenko directly would have been a safer and more effective way of harming his reputation than attacking Brezhnev, but the KGB files apparently did not contain potentially embarrassing material on Chernenko. Chernenko was one of the few highly placed Central Committee members not involved in corruption, bribe taking, or womanizing. Thus, the only route available to Andropov was indirect: to compromise Chernenko by compromising Brezhnev.

During the first months of 1982 (as recounted in my book *Policy*

Dilemmas and the Struggle for Power in the Kremlin: The Andropov Period) Brezhnev became the target of intricate intrigues replete with startling rumors (e.g. that Brezhnev had become senile), with charges of crimes (Brezhnev's children were said to be guilty of illegal currency transactions, stealing jewels, and attempting to flee abroad), with surprising revelations (Brezhnev's old buddy, the secretary of the Krasnodar *kraykom*, Medunov, was fired), and mysterious deaths (in the course of several months the deaths were reported of first secretaries of the *obkoms* of Yakutia and Tataria, of the first secretary of the central committee of Tadzhikistan, and of the chairman of the council of ministers of Georgia, all friends of Brezhnev). Chernenko was disturbed and distraught and his Politburo colleagues shocked (some also worried about their own fate) by the strong-arm tactics of Andropov, who previously had not been considered an aspirant to Party leadership because according to the rankings fixed by the recently concluded 26th Party Congress, he ranked only eighth or ninth in the hierarchy.

Chernenko's generation, which still dominated the political scene, was accustomed to other "more respectable" patterns of conduct, such as intra-Party plots, secret deals, intrigue, and manipulation. Now Chernenko had to respond to Andropov's challenge. Brezhnev's illness was serious and it upset the relative stability in the Politburo, which, deprived of leadership, split into several factions as well as some unaffiliated individuals. The latter included the two, Kirilenko and Suslov, who were most entitled to claim succession after Brezhnev, one because he was the second secretary of the Central Committee and the other because of seniority. However, their authority and influence were at that time already somewhat diminished, simply because in the whirlpool of Party intrigue, no Party career, no matter how promising it may look at the outset, is likely to last long. Furthermore, both Kirilenko and Suslov lacked sufficient ruthlessness and single-mindedness, and were incapable of continually currying favor with the general secretary. In this respect, they could hardly compete with Chernenko, who excelled in the latter respect.

Chernenko, however, faced the danger of finding himself isolated. Having staked his future on Brezhnev, he underestimated the power of the oligarchs. Without being general secretary, he was not in the position to undercut their power. He had failed to pay sufficient heed to the collective leadership principle and had demonstrated a tendency toward making decisions on his own authority. Paradoxical as it may seem, it was Andropov who helped Chernenko overcome his isolation. It was the speed, energy, and range of the measures resorted to by the head of the KGB that persuaded the entire clique of Brezhnev faithfuls to ally themselves with Chernenko. Seeing how power was slipping from the weakening grip of the infirm general secretary, they needed a substitute leader.

Of course, the Brezhnev cohort would have preferred someone with authority within the Party, with a more independent past, in short, somebody like Andropov, but the latter's growing power was frightening to the group. A man who challenged Brezhnev could not be expected to show any mercy toward his underlings. Kirilenko was already on the defensive and Chernenko sought his head in an effort to supersede him. Suslov was not even in the running for succession both because of his age and the role of arbitrator of factional disputes, which he assumed long before. Still in that role, he considered it his duty to ensure that succession be smooth. This precluded his own candidacy for general secretary. Thus, for lack of a better alternative, Chernenko received the support of Premier Tikhonov and the CC secretary of Kazakhstan, Kunaev. Another full Politburo member, Pelshe, and the candidate members Kuznetsov and T. Ya. Kiselev were also inclined to support him. Being so indebted to Brezhnev, they felt they could not refuse support to his heir designate. In the Party apparat Chernenko was supported by CC secretaries Kapitonov, K. V. Rusakov, and M. V. Zimyanin.

On the opposite side, all those who considered themselves overlooked by Brezhnev or were for some reason dissatisfied with Brezhnev rallied around Andropov. Their number included full Politburo members Romanov, Gromyko, and Ustinov, and candidate members Ponomarev, Aliev, and Shevardnadze. Among the junior CC secretaries Andropov could count on V. I. Dolgikh and on the editor in chief of *Pravda*, Viktor Afanasyev.[12]

Chernenko was counting on the formal status of his supporters: the general secretary (Brezhnev still held this position despite illness), the chairman of the Council of Ministers (Tikhonov) and the chairman of the Party Control Commission (Pelshe). Andropov, by contrast, was relying more on the *real* power of his allies in the army (Ustinov), the KGB (Andropov himself), and the diplomatic corps (Gromyko). The most powerful, indeed the decisive power, the Party apparat, remained meanwhile on the sidelines, restrained by the wait-and-see attitude or indecisiveness of Suslov. Still calculating the advantages of committing themselves one way or the other were Shcherbitsky, the secretary of the CC of the Ukraine, and Grishin, the secretary of the Moscow Party *obkom* (both full Politburo members), as well as the candidate member Demichev, minister of culture. Each of them wanted to make the best possible deal for himself. Shcherbitsky believed that in view of his own loyalty to the general secretary and his position, he was better qualified than Chernenko to head the Brezhnev camp. Grishin calculated that both factions would exhaust themselves in the contest, and that he would have ample time to join the victorious side. Demichev had his sights set on full membership in the Politburo and hence was prepared to join whoever would guarantee him that in advance, as well as a return from government work to the Central Committee. There remained Gorbachev, the youngest member of the Politburo: he remained loyal to the general secretary following the lead of Suslov, his patron.

Both camps studied the course of Brezhnev's illness, seeking the optimal timing for their initiatives. The denouement, however, occurred suddenly and from an unexpected quarter. Not Brezhnev but Suslov died first, whereupon Chernenko, taking advantage of his position within the Party bureaucracy, began carrying out Suslov's functions in addition to his own. This meant combining the duties of the second and third CC secretaries (i.e., respectively, those of the cadres and ideology). He performed these duties de facto pending official approval by a CC Plenum of their combination.

Chernenko should have pushed for the convocation of such a Plenum as soon as possible to confirm his assumption of responsibility for ideology. Instead, he launched an attack on Kirilenko, seeking the latter's dismissal from all Party posts. Meanwhile, he was unexpectedly aided in his struggle against Kirilenko by Andropov and his faction. But the latter had a completely different purpose in mind: to exploit Chernenko's intrigue in order to reenter the CC, but this became clear only later. At a Politburo session in early April Andropov (who tended to take the initiative) made a speech largely based on information from KGB sources. He painted a grim picture (which quite upset the Politburo) of the emergence of disconcerting tendencies in the portrayal of Soviet realities by Soviet literature. Brezhnev agreed with Andropov's criticism because he had his own score to settle with writers (a literary journal had published a work that committed lèse majesté in referring to him, albeit indirectly, with sarcasm). From newspaper reports of this period it appears that Andropov was proposing some kind of change in relation to literature. One would expect such a process to begin with an increase in ideological supervision, one of the two sectors for which Chernenko was responsible. Andropov thereby may have intended to imply that precisely there the Party apparatus was lacking strong leadership, a quality that he himself strove to project and embody.

Andropov continued to intervene in matters of ideology. At the April 22, 1982, meeting in Moscow commemorating the birth of Lenin, Andropov made a speech in which he laid very heavy emphasis on issues of propaganda and Communist upbringing. This was understandable because he had already raised these themes in the Politburo. Yet such "trespassing" was understood by those in the know as an attack on Chernenko. Then several days before the Plenum Andropov nearly lost his opportunity to enter the Central Committee. A careful reading of Soviet newspapers of this time suggests that Chernenko intended to have this Plenum remove Kirilenko from all posts in the Party apparatus while confirming Chernenko as second CC secretary—and thereby as the tacitly recognized heir of Brezhnev.

The transfer of power into Chernenko's hands was probably supposed to proceed in two stages. In the first stage Chernenko would gradually edge Brezhnev out of his Party responsibilities while leaving him the honorary post of chairman of the Presidium of the Supreme Soviet. In the second stage, in accordance with the "wishes of the workers" and the "will of the Party," Chernenko would be elected general secretary. The "coronation" of Chernenko as ruler, however, was scheduled to take place not at the upcoming but at the following Plenum, toward the end of December, on the eve of the celebration of the sixtieth anniversary of the establishment of the USSR. Meanwhile, the upcoming CC Plenum would deal with the vacancy of the post of CC third secretary. In this respect, the optimal solution for Chernenko would be to leave this post vacant until after he succeeded in consolidating his own position. Another option available to Chernenko was nomination to the post of one of the junior ideological secretaries: Zimyanin or Rusakov. However, Chernenko was not certain to what extent he could rely on either of them; therefore the filling of this post posed a problem for him. In general in the spring of 1982, his plans and hopes revolved around such personnel problems.

Then something happened to complicate matters. During a visit by Brezhnev to a tractor factory in Tashkent, a pedestrian bridge came crashing down near him. Was this an assassination attempt? Perhaps, but more probably the bridge buckled under the weight of the thousands of workers who had been called to greet the general secretary. In any case, Brezhnev's weak heart was affected and he entered the Kremlin hospital. Accordingly, the CC Plenum on which Chernenko pinned such hopes had to be postponed for several months.

Andropov exploited the time gained and Brezhnev's illness masterfully. At the Politburo meeting that took place a day or two before the CC Plenum held in late May, Andropov's supporters unexpectedly proposed their chief as CC secretary to succeed the deceased Suslov. This caught Chernenko off balance. He may have been puzzled by the apparent desire of Andropov to leave the KGB with its powerful machine of repression and blackmail for the sake of the far less tangible power of secretary in charge of ideology. However, he quite soon understood Andropov's motivation when at that very same Politburo meeting Andropov came out in opposition to the removal of Kirilenko. Kirilenko succeeded in remaining second secretary while Andropov moved into the post of third secretary. This meant a double failure for Chernenko. The CC Plenum of May 24, 1982, approved both appointments because neither contending faction wished to reveal the conflicts at the top in the broad party forum. Thus in one fell swoop Chernenko fell in the Party hierarchy from second place to fourth — after Brezhnev, Kirilenko, *and* Andropov. The return of Andropov to the Party apparat was a serious blow to Chernenko. By becoming a CC secretary in addition to being a member of the Politburo, Andropov patently established his qualification to run for succession.

Chernenko drew some consolation from Andropov's leaving the KGB because that was bound to (and did) lead to an ebb, or even termination, of the campaign of discrediting Brezhnev and thereby intimidating his supporters. Yet, the new KGB chairman, V. V. Fedorchuk, could not have been to Chernenko's liking. Being a veteran chekist from the Ukraine and not a Central Committee member, he remained under Andropov's supervision because the latter (as a Politburo member) continued to oversee the security services. Fedorchuk was also dependent on Shcherbitsky, his former Party boss.

Left to his own devices, Chernenko had only Brezhnev to count on. At this point the general secretary's health remained an important factor and for Chernenko his only remaining weapon in the struggle for power. In this situation Brezhnev suddenly felt well enough to appear in public and give interviews. Alternatively, he may not have felt any better than previously, but may have been set on his feet by Chernenko to appear in public, despite the state of his illness and even at the risk of its further deterioration, in order to demonstrate that he remained at the helm. It is difficult to say which was the decisive factor: Chernenko's determination, Soviet medical expertise, or Brezhnev's fear of losing power. In any case, Brezhnev's reappearance had the effect desired by Chernenko: it caused havoc in the ranks of Andropov's forces. Taking advantage of the changed situation, early in October Chernenko resumed pressing the Politburo for the removal of Kirilenko. Apparently, at this point the Andropov camp lacked the strength to resist the will of the general secretary in regard to his number two. Chernenko had succeeded; he was now second secretary *with* official approval. But, as it turned out, it was too late.

Seemingly sensing that little time was left, Chernenko put Brezhnev into high gear, saddling the general secretary with meetings, conferences, and trips around the country. This was a mistake. During a speech by Brezhnev in Baku someone handed him the wrong text to read. Doped up with medicines, the general secretary read what he was handed, and would have read it to the end without anyone's noticing the difference because such speeches are all so similar, but someone took the trouble to hand him the right text, which was somewhat more appropriate for the occasion. The result was that the general secretary made a fool of himself before millions of television viewers. He mumbled a confused apology: "Comrades, it's not my fault." It was obvious to the CC secretariat and the Politburo, as well as to the public, that Brezhnev's days were over.

Nevertheless, Chernenko persevered in his attempt to bring Brezhnev back to life. For example, he encouraged Brezhnev to convene a meeting of military commanders in Moscow on October 27. The effect was miserable. With the help of the half-dead Brezhnev, Chernenko attempted to coax the army into the succession struggle. The effort backfired because, to his chagrin, the army turned to the side of Andropov. Seeing the general secretary in a shape so poor that he could scarcely move his tongue, the more than 500 military commanders of all types of forces decided to support a strong man in the Kremlin—Andropov![13]

Chernenko raced against time. He headed to Krasnoyarsk to attend the plenum of the Party territorial committee. He was seeking support in a place where his career had begun. His purpose was to intimate to the people of Krasnoyarsk and to the citizens of the whole country how close his relations with the general secretary were. For this purpose, he began his speech with a reference to a conversation between him and Brezhnev during which the latter reportedly said, "Tell the Siberians in Krasnoyarsk that I still remember well my meetings with them."[14] Then Chernenko proceeded, as Party leader, to evaluate the May CC Plenum and to express his confidence in the solution of as yet unresolved problems. He spoke of the nature of these problems freely and, in an obvious attempt to gain popular support, promised major progress in the country. He cited neither facts nor figures concerning the development of the territory because their dry recital would serve no purpose in his attempt to turn to the people and to the Party directly over the heads of the Politburo. To the common people, he promised to build more inexpensive housing and to improve the food distribution supply. To the Party members, he promised stability in Party ranks, i.e. job security. He offered no new ideas (any innovation would be impolitic at the last stage of a succession contest), and contrary to what could be expected of him, criticized no one because naming names could only alienate potential supporters.[15]

Next Chernenko traveled to the Transcaucasus to cover his flank before his final thrust for leadership. The occasion was not a major one—the awarding of the Order of Lenin to the city of Tbilisi—and could have been dealt with by delegating one of the junior CC secretaries to preside over the ceremony. However, Georgia was the turf of Shevardnadze, a candidate member of the Politburo whose factional allegiance was not totally clear. Formerly, as head of the Georgian KGB, he had been close to Andropov while simultaneously maintaining close ties to Brezhnev. Chernenko wanted to ascertain the attitude of Shevardnadze toward his own bid for leadership.

Propitiating the proud, independent Georgians, who despised people who fawned on authority, would not have been an easy task for Chernenko. This is why he resorted to the best Georgian tradition of paying homage to their "glorious" and "inimitable" history. Nor did he spare the flattery when he exalted the activity of the Georgian Party leadership above that of all the republics. He enthused:

> Why not come out and admit it? Sometimes it happens that after a decision is made, Party members meet, discuss, and calculate the percentage of growth of whatever it was that was supposed to grow, and then they leave. But in Tbilisi the Party members have done otherwise, they have met a number of times, on all levels, and discussed not only the percentages, but also how they were attained, at what cost, and under what conditions practical work was being carried out and how it was affecting the situation in the collective. . . . That means that they considered not only everything that affects the material condition of people's lives but also the moral aspects, the whole moral atmosphere in the work collective.[16]

Chernenko reported that all was praiseworthy in the work of the "Georgian comrades": the creativeness of the work, their concern for maintaining cadre reserves, their open, frank, and timely appraisal of existing problems, and the solidity of their intelligentsia's backing for the positions of their Party. In short, the picture he painted was that of a veritable idyll. He even waxed nostalgic about the time when Tbilisi was the capital of Caucasia. (He said this without giving any thought to the feelings in the other Transcaucasian republic capitals.[17])

Chernenko's speech included another point, which was addressed neither to the Georgians nor even to the Soviet people as a whole but to the outside world. In an effort to depict himself as a moderate, the picture of international relations that he presented was multifaceted and laden with complexities, in contrast to the schematism and one-dimensionality typical of Brezhnev and vagueness typical of Andropov. Chernenko called on the world to renounce recourse to force, to sit down at the negotiating table, and to make an attempt to settle unresolved problems within the framework of Soviet-U.S. relations. In his speech, which contained nostalgic references to the period of detente, there was no sabre rattling nor the usual invective against the capitalists. The West was given to understand that were Chernenko to become general secretary, he would be a Soviet leader committed to the cause of peace and cooperation between

East and West.[18] Chernenko's Tbilisi speech was greeted with "thunderous applause"[19] as if he were already general secretary. But in Moscow, which was busily preparing itself for the November anniversary of the Revolution, the vision of political change he advocated aroused little enthusiasm.

Chernenko made preparations of his own for the November festivities. He brought Brezhnev to Moscow from his Kuntsevo *dacha* for the ceremony of the awarding of a second star of Hero of Socialist Labor to Tikhonov. For Chernenko, it was important that his main supporter, the premier, receive the award from the general secretary's own hand, for this could be interpreted as a sign of Brezhnev's approval of Chernenko as his heir. He also persuaded Brezhnev to appear in Red Square on November 7 to stand there on the mausoleum in the bitter cold and wind for several hours. This was followed by one more programmed ritual, Brezhnev's participation in a reception at the Kremlin palace, where he was seen by hundreds of diplomats and Party bigwigs.

The next move — which would have meant the ultimate fulfillment of Chernenko's fond hopes — was to be Brezhnev's gracious resignation for the sake of a "well-deserved rest." The optimal time for such resignation seemed to be December 21, the date of the joint session of the Central Committee and Supreme Soviet scheduled for the celebration of the sixtieth anniversary of the USSR. History ruled otherwise: Brezhnev died and Chernenko lost out.

Brezhnev's death may well have been the result of the excessive burden he took on at Chernenko's urging. Chernenko turned out to be ill-prepared for this surprise; not so Andropov, who had a plan of action ready. Before the corpse of the general secretary had time to grow cold, units of the Kantemirovskaya guards division were, on orders from Ustinov, stationed in Moscow along with the Dzerzhinsky division of the KGB. The participation of the latter evidently led to a protest from KGB head Fedorchuk; otherwise it would be hard to explain his rapid dismissal after Andropov's advent to power.

The sight of the tanks and armed units on the streets of the capital were a strong argument in favor of Andropov at the Politburo session convened on November 10 within hours of Brezhnev's death. The meeting was stormy. The Politburo was split. It was undoubtedly Tikhonov, probably backed by Kunaev, who proposed the election of Chernenko as heir to Brezhnev, while Ustinov, Gromyko, and Romanov called for the election of Andropov. Kuznetsov and Rashidov could be presumed to have supported Chernenko and probably to have voted for him. Because of the absence of two full members of the Politburo (Kirilenko and Pelshe), candidate members Kuznetsov and Rashidov obtained the right to vote, and this turned out to be decisive. Opinions were divided, and the situation was tense. In the case that the Politburo remained divided, the standard operating procedure was to refer the matter to the Central Committee Plenum for a vote. Chernenko undoubtedly made a mistake by not pushing for that, for there the Brezhnevites were in the majority. However, after being abandoned by Shcherbitsky, Gorbachev, Demichev, and Ponomarev, Chernenko preferred to come to terms with Andropov. What he feared was that if he were defeated by Andropov in an open vote, he would lose all his posts and might even end up being politically ostracized as an "anti-Party" figure, as had happened to Molotov and Malenkov after they opposed Khrushchev.

Thus, Chernenko acquiesced to Andropov's becoming general secretary but he did not demean himself. While recommending that the Plenum approve the election of Andropov (as required under the rules of "democratic centralism," which call for the subordination of the minority to the majority), Chernenko did nothing to prevent his supporters from advocating his candidacy for general secretary at the Plenum. Another rule of democratic centralism called for the subordination of the lower body (the Central Committee) to a decision made by the superordinate one (the Politburo). This worked against Chernenko's chances at the Plenum, and ultimately determined his defeat.

In fact, Chernenko had already lost to Andropov before the Plenum. His first defeat came when he yielded to him in the Politburo, and the second when, in clear violation of the Party protocol, Andropov was allowed to chair the Central Committee session. Neither Andropov nor Chernenko wanted to leave anything to chance. This explains why Andropov overstepped his authority by chairing the Plenum meeting. This also explains why Chernenko renounced his right as second secretary to preside at the Plenum, in which capacity he would be required to introduce Andropov as the Politburo's choice. All he did allow himself at the Plenum was cautious and indirect criticism of Andropov. Alluding to Andropov, Chernenko said: "Leonid Ilyich (i.e. Brezhnev) knew well that mere good intentions are devoid of value. It is insufficient to mouth correct ideas; it is necessary to match correct ideas with efficient organizational work. . . . "[20] And to this he added a reminder—and warning— that Andropov not only make demands but also have consideration for cadres, i.e. officials currently in office. In a transparent move to protect the Brezhnev crowd, including himself, he reaffirmed the principle of collective leadership: "Now it is doubly, triply important to conduct affairs in the Party collectively."[21]

Andropov had no intention of ruling in opposition to collective leadership. Initially, his options for exercising power in an autocratic manner were foreclosed, not just by his opponents but also by his supporters, who desired neither his too rapid rise (under the impact of which they might be crushed) nor his too rapid fall (which could entail their fall as well).

One choice that did face Andropov was the problem of how to try to change the Soviet Union. The transformation of society could be planned to occur piecemeal by increments or through more radical measures, in leaps. A second problem facing Andropov was the revitalization of the executive machinery that during the Brezhnev years had fallen into bad shape. There were many vacancies: the post of chairman of the Presidium of the Supreme Soviet was unfilled, and the Politburo and the CC Secretariat were both understaffed. In regard to appointments, a confrontation with Chernenko was inevitable. As a result of Brezhnev's death, Chernenko had amassed, even if not for long, a cluster of functions (the supervision of industry and ideology plus control over Party cadres) that he could not have held during Brezhnev's lifetime. To consolidate his power, Andropov had to reduce Chernenko's authority by taking away from him either the Party apparat or control over the economy, or better still, both. At the same time Chernenko's interest dictated that no additional CC secretaries be brought into the Politburo. Only in this way could he hope to preserve both the scope of his authority and his second rank in the Party hierarchy.

Chernenko was well aware that he had only a minority in the Politburo and that with time this minority was bound to shrink as the new general secretary began to deal with the opposition to himself. Yet, Chernenko suddenly received support from where he least expected it, from Shcherbitsky and Grishin. Their attitudes were formed by the experience of long years of intra-Party intrigues; they were resentful of Andropov's steamroller approach and had good reason to feel antagonized and frightened by the unseemly haste of a mere several months with which the new general secretary proceeded to restaff the Party apparat and to inject new blood into it. However, the power of the general secretary has its own dynamics independent of the will of the Politburo. At the November 1982 Central Committee Plenum Andropov promoted Geidar Aliev from candidate to full member of the Politburo, simultaneously with his appointment as first deputy chairman of the Council of Ministers. This meant that Tikhonov, Chernenko's most important ally, was from then on under the supervision and control of Andropov.

Chernenko's camp also viewed with dismay other appointments of Andropov's, such as that of Nikolay Ryzhkov as a CC secretary. However, despite pressure from Andropov, Chernenko's forces blocked Ryzhkov's appointment to the Politburo, thus preventing this protégé of Andropov's from gaining control over the economy. Still, supervision of the economy did not remain in Chernenko's hands because the general secretary himself was gradually assuming responsibility for it. He began right after he gained power: at the CC Plenum of November 22. In his speech there Andropov presented a broad program for the socioeconomic reconstruction of Soviet society, a goal that Chernenko shared but had failed to pursue. Chernenko's failure in this regard was rather transparently and caustically alluded to by Andropov when he said: "There are not a few leaders who extensively quote the lofty words of Leonid Ilyich [Brezhnev] about how our economy should be economic, [but] in practice do little to bring this about."[22]

Next, Chernenko lost control over Party cadres; this sphere of responsibility was up for grabs for a while. In early January 1983 it was assigned to Gorbachev in addition to his duties as CC secretary for agriculture. The appointment determined the factional allegiance of Gorbachev, who from then on became a fervent supporter of the new general secretary. It also greatly affected Chernenko, who was now left with only ideology.

The consequence was a reshuffle in the ranking order, with Chernenko falling from second to third (after Gorbachev) in the Party hierarchy. Very soon Chernenko realized that it would be quite difficult to distinguish himself in propaganda. This was due not to lack of expertise (because he could rely on the extensive and well-oiled agitprop machinery he had inherited from Suslov) but to the fact that within the overall scale of priorities set by Andropov, ideology ranked low. Finding himself on the fringes of Party work, Chernenko faced the prospect of being relegated to the sidelines of Soviet politics.

And in fact, for several months Chernenko was almost completely absent from the political stage. He did not appear at the CC meeting of heads of ministries (in January 1983) at which discussion revolved around labor discipline, an issue that certainly was of direct concern to his sector. He was also the only Politburo member absent from the important meeting of first secretaries of republic central committees held in the Kremlin in April 1983.

In such a situation Chernenko returned to his customary mode of self-expression, writing. In early 1983 he published *To Reaffirm the Leninist Style in Party Work*, a book that contained mostly pronouncements, articles, and speeches from 1981–82. While compiling this volume, Chernenko engaged in a covert polemic against the general secretary. Andropov was then attempting to remold Soviet behavior by advocating soberness, discipline, and conscientiousness. He was doing this by all means available, including intimidation and use of force, e.g. arrests of unauthorized absentees from work, firings, and limitations of rights and privileges. In his book Chernenko argued that a preferable means of influencing the masses was persuasion. He observed that "organizational work of the government which does not take individual psychology into consideration and does not rely on educating people is pointless and has little prospect of success." To substantiate this idea, Chernenko cited numerous examples, all showing that Andropov's hopes of instilling a work ethic through coercion and harsh rule enforcement were doomed to futility. Morality cannot be instilled immorally, noted Chernenko, covering himself with a quotation from Lenin to protect himself from Andropov's retaliation.[23]

In Chernenko's book one can also sense a cautious protest against the Stalinist methods revived by Andropov in Party work. Chernenko asserted that the style and methods of guiding the masses could not be left unchanged but needed to be adapted to specific conditions of people's life; hence his appeal (perhaps intended directly for the general secretary) to assess newly emerging conditions speedily, to analyze the findings, and to apply them accordingly.[24]

Chernenko stressed the redirection of the Party from attempts to solve economic problems to attempts to deal with ideological ones. This was a sign of his failure to comprehend the importance not of reforms (shortly before, when Brezhnev had still been alive, Chernenko did advocate reform, albeit in somewhat vague outlines) but of changing times. Andropov was in the process of unfolding his program for ruling, basing it on the reconstruction of society, and displaying contempt for theory; he had concern only for putting his ideas into practice. To support Andropov in such pragmatism would have meant Chernenko's renunciation of his valid claim to pioneering the idea of reform. If anything, his pioneership, which was rapidly being forgotten, needed to be reasserted. Furthermore, aware that the general secretary's dynamic and headlong methods of leadership generated much bureaucratic backlash, Chernenko wished to propose an alternative tactic. Chernenko took the field under the banner of conservatism, i.e. of the defense and preservation of the Soviet ideological heritage. But even in this conservative role, he managed to remain unorthodox: he insisted on the convening (for the first time in twenty years!) of a special CC Plenum to be devoted to ideological issues, on the crest of which he hoped to emerge as the supreme intellectual authority in the Party.

Exhortations about the importance of ideology did not carry the day because the country was preoccupied with the widely touted idea of economic reforms. Yet, Chernenko did achieve something tangible, for it was he, not Andropov, who gave the main speech at the Plenum. His speech determined the agenda; all the assembled Party activists were compelled to deal with the propaganda issues raised by Chernenko.

At first glance it might have appeared that Chernenko's speech reflected the spirit of Andropov. In regard to form, it conformed to the Andropov style: it was pointed (although not quite as sharply as Andropov's), problem-centered, and polemical. However, its contents were rather anti-Andropovist, although not to the degree of exceeding Party protocol. Chernenko quoted Andropov extensively, to the point of overdoing it. At the very beginning Chernenko said: "The effectiveness of ideological work depends directly upon the extent to which the specific features of the period our country is going through are taken into consideration."[25] This remark already signaled a clash with Andropov. In Chernenko's view progress was being slowed by the insufficient civic maturity of the Soviet people; this contrasted with Andropov's thesis that lack of progress was traceable to defective management and low labor productivity.[26] Actually, these views were not contradictory. Both Chernenko and Andropov were correct because the lack of "civic responsibility" was attributable to faults of the "administrative mechanism" and vice versa, but Chernenko purposely stressed the human factor at the expense of the sociostructural factor in order to highlight the general secretary's lack of theoretical background.

Chernenko also had good reason for selecting his specific targets for attack, namely, the Institute of Sociological Research in Moscow and the Central Economic-Mathematical Institute in Novosibirsk. Both research centers had actively aided Andropov. The former provided the general secretary with considerable data about public opinion, labor problems, and social participation, and the Novosibirsk institute, headed by Professor Tatyana Zaslavskaya, prepared various proposals for economic reforms. Chernenko's disappointment was clearly expressed: "We expected much from the Institute of Sociological Research and the Central Economic-Mathematical Institute of the Academy of Sciences established in the 1960s, but we have not yet seen major concrete research from them."[27]

Chernenko's speech contained no fewer original and bold ideas than the speeches of Andropov at the same and succeeding CC Plenums. Still, Chernenko's views, in contrast to those of Andropov, did not gain public attention for several reasons related both to the topic on which Chernenko spoke and to his personality. In the minds of Soviet citizens ideology (and everything connected with it) tends to arouse distrust, along with the firm conviction that ideology leaves no room for originality, that it is by its very essence rigid and petrified. In contrast, sociopolitical activity, the area of Andropov's concern, is more compelling for Soviet citizens, which explains why, after many years of political stagnation, every proposal of the new general secretary met with considerable interest and often an enthusiastic response. This led to the perception of Andropov's ideas as being original and, above all, bold.

Something similar can be said about the personalities of the two men. Chernenko was perceived as having been indelibly stamped with the hallmark of the Brezhnev era. In contrast, the image of Andropov was carefully crafted by KGB propagandists to fit the role of a dynamic Soviet leader of world stature. Thus, Andropov was projected as sophisticated and well-educated, a clever politician, a pragmatist, and even to some degree, a closet liberal!

In reality both were products of the same Soviet system. Chernenko was a product of its Party microstructure; Andropov was a product of its security police apparatus. Hence their similarities and differences. Equally ingrained in both Chernenko and Andropov were conformism and duplicity, and both were indoctrinated to perceive and evaluate life in the terms of Marxist dialectic. Both were ruthless and cynical. Andropov had spent many years in the KGB in command of the fates of millions of people; he knew how to instill fear. Chernenko, in contrast, had spent many years in the inner corridors of Party politics, many of them on the lower rungs of power; he had learned how to survive and advance by winning favor. The irony is that the Soviet people more readily accepted Andropov than Chernenko, who did not conform to their image of a real leader. This explains the basically skeptical and ironic attitude of the Soviet people to Chernenko and everything he said, wrote, and did. However, it does not diminish the historical importance of his views nor their importance as a source for helping us understand his personality.

Within the Soviet context it was quite astounding to call for a scientific study of international relations. It amounted to discarding dogma for the sake of an empirical approach. In Chernenko's call, one could perhaps detect his chagrin that during the first period of Andropov's rule, Andropov kept him at arm's length from foreign policy matters so that he hardly appeared at receptions for foreign guests or participated in negotiations with foreign delegations. Another of Chernenko's points was also quite surprising: he called for an analysis of sociopolitical realities in Western countries that would avoid relying on the common anti-imperialist stereotypes of Soviet propaganda.[28]

Chernenko espoused a similarly empirical approach in regard to domestic social relations. He believed that their study should be based on "existing reality" and not on outmoded ideological models. He proposed exploring Soviet society in all its complexities and contradictions. He opined that it was not valid to perceive or explain various social problems, such as drunkenness, hooliganism, bribery, or greed, as "relics of the past." Chernenko saw such problems as stemming from the present conditions and hardships of daily life in the USSR. He therefore concluded that purely economic measures (such as those of Andropov, of course) were insufficient because a social change was needed as well. The same recognition of the determinative role of social conditions was present in Chernenko's views on the crisis in agriculture.[29] He believed that it was not enough to industrialize agriculture (as Andropov had advocated) but that reconstruction of the villages and the improvement of housing and living conditions in the rural sector were no less needed. To Andropov's approach to developing the economy Chernenko juxtaposed an emphasis on openness of public debate (*glasnost*) and democratization: "Without considerable openness — *glasnost* — the development of socialist democracy is inconceivable. . . . We will continue this line, guaranteeing the maximum possible openness in debates affecting the interests of the people. Certainly, regular TV reports by ministry chiefs and by other authorities, [and] by Party committees will have to be made mandatory."[30]

It should be kept in mind that Chernenko conceived of "openness" and "democracy" in Soviet terms, as something to be exercised to a limit, encouraged but controlled from above. Still, Chernenko's concept of the prerequisites and consequences of social progress seems to have been considerably broader-minded than the economic determinism of Andropov with its simplistic reliance on order and discipline. Chernenko's approach was more humanitarian and more oriented toward social problems. Chernenko's speeches amply confirm these features. A further confirmation of his attitudes is provided by his comments on the Soviet press. Chernenko criticized its contents, language, and style, its stereotyped correspondent dispatches and articles that "lack both insight and originality."

Nevertheless, there is no point in idealizing Chernenko. His views were a product of totalitarian times and their boldness was greatly curtailed by his Communist socialization. Thus, when he sought to make deeds match the words, the words to be matched were to be the Party's words, the words of Soviet propaganda. This does not detract from his intellectual ability, nor from the fact that his views had a potential for promoting systemic integration. He sought to make the system more flexible, dynamic, and modernized; he also sought to make its ideology more sophisticated.

Thus, it is not surprising that in his speech at the Plenum Chernenko reiterated the idea that Party committees were duty bound to improve the quality of propaganda-agitation work inside the Party itself. The rationale he provided was not phrased in stale ideological clichés but in scientific terms. He observed that the social conditions of Soviet society were changing and that the Party had acquired a new demographic profile, for in its ranks there were "more than 3 million Party members under the age of 30."[31] Chernenko's attitude to his own work was exemplary: serious and thoughtful. He was cautious, reluctant to make quick decisions in moments of crisis or rapid adaptations to new circumstances, but once he did start something, he would bring it to conclusion thoroughly and solidly.

Chernenko wanted harmony and coordination. He wanted ideological work to function like a good orchestra, with each instrument having its own voice but performing jointly under the baton of the conductor (Chernenko himself). Harmony and coordination were in short supply, however, both in Marxist ideology and in Soviet politics. The fact that this did not prevent Chernenko from artfully executing his own score was astounding. He succeeded in playing that score with enviable mastery while accompanying Andropov's illness. At official political performances, e.g. at the session of the Supreme Soviet of June 16, Chernenko self-deprecatingly introduced Andropov, praising his intelligence, experience, and statesmanlike acumen.[32] But scarcely two days earlier at the CC Plenum, out of the public limelight and aided by his loyalists, Chernenko had succeeded in frustrating Andropov's plan to introduce new members into the Politburo, which after the death of Pelshe dropped from fourteen members under Brezhnev to a mere eleven.

By that time Chernenko had changed his tactics in his struggle against Andropov. He no longer attempted to unite his supporters on a common opposition platform to that of Andropov. Andropov was then at a peak of popularity and such an attempt would have failed. Instead, Chernenko's new tactic was to exploit the generation gap in the Politburo, to mobilize the old against the young. It turned out that the Politburo veterans had much in common: they all wanted to preserve their power and privileges for as long as possible. The result was the emergence of a group of Politburo members with shared goals, which, however, stopped short of either resisting Andropov or planning Chernenko's succession. The faction comprised Tikhonov, Kunaev, Shcherbitsky, Grishin, and Chernenko himself. Their first shared goal was to oppose the ascent of younger leaders, but they would not have succeeded in blocking the plan of Andropov to carry out a wide-ranging reorganization of the Party apparatus if a split over the issue had not occurred in the general secretary's camp.

One of the two "old men" in Andropov's camp, Ustinov, was jealous enough about his own prerogative to oppose injections of new blood into the Politburo. This meant a majority for Chernenko with six of the eleven

Politburo members on his side, and consequently, an opportunity for stopping Andropov from carrying out his personnel reshuffle. Under these conditions Chernenko withdrew his opposition to the appointment of Romanov as CC secretary (because the vacancy in the CC secretariat could be filled without any change in the Politburo balance). He was also willing to support the election of Andropov as chairman of the Presidium of the Supreme Soviet because the post added nothing to the general secretary's real power. What was important was that the total number of full Politburo members remained unchanged at eleven.

Soon Andropov gained another opportunity to humiliate Chernenko. On August 15 with great pomp, Andropov held a reception in the Central Committee for Party veterans. Andropov could either have addressed this group himself or assigned the task to a senior Politburo member, such as Chernenko. Instead, he entrusted it to Gorbachev. The latter introduced the general secretary to elderly Party activists who had long ago lost their political clout but whose prestige Andropov sought to exploit for the sake of legitimizing his rule. Chernenko was not invited to the ceremony. Furthermore, Andropov had no qualms about making fun of him in his absence. Personal slight to Chernenko was intended when Andropov ironically observed that one should care less about the ideological props for safeguarding the economy (the main concern of Chernenko's speech at the June CC Plenum) and more about the economic or, more broadly, social props for ideological work.[33]

Chernenko was not the only one not invited. Andropov did not invite other Politburo veterans, even those to whom he was indebted for helping him win the contest for leadership, like Grishin or Shcherbitsky, although as the secretary of the Moscow *gorkom* and as a representative of hundreds of thousands of Party members in the Ukraine, respectively, they should have been invited. Invited were only members of the younger generation in the Politburo, Gorbachev and Romanov (both Andropov's co-optees), along with several CC secretaries, Zimyanin, Kapitonov, and Rusakov, whom Andropov apparently trusted.

In contrast to Chernenko, Andropov did not have an adequate grasp of the mentality of the Party elite, of their affrontable and vindictive nature. Neither Grishin nor Shcherbitsky forgave the general secretary for slighting them. As long as Andropov was healthy and active, they sought no other avenues for expanding their influence than by assisting him subserviently. But as soon as his illness forced him to ease up on the reins, they discovered that they could choose between two major contenders for succession: Gorbachev or Chernenko. For a while they vacillated, seeking to exact maximal price for their support. Chernenko was someone they could easily understand. Gorbachev was an intellectual, a technocrat, not someone who shared their mental universe — they found him somehow unsettling.

Gorbachev had quite unexpectedly turned up in Moscow right after the death of Kulakov, yet in contrast to the restless and uncompromising Kulakov, he seemed, initially at least, to be nondescript, easily taking on any political coloration required by the leadership. In the Central Committee the impression was that Gorbachev was trustworthy and solid, that he could be counted on. He could always be found among those who rapidly and correctly readjusted themselves to the slightest, scarcely noticeable fluctuations in the Party line. But what seemed most estimable in Gorbachev was his apparent sincerity in identifying with whatever directives from above he received. Thus he remained, a perfect man to follow all the policies of Brezhnev's Politburo faithfully — until 1982. But as soon as the powerful gerontocrats began departing from the Politburo, some due to death, others due to the will of their more fortunate factional rivals, Gorbachev changed course. His complaisance disappeared. He became sterner and firmer in his commitment to the guidelines set by Andropov for the country's leaders. From that time on the politburo veterans were increasingly taken by surprise by manifestations of Gorbachev's new identity.

It is not a simple matter to evaluate this change. The problem is to decide whether it was due to mimicry or whether it revealed his real (even if previously scrupulously concealed) preferences. The contrast between his behavior during the long period of his rising Party career when he played, with considerable talent, roles assigned to him by others, and his behavior after he had already become the right hand of Andropov was striking. As soon as Gorbachev succeeded in getting close to the leader's chair, he began discarding the old roles; or perhaps the discarding of such roles was his new role. In any case, his hunger for political power now showed, and it could not fail to arouse the gravest apprehensions on the part of the Politburo veterans.

Andropov, whose illness increasingly paralyzed his activity in many ways, encouraged Gorbachev to act more assertively. For example, he first entrusted to Gorbachev supervision over Party cadres and then responsibility for the economy as well. In April Gorbachev was charged by Andropov with the task of chairing the instructional conference of first secretaries of republic and provincial Party committees. In June he attended a session of the Supreme Soviet of the RSFSR, where in the name of the Politburo, he recommended V. I. Vorotnikov as chairman of the Council of Ministers of the Russian Republic. Finally, Andropov assigned to Gorbachev the extremely important responsibility of running the Party reporting-before-the-elections conferences around the country.

Gorbachev thus gained an opportunity to install his men on various levels of the Party pyramid, from city to republic Party committees.

Attempting to strike a balance between bureaucratic inertia and reform, Gorbachev tried to convey the impression of being a conservative liberal or, depending on circumstances, a liberal conservative. Quite alarmed about what he was up to, the Party apparat reacted with suspicion, anxious to restore what Andropov had disturbed, namely, their relatively tranquil and gratifying existence. The apparat gradually began to identify with and pin its hopes on Chernenko, with whom it had much in common. Like Chernenko, these apparatchiks had risen to power under Brezhnev and therefore came to regard Chernenko as the best guarantor of the stability of their positions and privileges.

Meanwhile, the purges of the Party were in full swing. Almost one-third of high officials fell: 31 percent from the Moscow Party organization; 34 percent (including nine of twenty-five first secretaries of city committees) from the Ukraine; 32 percent (including seven of twenty-nine first secretaries of city committees) from Kazahkstan; and so on.

The Central Committee bureaucracy, in particular its "elected" component, which could be really reshuffled only at a Party Congress, still remained relatively less affected by the purges. In apprehension of the upcoming Congress, CC members and secretaries, heads of departments, high officials of the government bureaucracy, and first secretaries of republics, territories, and provinces (including those already dismissed) looked to Chernenko in the hope of preserving the posts they were still holding or of regaining ones they had already lost.

In the Politburo itself the balance of power was not clear. Andropov supporters were still in the majority, but Gorbachev could not be certain whether all of these would support him. There was neither unity nor concord in the ranks of either the older or the younger generation of the general secretary's supporters. Romanov, for instance, would have welcomed the candidacy of Chernenko for general secretary in preference to that of Gorbachev. His rationale was clear: Chernenko could be expected to rule a relatively short time during which Romanov could gather his strength to make his own bid for power. Similar considerations prompted Shcherbitsky and Grishin to support Chernenko. It was still far from certain what constellation of forces would emerge in the Kremlin when Andropov was no longer in control. Meanwhile the intrigues and conflicts of various interests determined the pattern of the succession struggle already under way. Several stages could be discerned in this process.

The first stage began no later than three months after the selection of Andropov as general secretary. As soon as Andropov's health took a turn for the worse, covert preparations were undertaken in the Politburo for a transfer of power. It was in fact Andropov himself who encouraged this development by beginning to concern himself overtly with the nature of the regime and the leadership after his death. The very raising of the succession issue already imposed certain restrictions on his power. In the face of his imminent demise, Andropov began seeking ways of ensuring that his ideas, in particular his reform plans, would be carried on. For this he would need an alter ego capable of continuing the transformation he had begun. Because Gorbachev appeared a plausible candidate, Andropov began to promote him unofficially as second secretary of the Central Committee. During this period Chernenko's domain of authority was progressively restricted until Andropov, with Gorbachev's help, reduced it to practically nil. Chernenko was not seen on public occasions from January to mid-May; among his striking absences were those at the evening devoted to Lenin's memory and at the May Day Parade. In July Chernenko missed the commemorative assembly dedicated to the eightieth anniversary of the 2d Congress of the Bolshevik Party (at which the Russian Social Democratic Party had split into Bolsheviks and Mensheviks) and meetings with the general secretary of the Portuguese Communist Party, Alvaro Cunhal, and American labor union representatives.

The second stage of the struggle for succession began as soon as Andropov withdrew from political activity in September. Chernenko then immediately went on the offensive. He once again appeared in print. In October *Kommunist* carried an article of his on changing the style of Party work, and in November he published an article (in *Problemy mira i sotsializma*) on the development of a creative approach to the problems of Soviet society. Moreover, writings of his on foreign policy also appeared in print. His visibility in print coincided with his visibility at public events: in October he received an Algerian delegation; in November he conducted discussions with Lebanese Communists; and in the same month he stood in place of Andropov on Lenin's mausoleum to review the November 7 parade on the anniversary of the Revolution. Two days earlier, at a festival evening in the Kremlin, he occupied the central place among the Politburo members at the Presidium table.

Chernenko also sought popularity outside the Party apparatus. At a Politburo session at the beginning of January 1984 he proposed the abolition of boarding school fees for children of single mothers and low-income families. The public subsidy for this purpose was minuscule: 40 million rubles for 1 million student boarders. Insignificant as the measure actually was, it was useful in establishing the reputation of Chernenko as a public figure who cared about people.[34] During this period the Soviet newspapers published the draft of a school reform prepared under Chernenko's supervision. The transparent goal was again to win the support of ordinary citizens, who were promised a "radical improvement in the conditions of labor education" "to provide students with knowledge and skills in the use of contemporary technology," and "an improvement in the forms, methods and devices of instruction."[35]

The hectic pace of Chernenko's pursuits spurred Gorbachev to assume greater control over various levels of the Party hierarchy. He began with long-postponed matters, such as promoting two promising supporters to key posts in the Central Committee bureaucracy: Egor Ligachev became head of the Department of Organization of Party Work, and Nikolay Kruchina became head of the Administrative Division. In this way Gorbachev gained control over the appointment of high Party officials. He immediately made personnel changes in provincial and republic Party committees. In August–September two important changes on this level took place; in September–October, three; in November, four; and in December–January, sixteen.

Personnel changes carried out at the CC Plenum of December 26–27 were symptomatic of Gorbachev's increase in power. His friend and colleague E. G. Ligachev was named CC secretary for cadres in place of the veteran Ivan Kapitonov. Vorotnikov, earlier brought to prominence by Andropov, became a full Politburo member, and another of Andropov's protégés, Viktor Chebrikov, became a candidate member. Additionally, full Politburo membership was conferred on Mikhail Solomentsev. For a considerable time the latter's political identity remained unclear: in age and Party experience he belonged to Chernenko's generation, but the ascent in his Party career (which came late and would be rather brief) was engineered by Gorbachev. Hence both main rivals sought Solomentsev's favor.

December was the time when the rivalry between Chernenko and Gorbachev finally came to a head. Gorbachev again attempted, this time indirectly, to discredit his contender. On the basis of evidence presented by Ligachev, the Central Committee passed a sharp denunciation of the method and style of work of the Party organization of Moldavia. (It should be recalled that Moldavia was a republic with which Chernenko had been intimately connected for long years.)

The Moldavian affair signified a new political departure for Gorbachev. Instead of mobilizing the Party for the solution of social problems that (because of Andropov's illness) remained unattended to after many years of negligence, Gorbachev directed his wrath, which by even Soviet standards was merciless, at a minor republic. The formulation of the problem was quite unusual. The Central Committee resolution did not denounce any specific administrative subunits of the Party (e.g. city or provincial), as is the standard Soviet practice, but demanded the investigation of the Party organization of the entire republic!

The form of the CC resolution was also unusual. It deviated drastically from the accepted standard. Normally, such resolutions first note the successes and achievements of the Party organizations, then proceed to listing the difficulties under which they operate (e.g. in regard to growth, unsolved problems, and the like), and only then, in "constructive" terms, do they criticize specific failures. However, the performance of the Party leadership of Moldavia was depicted solely in dark hues without any extenuation. Failures in its performance were commented on in sharpest terms possible. "Energies of the Party activists were wasted on working out meaningless plans." Note was taken of the leadership's inability to take measures "for the adoption of a real Party-like, serious operating style." The resolution pointed out the "systematic failure to fulfill assignments related to the growth of work productivity." The structure of management and of decision making was said to "often lack the requisite sophistication, practicality and purposefulness in the resolution of critical economic and political problems."[36] The Central Committee called for a "decisive halt" to manifestations of superciliousness and nastiness, but paradoxically, the tone and style of its resolution expressed (and thereby implicitly encouraged) scornful, boorish, and nasty attitudes.[37]

The CC resolution also broke another taboo: the assumption that each Politburo member had his own geographical power base in the republic, province, or city from which he rose as a Party functionary and on which he relied for recruitment of loyal associates. Such preserves of personal authority had always been immune to criticism. Gorbachev departed from this tradition in order to undermine Chernenko. He believed that nothing short of putting Chernenko's professional competence and integrity in doubt would serve his purpose.

Gorbachev also attempted to strike at Chernenko's flank, by attacking his most important ally, Tikhonov. He did so at the Politburo session in December when the performance of the Council of Ministers was criticized and a number of ministries severely reprimanded.[38]

Yet, in the end Gorbachev defeated his own purpose. Instead of revealing his power, his attack on Chernenko revealed his limitations. Chernenko's position was then still strong enough to protect his dependents from being routed. The second stage of the Chernenko-Gorbachev struggle thus ended in a standoff. The third and final round was about to begin.

The influence of Chernenko remained strong enough to cast a long shadow over the head of the dying general secretary. During the first weeks of 1984 this influence increased even further. The anthology of

Chernenko's speeches was issued in a second edition and the press reviews (in *Pravda*) for the first time noted Chernenko's "outstanding contribution to the elaboration of Marxist theory." This contrasted with the more modest earlier praise, when Chernenko was merely credited with a "great contribution to the development of Party building."[39]

But most important, Chernenko at that time succeeded in advancing Tikhonov. Tikhonov was head of the government; in this capacity he now presided at Politburo sessions, headed the Soviet delegation to the Council of Mutual Economic Assistance (Comecon or CMEA) talks in Berlin, conducted bilateral negotiations with the leaders of East European countries, and hosted the prime minister of Finland. In short, he became virtual leader for a while. The possibility loomed large that Tikhonov, using his newly won authority and visibility as leverage, would bring Chernenko to general secretaryship.

While Andropov was still functioning, Chernenko was in the minority in the Politburo, with only three, then four, of his supporters to eight of his opponents'. But during Andropov's protracted absence the quality represented by Chernenko overshadowed the quantity of the rival faction.

Andropov attained power too late for himself and too early for his country. The program of extensive reforms he hoped to carry through remained unfulfilled. Feeling that the time allotted to him by history was running out, he attempted to squeeze in eight to nine months of intensive activity during his terminal illness. Andropov accelerated change on a scale and at a speed comparable to those of the first years after the Bolshevik Revolution. Within several months he traversed a distance equal to that which all his predecessors, including Stalin, took years to cover. He concentrated enormous power in his hands as general secretary, chairman of the Presidium of the Supreme Soviet, and chairman of the Defense Council. He even turned his illness to advantage. Under its impact the rivalries in the Politburo abated for some time because everyone wanted to forestall a rapid change in the leadership. His supporters, who brought both him and themselves to power, were not yet prepared, whereas his political rivals, all in their seventies, understood that under conditions of radical change their ages might well be their vulnerability. Around Andropov's sickbed, both his supporters and rivals gathered, providing him with the opportunity to co-opt new members to the Politburo to bring it up to complement. Were he healthy, this co-optation would have been blocked.

Andropov was then at the very pinnacle of power. All he needed was to rise from his bed and survive another year or two. A formidable economic experiment was being launched in the country. An educational reorganization was in the offing, intended to satisfy industry's demand for millions of production workers. A change in the Party program was being proposed exactly as Andropov had envisaged it. Andropov's prospects for becoming a single, unchallengeable ruler, perhaps even the undisputed *vozhd*, or leader, in the manner of Stalin, were most promising. Although Andropov was not well enough to attend the December CC Plenum in person, his spirit held the day, and his will prevailed. Because he did not wish to share his primacy with anyone, at the Plenum the speech of the absent general secretary was read aloud. The listeners were given to understand that Andropov was not Brezhnev, that even when handicapped by illness, he would not let power slip from his hands. But his illness was terminal. Andropov died on February 9.

Public notification of the leader's death was delayed for a day, longer than after the passing of Brezhnev. The purpose was to give the Politburo enough time to decide on the next ruler of Russia. For the Politburo this was not time enough. Only after many more hours was the announcement made that Chernenko had been named chairman of the committee to arrange the general secretary's funeral. Those familiar with Kremlinological logic correctly assumed that Chernenko would be named the new general secretary. This turned out to be indeed the case, but the decision to this effect was made no earlier than February 13, after a round-the-clock battle lasting three days.

As soon as Andropov was no more, the coalition of his supporters fell apart. Nothing, or rather no one, held it together. Each of its members sought the best tactic for advancing his own interests. In the Politburo there ensued a situation in which six supporters of Gorbachev were countered by five opponents: Shcherbitsky and Grishin could not overcome the psychological barrier that barred the way to power to the generation of young partocrats headed by Gorbachev, which could be expected to hold onto it for a long time to come. So, following their instinct for political self-preservation, they joined forces with Chernenko, Tikhonov, and Kunaev. Nevertheless, the outcome of the contest would have been a victory for Gorbachev except for the role of Romanov.

Romanov wanted neither Chernenko nor Gorbachev as general secretary, but considered Chernenko the lesser evil. The ascent of Gorbachev would have meant blocking his own ambitions for general secretaryship for many years. Thus, Romanov betrayed Gorbachev at the most critical moment: when the Politburo came to vote.

In November 1982 the Politburo had been able to recommend a specific candidacy to the Central Committee Plenum for approval. In February 1984 this was not possible because the Politburo vote was evenly split between Chernenko and Gorbachev. Now the CC Plenum would have to choose between the two. It turned out that all the Politburo needed to be completely paralyzed was to have one head fewer, especially if it was the head of the general secretary, to which all other heads in the Soviet Union are duty bound to bow.

In the Gorbachev camp only Gorbachev himself had deep and firm ties with the Party apparatus, and Ustinov had vast experience in government work to an extent unmatched by any other Politburo member. (Way back in Stalin's time when some of Ustinov's later Politburo colleagues were just taking the first steps in their careers and others were just beginning to learn the basics of Soviet political life, he was already an influential minister.) In his long life in public service Ustinov had been first deputy chairman of the Council of Ministers, chairman of the Higher Economic Council, and a secretary of the Central Committee. He had also been awarded the State Prize and the title of Hero no fewer than three times. Despite all this, in the Central Committee he remained an outsider. Gromyko, another influential supporter of Gorbachev, despite being minister of foreign affairs and first deputy chairman of the Council of Ministers, did not carry any weight in the Party apparat, where he had neither connections nor influence. He owed his career success to his capacity for work and to purges that invariably placed him in the posts of those who had been purged. Always prepared to carry out his assignments faithfully, well disciplined and intelligent, he pursued his career in the Ministry of Foreign Affairs, advancing to the post of ambassador and ultimately to minister. Because the usual Soviet career advancement is via the Party bureaucracy, Gromyko's was an atypical career for a major Soviet leader. This explains the reserved attitude of the professional partocrats toward him, reflecting the estrangement Gromyko was not able to overcome even after having gained Politburo membership. From the perspective of the Central Committee, Aliev appeared as a newcomer from a completely different, subordinate apparatus, that of the security organs. He also remained culturally alien to the Central Committee as a native of a Muslim region who quite unexpectedly—at the whim of the general secretary—was brought into the power center of Moscow. Solomentsev was considered a failure, who shortly before, after twelve years of being "frozen" as a candidate member of the Politburo, was suddenly "thawed out" and brought to the pinnacle of power by Andropov.

While Andropov was alive, Party functionaries curried favor with Aliev and Solomentsev and feared them, but neither respected nor trusted them. It should be kept in mind that the Party bureaucracy remained Brezhnev appointees. All Andropov managed to do was to replace its top echelon. This explains why the Central Committee members, hastily summoned to a Plenum meeting on February 11, were hardly willing to support Gorbachev. They were quite well aware that all reforms started with personnel replacements and that in one year of his rulership Andropov had replaced a good dozen top CC members and many dozens of first secretaries of provincial and city Party committees. They also knew that at the next Party Congress in several years' time or possibly even earlier, a radical personnel reshuffle could be expected to shake the entire Central Committee membership. This was dictated by the rules of the game that every general secretary played by. At this moment, however, the members of the Central Committee were given an unusual opportunity to reverse the game by stalling personnel changes that Andropov's supporters were anxious to pursue at their expense.

Meanwhile, Chernenko was not idle. During the last weeks before Andropov's death he carried on frantic discussions with *obkom* secretaries and with important members of the Central Committee to sound out the shape of alliances and splits to emerge in the event of Andropov's death. After Chernenko narrowly lost the contest for succession in the fateful days of November 1982, he had learned to be even more cautious than before. In February 1984 he suddenly found an "ally" in the already deceased Andropov or, rather, in his former supporters. Badly scared by the prospect of further personnel changes, Party functionaries turned to Chernenko for salvation. Their interests and his now coincided.

Gorbachev faced a hostile CC Plenum that only one year previously had supported Andropov but now refused to support his heir designate. This was the result of the first failure in Soviet history by an incumbent general secretary to carry out a wholesale purge of the Party machinery. Also for the first time in Soviet history the CC Plenum, independently of the Politburo, was determining the outcome of a succession crisis and thereby making its bid to be the sovereign authority in the country in place of the Politburo.

Thus, Chernenko became general secretary by the mandate of the Plenum. His dependence on the rank-and-file CC membership was bound to (and did) determine the nature of his rulership. In his speech at the Plenum Chernenko undertook to restore to the Party apparat the self-confidence that it had gained under Brezhnev but that later had been undermined by Andropov. He also undertook to restore tranquility and stability to its ranks.

By promising the CC members not to produce surprises either in domestic or foreign policy, Chernenko courted their support, which he received in abundance. This is why his speech at the Plenum was so different from the speech Andropov had made after Brezhnev's death. Andropov had delivered a speech appropriate to the occasion: brief, laconic, containing almost nothing apart from a eulogy of the deceased leader and an appeal to remain faithful to his legacy.[40] Chernenko's speech, however, departed considerably from the pattern of a funeral eulogy. Impassively, even somewhat coldly depicting the life and career of Andropov, Chernenko emphasized the issue of reform. In this way he made it abundantly clear how differently from his predecessor he understood the nature of reforms. Andropov had always stressed societal progress and its speed and effectiveness. Chernenko, in contrast, stressed the human aspect of progress, conceiving it in terms of its contribution to the improvement of the conditions of labor and standard of living. He expressed doubt as to whether it was possible to accelerate development via only such methods as better organization of labor and increased discipline. In his view, the crucial factors were material incentives and social justice. His view of the context of envisaged reforms was also different. As Chernenko presented it, their success depended on other factors, such as reform of administration, indoctrination in Communist values, and peaceful cooperation with the West.[41]

Of course, many of Chernenko's statements were largely propaganda intended to promote his popularity both abroad and among his own people. However, some of his ideas were a genuine reflection of his own worldview as previously reflected in his writings. The time was approaching when his worldview could be translated into action that he, as general secretary, would determine.

The Plenum was in no hurry to accept and support the new general secretary's ideas. Tikhonov echoed and supported Chernenko by assuring the partocrats that the new general secretary was the genuine guardian of not only Andropov's but also Brezhnev's legacy. Because under Andropov Brezhnev's name had practically been banned from the accepted political discourse, Tikhonov's speech was meant as a signal of a turning of the tide.

The rehabilitation of Brezhnev was an imperative for Chernenko. It served to reassure the Party bureaucrats that whatever direction the political changes might take, the changes would not be detrimental to their interests and privileges. On this condition they were willing to grant power to Chernenko, a political Janus who looked both toward the past and toward the future. Chernenko would try to combine two approaches that had been used in Soviet history: the traditionalist-conservative approach and the reformist one. The Moscow events of February 1984 did not yet provide a clue to the chances of his success in this attempt.

Notes

1. K. U. Chernenko, *Voprosy raboty partiynogo i gosudarstvennogo apparata* (Issues concerning the work of the Party and state apparats) (Moscow: Izd-vo politicheskoy literatury, 1980); K. U. Chernenko, ed., *V. I. Lenin, KPSS i*

rabota s kadrami (V. I. Lenin, the CPSU, and work with cadres) (Moscow: Izd-vo politicheskoy literatury, 1980); K. U. Chernenko, *KPSS i prava cheloveka* (The CPSU and human rights) (Moscow: Izd-vo *Novosti*, 1981).

2. "The Lenin Style in the Activity of the Party and Government Apparats," *Partiynaya zhizn'*, no. 20 (1980): 11–14.

3. Chernenko, *V. I. Lenin, KPSS i rabota s kadrami.*

4. "The Leninist Cadres Policy of the CPSU," *Mezhdunarodnaya zhizn'*, no. 5 (1980): 9–15.

5. Chernenko, *Voprosy raboty.*

6. Chernenko, *KPSS i prava cheloveka.*

7. Speech delivered at the commemorative session in Moscow devoted to the 111th anniversary of the birth of V. I. Lenin, April 22, 1981, in Chernenko, *Narod i partiya ediny. Izbrannye rechi i statyi* (The people and Party are one. Selected speeches and articles) (Moscow: Izd-vo politicheskoy literatury, 1984), p. 228.

8. Speech delivered at the commemorative session in Moscow devoted to the 112th anniversary of the birth of V. I. Lenin, April 22, 1982, in Yu. V. Andropov, *Izbrannye rechi i statyi* (Selected speeches and articles) (Moscow: Izd-vo politicheskoy literatury, 1983), p. 203.

9. *Pravda*, February 24, 25, 1981.

10. *Pravda*, October 15, 1976.

11. Ilya Zemtsov, *Policy Dilemmas and the Struggle for Power in the Kremlin, The Andropov Period* (Fairfax, Va.: Hero Books, 1985).

12. Ibid., pp. 33–56.

13. "Conference of Military Commanders in the Kremlin," *Pravda*, October 22, 1982.

14. "For the Good of the Soviet People," from the speech at the Plenum of the Krasnoyarsk *kraykom* of the CPSU on June 15, 1982, in Chernenko, *Izbrannye rechi i statyi*, p. 519.

15. Ibid., pp. 519–35.

16. "The Fruitfulness of Leninist Friendship of Peoples," from speech delivered on awarding to the city of Tbilisi the Order of Lenin on October 19, 1982, in Chernenko, *Izbrannye rechi i statyi*, p. 545.

17. Ibid., pp. 544, 546, 547.

18. Ibid., pp. 550–54.

19. Ibid., p. 555.

20. Speech at the Extraordinary Plenum of the Central Committee of the CPSU of November 12, 1982, in Chernenko, *Izbrannye rechi i statyi*, p. 555.

21. Ibid., p. 556.

22. Speech at the Plenum of the CC of the CPSU of November 22, 1982, in Andropov, *Izbrannye rechi i statyi*, pp. 209–18.

23. K. U. Chernenko, *Utverzhdat' leninskiy stil' v partiynoy rabote* (To reaffirm the Leninist style in Party work) (Moscow: Izd-vo politicheskoy literatury, 1983).

24. Ibid., pp. 118–26, 215–30.

25. "Current Issues of Ideological, [and] Mass-Political Work of the Party," report at the Plenum of the CC of the CPSU on June 14, 1983, in Chernenko, *Izbrannye rechi i statyi*, p. 576.

26. Speech at the Plenum of the CC of the CPSU of June 15, 1983, in Andropov, *Izbrannye rechi i statyi*, pp. 284–99.

27. "Current Issues," p. 577.
28. Ibid., pp. 590–92.
29. Ibid., pp. 591–600.
30. Ibid., p. 600.
31. Ibid., p. 593.
32. Speech at the 8th session of the 10th Supreme Soviet of the USSR, on June 16, 1983, in Chernenko, *Izbrannye rechi i statyi*, pp. 602–3.
33. "Speech of Comrade Yu. V. Andropov," *Partiynaya zhizn'*, no. 17 (1983): 5.
34. "In the Politburo of the CC of the CPSU," *Pravda*, January 7, 1984.
35. "In the Politburo of the CC CPSU," *Pravda*, January 4, 1984.
36. "In the Central Committee of the CPSU," *Pravda*, December 13, 1983.
37. Ibid.
38. "In the Politburo of the CC of the CPSU," *Partiynaya zhizn'*, no. 24 (1983): 6.
39. *Pravda*, February 8, 1984.
40. Andropov, *Izbrannye rechi i statyi*, pp. 204–6.
41. Speech at the Extraordinary Plenum of the CC of the CPSU of February 13, 1984, in Chernenko, *Narod i partiya ediny*, pp. 414–22.

6

Leader for the Meanwhile

Andropov died as he lived — wrapped in mystery. He died on February 9, 1984, but his death was not even mentioned in the next day's morning papers. *Pravda* published on its first page a detailed report on government activity concerning increased production of consumer goods, material on the preparations for elections, and foreign news, but nothing else. The Kremlin needed to give the impression that Andropov was still alive because the struggle for power in the Politburo had not been resolved. Without as yet a new general secretary, the Soviet leaders were trying to keep the shadow of the old one in operation. Andropov was assigned this posthumous task for almost twenty-four hours after his death.

One could have assumed that Andropov's protracted illness would have given the Politburo sufficient time for designating a successor. Nevertheless, even more time was needed to elect a new general secretary than had been the case after Brezhnev's demise. During the four days until the election of Chernenko, from Friday until Tuesday, the Old Square and the entire neighborhood of the Central Committee building teemed with military patrols, uniformed as well as in plain clothes. During the days when Andropov's body lay in state in the Hall of Columns, few people came to pay their respects. The public's mood was indifferent. When the Soviet leaders arrived for the first time in the Hall to pay their respects to the deceased, they were tired and irritated, as could be clearly seen on television.

The intensity of internal friction within the Politburo was expressed in the manner in which the funeral cortege moved. It was headed by Chernenko, who kept a distance from the others, walking a few steps ahead of Tikhonov, Ustinov, Gromyko, and Grishin. Behind them, Gorbachev and Romanov marched side by side, as if to deny the rumors of their enmity. Upon reaching the coffin, they all stood silently, apparently just as they congregated during the Politburo meetings — not according to their hierarchical order but according to their political views. In one group were Chernenko, Kunaev, Shcherbitsky, and Tikhonov; in the other, Gorbachev, Aliev, and Vorotnikov. Between them stood Ustinov, Grishin, and Gromyko,[1] as if to separate the adversaries.

Chernenko was at that time officially appointed head of the funeral commission. His appointment to this purely ceremonial function was in keeping with protocol because he was second secretary of the CC. It therefore did not have the same symbolic significance as the similar appointment of Andropov after Brezhnev's death. Yet, a new tradition was already in the making by which heads of funeral commissions of general secretaries were thereby slated to assume the vacant general secretaryship. Cases in point were Khrushchev after Stalin, and Andropov after Brezhnev. In the present case commission membership had an importance because, besides Chernenko, it included those other Politburo members who were potential candidates for the top position.

Having fixed the day of the funeral for Tuesday, the Politburo had set a limit to the opportunities for maneuvering prior to the election of the new general secretary. It thus became imperative to convoke a Plenum in order to proclaim the new leader. A longer delay would have been ill-advised, even dangerous, for in the USSR a change of guard at the top entails the danger of a government breakdown. It would have also held back another important state function, namely, the grand reception for the diplomatic corps and foreign guests arriving to express their condolences to the bereaved government. If such a reception were to take place in the Georgievsky Hall in the Kremlin without the new leader, the assembled foreigners, both allies and foes, would have cause to doubt the stability of the regime.

Chernenko appeared unruffled and had every reason to be optimistic. It was expected that no fewer than fifty top officials ousted by Andropov would attend the Plenum in accordance with Chernenko's wishes (and likely prearrangement). These were the surest ones to support him and to carry along others — those whom Andropov had not had enough time to oust but who feared that they were next in line for ouster — with them. All these had good reason to fear that the power might fall into the hands of Andropov's chosen successor.

It was Chernenko's aspirations, rather than their fears, that were realized. Chernenko became general secretary. The hierarchical order within the Politburo was now rearranged. In the Hall of Columns on Tuesday morning the members took their locations around the coffin strictly according to their new order. There was no improvisation. Chernenko stood at the center, with Gorbachev to his right, a confirmation of the latter's having become number two in the Party. At Chernenko's left was Tikhonov, by virtue of his being head of the government. Next to Gorbachev stood Romanov; because Chernenko had failed to make Romanov second secretary, the latter had to content himself with being number three in the Party hierarchy. Behind Chernenko stood Gromyko, who had lost nothing of his status, and behind him was Ustinov, his position indicating his continuing power and authority. Shcherbitsky had risen in status and was assigned a place next to Romanov and Grishin was standing behind Ustinov. Both Shcherbitsky and Grishin were men whom Chernenko trusted. The following Politburo members completed the row: Aliev on the left, a sign of his decline in status as compared to that he enjoyed under Andropov, and Solomentsev on the right, with his status unchanged.

The configuration reflected the hierarchic ranking order of Chernenko's Politburo.[2] Its power and personal allegiance were split half and half between Chernenko and Gorbachev. This imposed a limit to the support Chernenko could command.

Although he succeeded in gaining a majority in the CC Plenum, Chernenko lost out in the Politburo. There he could count on the support of only six members: himself, Tikhonov, Kunayev, Shcherbitsky, and Grishin absolutely; Romanov partly. The support was obviously insufficient to enable him to exercise power as he wished.

Gorbachev, on the other hand, lost in the Plenum, but won in the Politburo. Out of twelve Politburo members, he could rely on six: himself, Gromyko, Ustinov, Vorotnikov, Aliev, and Solomentsev. This was enough to block any decision of which he might have disapproved. Grand maneuvering by both sides began at the first meeting of the Politburo on Thursday February 16, shortly after Andropov's burial, but before that Chernenko did his best to make the burial ceremony solemn and impressive.

The lengthy ceremony that Chernenko presided over began in the Hall of Columns. Chernenko approached Andropov's wife (the West had not even known for certain whether Andropov had had a wife!) and kissed her. His gesture indicated to the world that the two general secretaries had been reconciled, albeit over the coffin of one of them. Then he delicately touched the shoulder of Andropov's son, Igor. The latter, overcome with emotion, covered his face with his hands, sobbing quietly.

The performance then shifted outdoors, to the streets filled with warmly dressed Muscovites where a gun carriage awaited Andropov's coffin. The carriage was draped in red and black. Chernenko and his Politburo colleagues wore identical gray overcoats and fur caps.

The cortege passed by the Gosplan (State Planning) building, continued past the Hotel Nasional and the Museum of History, and reached the Kremlin wall. The itinerary had become traditional since Brezhnev's death. There was a seemingly endless number of wreaths, perhaps a thousand, followed by some thirty officers carrying Andropov's orders and medals pinned on purple cushions. There were fewer decorations than in Brezhnev's case, yet their number was more than impressive for someone who had been in power for only a year. In ritual procession behind the coffin walked the deceased's family and after them at some distance the Politburo members, with Chernenko in the center. These were followed by a large crowd of carefully chosen workers, who later would scatter throughout Red Square, toward which the burial procession was moving slowly.

Chernenko marched all the way from the House of Unions to Red Square without any assistance and, for his age, at a fairly rapid pace. He breathed with difficulty. When the mausoleum was reached, he ascended the tribune by the elevator while the other Politburo members plodded up the stairs, all breathing heavily.

He then had to face the ordeal of making a speech outdoors, in a freezing temperature, before a huge crowd. He spoke or rather read his short speech hurriedly, and in a cracked voice. Only a year earlier, Andropov had carried himself in a more dignified manner. "Good bye, our dear friend and comrade, Yury Vladimirovich Andropov!" was Chernenko's concluding phrase.

He was nervous and dejected when standing by Andropov's grave; his hand saluting could be seen to tremble. Several times he let it drop. Those very moments marked the ultimate accomplishment of his lifelong ambitions. Could he or anyone else have imagined that a lad of common peasant stock from a remote Siberian village, who had dropped out of school in order to work for rich peasants and who had no formal education, would one day become the ruler of a superpower? Yet Chernenko did not appear to be enjoying these moments. Looking toward the grave into which Andropov's body was being lowered to the accompaniment of Chopin's music, he appeared terrified. What was he thinking about? Perhaps he realized that he had come to power too late, too old, too worn out, and sick; that the day was not far off when he himself would be like Andropov, the center of attention at his own burial with pomp and circumstance. Then the atmosphere of mourning changed as a rousing march was played and the gloom receded. On Red Square the Moscow garrison began to cheer the new ruler. The old general secretary was dead — long live the new one!

Chernenko was eager to take up Soviet political life with its theatricality, and even its masquerade character. As an actor, now the main one, he had to change his disguises constantly and with proper timing. The masquerade was to begin with his playing host at a grand reception for foreign guests that was to take place in the Georgievsky Hall in the Kremlin. The reception required considerable organization and was calculated to impress. Despite the nervous strain and exhaustion of the previous days when he hardly had had time to sleep, Chernenko was required to display poise and charm.

A customary concern of Soviet politics is "What will the West say?" It was imperative for Chernenko to make a good impression on the outside world and thereby indirectly also on the Soviet people. Doing so was particularly important for him because his personal reputation in the Free World had been poor. He may have known of United States Ambassador Malcolm Toon's description of him as an obtuse paper shuffler or of Henry Kissinger's disparaging reference to him as no more than an "obliging and crafty servant." In any case, he certainly knew of the expressions of disdain for him that abounded in the Western press. The dislike was mutual. Chernenko resented the West, fearing it and looking down at it at the same time. He never really knew much about it. Even when he had traveled abroad on assignment (to the United States, Greece, Denmark, Finland, France, and Austria), he had had little opportunity to learn anything about the social or cultural lives of these countries.

During his travels he usually saw cities through the windows of his armored limousines. The superficial impressions he gained at conventions of "fraternal" Communist parties fitted his ingrained ideological preconceptions. He knew that a fierce class struggle was going on in the capitalist world, where inequality and exploitation were rampant. Any information that did not accord with his preconceptions he would dismiss as propaganda intended to fool the credulous, with the effect of reinforcing his conviction that the cause he was serving was just. He never attempted to learn more about the West, which to him always remained alien and inimical. Still, like so many other Russians, he had a grudging admiration for the United States, with its power and glamor.

When on a private visit to the United States as the personal guest of the Soviet ambassador to the UN he took great interest in the stenographic techniques used at the UN and in the State Department's computerized files. He fully acknowledged the technological superiority of the United States, but when he was in Europe he had neither time nor curiosity for anything apart from performance of his duties. Foreign statesmen and politicians, who saw him as a permanent fixture at Brezhnev's side, believed that he had scant understanding of international politics and that he kept a low profile because he had nothing interesting to say. That was how he was assessed by former U.S. Secretary of State Cyrus Vance after the two met in Helsinki. Zbigniew Brzezinski, who was national security adviser to President Carter, also considered Chernenko as a man of limited understanding, albeit crafty and devious.

It would be wrong to assume that Chernenko did not care about how others saw him. He tried to improve his reputation, but rarely with any success. He did, however, succeed with Vance, who ultimately admitted that Chernenko was a strong character, a man who bravely spoke his mind and did not hesitate.[3] But this was an exception: negative opinions about Chernenko continued to predominate.

Right after Andropov's funeral Chernenko presided over the reception in the Kremlin. He appeared imperturbable, playing the host with dignity and assurance against the background of the tsarist splendor of the Georgievsky Hall with its glittering crystal chandeliers, brilliant silver candelabra, and precious carpets. As Andropov had done before, Chernenko welcomed the guests representing over a hundred governments and various political orientations who arrived in Moscow. He stood with Tikhonov, Gromyko, and Kuznetsov behind him. Gorbachev was not there; his absence was noticed and much conjectured about. Unlike Andropov, Chernenko did not try to charm. There was no smile fixed on his face. He greeted everyone in the same manner: a short handshake and an exchange of greetings, with the postponement of serious talks for later.

The difference between Chernenko's and Andropov's behavior at these receptions was striking. Andropov had assumed an individualized approach, varying his response depending on the identity of the delegation he was receiving; he displayed his own brand of diplomacy, making remarks as appropriate and cracking an occasional joke; he took the time to speak for several minutes with China's minister of foreign affairs, and surprised the president of Pakistan by inviting him for a conversation.[4] Chernenko behaved with greater restraint. Each guest was allotted less than a minute. The guest from China, who, unlike the Chinese guest at Andropov's reception, was a full member of the Politburo, was referred to Geidar Aliev. The president of Pakistan was not honored the way he had been by Andropov.

Yet, like Andropov, Chernenko made exceptions for the vice president of the United States; the prime ministers of France, Great Britain, and Canada; the president of Italy; and the West German chancellor. With all of these he chatted. Unlike Andropov, however, he refrained from saying anything controversial and thereby conveyed the impression of his flexibility in contrast to the uncompromising stance of his predecessor. He thus proved that he understood the Western leaders' mentality. They were all impressed to see in Chernenko a statesman to be reckoned with, and anticipated that it would be possible, even pleasurable to deal with him.[5]

Vice President Bush said that Chernenko was a potentially strong leader, had a sense of humor, and gave a clear and succinct account of Soviet views. Italy's President Alessandro Pertini declared that he considered Chernenko a rational statesman, capable of objective decisions. The German chancellor, Helmut Kohl, described him as open and sincere, and as someone who could express himself without double-talk. The United Kingdom's prime minister, Margaret Thatcher, was no less positive in her evaluation. Without revealing the contents of her conversation with Chernenko, she expressed her certainty that Chernenko bore no animosity toward the West. The French premier went even further, expressing confidence that "the Russians would soon join the nuclear disarmament talks." His optimism was shared by the Canadian premier, Pierre Trudeau, who said, "Once again there is Brezhnev's detente in the air," and that Chernenko was laying the foundation for mutual understanding.[6]

Having overestimated Andropov, Western politicians were this time wary of underestimating Chernenko. Under the impression of the latter's restraint and forbearance, they failed to discern his dogmatism. This characteristic, however, soon showed when he categorically told the representatives of Bonn that in the future as in the past, the Soviet government intended to focus on East rather than West Germany. Nor did they appreciate his conservatism, in particular his fear of taking political risks and therefore his initial preference to rely on Gromyko's experience and Ustinov's competence. They further did not realize that Chernenko was a beginner in the world of foreign policy and diplomacy. He lacked assurance, could not improvise when dealing with Western leaders, relied on prepared notes, frequently repeated himself, faltered, and often was at pains to find the right words. Whenever the talk turned from generalities to concrete offers or suggestions, he endeavored to refer matters to his aides.

It did not take long for the West to realize that the personality of the new Soviet leader was no less inscrutable and mysterious than the Soviet system. It is true that Chernenko had once surprised the world, so now the world was waiting for another surprise. But this did not occur. The unlikelihood of further surprises became obvious as soon as the paraphernalia of mourning disappeared from the streets of Moscow.

Most Soviet leaders do not last long in people's memory. They tend to disappear from history soon after their death. The illusions built up around the person of Chernenko disappeared while he was still alive. His rule was symbolized by the catchword "continuity," which reflected the Soviet leader's basic notion of what it takes to maintain power. By this he meant to "hurry slowly." To be sure, such an approach could not but immediately generate strains and contradictions.

As an enterprising and resolute individual, Chernenko endeavored to rule energetically and efficiently. His experience and his career indicated an orientation for change. Although he wanted to be remembered by posterity, the main thing for him was the opportunity finally to realize his own theories and views, many of which he had been unable to put into practice during the terms of office of Brezhnev and Andropov. His interest in change might have led to his receiving support from the Politburo's younger generation, but the support was not forthcoming because Gorbachev was not interested in having reforms carried out by Chernenko. He was just waiting for him to die. Chernenko tried the proven Soviet way of bribing Gorbachev's supporters. As general secretary he had the requisite influence and good chances of success. Yet, he had to treat his own supporters with care so as not to antagonize them by hasty or ill-conceived innovations. Chernenko was caught in a dilemma, his predicament being that he had to propitiate his own supporters on the one hand and share his power with his opponents on the other. This was the situation of "collective leadership" writ large: a phenomenon recurrent in Soviet history at times of change of leadership.

Chernenko admitted openly to the leader of the West German socialists, Hans Vogel, that he represented nothing more than a "collectively agreed on political line of the Politburo."[7] He reiterated the same idea in his campaign speech before the elections to the Supreme Soviet,[8] and again at a meeting of the CC apparatus members.[9]

Chernenko's predecessors from Khrushchev to Andropov had also been forced to profess that they had been acting in the name of the collective. Yet, they never stated it so openly, frequently, and emphatically as did Chernenko. This was a manifest indication that the general secretary's position was insecure. Although clear signs of conflict within the Soviet leadership were still lacking, the weakness of its top leader was patent, as revealed during the visits of other Soviet leaders abroad when they read out greetings in the name of Chernenko, Tikhonov, and Gromyko.[10] This kind of formula was not in line with the accepted custom because previously the general secretary was always supposed to be solely in charge of Soviet foreign policy.[11]

Power sharing within the leadership for a time after the arrival of a new ruler is customary, but there was no precedent in Soviet history for the sharpness of the conflict between the old guard supporting Chernenko and the young leadership standing behind Gorbachev. The former were openly enthusiastic about Chernenko's election; the latter, hardly so. The speeches made by the senior Soviet leaders at the meetings preceding the

Supreme Soviet election clearly reflected one or the other attitude. An additional indication was that the flatterers of Chernenko were noticeably cool, even disapproving whenever they referred to Andropov. They stressed Chernenko's "outstanding contribution to the solution of practical and theoretical problems," "highly acknowledged authority," and "international recognition." The deceased Andropov, by contrast, was merely mentioned as someone who had "devoted his entire life to the service of his people" but who had "died too early." Grishin presented Chernenko as the "head of the Party," i.e. in a way Soviet leaders were rarely described. Tikhonov even attempted to compare Chernenko with Lenin, speaking of him as "a leader of Leninist stamp."

Chernenko's supporters exceeded the norms when they praised his "brilliant abilities and talents." Such adulation is normally expressed only after the general secretary has already won undisputed power. However, referring to Chernenko as an "outstanding statesman and leader of the Soviet Union" remained within the bounds of Soviet tradition. Every general secretary is customarily referred to as "outstanding leader," and leaders of lesser rank are merely touted as "exceptional organizers" or "talented propagandists." The reluctance of such Gorbachev followers as Gromyko, Ustinov, and Vorotnikov to call Chernenko an "outstanding leader" is to be understood against this background. It reflected their disappointment with Chernenko's appointment as general secretary. It also revealed Chernenko's lack of authority.

There was one exception: Aliev. He was the only Politburo member affiliated with Gorbachev's faction who spoke highly of Chernenko, to the extent of praising him with oriental gusto and servility.[12] Aliev's behavior served as a useful reminder that within the Politburo allegiance need not be permanent.

Chebrikov and Shevardnadze divided their support between both factions: the former, carefully and circumspectly; the latter, openly. Chebrikov, a former head of the state security services, remembered the appreciation the general secretary had shown for the KGB, and the CC secretary from Tbilisi was mindful of Chernenko's earlier ties with Georgia.[13] The wavering sympathies of the two prefigured the possibility of a scramble for power in the current Politburo. This prospect remained for the future, possibly to materialize only if Chernenko emerged from the transition period strengthened.

In the meantime Chernenko's real power was not commensurate with his formal position. He tried but did not succeed in minimizing Gorbachev's significance at the CC Plenum. The press originally reported Chernenko's and Tikhonov's speeches without mentioning Gorbachev's at all.[14] Yet, only several days later, when the booklet containing the minutes of the Plenum in full was published, it turned out that it was Gorbachev, not Chernenko, who closed the meeting and that he made his speech without uttering a single word of commendation for the general secretary.

Gorbachev's dry, businesslike speech revealed that the top leadership in the Soviet Union was still in dispute.[15] It also implied that in the event of Chernenko's death, succession would be assumed not by members of the generation of functionaries born in the 1920s whose time for power bidding had passed but by a new generation of leaders exemplified by Gorbachev. This explains why Chernenko found it so difficult to consolidate his power and to function as a decisive leader. He also discovered that the upper crust of his administration comprised appointees of his two predecessors, i.e. people with different beliefs, habits, and principles. They tended to act independently, and he found himself unable to control their various and often mutually conflicting interests. Contrary to what is often assumed, Chernenko had no desire, at least initially, to return to a Brezhnev-style rule with its slow-motion bureaucratic atmosphere, self-contentment, and predilection for window dressing.

As general secretary, Chernenko did his best to put up with the exhausting schedule of official meetings and events. On the surface, there was no seeming difference between Chernenko's and Andropov's conduct. Both had to cope with the same problems, and both found little room left for economic maneuvering and social experiments. The same problems dictated the same solutions. An important difference, however, lay in their respective power bases: Andropov's mainstay was the KGB; Chernenko was seeking support from the Party apparatus, strictly speaking from its ranking secretarial corps.

Chernenko's program, problems, and ideas (enunciated soon after he became general secretary at a meeting with the members of the CC apparatus) were calculated to appeal to the ranking secretarial corps. His address created the impression that he would not allow a return to old times with their stagnation and inactivity. It looked as if he intended to impose his own political line; to improve the style and methods of government, raise productivity, and develop the economy. As he himself put it: "Nowadays it is important to work so as not just to fulfill quotas — but to overfulfill those established for 1984."[16]

Being seventy-two, Chernenko realized that he did not have much time left for consolidating his power; hence he tended to work on the problems of his country collectively, usually in consultation with, and with the help of, the entire government. The cooperation often freed him from tiresome and exhausting intrigues. He stressed that the announced policies were not his own initiative but "decisions arrived at collectively."[17]

It turned out that Chernenko had very little to offer to society. In-depth criticism would merely mean the continuation of an Andropov-initiated practice without the chance to display his own originality. The absence of tangible change would confirm the general opinion that he lacked independence and originality, and was drifting back to Brezhnevism. Chernenko chose a third way, which turned out to be the worst. He strove for a happy medium between Brezhnev's orientation toward continuity and Andropov's orientation toward change.

In justice to him, it should be noted that Chernenko's choice was not really free. It was a compromise dictated by Brezhnev holdovers and Andropov supporters in the Politburo. Once Chernenko accepted their joint demands, he began gradually to lose his initiative and independence and content himself with speechmaking and verbal declarations, many of which merely reiterated points made previously in his books. He invariably called for "tightened organization and discipline" and for "wider application of the rapidly developing technical-scientific progress," as well as for "setting in motion a more extensive program of fully exploiting productive resources" and of saving raw materials.[18] The ideas, conceived of by Chernenko in the midst of stagnation of the Brezhnev era, had once been remarkably daring, but a reiteration of the same old slogans without following them up with a well-defined and effective policy had the effect of making them banal clichés. Between his intention and reality there was a gap.

Incantations could not suffice to set straight the unwieldy mechanism of Soviet bureaucracy, let alone make it work. For that, acts were needed. Andropov understood this and made the nation feel it by a swift succession of campaigns, decrees, decisions, and remedial measures. Chernenko, too, dreamed of action that would at least be daring and impressive, if not efficacious. What he might have done was dismiss a few senior officials and replace them by others sufficiently competent to manage industry and industrial production, and arouse the interest of the masses by the prospect of controlled democratization and an openness to critical discussion. That would have amounted to implementing some of his own ideas. Chernenko might thus have succeeded in changing his image — from a conservative to a reformer.

But Chernenko did not take the necessary risk. Perhaps he was incapable of translating his ideas into practice or perhaps he was defeated by the setting he operated in, by people who did not want change and did their best to frustrate his projects. His obstructors had various motives. Gorbachev wanted to discredit Chernenko as a do-nothing. Romanov feared that Chernenko's projects would be realized by the Party apparatus controlled by his rival Gorbachev; he wanted to nip all such projects in the bud in order to prevent Gorbachev from gaining in reputation and power. Under such circumstances, Chernenko's good intentions remained no more than that, and were met with the Soviet society's usual apathy. The society had long ago ceased reacting to words and responded only to actions. Yet, all the Soviet people could see were palliatives: calls for realizing decisions already taken, stress on detailed planning before implementation, and looking ahead to longitudinal plans for the twenty-first century. All they could hear were the old refrains: "raising the standard of Party activity" and "strict adherence to Leninist principles." And to complete the list, Chernenko offered elaborate respect paid to the Party apparatus, whose support he badly needed. The Central Committee, which was used to demands rather than appeals and to punishment rather than persuasion, refused to give its support to a general secretary who was too obliging. It declined to cooperate with a leader lacking in assurance, who failed to be a master. Without CC support, Chernenko did not dare to introduce radical reforms. The CC knew this, and this is precisely why it refused to support him.

Chernenko's inertia, which ultimately satisfied many top officials, not only stemmed from the choice of a wrong policy but also reflected the political balance in the Politburo, with the number of his supporters being equaled by the number of his opponents. Thus, Chernenko found himself dependent on both sides to the same degree. Chernenko's age was also a factor. Not expecting to live much longer, he could not embark on radical personnel reshuffles. Therefore, his failure to play by the harsh rules of the Party game had the consequence of rendering him ineffectual. He remained ineffectual until his death.

Here we come to an astonishing paradox that regularly recurs in Soviet history. The weakness of a general secretary correlates with the stability and strength of the regime. Chernenko's general secretaryship contributed to the stabilization of "partocracy" rule with its collective power. The Soviet system did not need a powerful autocratic ruler. It was quite content with a figurehead leader who did not challenge the rights and privileges of Party elite. The system was stagnant, resistant to constructive change. To direct the system, it was not necessary to believe in its ideology but merely to pay lip service to it. The appearance of an independent and enterprising leader had always threatened the Soviet state with crisis likely to destabilize its conceptual foundations. Chernenko fit the exigencies of the partocratic system on the wane better than any other Soviet leader. This can be clearly demonstrated by comparing him with his predecessors.

Lenin shaped the realities of Communism by trial and error. Hence, the inconsistency of his rule and the instability of his regime, which experienced uprisings, mutinies, riots, and revolts. Stalin had no regard whatsoever for the Communist system. He either undermined it or molded it as his lust for power dictated. Khrushchev was reckless to the point of placing himself above and beyond the system, and therefore lost all power. Brezhnev, on the other hand, was hopelessly behind it, and Andropov had no time to adjust himself to it. Only Chernenko became fully integrated into the system as it looked in the early 1980s, with its inertia and incapacity to change. He came to power too late for his age and health and for the already waning regime, well past its former glories. The regime at that time was at a crossroads. Its archaic institutions and outmoded doctrines needed a radical overhaul. Yet, neither Chernenko nor the regime was ready for that overhaul—hence both Chernenko's weakness and his strength.

Chernenko's weakness was due to the fact that the task he envisaged for himself, to bring the Communist system to the twenty-first century by means of old or at least insufficiently up-to-date methods of governing, was a mission impossible. His strength consisted in having been elected general secretary, and in the skillful use of a powerful and ramified ruling apparatus for his purposes. He was by no means an honorific titleholder.

At the first meeting of the Politburo under his command, on February 23, 1984, Chernenko defined the most important directions of his policy: development of the economy, strengthening of Soviet defense capability, and improvement of the country's planning. He also stressed the "growth of technical progress" and "improvement of order and discipline." Because all of these had been Andropov's slogans, their reiteration detracted from Chernenko's originality. Like every new general secretary, Chernenko reacted to his elevation by first seeking the support of, and popularity among, the masses. He declared that "permanent concern for the welfare of the masses" must decisively guide the Party's activities. It is a foregone conclusion that it was his goal as well. He proclaimed his desire to "raise the workers' standard of living," "strengthen ties with the masses," and "improve educational work," as well as the country's economic performance. His mention of educational work echoed his previous preoccupation with the field of ideology.[19]

Even during the first days of his general secretaryship, Chernenko's health was noticeably poor. There were visible indications of enlarged lungs. He walked uneasily, moved slowly, and dragged his feet. He could not stand for long and needed help when walking upstairs. His breath was short, and even reading short sentences from a prepared draft was obviously a strain for him. His voice was heavy and often faltering. He coughed much.

The mad whirl of receptions at which he had to appear was far too strenuous for him. In March he had a number of long talks: with the defense minister of East Germany, G. Hoffmann; with the president of the socialist caucus of the West German Bundestag, H. Vogel; and with the Ethiopian ruler, Mengistu Mariam.[20] Many more meetings were scheduled for the forthcoming months: with the king of Spain, Juan Carlos; with General Wojciech Jaruzelski; with the North Korean leader, Kim Il-Sung; and with West Germany's minister of foreign affairs, Hans Dietrich Genscher.

In February Chernenko appeared almost daily on television, and the newspapers published his addresses and replies to various foreign statesmen. His mail brought a flood of letters and congratulations from heads of state, statesmen, and other notables, and from simple "Soviet working people."[21]

Chernenko's burst of activity and the publicity around it were needed as compensation for the long periods of enforced inactivity on the part of his ill predecessor. Moreover, the publicity surrounding Chernenko was needed to offset his low esteem among the masses. The Soviet people are wont to joke about their leaders but rarely dare refer to them disrespectfully in public, not only out of fear but also out of some residual respect. The rulers of Russia/the Soviet Union had for centuries inspired fear. This was no longer so under Chernenko, due both to his personality and to the manner in which he had become ruler of the USSR. The Soviet public could not respect a ruler who gained power via servility and readiness to kowtow to others.

Moreover, the prestige and authority of the Soviet ruler had already been undermined by his predecessors. Khrushchev had been rough and uncouth, and evoked little sympathy when he was ousted as brutally and inconsiderately as he had ousted others. The aura of awesome leadership was further undermined by Brezhnev with his boundless thirst for flattery and his ridiculous vanity. The long months of Andropov's illness encouraged the public to feel sympathy for him as a person but detracted from the authority of leadership. Chernenko merely finished the job, finally stripping the general secretaryship of its last remnants of charisma. He was quite an ordinary sort of person, as became readily apparent.

As the flaws of Chernenko's character became obvious to all, he began to be perceived as being much like the fellow next door; this hardly was conducive to respect from the Soviet public. It was thus no wonder that people nicknamed him "Kucher," which means "coachman" (although it also stemmed from his initials K.U.Ch.), evoking the familiar Russian image of a tired, elderly man sitting precariously on his seat, reining his horses in with great effort. No such condescension toward a leader had ever been known before in Soviet popular lore; nor had Soviet apparatchiki ever permitted themselves to refer to their leader in such disrespectful terms. Suddenly there appeared a reference to Chernenko as a "muzhik" (peasant), after which followed the quite astounding suggestion of *Pravda* editor Afanasyev that Chernenko was an embarrassment as a leader.

Why was this general secretary criticized for his inability to make a speech or for his behavior? Neither Khrushchev nor Brezhnev was known for his particularly refined behavior and obviously neither excelled in oratory. Chernenko alone was disparaged because he had lost control over certain groupings of the Politburo that were plainly interested in discrediting him. To counteract them, the supporters of the general secretary went out of their way to lend some luster to his lusterless image. They knew that as soon as the last of Chernenko's authority and credibility were gone, their own power and privileges would also be gone. Furthermore, they knew that the very ability of the Party, in whose name they were acting, to stay in power would be seriously endangered.

However, attempts to improve Chernenko's image were often futile and sometimes counterproductive. He invariably appeared in public together with a large retinue of supporters, making speeches devoid of all originality. All that changed was the identity of his visitors: the Italian minister of foreign affairs; the president of Finland; the head of the Greek Communist Party. But the manner of publicizing these encounters was highly routinized: in photographs Chernenko always appeared serious and attentive in conversing with his visitors.[22]

Whatever appears new in the Soviet Union is usually something old that has already been forgotten. This applies to Chernenko's public behavior as well. He just kept repeating the familiar words and outworn phrases and gestures of Brezhnev. He was shown receiving cosmonauts, who stood expressionless in a row, or sitting at a table presiding over a meeting of the Supreme Soviet Presidium with a stony face and with crossed arms.[23]

All newspaper pictures of Chernenko look so much alike that one gets the impression that they were all developed from old negatives, perhaps even of his predecessor, with Chernenko's figure replacing that of Brezhnev in various poses. His words to others were just as banal and colorless as those spoken to him. All conformed to the same pattern. Chernenko "acknowledged the achievements" of someone or other, whereupon those thus honored expressed their "heartfelt gratitude for the high appreciation of their activity."[24]

The Soviet public was long since familiar with that kind of cant. Having gotten used to it during the tedious rule of Brezhnev, the people learned to disregard it. By diligently copying his master, Brezhnev's pupil likewise raised no enthusiasm. CC propagandists had little success in making credible Chernenko's concern about the people's welfare. In reality he was as remote from such concerns as his predecessors. All were confined within the tight, largely restricted circle of Party business and power games, and to their world of villas, expensive cars, brilliant receptions, and attendance at opera and theater premieres. Of real life in the USSR they knew no more than they read in the press. Consequently, instead of ordinary Soviet reality with its contradictions and problems, they saw little more than a world of luxury and privilege. No wonder that when Chernenko visited a metallurgical plant he could find no common language with the workers. Instead of asking about their daily life, productivity, earnings, and the like, he confined his interest to fictions that he mistook for reality. He inquired about the organization of socialist activities, Party organization achievements among workers, and so on. Then he proceeded to instruct the workers in socialist ideology and the significance of the East-West conflict.

The workers of that particular plant, as well as the rest of Soviet society, remained indifferent to such encounters, which had already developed into a familiar routine. Chernenko walked the trail blazed by Andropov. In the latter's time a face-to-face encounter with the national leader was a novelty; in Chernenko's time it was already routine.

Another reason for Chernenko's being received with indifference was that his inability to find the right approach to the workers added to his unpopularity with them. He relied on clichés dry enough to kill all intended meaning if there was any. His physical handicaps further added to his pitiful performance. He had difficulty in standing and, even while sitting down, he breathed heavily and stopped frequently while speaking. He usually read his speeches from a text. Nevertheless, they were not totally devoid of meaning. He had one interesting idea: developing the country's economy intensively. "We do possess considerable resources but, as is known, they are not being renewed by nature." He advocated teamwork organization of labor: "This system of work stimulation has already proven itself." He suggested a progressive system of payment for workers, and called upon his audience not to wait for the end results of those experiments to be announced by the State's Work Committee. The workers themselves should carry out the experiments "wherever conditions permit."

Trying to win the goodwill of the workers in the plants he visited, he would thank them for their good performance: "In the name of the Politburo, the Central Committee and the Government I wish to thank you all briefly but sincerely: Thank you, comrades. Thanks are due to your collective and to the entire working people." Then he would proceed to mention the snags in production, just the way Andropov had done. He spoke of the problems that had arisen in the Soviet economy in the years 1970–80 and waxed indignant at the slackness and unconcern of leaders. Yet his criticism of leaders' attitudes sounded different from that of Andropov because it was largely abstract, devoid of specifics. Nor did he mention the need for reform. The word *reform* nevertheless reappeared in a different and somewhat surprising context, that of educational organization. Chernenko spoke of "new frontiers," but he envisaged reaching them by old and ineffectual means: by appeals for higher productivity and greater civic involvement in the country's economy. Most unexpectedly, Chernenko also mooted the idea of "justice" in the setting of wage scales; for all its merits, this suggestion remained unelaborated, drowned in the usual propaganda sloganeering.

There was no spontaneity in his speech. Every idea was carefully phrased in terms of ideological rectitude. There was no humor; everything was respectable and pompous. At the end his audiences would predictably rise to give what was—ostensibly—an "enthusiastic and prolonged ovation." This was followed by the stereotyped obligatory commendations of the general secretary delivered by the plants' directors, the secretaries of the Party committees, and several carefully chosen workers. All these praised the "outstanding political talents," the "great experience" of the general secretary, and so on. (This was not the kind of flattery showered on Brezhnev, whose credentials had been much more impressive.) But Chernenko was also praised for his humanity and concern for the working people. He was thanked as well for his role in spreading peace in the world (literally "for spreading a peaceful sky above us").[25]

One wonders whether Chernenko experienced any satisfaction when listening to this flattery lavished on him by apathetic speakers in the presence of no less apathetic listeners. He was sufficiently experienced to realize that all the ritual was prepared and rehearsed in advance. Yet, to doubt that he indeed did experience satisfaction would be to fail completely to understand the essence and character of the Soviet way of life, wherein flattery and hypocrisy play such an important role.

Chernenko's followers were not fully satisfied with the actual performance at the plants. They wanted something more grandiose that would allow Chernenko to bask in the glory of past general secretaries as heir and equal.

For this new performance the main role, according to Moscow's rules of the political game, was reserved for Gorbachev, who, as a result of his failure to defeat Chernenko, was chosen to announce his rival's election as the new chairman of the Supreme Soviet. He did this on April 11, 1984, at the joint meeting of both chambers of the Supreme Soviet of the USSR. He announced the appointment in his smooth baritone, with apparent enthusiasm. He extolled Chernenko as a "faithful and persistent fighter for Communism" and referred to him—for the first time—as an "outstanding leader."[26]

The members of the Supreme Soviet hardly needed Gorbachev's commendation of their new leader, but reiteration of the general secretary's virtues was required to educate the masses. Gorbachev had barely finished his speech when thousands of hands were raised in unanimous approval of Chernenko's appointment; whereupon the Politburo members rose and applauded "loudly and enthusiastically" the arrival of their new chief. This was the moment of Chernenko's greatest triumph. Brezhnev had waited thirteen years to become head of the Supreme Soviet; Andropov, who had succeeded in compressing to the utmost the time needed for his power accumulation still needed seven months after becoming general secretary. Chernenko made it in two months. He made the most of that moment, savoring it to the full, raising his locked hands like the winner of a boxing match. He was oblivious to the fact that this success was not due to his individual merits and achievements but to the machinery of power operating still as programmed by the Communist system almost seventy years previously and engineered to enhance the ruler's personality cult. This was implied by Gorbachev in terms that were almost the same as those used by Chernenko when he was recommending Andropov for that position. Gorbachev said: "The assumption by the general secretary of the function of head of the Supreme Soviet's Presidium derives from the spirit of the Soviet Constitution, which proclaimed the Party the main moving spirit and determining factor of Soviet society and is dictated by the highest of state interests."[27]

Chernenko, appreciating the importance of this moment of triumph, took his place at center stage. On both sides he was flanked by members of the Kremlin's old guard, who were over seventy, and some nearly eighty: Ustinov, Gromyko, Tikhonov, Grishin, Shcherbitsky, Solomentsev, Kunaev. Both friends and foes, these masters of intrigue who managed to reach the Party Olympus were now bowing before him. Only one detail spoiled the joy for these veterans who had fought many political battles to become the top power elite in the country: the presence next to Chernenko of the young and conspicuously healthy Gorbachev, who hardly fit in with the general geriatric environment. Yet, it was he who was given the honor of announcing the general secretary's new responsibility. His prominence indicated the existence of a new tendency (as yet largely latent) within the Politburo, the tendency to favor the younger generation.

Nevertheless, Gorbachev's time had not yet come. He had to be cautious and conduct himself properly so as not to provide Chernenko with cause to oust him from the CC. Wearing a dark-gray well-tailored suit and glasses in elegant golden frames, Gorbachev nervously turned the pages of a red, bound file containing his already delivered speech. Two hours earlier the neoclassical hall had been mostly empty after a long and boring morning session. When there were only a few delegates left, Gorbachev was nominated as chairman of the Supreme Soviet Commission for Foreign Affairs. The appointment was significant: the post had usually been reserved for the second Central Committee secretary, to provide him with an opportunity to acquire some experience in international affairs, which he usually lacked. But important as it was, the honor disappointed Gorbachev, who had previously been groomed by Andropov for the first rather than the second secretaryship. But Andropov was now gone, and Chernenko was in his place.

To present a more impressive image of the new general secretary, the Soviet press — first *Krasnaya zvezda* (Red star, the newspaper of the Defense Ministry) and next *Ogonyok* magazine — published articles intended to "fill in" retroactively the holes in the military career of the new general secretary of the Party and president of the state. The description of his fight against bandits in the steppes of Kazakhstan at the beginning of the 1930s was both picturesque and poignant. The article featured a photograph of a group of border guards, which included the young Chernenko standing inconspicuously in the last row of the group. The article also reported that the future ruler of the Kremlin was an excellent rider and a good shot.[28]

To enhance the general secretary's authority and to emphasize his "humanity and modesty," TASS distributed a picture of the "informal Chernenko," showing him with his wife, daughter, and grandson. Unlike Andropov, who never permitted the press to touch upon his family life (as noted above, his wife was seen in public for the first time at his funeral), Chernenko liked to appear as a good paterfamilias. It is known that Chernenko's first marriage was not a success and was dissolved, and that his son Vladimir, like his father, opted for a Party career but, unlike his father, remained a modest official, a propaganda chief in the city of Tomsk (in Siberia). Chernenko's second marriage, however, was lasting. His second wife had a strong influence on her husband. Neither beautiful nor possessing particular social graces, she provided him with care and affection. Still, their home and their entire style of life did not reflect her personal taste but rather that of the standard typical of Party functionaries living in the prestigious areas of luxury villas and furnished accordingly, in imitation of the style set by Brezhnev. Chernenko did not feel at home on the noisy Kutuzov Avenue, in the building of steel and glass. He often took refuge in his *dacha* in a Moscow suburb, where the conifer forests and lawns reminded him of his native Siberia. Whenever possible, he liked to invite friends to old-fashioned Russian dinners, with many traditional courses and much drink. Sometimes he even cooked those meals himself. Were it not for his thirst for power, Chernenko would most probably have been content with the life of the Soviet middle class. And his children were model Soviet citizens, untainted by characteristics common to children of the Soviet elite families, such as dissoluteness and extravagance. After graduating from the Institute of Foreign Affairs, his son worked in Goskino (State Film Industry) in the humble capacity of editor. His daughter had an advanced graduate degree, but not the prestigious doctorate in philosophy, from the Institute of Marxism-Leninism.

And yet Chernenko's apparent "simplicity" was in a sense deceptive. Like all other apparatchiki of high rank, he was estranged from the common people, did not understand them, and feared them. He had not the faintest idea of overcrowded communal dwellings, endless queuing, hassles with bureaucracy, the "free" but poor-quality medical services—in short, of the whole miserable, daily life in poverty of millions of Soviet citizens.

For all Chernenko's simplicity, when he became general secretary and had at his disposal fashionable villas, yachts, jets, and the like, he did not object. He was not a hypocrite and realized that all these luxuries stemmed from his power rather than hard work. He acquiesced even when a doctor began to take the temperature of the sea before Chernenko would go for a swim. He understood that the practice was part of the established hierarchical system, under which the general secretary, including his health and way of life, was state property. He accepted this because he had always respected law and order. His entire life indeed was law and order: two substitutes for reality. His intellectual and cultural needs were perfectly gratified by Party work. His mental world began and ended with it. He never attempted to widen the scope of his interests. His required presence at the Bolshoi Theater, where he had to sit through dozens of performances of Khachaturian's "Spartacus" and Tchaikovsky's "Swan Lake," he perceived as a duty, but he preferred the sentimental films arranged to be shown by his wife for the enjoyment of the wives of the Kremlin leaders.

Chernenko also had more rustic hobbies; he loved fishing, swimming, and riding as long as his age and health permitted. Influenced by

Brezhnev, he had acquired a taste for hunting; in the Kremlin hunting was considered chic.

The most formative educational influence of his life had been the Party. In that he resembled Brezhnev; however, the two may have differed otherwise. The resemblance was clearly noticeable in their speeches. Both believed that capitalism was a system of cruel exploitation and that its days were numbered. They also believed — although Brezhnev probably less so than Chernenko — that communism was the panacea for humanity's problems and would lead the world to freedom and affluence. One difference between them was that Brezhnev was fortunate; his career developed smoothly from success to success. He never had to remain under the domination of a master for any length of time, nor was he forced to behave in a subservient and sycophantic manner. He was proud, secure, and independent. He loved women and they loved him.

Chernenko, on the other hand, had to endure humiliations and the caprices of others. For a provincial Party worker, he had an unusual inclination toward experimentation, toward seeking new solutions and directions. Having remained for the greatest part of his life under the shadow of leaders stronger than himself, he had not dared to display his real convictions or to defend them. When he finally became free to test his ideas and theories in action, it turned out that they were already obsolete in many aspects. Brezhnev was a sybarite; his main concern was comforts, recreation, and pleasure. He loved himself more than his work or his friends. Chernenko was practical and realistic, but he sacrificed himself completely in service to ideas and also to people. Brezhnev considered Chernenko a pedant, taking it for granted that the latter would never forget anything, not even the smallest detail. Chernenko, however, had a more generous character. In addition to not forgetting anything, he also never forgot *anyone*.

Chernenko did not share Andropov's attitude toward discipline and legality. He considered personal relationships more important than slogans. This attitude is not to be equated with the absence of principles or convictions; rather, it stemmed from his sense of duty, which amounted to as much humanity and decency as Soviet standards allowed.

Chernenko understood that the motives of Andropov's anticorruption campaigning were far from unselfish, that Andropov's true goal was to accumulate personal power, and that sacrifices were demanded from the populace not for its own future welfare but for strengthening the system. People in the Soviet system are basically considered cogs in the machine of labor exploitation and perpetuation of human misery. Chernenko, in contrast, was unwilling to magnify purposeless harm, and willing to help some people, for example, people with whom he had previously been in contact or to whom he was indebted in some way. He remained faithful to Brezhnev's slogan of live and let live.

Following that philosophy, Chernenko recalled from exile Brezhnev's daughter, Galina, who reappeared in Moscow. She attended a reception given by Chernenko's wife, Anna Dmitrievna, in April 1983, at which Gorbachev's wife appeared covered with glittering jewelry and caused a sensation. Galina Brezhnev had been exiled since November 1982, after repeated interrogations by the KGB in connection with the theft of some diamonds involving a friend (a circus performer) who ultimately committed suicide. The affair had been highlighted by the late Brezhnev's opponents with the aim of discrediting him posthumously. And it had had tragic consequences for Galina's husband, General Churbanov, then first deputy minister of interior: he had been dismissed and dispatched by Andropov to Murmansk, beyond the Arctic Circle, to head the local militia administration there. It was rumored that Galina had tried unsuccessfully to retain their apartment in Moscow, until she had eventually been forced to join her husband.

Chernenko also rehabilitated a number of well-known party functionaries framed or scapegoated by Andropov. In April the leader of Moldavia, Semyon Grossu, who two months earlier had been harshly criticized "for inertia and bureaucratic methods in his work," was awarded the Order of Lenin. Investigations were stopped against the former chairman of the All-Union Council of Trade Unions, Alexey Shibanov, and the dismissed secretary of the Krasnodar Territory Party committee, Sergey Medunov. Both Shibanov and Medunov had been accused of underhanded financial dealings and embezzlement. The criminal investigation of Petr Neporozhny, former minister of energy and electrification, was also halted and he was allowed to retire.

Although he discontinued a number of Andropov-initiated prosecutions against prominent public figures, Chernenko did not, as is widely believed, mean to return the country to the stagnation of the last years of Brezhnev's rule. My surmise is that he had different considerations. He apparently recognized that scandalmongering only helped increase arbitrariness and coercion, and considered corruption to be less a product of individual dishonesty than a feature of the system[29] — not, however, in the clichéd sense of the supposedly "socially determined nature of crime" but rather in the sense that the power elite had always been encouraged and compelled to break the laws. This phenomenon has its objective and subjective causes. The former includes a corrupt social system, lawlessness, the absence of guaranteed individual rights, arbitrariness of Party rule, the concept of the individual person as a servant of the system, disregard of due process, and suppression of information that elsewhere would be normal news.

The subjective causes of criminality have to do with the atmosphere that surrounds the elite families. Restricted-access stores selling otherwise unobtainable goods at reduced prices, as well as restricted-access hospitals, rest homes, sanatoria, exclusive clubs, and the like generate this atmosphere. In the Soviet state such privileges are not inheritable, and they can be enjoyed only as long as their beneficiaries remain in power. This means that the elite hastens to make hay while the sun shines. Before the sun stops shining on them, the *nomenklatura* have the motive to use their temporary power for the sake of accumulating durable wealth that can be amassed in the Soviet Union only by illegal means: bribes, embezzlement, and various shady business deals.

Soviet society is closed, not only to foreigners but also to its own people. The barriers between the people and the "partocracy" lead to consequences such as extremely tight censorship; criminal penalization of any criticism of authority (commonly known as "criticism of the Soviet social structure and state regime"); and the state monopoly on media information. Such institutions give the elite the sense of being socially protected, of immunity, even of ownership of the law and its enforcement.

It would have been more justifiable to increase the remuneration of the ruling class, even by a great amount, rather than feed it covertly—and thereby corruptly—by open-ended bank accounts such as all Politburo members have; by apartments received out of turn, ahead of the waiting line (which for ordinary people may take many years); private chauffeurs; free or token-price restaurants; free transportation; and free vacation facilities. Actually, all those privileges are unconstitutional, regulated by secret ordinances that may remain at odds with the public law and that always remain at odds with morality.

In the Soviet Union, where there is a permanent shortage of almost everything, acquisition becomes a universal obsession. One grabs what one can: for oneself and for one's children. Because might is right, nearly every high official is on the take from the underworld. Buying security against detection or prosecution, criminals deposit thousands of rubles into the accounts of officials; the sums may reach from tens of thousands to millions of rubles, depending on the official's rank in the hierarchical ladder. The higher an official is placed, the larger is his "compensation" and the more likely his chances of avoiding detection.

At the very pinnacle of the Soviet social pyramid there operates a system of indirect purchase of the partocracy's favors through providing for its children. The children of Brezhnev turned out to have been involved in the web of criminal business. Bribes worth millions were given to them. "Tokens of appreciation" were often forwarded: diamonds, antique jewelry, paintings, and precious carpets, as well as foreign currency, gold ingots, and gold coins. All that booty was expected and was given in exchange for no more than a kind word to their father, sometimes on matters as trivial as an invitation to see the general secretary. No motives were involved at this point other than the opportunity to pay one's respects and to remind Brezhnev of one's existence in the event that one later needed to be saved from trouble.

Truly large-scale business was also blossoming. Prime Minister Kosygin's son-in-law, Dzhermen Gvishiani, deputy chairman of the Science and Technology Committee, was highly active in that regard. Assisted by a fellow Georgian, Secretary of the Presidium of the Supreme Soviet, M. P. Georgadze, he arranged pardons for some convicts sentenced to death for sums starting at 100,000 rubles.

Members of the families of nearly all the Politburo members and CC secretaries participated in more modest ventures. Bribes in services could assume quite sophisticated forms. Gromyko's son arranged prestigious foreign travels for influential scholars and scientists until with their help he eventually became a scholar himself, and was appointed director of an academic institute and a corresponding member of the Academy of Sciences. Some ingenious businessmen considered it worth their while to finance a resplendent wedding reception for Romanov's daughter and furnish her apartment. Other children of the elite, such as the sons of Kirilenko, Podgorny, Polyansky, and Shelest, did not let themselves be outpaced. During their trips abroad they vied with sheikhs of Arabia in their lavish spending, living in royal suites of the best hotels, and giving hundred-dollar tips. Grishin's son was a gambler, and while in Monaco lost thousands at roulette. In the private life of the Soviet elite, the sky was the limit.

The higher the father's official position, the more money was available to throw around and the lower was the risk of being apprehended. Deviant or asocial forms of conduct were pursued quite openly. The offspring of highly placed parents smoothly and rapidly ascended the ladder of success. The son of Minister of Internal Affairs, Nikolay Shchelokov made a brilliant career in the Komsomol until he was thrown out of his post when Andropov succeeded Brezhnev. Andropov's son was a successful diplomat until his father's death; his daughter was the editor of a well-known periodical. Khrushchev's son-in-law, Adzhubei, was being groomed for the post of minister of foreign affairs before his father-in-law fell from power.

By such standards it appeared quite natural for Brezhnev's son and son-in-law to be made members of the CC and first deputy ministers: Yury Brezhnev in the Ministry of Trade; Yury Churbanov in the Ministry of Interior. It was a foregone conclusion that such figures would abuse their power positions. The former did so by accepting "tokens of appreciation" for helping foreign firms obtain advantageous commissions from the USSR; the latter, by receiving generous gifts for providing pardons. Churbanov also engaged in a lucrative trade in automobiles, supplied by the West German firm Mercedes-Benz on the order of the Soviet Ministry of Interior.

In a corrupt society infringements of law cease to be exceptions and become the norm prerequisite for the system's functioning. This is why a war against corruption may at a certain stage transform itself into a war against the regime. The latter, trying to save itself, seeks a compromise between its own prosperity and the law, as a result of which certain crimes become lawful privileges of the select few. This puts the elite above the law by the simple expedient of their power to transgress it in fact, if not formally.

It is the system, therefore, rather than human will that blurs the borders between law and lawlessness. The consequence is immorality writ large, extending from the authorized licentiousness of the elite to exploitation of the masses. Overcoming this criminality can therefore be achieved only by overcoming the system, its institutions and its philosophy. Not a single Communist leader had ever been ready to attempt that. Nor was Chernenko.

Chernenko's loyalty toward the "Moldavian mafia" and the "Dnepropetrovsk clan" cannot be seen as a policy choice, whether moral or immoral (any more than were Andropov's highly selective prosecutions), yet it had the advantage of sincerity. Chernenko remained true to the mafia ethic, which requires the protection of one's own and which represents a morality consistent with the worldview of the Soviet ruling class.

It does not follow that Chernenko wished to abandon the struggle against corruption as a feature of the Soviet power system. He only saw to it that the struggle would not turn against his own supporters. Two death sentences were carried out against officials of the Ministry of Foreign Trade: the head of Tekhnopromexport (Technical Industry Export), Yu. Smelyakov, and his assistant, head of the import department, V. Pavlov. These were the highest Soviet officials to receive the maximum penalty for embezzlement and bribery in the post-Brezhnev era. The director of the Eliseyev delicatessen, after being kept for several months in a prison hospital, was also executed. The option of pardoning him was probably considered because he was close to Galina Brezhnev and supplied special foodstuffs to her household. Nevertheless, the consideration that turned out to be decisive was the desire to issue a warning to lesser crooks. Particularly offensive was this embezzler's greed: he was charged with embezzling a sum — 1,500,000 rubles — far larger than befit his rank.

Several municipal committee secretaries and several state ministers were dismissed from their posts in Uzbekistan for such crimes as bribery and embezzling. Likewise dismissed and put on trial were several deputies of the republic Supreme Soviet, as well as a dozen officials of local soviets in that republic.[30] Over a hundred senior party activists were expelled from the Party in Latvia, where a large-scale embezzlement scandal came to light in the Ministries of Agriculture, Construction, and Welfare; there were altogether 260 defendants at the ensuing trial. A criminal network was also uncovered in Rostov, and as a result 76 persons were arrested for selling butter and meat of inferior quality. A large group of people in higher education institutions in Odessa were found guilty of taking bribes ranging from hundreds to tens of thousands of rubles.[31]

On the basis of the economic crime statistics published, one might conclude that the people of the Soviet Union are particularly prone to cheating, stealing, and other underhanded pursuits. This, however, would be to misunderstand the meaning of the statistics because such behavior is a *systemic* feature that can disappear only with the disappearance of the system. To demonstrate that, however, was not Chernenko's purpose. Detection and punishment of crime had to serve as deterrent and as proof of the fact that he, Chernenko, was in step with the realities of life. The campaign resulted in an enormous number of prosecutions, amounting to tens of thousands. This was Chernenko's way of experimenting with measures to improve the "mechanism of social regulation." Instead of Andropov's efforts aimed at overcoming alcoholism and absenteeism from work, Chernenko came up with the slogan "The struggle for legality." The purpose of both was the same: to make the masses believe that the Party cared for the people, and that all social problems, whether material deprivation, food shortages, or low quality of industrial goods, and so on, were the fault of careless and dishonest individuals, not of the system. That was what Andropov sought to impart to the people. Chernenko was following suit.

The struggle against corruption had another curious feature. Even though it was supposed to be "new," it consisted of a revival of old institutional forms. Chernenko decided to reinstitute the system of political sections within the militia that had been discarded shortly after Stalin's death. From then on the *politruks* (political instructors), actually commissars attached to units, were charged with the inculcation in the enforcers of law and order of "political-ideological consciousness."

V. V. Fedorchuk, a KGB man, understood the task of reordering the prison services. Sometimes he tested his subordinates by appearing incognito. Once, dressed in a shabby jacket and a scruffy cap, he appeared at one of the militia stations of Moscow and asked to see the head of the department. He was kept waiting until he gave up after two hours.

Fedorchuk was obviously out for popularity. Little known in Party circles, not even a member of the CC, he was seeking to gain the reputation of an efficient KGB official who gave no special consideration to anyone regardless of personal rank and social status. His entire career involved security work. He served in the SMERSH (the military counterintelligence; contraction of the Russian words *Smert Shpionam*, "death to spies") in World War II and after the war with the Soviet occupation army in East Germany. In 1970 fate—and the right connections—made him chief of the KGB in the Ukraine. There he soon became known for his ruthlessness in preparing cases (and their outcomes) against dissidents. Thanks to his diligence, the Ukrainian opposition movement was broken with a ferocity hitherto unknown even in the Soviet system. He tried to introduce the same standards on a national scale when, as a result of complex intrigues, he was promoted to the post of head of the KGB for the entire country. Then he suffered a serious setback. His style and manner, which may have been good for Kiev, could not be tolerated in Moscow. There, on the political Olympus, greater finesse and resourcefulness were required. These were qualities he lacked, and therefore he was transferred by Andropov to the Ministry of Interior. There too he displayed great zeal, but it seems that he had not understood that with the advent of Chernenko the "line" had changed: it had become more subtle, more cautious.

But Fedorchuk proved unable to change: his style resembled that of the former secretary general, much to the displeasure of the new one. Furthermore, in the case of Shchelokov, the most sensational in recent years, Chernenko was pressured by Fedorchuk to agree to strip his friend of his general's rank. Chernenko very much wanted to save the skin of a man he had known since his Moldavian days. He attempted to "hide" the former minister of interior within the ranks of the army by attaching him to a group of inspectors general of the Ministry of Defense.[32] But Fedorchuk, as the new minister of interior (appointed by Andropov and apparently confident of Gorbachev's support), decided that Shchelokov should not be pardoned. Thus, information about the latter's abuses of power found their way into the press, making it imperative to sacrifice him. Toward the end of 1984 Shchelokov shot himself, thereby ending the life of a close friend of Brezhnev's, from whose hands he had received his first appointment in the Moldavian Ministry of Interior. Under Brezhnev's patronage he reached the position of deputy chairman of the Council of Ministers of that republic, was later appointed second secretary of the CC, and eventually (in 1966) became the minister of interior of the country. He remained in that post until 1982, when the Dnepropetrovsk clan of Brezhnev's supporters disintegrated.

Shchelokov's downfall was an indicator of important changes occurring not only within Chernenko but also in the balance of forces in the Kremlin. What apparently happened was that this time Chernenko put rationality, or ordinary calculation, above the obligations of friendship. Also, his ability to shield his faithful supporters had its limits. He not only had to please his supporters but also felt the need to avoid antagonizing his opponents, who were demanding the head of the minister of interior.

In the meantime Chernenko's praises continued to be sung. The more limited his real power was becoming, the louder the singing was. Thousands of his portraits were carried during the May Day parade. Red Square became literally red, filled with red flags and red posters displaying quotations from his speeches. Chernenko looked younger than his years and enjoyed the occasion to the full. Dressed in a heavy black overcoat despite the balmy weather, he greeted the demonstrators by raising his hands and engaged in lively conversation with Tikhonov.

Chernenko thirsted for fame and esteem. Why not? Brezhnev, his mentor, had believed that the need for esteem and respect was a sign of mental health. Now, when Chernenko himself became general secretary, who would dare reproach him for such a desire? It would have been natural for him to try to forget his thorny uphill path to power, and his entourage was ready to help him in this. Shevardnadze, of all people, exhibited special zeal in that regard despite the fact that he had only recently been among Gorbachev's supporters. In one of his speeches Shevardnadze said: "The working masses consider him [Chernenko] the beacon of our country. His authority is immense. His instructions and ideas served to lay the foundation for the realization of the most important projects in Georgia."[33]

Chernenko also received some recognition from Aliev, although the latter had not yet gone over openly to his side. He was too crafty and prudent to commit himself prematurely. Aliev did stop opposing Chernenko at Politburo meetings and consequently was rewarded by the increasing references to himself in the press. He also began to attend official receptions and even receive important foreign visitors. One noted that in group photographs he had moved from the ninth or tenth place in proximity to the secretary general to sixth or even fifth.

The Soviet social system appears very complex and intricate, with its immense bureaucracy and plurality of competing interests. However, its diversity may well be more apparent than real because the regime "homogenizes" personalities. The rule is that the closer one is to the top of the political pyramid, the less different one is from the others. At its very top, in the Politburo, the standardization of traits is so extreme that even differences in skills or fields of competence largely disappear. Politburo members who as Central Committee secretaries supervise agriculture can easily be shifted to the supervision of ideology or industry or, if need be, administrative or military personnel.

The apex of Soviet power resembles a portrait gallery of dull and immobile figures who are almost look-alikes. The faces are rather common, stern and gloomy, with heavy chins. Missing among them are people prominent in any field, be it outstanding scientists, talented actors, famous physicians, or renowned poets. The ferment of creativity or of the search for truth are unknown to them. The driving force in their lives is the pursuit of power; only in this process are their individuality and amour propre revealed. Several decades of living in the milieu of the power elite have left an imprint on them, shaping their appreciation of luxury, their taste for quality goods and expensive residential facilities. But they are very far from any refinement in manner. They remain rude and arrogant, quick to lose their temper and reveal their coarseness. They invariably derive pleasure from flattery and the kowtowing of others to them. Nevertheless, in cases of necessity, they are skilled at hiding their real thoughts and feelings. The unsurpassable master of this art has been Gromyko. His superb skill in dissimulating his real thoughts has permitted him to survive almost fifty years in the Kremlin, untouched by all the purges and changes of political course.

Gromyko was born in Belorussia in the village of Starye Gromyki, hence his name. He studied in a technical school in Minsk and later at the Academy of Agriculture in Moscow, where he obtained a doctoral degree and was appointed university lecturer. He was about thirty when he was noticed by Molotov, who, as the new commissar for foreign affairs, was forced by Stalin's purges to look for replacements that could be considered loyal to the leader. The required qualifications were peasant or working-class origin, unquestioning obedience, and assiduity. These were precisely the qualities that Gromyko had in abundance. After only two years as a minor official in the diplomatic service, he rose to become adviser at the Soviet Embassy in Washington. After two more years he became the youngest Soviet ambassador, also in Washington. He owed his rapid advancement not only to the appreciation of Molotov but also to the constant purges in the Party ranks. Purges enabled people like Gromyko, who were kowtowers devoid of self-respect, and either unthinking or skillful at concealing their thoughts, to rise rapidly to prestigious and influential positions.

In 1946 Gromyko became the first Soviet representative in the UN Security Council. The war was over. Times had changed, and Gromyko himself underwent a change. From a champion of friendship with the United States he became a fire-breathing execrator of the United States, a denouncer of its imperialism, and unmasker of its evil designs. During his diplomatic career of nearly a half century Gromyko changed the views he expressed countless times, but always in conformity with the political interests of his superiors.

In 1947–48, on Stalin's instruction, Gromyko demanded recognition of the right of Jews to have an independent state of their own. He then marshaled his arguments logically and convincingly. Later he was capable of arguing, also logically and convincingly, in favor of breaking diplomatic relations with the state of Israel when, in 1952, Stalin considered that expedient.

Having survived under Stalin, Gromyko managed to hold his own also under Khrushchev. The latter appointed him minister of foreign affairs when Molotov, his former chief and patron, fell into disgrace together with the incumbent foreign minister, Shepilov (who was believed to have joined the conspiracy against the first secretary). Then the man who formerly espoused global conflict and cold war became overnight an ardent advocate of the new policy of "peaceful coexistence." What this term meant in practice was a policy of vacillating between suspicion and trust, and of fostering relations with the West while expanding into the Third World.

Having successfully survived the mercurial and moody Khrushchev, Gromyko safely navigated the stormy waters of Brezhnev's intrigues and was eventually promoted to the Politburo. He was now a statesman, a policymaker, not a mere executor of policy. His appointment was due to two rather fortuitous factors: first, to vacancies in the Politburo after one of Brezhnev's purges, and second, to Brezhnev's poor health, which limited his ability to conduct foreign affairs by himself. Initially, Gromyko did not aspire to top-rank position: he was content to belong to the body of top policy decision makers that included the minister of defense and the CC secretary for ideology. Gromyko's devotion was something Brezhnev took for granted, as did Khrushchev, who once went so far as to say that should Gromyko be ordered to take off his trousers and sit on the ice, he would sit there until instructed to get up. Gromyko served faithfully the institution of general secretary. Thus, after Brezhnev's death, he did not consider himself bound by the deceased man's will and switched his allegiance from Chernenko (Brezhnev's choice of heir) to Andropov. That choice almost led Gromyko into a dead end; the ambitious new general secretary intended to keep foreign policy under his personal control but once again fate, in the form of illness, intervened to Gromyko's advantage. For many months prior to his death, Andropov was bedridden. This circumstance propelled Gromyko once more into the role of the actual maker of foreign policy.

Common sense should have prompted him to support Chernenko, who, without any experience in foreign policy, would have to rely on his help and knowledge. This would have guaranteed Gromyko a measure of power. But this time he did not wish to bow to a man who was a late arrival on the Kremlin heights. Having shown so much compliance and servility to all the former general secretaries, Gromyko did not want to bend his knee before someone like himself who had been assiduous in execution of the will and whim of others. Besides, he considered Chernenko his intellectual inferior, despite the fact that he himself lacked a broad intellectual horizon.

Having frequently met with many Western politicians, Gromyko was well aware of their weaknesses and shortcomings. However, his knowledge of the West, and its sociostructural characteristics and philosophical traditions was rather superficial. Gromyko understood fairly well how the Western polities functioned but he hardly knew a thing about daily life in the free world and its organizing principles. In that respect he was a prisoner of the outdated and banal preconceptions of Marxist ideology. He never walked the streets of a Western city, whether European or American. But then he has hardly ever appeared on the streets of Moscow either. Abroad, his walks were circumscribed by the walls of Soviet embassy compounds, and at home by the high fences surrounding government-provided dachas. He might have aimed his ambition toward other goals: he could have been a scientist for instance, enjoying the seclusion of his study or laboratory. However, because he had become a political figure, he could not avoid contacts with people he would have preferred to avoid.

In private he was rather affable, a good conversationalist, courteous yet reserved, wary of alcohol and overeating.[34] He lived his entire life in harmony with his wife Lydia Grinevich, who bore him a son and a daughter. When at work, he was quite the opposite: rude, petty, and brutal toward his subordinates. His working style gradually spread throughout the Soviet diplomatic corps paralleling the growth of his personal influence in the Soviet ruling class and the growth of Soviet influence in the world. He made it a habit of expressing himself harshly, cuttingly, without attempting to control or conceal his moods and temper tantrums. Whenever a diplomatic encounter touched upon U.S. policy, the European Community, or disarmament, he more often than not shocked the Western diplomats of his rude outbursts and unfounded accusations. Yet, strange as it may sound, he remained in some ways pro-Western, as an advocate of policies oriented toward placating the USSR's main adversaries: Europe and the United States. In regard to the Third World, in contrast, he counseled that it not be given priority and, accordingly, avoided visiting Africa, Asia, and Latin America. Despite all this, Gromyko never had the opportunity of conducting foreign policy strictly on the basis of his personal views. The decision-making process in the Soviet Union required him to defer to the will of the Party leaders. Pedantically, he executed the orders of Stalin, Khrushchev, Brezhnev, and Andropov.

It was only Chernenko whom he refused to follow. He realized the latter's weakness in relation to the power of the Politburo, and Chernenko's need to consult Ustinov, Romanov, Gorbachev, and Aliev, and to take into consideration the interests, opinions, and preferences of each of them. This situation prompted Gromyko to assert his independence. When meeting foreign statesmen, Chernenko read from a prepared text of a general nature, possibly because he lacked the strength to stand up and expound at length. In any case, all the real negotiations were delegated to Gromyko. He was the first to meet foreign visitors at the airport and the last to bid them goodbye. Having held the post of minister of foreign affairs for twenty-seven years—longer than anyone else—he found himself at last in a position to impose his will on the general secretary.

Andropov had not become a statesman of international stature because he died too soon. It was Chernenko who was intent on overcoming the stagnant state of long-neglected Soviet foreign relations. In June he was host to the president of France, François Mitterrand. The importance of this visit lay in the very fact of its occurrence rather than in any substance achieved. Mitterrand expressed the wish to come to Moscow, and Chernenko, as it happened, was physically able to receive him. The general secretary recognized that he was being presented with a long-sought opportunity to enhance his international prestige and to convey the impression that (despite the standstill in Soviet-U.S. relations) he was ready for a rapprochement with Europe. The ritual of the reception was carefully prepared, direct broadcasting of the leaders' speeches was arranged, and a joint communique drafted. That carefully planned event was spoiled by Gromyko, however, when Mitterrand invited Chernenko to visit Paris. Chernenko responded immediately, professing to accept the invitation with pleasure. At that moment Gromyko interfered and, turning to Mitterrand, rudely informed him that in the foreseeable future

Chernenko would not be able to find time for a return visit. Gromyko's tactless remark had a purpose: it revealed to the West the ineptitude of the new Soviet leader and his inability to take independent decisions.

Gromyko also acted in a similar manner when openly putting words into his boss's mouth during his meeting with the foreign minister of West Germany, Hans-Dietrich Genscher. Chernenko was certainly not the first Soviet leader to follow his minister's advice, but Gromyko was the first foreign minister to dare to reveal the incompetence and ineptitude of his leader in matters of foreign policy. The maneuver of Gromyko would not have been possible without the support of the minister of defense, Ustinov. The latter, unlike the minister of foreign affairs, did not have opportunities to make public statements, so he had no opportunity of hinting at Chernenko's dependence on himself. His influence on the general secretary was nevertheless strong, and it was he who maintained the precarious equilibrium in the Kremlin. In policy discussions his opinion tended to be decisive. Besides, it was Ustinov's vote that gave the Chernenko camp a majority in the Politburo.

The power of the minister of defense, however, stemmed not merely from his ability to tip the balance between the rival factions. A no less decisive factor was his control over the armed forces, a multimillion-strong segment of Soviet society. The army has no noticeable influence on day-to-day Soviet politics or society. As a rule, it assumes power in the midst of crises caused by shifts of power. In such instances it transforms itself from a military institution into a political one, and the army was thus used for political purposes by all Soviet leaders from Lenin to Andropov. Chernenko's coming to power was in a way an anomaly because it occurred without the army's support. In this instance the support of the Party apparatus proved sufficient. But even Chernenko could not ignore the army. Constant expansion is inherent in Communism. That systemic trait of Communism has forced all general secretaries to defer to the army, and to the minister of defense. All of them have been anxious to cultivate good relationships with the defense minister, especially because the most extremist circles of the Party apparatus have traditionally received backing from that very same quarter. Ustinov was supported by Romanov, and reciprocated by backing the latter's personal ambitions. Ustinov's other supporter was Aliev, whose career had long been associated with the KGB, and thus he tended to favor military measures and forceful solutions.

Ustinov himself tended to defer to the views of the General Staff, fought for privileges for its members, and respected its advice. He himself had never been a professional soldier. Ustinov was a worker's son who had been apprenticed to a locksmith; he had served in the army for only several months in 1922. Much later, in 1944, after serving as minister of armaments for several years, he had been given the rank of colonel-general. Twenty-two years later he had become minister of defense and was raised to the rank of marshal. In a rare but not unique episode in Soviet history, a civilian had risen to the highest military rank in the USSR. Ustinov's civilian background (perhaps as a kind of compensation) impelled him to zealously concern himself with strengthening the army and increasing its influence. He had actively supported the Soviet invasion of Afghanistan and advocated the deployment of operational missiles (between 500 and 1000 km in range) in Eastern Europe.

Ustinov owed his military career entirely to Brezhnev and had no particular regard for Chernenko, whom he considered incapable of managing the Soviet economy as toughly and decisively as was required to facilitate the growth of Soviet military might. Ustinov was a crafty and experienced politician. While supporting Gorbachev's claim to power, he nevertheless let him understand that this support was not something to be taken for granted. At Politburo meetings he did his best to keep all his options open; this encouraged Chernenko to hope that with time Ustinov could be won over to his side. Chernenko also drew some hope from Ustinov's close ties with his ally, Romanov. The two had much in common, sharing a highly conservative attitude toward the development of Soviet society. Romanov must have appeared to Ustinov as the best possible Party leader: purposeful and uncompromising. He had come to the forefront of Soviet politics under Andropov, who had appointed him CC secretary and thus placed him in the position to compete for succession.

Romanov, a shipbuilding engineer, began his Party career by becoming a *raykom* first secretary in Leningrad. In 1970, at the age of forty-seven, he became first secretary of the Leningrad *obkom*, replacing Vassily Tolstikov, who was "exiled" from the centers of power to China as Soviet ambassador. By the age of fifty-three Romanov was a full member of the Politburo. Elegant, well groomed, and self-assured, he was arrogant and brutal. He had preconceived opinions on everything and did not tolerate any opposition to them. He liked to show off and to impress people by his ostentation. For example, he was fond of throwing raucous parties in old palaces and, on one occasion, created a scandal when on the occasion of his daughter's wedding, his guests were served meals on a priceless set of china that had belonged to the tsars. Broken pieces of that chinaware provided a memorable symbol of his unrestrained willfulness. Unlike most members of the Politburo, he was fond of traveling; he had been to Finland, Greece, Italy, Norway, and West Germany. The trips, however, did nothing to relieve his abysmal ignorance. For instance, he could never understand why the leaders of democratic governments did not call to order or discipline the dissenting members of their own parties. Romanov's narrow-mindedness did no damage to his reputation as a good administrator. On the contrary, in the milieu of the Kremlin "old guard," such a perspective was identified with and appreciated.

The road to the top power post for Romanov was still blocked by two obstacles. One was the curious fate of all past leaders who originated from Leningrad. All of them made careers rapidly until they became members of the Politburo or secretaries of the CC; whereupon they either died suddenly, often under mysterious circumstances or, without any particular mystery, lost their high positions. Romanov was determined not to let such a fate repeat itself in his case.

The other obstacle was Gorbachev, whom it was necessary to remove or to bypass. One possibility was for Romanov to build a political support base stronger than that of his rival's. It was a possibility that was unlikely to materialize, for Romanov had neither roots in Moscow nor the necessary connections in the Central Committee. Consequently, Romanov followed a different strategy: betting on Chernenko and attempting to make himself irreplaceable, in the hope of eventually winning the allegiance of at least some of Chernenko's supporters. In this, however, he was handicapped as an outsider. Besides, the Party veterans, who could by no means be accused of liberalism, were put off by Romanov's political extremism.

Romanov therefore had to adapt, to provide demonstrations of an ability and willingness to work in concert with the collective. He was not a bad actor; he succeeded in appearing to be less high-handed and categorical than previously and to be able to listen to others. His attitude toward Chernenko was respectful but not servile. He remained on correct terms with Gorbachev, even though the latter quickly saw through his games. Romanov also exhibited a change in foreign policy views as he began to advocate an improvement in Soviet-U.S. relations and a kind of mutual tolerance and coexistence. In this way he both accommodated himself to Chernenko and simultaneously improved his image in the West.

Romanov's efforts were noticed and appreciated. He began to appear more often at the airport together with Tikhonov, welcoming and seeing off foreign delegations, and to participate in various international negotiations. Press photographs showed him standing in the first row, which moved Gorbachev to a less central location. Basically Romanov had not changed; this was indicated by his continuing use of the same expressions and slogans as ten years earlier. His goal remained to protect his country from any liberalization and to maintain a strictly authoritarian and disciplinarian line. In that he was of one mind with both Ustinov and Aliev, though the latter seemed to him the more promising as an ally.

Aliev had been living in Moscow since 1982, when Andropov made him a member of the Politburo and deputy chairman of the Council of Ministers. He was capable of working hard for as many as twelve to fourteen hours a day. In this way he coped with his responsibilities for transport, health, culture, and education. Yet still more duties were heaped on him. When the targets for production of consumer goods were not reached, he was made head of the interministerial commission responsible for the fulfillment of the targets. He was also charged with drafting the new law dealing with workers' collectives. In addition, he carried out diplomatic duties, such as heading a Soviet delegation to Vietnam, visiting Syria, and gaining expertise on the Middle East. Despite all this, he remained a "lone wolf" in Moscow, a victim of the nationalistic prejudice that is rampant in the Soviet capital. The disdain for Aliev's Moslem background was combined with fear at his having come from the Caucasus, which had already produced one despot who subjugated the entire Party. Every newcomer from that region was suspect as a potential new Stalin.

Aliev had been a Gorbachev supporter from the time of Andropov's rule. His factional affiliation was forced on him by his indebtedness to Andropov, whose patronage had been the decisive factor in his career. He was allowed to head the state security service in Azerbaijan in contravention of the rule that no member of a national minority be appointed chairman of the KGB in his own republic. He was then the first Azerbaijani to be made a member of the Politburo and to be promoted to first deputy chairman of the Council of Ministers. When after Andropov's death his faction shifted its allegiance to Gorbachev, Aliev went along, perhaps reluctantly, but without protest. This was the result of his Oriental respect for power. Furthermore, the wish of his deceased patron was sacred, and the habit of military discipline only confirmed this loyalty.

For the greater part of Aliev's life he had been an intelligence officer, first in the army and later in the KGB. As a young officer, he had participated in the efforts to detach a part of Azerbaijan from Iran and annex it to the Soviet Union. When that adventure misfired, he had been transferred to Turkey and from there to Afghanistan, with the assignment of maintaining contact with pro-Soviet Iranian exiles from the Tudeh party. Many years later he had succeeded in capturing the attention of Andropov (who was at that time, in 1959, in charge of the "fraternal parties" in the Central Committee) by establishing a number of underground radio stations in Sophia that broadcast in Turkish and Persian. The fact that in Khomeini's Iran a fair number of Soviet agents operate today is also due to Aliev. He had made contact with the Ayatollah when the latter was still living in exile in Nedjif, the sacred Iraqi city of the Shi'ites, and he had prevailed on the Tudeh party to disseminate Khomeini's subversive, anti-shah proclamations from its headquarters in exile in Leipzig.

Service in the KGB, in which Aliev had been very successful (colonel at the age of forty-two and first deputy chairman of the Azerbaijan KGB) did not satisfy his ambitions. Because he was fluent in Russian, Persian, and Turkish, when World War II broke out, he had been assigned to the security services. But the KGB career was never fully to his liking, and the necessity of suppressing some of his own inclinations was bound to have traumatic effects upon his personality. His openness and spontaneity were replaced by cupidity and an unquenchable thirst for power. His natural energy found an outlet in aggressiveness; his irony, in stinging sarcasm. His insecurity made him suspicious and vindictive.

Aliev was a master of dissimulation, which he practiced especially in the presence of Semen Tsvigun, his immediate superior. He never lost his temper or allowed his conceit to show. He used to stay in his office until late in the night reading the reports of agents, for he never entrusted such jobs to his subordinates. Contrary to what was expected of a man of his status, he also traveled to remote districts to meet his agents. In such instances he always tried to appear an appreciative listener. He was also a superb host, entertaining his guests in the grand and lavish Oriental manner. Tsvigun loved to attend Aliev's parties, where he could always meet interesting people. When Tsvigun was appointed deputy chairman of the All-Union KGB, no better candidate than Aliev could be found for heading state security in Azerbaijan.

Moscow was not disappointed. Aliev remained dedicated and continued to perform with distinction. Not confining himself to building up evidence in criminal cases, he sought to understand the motives and causes of crime. This approach helped disclose the extent of complicity of the Party leadership, especially of local-level authorities (i.e. district, region, or municipal), in unlawful behavior. Due to the extensive involvement of the Party elite, a great danger was posed to the system, and Aliev was called upon to remedy that state of affairs. Understandably, he neither could nor wished to lessen the inherent arbitrariness of the Soviet authority system, but he did manage to replace the self-serving arbitrariness of local leaders by a centralized arbitrariness of the state. As a result he succeeded in stopping the disintegration of Azerbaijan's economy.

Andropov had hoped to apply Aliev's methods in Moscow; Chernenko considered the methods unnecessary. After Andropov's death, Aliev's dynamism was no longer in demand, even though Chernenko was by no means averse to using Aliev's energy and experience for the sake of revitalizing the economy. Chernenko never criticized Aliev's methods; on the contrary, he considered them effective and even humane. He had particular appreciation for one device that Aliev had applied in Azerbaijan extensively when thieving ministers were caught red-handed: Aliev would not prosecute them but merely disclosed to them the evidence of their misdeeds. Then he would let them remain at their posts. The effect was that scared to their bones, they turned into hardworking, honest, and efficient executives.

Chernenko knew that Aliev was not to be relied upon, but he was hardly in a position to rely on anyone in the Politburo. Collegiality in the Politburo hardly existed anymore; it had been destroyed by factionalism, with each faction assuming the role of a fiefdom, headed by a minister or CC secretary able to exact from Chernenko a degree of independence in exchange for his pledge of support. The rule was, the more independence they exacted, the more they demanded. Chernenko found that his supporters did not differ from his opponents in this regard. Grishin and Shcherbitsky were no less zealous in guarding their special interests than were Gromyko and Ustinov.

Such a situation could not last indefinitely. In the end either the fiefdoms had to be curbed or the general secretary could not last. Abnormal as this situation was, it was typical of leadership transition periods in Soviet history. Shifts of power have invariably led to a crisis of authority. For general secretaries, time has always worked in their favor because it provided them with opportunities to get rid of the rebels against their authority. Peace and quiet would then return to the Politburo until the next crisis. Chernenko's misfortune was that he just did not have the time. With his advanced age and ailments, he knew that he was living on borrowed time. Realization of this fact was shared by all of his Politburo colleagues, and hence they all made efforts to obtain as wide a scope of authority for themselves as possible. For them, this was their hour of triumph. Foreign relations became the fiefdom of Gromyko, defense that of Ustinov, and industry was divided between Romanov and Aliev.

Nor was there any way to control Shcherbitsky and Kunayev; they behaved in their republics as they deemed fit, tolerating corruption, toying with nationalism, and revising economic targets. Freedom of action in their respective republics was their price for supporting Chernenko. Even worse, Chernenko was losing control over the Party apparatus where the new arrivals of the Andropov period were assuming ever greater influence and authority. Their connections with Gorbachev were impossible to pin down, but they were obviously attracted to the young and energetic CC secretary more than to Chernenko. Gorbachev, like Chernenko, had no well-defined area of responsibility in any particular policy area; the only exception was ideology, with which he dealt reluctantly and superficially. There was a danger here for Chernenko because without a particular area of responsibility, he was like a king without a kingdom. His predecessors feared that situation and thus endeavored to retain control over some key sector of public administration. Khrushchev and Brezhnev personally supervised industry; Stalin and Andropov supervised cadres. In Gorbachev's case, however, his lack of specialized responsibility paradoxically proved a certain advantage because he was perforce considered Chernenko's number two.

Chernenko had no option other than to use the means still at his disposal to make personnel changes that he hoped would solidify his position. If Andropov's purges had, as a rule, been prompted by efficiency considerations to bring the country out of its economic and spiritual stagnation, Chernenko's considerations were personal. He selected people for dismissal or appointment depending on how it would affect his personal power. Having put his confidence in men who opposed change and having become in turn increasingly dependent on such men, Chernenko had to acquiesce in ruling a stagnant society without pursuing change.

In any case, he could have changed very little because his wings had already been clipped by his pact with the Party elite that had brought him to power. The agreement formally secured the Politburo's privileges, which Chernenko had no right to alter, even by co-optations of new members or by reassignments of the functions of the old members. In practice the arrangement was extended to cover also the CC Secretariat, the Party leaders of the various republics, and to a considerable extent, even the regional Party committees. Chernenko's room for maneuver was confined to the second echelon of Party elite, heads of the CC departments, ministers, and in certain cases even secretaries of *obkoms*. Chernenko had limited options. He had to operate without prejudicing the interests of any of the Politburo's factions. It would have been a mistake to oust anyone securely established in the Party apparatus during Brezhnev's rule because such holdovers were now Chernenko's firmest supporters. However, Gorbachev supporters who had made their careers under Andropov were also untouchable, as were those with close ties with Gromyko, Ustinov, and Grishin.

Only men who had been promoted by chance, or who had no connections with anyone in the Politburo were vulnerable. Such high officials were now to become targets. But even their cases posed problems. The consent of the Politburo to the firing of a Party official did not imply that Chernenko was free to choose one of his own factional allies as a replacement. Every candidacy for appointment to any post of importance was thoroughly investigated, first by the Central Committee Secretariat and then by the Politburo, and approved only if it did not upset the existing balance of factional forces. The fear of upsetting the status quo in this respect dictated frequent appointment compromises whereby approval of a representative of one camp for one post was counterbalanced by approval of a representative of the opposite camp for another post.

Personnel changes satisfying to more than one faction did occur, but such events were rare. A case in point was the firing of Colonel-General Semen Romanov, who, one year earlier (when holding the rank of head of the general staff of the air defense forces), had given the order to open fire at the Korean airliner in the vicinity of Sakhalin Island. Irrespective of the real reasons behind this order, the downing of the civilian aircraft cast doubt on Secretary General Andropov's control over the country. Objectively, discreditation of Andropov could work only to Chernenko's advantage. Yet, after Chernenko found himself in Andropov's shoes, he could not permit the military to interfere in politics so blatantly and brusquely. In this respect, the Politburo was unanimous in its fear and distrust of the armed forces.

Because Chernenko could not afford to make radical personnel changes, such changes as he did make were usually selective, following a certain pattern. Representatives of Moscow, usually functionaries of the Party Organization Department in the CC, were dispatched to the provinces to convene assemblies of the local Party activist ranks at which they would voice criticism of local authorities, thus targeting them for removal. In fact, such targets were selected from the files of the KGB, which contained abundant documentation of corruption and abuses of authority of all *nomenklatura* officials.

The leaders of two important Party committees—those of Rostov and of the Checheno-Ingush ASSR—were ousted in precisely this manner. The decision to dismiss the comparatively young I. A. Bondarenko from his long-held post as first secretary of the Rostov *obkom* was reported to be due to his poor health and consequent retirement. This was a formula that had been frequently used by Andropov. In fact, his dismissal should be viewed in the context of the new configuration of interests within the Politburo. Chernenko accused Bondarenko of "wrongly" choosing his personnel cadres, i.e. "wrongly" in terms of Chernenko's interests. Gorbachev, on the other hand, stressed the official's abuses of power. In reality both charges were but a screen. Had Bondarenko been supported by a highly placed and strong patron in Moscow, he would never have been held responsible for the very poor performances of his regional committee. Chernenko was in a position to challenge the Rostov secretary simply because Gorbachev did not oppose this move. Yet, Gorbachev subsequently successfully opposed the filling of that post by anyone from the Chernenko entourage. In the end the post was filled by the fifty-two-year-old Alexander Vlasov, who since 1975 had been first secretary of the Checheno-Ingush *obkom*. The appointment of an outsider as leader of the Rostov district was a result of a "compromise" reached in the Politburo. The idea was to ensure the appointee's equal loyalty to the contending factions.

Chernenko apparently did not know of Vlasov's past ties with Gorbachev. Vlasov had made his career in Irkutsk, first in the Komsomol and later as a Party official. From 1975 he had headed the Party committee of the Checheno-Ingush Republic, which adjoined the Stavropol Territory, where Gorbachev was head. Failing to be aware of this was a mistake on Chernenko's part. The close ties between Vlasov and Gorbachev were revealed only later, after Chernenko's death. In the meanwhile Chernenko mistakenly believed that he had succeeded in removing the Rostov district committee from the arena of factional contests within the Party. In the Checheno-Ingush Republic Vlasov was replaced by V. Fotiyev. Chernenko hoped that Fotiyev, who had been secretary of the Kuibyshev *obkom*, and thus jumped from a low-ranking post to a quite high one, would in the future be grateful to him. This would probably have been so if Chernenko had lived longer.

Chernenko never had any close relations with state security, and those few ties he had were abruptly severed by the mysterious death of Tsvigun. The promotion of Chebrikov to headship of the KGB had been the idea of Andropov. Chernenko therefore needed to introduce within that organization his own man, or "eye," on whose services he could rely. The "eye's" role was, first, to strengthen control, and second, to take over part of Chebrikov's work load. In spring 1984 a new first deputy chairman of the KGB, Nikolay Yemyakhin, was appointed.[35] Then Chernenko could proceed to avail himself more of the KGB's services and at the same time gain its favor. He soon found a suitable opportunity.

The situation in Latvia had become alarming because neonationalist movements were spreading and, together with them, advocacy of citizens' rights. The circumstances called for a stern and implacable leader, preferably to be sought in the ranks of the KGB. Such a man was found in the person of Boris Pugo, the head of the Latvian KGB, who was appointed Latvian CC first secretary. To Moscow, this appointment was the best guarantee of a strict and meticulous adherence to its policy; to Chernenko personally there was the additional factor of expected gratitude and devotion on the part of an appointee likely to become a member of the CPSU Central Committee.

Another problem for Chernenko was the subjection of the military establishment to stricter control. Unfortunately, among the numerous deputy ministers of defense none was under any personal obligation toward him. That was undesirable and could be dangerous in a crunch, e.g. at the time of appointing a new minister of defense in place of Ustinov, who was already seventy-six. Infiltration of the army command by Chernenko—at the top leadership, not the secondary level—became an urgent necessity. The retirement of the chief inspector, deputy minister of defense, the eighty-two-year-old and obviously ill Marshal K. S. Moskalenko, was approved without demur by the Politburo. Equally unopposed was his replacement by General Vladimir Govorov.[36] Chernenko could now be certain of the support of the new deputy minister of defense.

Govorov, the son of a famous commander in World War II, had come to the notice of the future general secretary some ten years earlier when he commanded the Moscow military district forces; he was then elected, not without Chernenko's help, a CC candidate member, and then in 1981, a full member. Because Govorov had not yet reached the peak of his career and was not yet sixty, Chernenko apparently planned to use him to infiltrate further into Ustinov's citadel.

Another initiative of Chernenko's was to introduce his own order into Andropov's "patrimony," i.e. Karelia. This republic was the focus of his predecessor's special concern. Chernenko pushed a change of local leadership there without the ritual of "criticism" and prosecution, as if it were merely an ordinary affair of personnel change. The first secretary of the *obkom*, Ivan Senkin, who had ruled the republic for twenty-five years, was transferred to chairman of the Supreme Soviet Presidium of that republic. Vladimir Stepanov, who had worked as one of the *obkom* secretaries, was appointed in Senkin's place.[37] Everything went quietly and smoothly and would have gone unnoticed except for one detail. *Obkom* first secretaries were very rarely recruited from the ranks of the local apparatus; this practice was intended to prevent the establishment of power centers that could serve as foci of local loyalties. For that, the new leader of Karelia had reason to be grateful to Chernenko.

What appeared in the press at the time was not always in tune with the new policy. This may have been due either to propagandistic inertia or the will of the editors. In any case, the press continued in the style of the late Andropov. It contained appeals—probably much too frequently for Chernenko's liking—to gifted young people to join the Party. Revelations proliferated in the press on such social ills as negligence at work, bribery, profiteering, stealing, and drunkenness. Chernenko considered such revelations too detailed. He also considered superfluous the insistent advocacy of a thorough and extensive overhaul of the economic structure and its operating principles. Chernenko inclined toward the position that limited reforms, such as contractual teamwork and basing salaries on the team's efficiency, would suffice, at least for the time being. Yet, the press was led by *Pravda*, with the rest of the Party newspapers following suit. Although it was the traditional mouthpiece of the general secretaries, *Pravda* opposed Chernenko. Its editor, Victor Afanasyev, fully identified himself with Gorbachev so openly and cleverly that the slightest criticism of his performance would immediately be interpreted as a thrust against the second secretary of the CC. Chernenko was not yet ready for a major skirmish with his main rival.

Afanasyev's dislike for the general secretary had a personal cause. Both were writing books on the same subject, social administration, and apparently there was no room for more than one in so narrow a field of expertise. Chernenko was writing about Party organization; Afanasyev was busy attacking Western sociology. Given the proximity of their respective interests and Chernenko's superior position, Afanasyev could not avoid frequent references to and quotations from him. Each man had managed to use his respective writings as a leverage in his bid for power. But Chernenko had gotten the best — both politically and academically — of Afanasyev, who was a less acknowledged authority than the general secretary. Although Afanasyev became a member of the Academy of Sciences, the State Prize he received for his book was no match for Chernenko's Lenin Prize. Hence, the jealousy of Afanasyev was of sufficient intensity to make him risk publishing in *Pravda* comments quite unsuitable for an editor of a Party organ. Had he not been supported by Gorbachev, his head would have rolled.

It was Afanasyev who introduced into the political vocabulary the term "Second General Secretary of the Politburo," coined with the obvious intention of elevating the position of Gorbachev. Afanasyev also encouraged leaks from the Politburo meetings that were designed to reveal Chernenko's weakness and indecision. The general secretary had no option but to ignore both *Pravda* and its editor and hope for a reversal of fortune. He turned to *Izvestiya*, second in importance and authority to *Pravda*. The former newspaper was closer to the government than to the Party, although the Party apparatus never completely relinquished its control over it. Chernenko decided to use *Izvestiya* to espouse his own ideas.

Chernenko's decision was well timed, for he intended to submit to the Central Committee a number of projects for social development that required extensive and skillful publicity. The tactics he chose were also successful. He got rid of the chief editor of *Izvestiya*, L. N. Tolkunov (who had been supported by Andropov), by promoting him and making him chairman of the Soviet of the Union in the Supreme Soviet. The chief editorship of *Izvestiya* was given to a longtime rival of Afanasyev, Ivan Laptev, an experienced apparatchik in the guise of a writer and philosopher.[38] He did not disappoint his patron. Very soon the pages of *Izvestiya* presented numerous "letters from the working people" abounding in expressions of gratitude and support addressed to the general secretary.[39]

Chernenko's great desire was to be heeded by the masses. Another desire, noticeable in the text of his reply to the leader of the Socialist International (Willy Brandt), was to prove himself capable of wider and more active cooperation with the West.[40] His letter to Brandt appeared to him too limited in the scope of possible impact. Chernenko wanted the entire world to know that with his ascent to power, the barriers obstructing negotiations toward the reduction of nuclear armaments would begin to disappear. Consequently, he also arranged for *Pravda* to interview him in order to present his assessment of the current international situation, relations with the United States, cooperation with Europe, and so on.

In the interview Chernenko attempted to break loose of the usual Soviet rhetoric. He marshaled his arguments and weighed his proposals carefully. He tried to demonstrate the need for dialogue and pointed to the bipolarity of the two hostile blocs as the source of the present stalemate and future dangers. Projecting a realistic approach and qualified optimism, he evaluated the possibilities of reaching an agreement on reduction of nuclear testing and on slowing the arms race in space. Yet, his new vocabulary did not mean a new policy; in the latter respect Chernenko did not have freedom of choice. He could only repeat old Soviet proposals (even if somewhat softening, redefining, or qualifying them), such as the Soviet position regarding the deployment of medium-range missiles in Europe, which one year previously had caused cancellation of the Geneva talks.

The totalitarian structure of Soviet society endows the system with a large measure of uniformity and continuity. This is why the role of an individual, his character, opinions, and principles count for little when he stands at the top of the power pyramid. What is important is his status, for this determines his goals and priorities. It would therefore be a mistake to see Chernenko's policy as a reflection of his individual preferences. Hence, the new general secretary was unable to present his point of view at the CC Plenum, which began on April 10 in Moscow. Nor was he able to voice his disapproval of his adversaries or of the past leaders. Yet, it was precisely the dead weight of the uncriticized past that for thirty years had prevented Soviet leaders from attempting any radical changes.

In his address to the Plenum Chernenko endeavored to do the impossible by attempting to synthesize the past with the present, to combine stagnation with development, hopes for change with hopes for the preservation of the system without any change. In effect his speech abounded in contradictions. Instead of searching for real innovation, Chernenko contented himself with make-believe. The CC members were flabbergasted when he suggested that mobilization of reserves needed for the activation (the term used today is *acceleration*) of changes be achieved via the medium of the soviets (or councils). The soviets! Lenin used them for the benefit of the workers at the beginning of the century; subsequently, Stalin succeeded in turning that instrument of workers' authority into an authority without workers. And thirty years after Stalin, Chernenko suggested improving the very same institution, to use it against the working people's interests.

Unforeseen as his suggestion was, it was understandable in terms of his expected — already approved by the Politburo — election to the chairmanship of the Supreme Soviet a few days later. He was anxious to display his familiarity with and knowledge of the soviets, especially with his background of five years' work in the office of the Presidium of the Supreme Soviet.

It is hard to say whether Chernenko really believed that the soviets could provide the solution to the dilemmas of Soviet economic development. However, the CC members attending the Plenum did not believe that the soviets could provide a remedy for the all-enveloping inertia, incompetence, and bureaucracy. Chernenko did not understand that it is impossible to forge a new policy by means of outdated concepts and tools.

Chernenko's attempt to link the malfunctions of the society to the activity of the soviets was, despite its implausibility, not devoid of some logic. Because Chernenko held the soviets responsible for unsanitary conditions in cities, unheated apartments, deficiencies in industrial production, and rampant delinquency, it was not farfetched for him to seek a remedy in improving the soviets' work. In fact, this was totally unconvincing. His proposal to improve the economy was equally unconvincing. The remedies he suggested were based less on ideology than on an exhortation to idealism. He appealed to leaders to "forswear" any kind of weakness and to "revive" their concern for the state plan. He also tried to involve them in a peculiar form of "social contract": "Let us agree that for every failure, every incompetence and delay that occurs in the current year, the penalty will be harsher."[41]

Many years earlier Chernenko had conceived a serious social administration program that contained fresh ideas and courageous commitments. Now it was all forgotten and, instead, a nebulous program was being offered to salvage the economy: "Personal creative activity coupled with initiative; the ability to organize harmonious work and cooperation;

efficient working relations; solicitousness of the needs and interests of the workers."[42]

How would Chernenko of the 1970s have reacted to this kind of naive cant? His incisive common sense and predilection for activism would have doubtless been offended. In all probability his advanced age and illnesses had damaged his mental alertness over the intervening five or six years. Or perhaps the system itself, which was also old and sick, via its Party apparatus forced the general secretary to parrot its views. In fact, he seemed to be delivering a text dictated by others. Whenever Chernenko began to speak about administration, the words sounded as if they were someone else's; they hardly resembled the fresh ideas that abounded in his books. His former ideas now appeared in his speeches only sporadically, like furtive and timid shadows, in the form of suggestions to reduce and reorganize the administrative apparatus, to strive for higher productivity, to apply scientific methods for recording the amount of time wasted, and so on.[43]

Only once did Chernenko become animated, when he touched on the subject of school reform. He had been involved with a plan for such a reform for years, both prior to the Andropov era and later when he headed the school reform commission. He secretly hoped that this reform would become the point of departure for the realization of his dreams for reconstructing Soviet society. His ideas on moral upbringing, professional training, and instruction in the basics of industrial production portended fairly comprehensive change. That was to be his answer to Andropov's economic plans, which he believed were too narrow in scope and aim.

There had been innumerable school reforms previously in Soviet history, but none so comprehensive and radical as Chernenko's. In place of Lenin's slogan "To study, study, and study," Chernenko proposed "From school classroom to the working class." His reform was intended to be carried in two consecutive five-year plans. It was to provide millions of additional industrial workers, to acquaint school children with unskilled physical labor, to lower their expectations for intellectual accomplishment, and to reduce the opportunities to acquire higher education. In other words, the reform was meant to ensure maximal proletarianization in both cities and villages and thus to bring society closer to the ideal of a socialist revolution.

The reform also had a more immediate objective, namely, to obtain revenue from the exploitation of schoolchildren's labor. Chernenko recommended that "part of the money earned by school children be paid to the school collectives for their disposal." This was nothing other than camouflaged school fees. Chernenko's imagination soared when he envisaged that in the future school factories, plants, and farms would put the entire school system onto a basis of economic self-sufficiency. He declared: "We expect this reform to result in money and personnel savings. Each job created for the students of higher school grades must yield a concrete result—let it be modest but it must be real."[44] Those last words were dictated by circumspection. He knew that a great many of his high-minded plans and noble hopes were doomed to remain unimplemented, and eventually to be shelved. Yet, he continued to believe in the salutary effects of the school reform, even if it were only partially implemented. Hundreds of thousands of school graduates, after having acquired the necessary skills at school, would begin working in factories and plants that suffered seriously from labor shortages. This was why he decided to submit his reform project for nationwide debate. He judged the mood of the public as sufficiently anti-intellectual to accept his ideas readily. Besides, the shortage of labor was acute and rising.

School reform was indeed the key to deal with social problems of extraordinary complexity. Society was rife with disdain for unskilled labor. Parents were anxious to ensure higher status for their children, which entailed training them away from productive occupations. The chronic shortage of workers was conducive to low productivity while labor reserves were distributed unequally, with acute shortages in the central parts of the USSR and excess supply in the peripheral regions of the country.

No matter how paradoxical it may sound, this reform was unimplementable precisely because it was comprehensive. Social development in totalitarian systems cannot be effective because whatever is gained in speed is only lost in quality or vice versa. There is no way of reconciling this opposition or effecting multidimensional change. Adverse consequences of such a reform would be inevitable. Corruption would grow as many families would strive, by fair means or foul, to provide higher education for their children. Migration of young people from the center to border areas would also grow, for it would be easier to enroll in a university there. There would also be a flight of skilled labor from industry to services, which offer greater chances for amassing enough money to afford bribes to enroll one's children at a university. The quality of school education would be lowered if its purpose became training manpower for industry. Overall, this school reform could only lead to even graver social malaise and discontent. Pressures to achieve would lead to increased social inequality, which in turn would lower the nation's moral standards. Alcoholism and drug addiction would rise to even more alarming proportions, and social divisions would become even more pronounced.[45]

Chernenko refused to listen to the arguments of the opponents of this reform, regardless of the practicality of their considerations. Yet, the opponents were numerous enough to gain exposure for their views in the press. It turned out that despite his materialistic outlook, Chernenko remained idealistic insofar as he refused to be bound by existing realities.

Past master of political intrigue, Chernenko was expert in the technology of power yet unable to understand the art of administering society. His abstract knowledge and theories did not withstand contact with real life. He became confused and began to confuse others. In disorientation, he fell back on such meaningless formulas as "broader, more general and farther reaching ideas are needed more than ever."[46] Beyond the reiteration of such vague banalities of Lenin, Chernenko had nothing more to offer the Plenum. At this point Soviet society required the implementation of concrete and well-thought-out plans of action.

Notes

1. "The Leaders of the Communist Party and the Soviet State Take Farewell of Yuriy Vladimirovich Andropov," *Pravda*, February 12, 1984.
2. "Participants in the Plenum of the CC CPSU Take Farewell of Yuriy Vladimirovich Andropov," *Pravda*, February 14, 1984.
3. Reports from Moscow, *New York Times*, February 14–20, 1984.
4. Ilya Zemtsov, *Policy Dilemmas and the Struggle for Power in the Kremlin: The Andropov Period* (Fairfax: Hero Books, 1985), pp. 55–60.
5. Reports from Moscow, *New York Times*, February 14–20, 1984.
6. Ibid.
7. *Pravda*, March 13, 1984.
8. "Speech of Comrade K. U. Chernenko at a Meeting with Voters of the Kuybyshev Electoral District of the City of Moscow on March 2, 1984," *Pravda*, March 3, 1984.
9. "In the Central Committee of the CPSU," *Pravda*, March 7, 1984.
10. Section "Khronika" (Chronicle), *Novoye vremya*, nos. 22, 28 (1984).
11. *Leonid Ilich Brezhnev* (Moscow: Izd-vo politicheskoy literatury, 1981), pp. 158–73, 190–95.
12. "Pre-election Meeting of Workers. Meeting of the Voters with D. A. Kunaev, V. V. Shcherbitsky, V. V. Grishin, M. S. Solomentsev, N. A. Tikhonov, G. A. Aliev, M. S. Gorbachev, G. V. Romanov, A. A. Gromyko, D. T. Ustinov, E. A. Shevardnadze, V. I. Vorotnikov," *Pravda*, February 21–28, March 1–3, 1984.
13. Ibid.
14. "Plenum of the CC CPSU," *Pravda*, February 14, 1984.
15. *Partiynaya zhizn*, no. 5 (1984): 12.
16. "In The Central Committee of the CPSU," *Pravda*, March 7, 1984.
17. Ibid.
18. Ibid.
19. "In the Politburo of the CC CPSU," *Pravda*, February 25, 1984.
20. "Negotiations in the Kremlin," *Pravda*, March 13; "Meeting in Moscow," *Pravda*, March 21, 1984.

21. Section "Pis'ma i pozdravleniya" (Letters and greetings), *Pravda*, February 16–24, 1984.
22. Section "Vstrecha v Moskve" (Meeting in Moscow), *Pravda*, April 25, 27, 29, 1984.
23. "Session of the Presidium of the Supreme Soviet of the U.S.S.R.," *Pravda*, April 14, 1984.
24. "To Heroes of Orbiting the World and of Cooperation," *Pravda*, April 21, 1984.
25. "The Meeting of K. U. Chernenko with the Workers of the Moscow Metallurgical Plant 'Hammer and Sickle.' Speech of Comrade K. U. Chernenko," *Pravda*, April 30, 1984.
26. "M. S. Gorbachev, Speech at the Session of the Supreme Soviet of the U.S.S.R.," *Pravda*, April 12, 1984.
27. Ibid.
28. B. Sopel'nyak, "At a Distant Frontier Post," *Ogonek*, no. 22 (May 1984): 7.
29. K. U. Chernenko, *Avangardnaya rol' partii kommunistov* (The avant-garde role of the party of Communists) (Moscow: Izdanie Akademii Nauk SSSR, 1982), pp. 12–70.
30. Section "Khronika" (Chronicle) in *Pravda Vostoka* and *Sovet Uzbekistana*, July 15, 22, 24, 26, 29, 31, 1984.
31. *Izvestiya*, March 22, 1985.
32. *Voyenny entsiklopicheski slovar'* (Military encyclopedic dictionary) (Moscow: Izdanie Ministerstva oborony, 1983), p. 825.
33. Lead article, *Pravda Vostoka*, April 23, May 2, 1984.
34. Arkadiy Shevchenko, *Razryv s Moskvoy* (Breaking with Moscow) (New York: Liberty Publishing House, 1985); English translation, *Breaking with Moscow* (New York: Knopf, 1985).
35. Moscow radio, "First Program," April 14, 1984.
36. "Khronika" (Chronicle), *Krasnaya zvezda*, July 28, 1984.
37. "Khronika" (Chronicle), *Pravda*, April 19, 1984.
38. "Khronika" (Chronicle), *Zhurnalist*, no. 6 (1984).
39. Section "Pis'ma v redaktsiyu" (Letters to the editor), *Izvestiya*, September 6–14, 18–29, 1984.
40. "The Answer of K. U. Chernenko to the Leaders of the Socialist International," *Izvestiya*, April 5, 1984.
41. "Speech of Comrade K. U. Chernenko at the Plenum of the CC CPSU on April 10, 1984," *Izvestiya*, April 11, 1984.
42. *Izvestiya*, April 11, 1984.
43. E. Levin, "What Is Not Expected from the School Reform," *Byulleten' radio "Svoboda": materialy issledovatel'skogo otdela*, March 1, 1984.
44. See note 41, above.
45. See note 43, above.
46. See note 41, above.

7

The Brezhnev Era Replayed

> *New ideas adopted under the pressure of circumstances resemble false teeth; no matter how perfect they are, they never become part of the flesh.*

The Soviet people, as the Russian people before them, are always asking themselves two perennial questions: "What is to be done?" and "Who is to be blamed?" Chernenko could not evade these questions. He could not help being disturbed by the fact that his society, which had not long previously aspired to catch up with and surpass the West in development, found itself on the eve of the twenty-first century in a deep depression; nor could he help seeking the factors — or persons — responsible for the sorry state of affairs. Obviously, the malady originated with the economy, paralyzed by its central planning and lack of labor, and from there it spread to a social fabric pervaded by corruption, mendacity, and apathy. The country, larger than the combined territories of the United States and Canada — not counting the millions of square kilometers of virgin taiga and vast tundra — turned out to be incapable of feeding and clothing its own population.

The heroic period in Soviet history was over, replaced by a universal mood of apathy and cynicism. At worst it was an inconvenience that posed no threat to the regime. This is why Chernenko believed that dramatic appeals and exhortations to the people — à la Andropov — were superfluous. As a society, the Soviet Union retained an impressive degree of stability; it functioned and developed well, even if according to laws different from those applicable to free countries.

The Western view was that after a series of disasters in agriculture, the Soviet state was on the brink of disintegration. However, the shortfall in foodstuffs had an advantage for the regime because it distracted the masses, continually preoccupied with the daily pursuit of food, from more threatening concerns.

Without the benefit of domestic competition, Soviet industry remains inefficient and unprofitable. Yet, inefficiency has benefits for the regime because it guarantees employment, job security, and a concomitant satisfaction, and a nonnegligible consensus that goes with such satisfaction. Furthermore, low wages, difficult living conditions, and a poor quality of life should not be viewed as indications of poverty. In the closed society of the USSR living standards should be measured differently, in terms of relative rather than absolute magnitudes. Nor should corruption be considered an anomaly. It is rather intrinsic to the Communist principle of redistribution.

Thus, the social philosophy of Chernenko could be encapsulated in a formula: the Soviet system is not ideal, but it is the best there is. Such a formula obviated the need to subject the system to deep or radical change. It justified the preservation of its basic structural features and the limitation of change to seeking new ways to solve old problems. In this vein did Chernenko grapple with the perennial question, "What is to be done?"

Any changes in the economy he envisaged would be piecemeal, and of a technical rather than a fundamental nature (e.g. the use of new plan indicators or of new methods of planning). In addition, he wanted to split unwieldy industrial conglomerates into smaller units, more flexible to manage. In conformity with these assumptions, Chernenko assigned higher priority to indicators of efficiency that would reflect the profitability of industrial production. He also advocated contractual relationships between enterprises and a redistribution of the work force intended to increase the production of consumer goods.

Administrative reorganization is a common occurrence in the Soviet Union. Its necessity is espoused by each new leader. In this Chernenko was no exception. In contrast to Andropov, who had relied on administrative measures such as tightening up labor discipline, assigning personal responsibility for each task performance, and severely penalizing absenteeism, tardiness, and disruptions of work routines, Chernenko preferred to rely on incentives.

Chernenko realized that not one of the numerous past reforms had led to any meaningful improvement of the economy. This is why instead of talking about "reforms" he preferred to talk more vaguely of "improvements in management techniques." In view of the fact that the term *reform* evoked associations with the glories of the Revolutionary period, its rejection was not a chance matter. It indicated that Chernenko recognized the Soviet Union's lag behind the world's leading industrial powers. Chernenko considered it advantageous to save research and development expenditures by copying Western technologies instead of having the USSR conduct its own experimentation randomly and to learn by trial and error. The saved resources could be allocated to adapting Western technology to Soviet conditions.

Unattractive as Chernenko's strategy was in terms of "national pride," it *was* economical and it gave him time to try small variations on the old theme of the "extensive" development of society. Such tinkering entailed one serious danger: the continuous decline of productivity. But even with chronically low growth rates (about 2–3 percent), gradual progress was possible. What was required was to raise production to match the demand for consumer goods rather than allow it to fall below the levels at which discontent over the shortages could lead to an outbreak of public unrest. But in this respect Chernenko had no grounds for particular alarm. The Soviet people have a great capacity for adapting to hardships and deprivations, and the state has at its disposal considerable means of cushioning discontent by satisfying rudimentary needs of the citizens from time to time. Protracted exposure to indoctrination has made the people susceptible to manipulation and has largely paralyzed their capacity for resistance. Whenever incidents of spontaneous and unorganized resistance have occurred, the state has had an easy way to suppress them: feeding the people. In such instances food could be provided from strategic stockpiles that had been prepared for the event of the outbreak of war, or obtained in the West, which was more interested in selling food than considering its benefits to the Soviet regime. Thus, Chernenko had a clear conception of how to maintain an equilibrium between people's needs and systemic constraints. His whole scenario could be clearly discerned by studying the Soviet press.

Two consecutive reports of the Central Bureau of Statistics of the USSR reveal that under Chernenko (1984) the rates of economic growth were higher than under Andropov (1983),[1] and that under Andropov they had been higher than under Brezhnev. The sources of these data, however, were less economic than political. Each time the incumbency of the top Soviet leadership changes, the rates of growth, at least according to the reports, increase. The explanation is that each new leader needs to demonstrate his achievements in order to consolidate his position. This is something everyone (from directors of enterprises to ministers and chief administrators) understands. The intricate and confused accounting system allows them to doctor statistics without particular difficulty or great effort. The true figures can be easily transformed into what the Kremlin wants to hear, and the results can be strangely inconsistent. For example, the Ministry of Petroleum Industry reported that the target for supplies of crude oil to the state for the first six months of 1984 had been fulfilled by 100.3 percent. Unfortunately, another report indicated that the extraction of crude oil had fallen and barely reached 97 percent of what had been planned.[2]

Because Andropov wanted to be credited for progress in the area of transportation, the rates of growth in this sector for 1985 were reported to be higher than under Brezhnev. Chernenko's ambitions related to consumer goods; consequently, his "achievements" in this sector exceeded those of Andropov.[3]

If one were to judge from the Soviet press, the Soviet economy had been growing at a reasonably good pace over the years. But, if so, it would be incomprehensible why, for example, Andropov chose to make the following comment in a discussion with Moscow workers: "You are all familiar with the expression 'to correct the plan.' I must confess that I have never heard of correcting the plan targets upward. He who says, 'We have to correct,' means *lowering* a target."[4]

Chernenko would not make such admissions. The following comment illustrates his unflagging optimism:

> Our national economy has reached the level at which it is imperative to move to the track of intensification. You know that the Party is energetically supporting all initiatives aimed at increasing the efficiency of production, the growth of productivity. . . . The task is to structure production according to the latest word in science and technology, to introduce all that is new, advanced.[5]

It is hard to resist the conclusion that it is not worth looking to official statements for a hint about what the Soviet leaders are concerned about. One might rather try consulting the Soviet press. It should, however, be borne in mind that the Soviet press reports no more than a small fraction of what can be learned in the USSR via the grapevine; it concentrates rather on what the Party wants the people to know. Still, the economic situation of the country was too grave to allow total concealment of successive disasters. Hence, during 1984 the Soviet press was more outspoken than usual about failures in production and professional incompetence. Not merely sporadic reports but whole series of articles were devoted to these topics. The impression conveyed was that the issue was not isolated incidents of negligence or disorganization but mismanagement on a countrywide scale due to specific features of production organization. What was being revealed was a systematic failure to fulfill contracts and supply raw materials. Plants and factories were unable to produce the goods they were expected to produce and therefore were far from fulfilling state production plans. A chain reaction took place that paralyzed the whole economy.[6]

Chernenko, of course, was more cautious in his conclusions. At a July session of the Politburo he merely noted that "enterprises do nothing to increase productivity of labor, to reduce the costs of the production and to conserve resources."[7] The newspapers discussed the crisis more critically, and in much greater detail. It was reported that in many Soviet cities hundreds of millions of rubles' worth of imported equipment was lying idle and subject to irreversible damage while the construction of the plants was halted due to the lack of ministry funding to build them.[8] A devastating case cited was that of an electropower station inadvertently using vegetable oil as fuel, due to carelessness.[9]

For decades Soviet industry had developed extensively. Progress was assessed in terms of quantitative indicators: how many lathes or machines produced, how much coal or oil extracted, how much steel or cast iron turned out. Accordingly, the bulk of resources was allocated for construction of new plants and digging of new mines. As a consequence, funds for the renovation of existing enterprises, the modernization of equipment, and technological advancement were perennially scarce. This explains why, despite the overall growth of production, there were persistent and growing shortfalls in such production sectors as energy and equipment. A change in priorities entailing the redirection of funds from the construction of new enterprises to the modernization of existing ones appeared a logical solution. However, a number of factors militated against this solution. First, reconstruction did not benefit the enterprises. The price of domestic equipment grew two to three times faster than productivity. And, the equipment was in short supply. In 1984 only 3 percent of existing machinery was replaced by new machinery.[10] Pursued at this rate, modernization would take thirty-three years, which would mean that Soviet industry would be doomed to obsolescence for another third of a century.

Judging from official statistics, Soviet agriculture has been developing rapidly and successfully. Each year hundreds of thousands of tractors and cotton harvesters, and millions of tons of fertilizers were devoted to it. In light of this it may appear strange that grain harvest figures for 1984 were not published. Nevertheless, the total can be estimated indirectly: 195 million tons, a great deal short of the official target of 240 million tons. Soviet statistical reports nevertheless claimed, in keeping with their habit of stressing annual growth, that the 1984 harvest exceeded that of 1983.

Given the scale of the current calamity, it is not surprising that Soviet newspapers occasionally recall almost with nostalgia the time of individual land ownership prior to the establishment of state and collective farms. As the press expressed it, "There it is, the wall of China which separates the two worlds: your own land and that which is not yours. On your own land you see to it that whatever you plant flourishes."[11]

An additional serious agriculture-related problem much talked about in the Soviet Union is lack of labor. Twenty-three million people are employed on collective and state farms, i.e. three times as many as on U.S. farms. It can be therefore seen that the issue is not the lack of labor but, rather, the low degree of mechanization and the faulty organization of labor. The Soviet authorities do not wish to admit such a situation but they try to meet the crisis in agriculture by mobilizing help from the cities. Every year millions of workers and students, along with hundreds of thousands of vehicles and tractors, are dispatched to the countryside to help in bringing in the harvest and to deal with various agricultural crises. How do the rural areas respond? If one believes official reports, the supply of foodstuffs to the population increased under Chernenko. Here, the statistics are again self-contradictory: in the first half of 1984 the supply of meat and milk products is said to have increased by many billion rubles but the sales of these products were reported to fall short of plan targets. In order to "save" the sales plan, trade organizations stepped up the sale of vodka! As a result sales of alcoholic beverages were three times higher than the sales of foodstuffs.[12]

Although the shortage of food was mentioned rather sparingly and, at best, indirectly, shortages of consumer goods were commented on openly and even with humor (in fact, there was even an exhibition that featured a pavilion of goods unavailable on the market: scissors, forks, knives, frying pans, teapots, meat grinders, brushes—a sum total of 1,500 such items[13]).

One may seek to explain the disruptions in supply by the fact that the authorities were ultimately compelled to devote their efforts to improving living standards and the quality of life. Soviet newspapers do not corroborate this explanation. People were waiting many years for their turn on the list of applicants for an apartment. Transportation was getting worse, more disorganized, more overcrowded, more uncomfortable. The quality of services was hardly something to brag about, either; it was impossible to have repairs made in one's home, to have one's car repaired, and even to have one's laundry done on time. And in trade, sales personnel were either condescending or apathetic, offending customers by their indifference or rudeness.

As customary in the USSR, the blame was placed on "ill-intentioned" or "insufficiently conscious" citizens: embezzlers who steal from factories and plants, directors who appropriate state property, comptrollers and supervisors who accept bribes, and the large throngs of practitioners of the art of falsifying accounts, known in Russian as "whitewashing" (*ochkovtiratel'stvo*) or "write-ups" (*pripiski*).

A common practice was to retroactively "adjust" the planning targets to actual results. This created the illusion of well-being and order through statistical information that was distorted and that concealed the fact that production was in shambles. *Ochkovtiratel'stvo* was classified into several categories according to intent, e.g. to prove that the plan had been fulfilled, to gain bonuses, to cover up acts of theft, and to meet the demand of higher-ups for mendacious reporting. So much for the answer to "Who is to be blamed?"

Neither the Soviet press nor Chernenko was willing to undertake a fundamental analysis of these (and many other) defects of production. The reason was obvious: the malfunctions were due not to bad work of individual directors or managers but to the very principles on which the Soviet economy rested. The familiar phenomenon of permanently obstructed circulation of resources, the recurrent shortage of services and goods on the market, the wastefulness of managers, the producer's diktat over the consumer, the poor quality of industrial products, and even the falling growth rate are merely outward manifestations of systemic strain afflicting the entire Soviet economic organism. The economic realities in the USSR are very different from what the Soviet authorities would like to see. In the first place, there is much disorder caused by unauthorized, private production and decentralized decision making, not at state enterprises, in which the opposition of the Party members in the management has sufficed to prevent any decentralization, but on the black market, where no supply problems exist and where one can buy (or "get" in Soviet slang) anything to one's liking, from automobile parts, video recorders, and top-brand computers to chandeliers, good-quality tea, and popular books. It is a market well attuned to the existing demand. Rationality, practicality, and serious thinking about consumer needs reign there. Ugly and unfashionable junk ceased to be peddled there long ago.

The conventional notion of the Soviet black market conjures images of speculators noisily and obtrusively bustling around entrances to hotels and department stores, of dilettantish amateurs whose brash appearance marks them as shady characters. In fact, such operators are only the most visible segment of the black market and conceal its true essence. It has penetrated the system of state trade and has at its disposal broad underground channels of supply, such as resale of goods brought in from abroad and of goods obtained in the restricted government stores for the privileged elite. One does not simply enter the Soviet black market; first one has to make the necessary "connections." The network of interpersonal "connections" of this sort gives rise to yet another variety of the black market: the so-called gray market. Goods are exchanged for services there — and vice versa — on a barter basis, according to the principle "You scratch my back, I'll scratch yours."

Illegal commerce in the USSR has its own strategy, geography, and standard operating procedures. First-rate, top-quality goods are imported from abroad, primarily from the West but sometimes from Eastern Europe. The goods are purchased by officials who go abroad on business trips or are stationed abroad. They "import" items: for themselves, whatever they want; for sale, whatever brings the largest profits. In contrast to state commerce, the black market is remarkably responsive to demand. In the 1960s there was considerable demand for mohair goods and for transistor radios from Holland or Japan. Twenty years later, at the time Chernenko came to power, the greatest demand was for stereo systems, video recorders, and computers. Profits from the resale of such goods could run to ten times their cost.

The nature of goods determines with exactitude the division of labor. The principle of specialization, which does not find consistent application in the state economy, thrives in the black market. Sailors, chauffeurs, train conductors, and flight attendants bring in from abroad various "small-calibre" items that can be concealed in luggage or clothing, such as gold pins, silver chains, watches, bras, stockings, scarfs, the smuggling of which usually brings quite handsome payoffs. The turnover in such items runs to millions of rubles, with profits amounting to 80 to 90 percent, quite an incentive to run the risk of detection. If a smuggler is caught, he may be forbidden to travel abroad for many years, in some cases is jailed, and in any case is expelled from the Party. In much the same way working capital is accumulated by "moving" goods. In this case the "movement" goes not from West to East but in the reverse direction, from the USSR westward. Such trade involves antiques, rare coins, stamps, religious objects, including valuable icons and paintings, and so on. The profits on these run to four- and five-digit figures.[14]

Soviet officials of high standing, from the Ministry of Foreign Affairs or the Ministry of Trade for instance, or Party officials of corresponding levels tend to import radio and electronic equipment. The profit on the resale of two stereos can buy a two-room apartment in a Moscow housing cooperative.

Athletes, performing artists, and writers tend to prefer to deal in clothing, which can be bought abroad cheaply on sale or in discount stores. The profit from such items is not high, but little investment is required. Because Soviet tourists are allowed to take only a minimal amount of cash abroad with them, this type of "business" is an option for many of them.[15]

In contrast to government-set prices, the prices on the Soviet black market follow supply-and-demand shifts swiftly. When supply becomes excessive, prices fall or, as happens much more frequently, capital moves to areas of higher demand.

Goods can be sold via several channels. The simplest and most convenient (although not the most profitable) is the commission stores. Such operations are perfectly legal and the profit there comes from the difference between the prices of foreign goods (which the demand sets) and of domestic goods (which the state sets). However, commission stores do not deal with all types of goods, which is why the bulk of illegal imports of value are marketed via "black" channels, which again means "through connections." There exist apartments specially rented for the purpose of effecting such transactions. Usually, anonymity is observed; the not too frequent exceptions are "orders" placed in person. Profit is then higher, but so is the risk.

The most important operations of the black market take place on a solid business basis, conducted not directly but via a wide network of middlemen. Their ranks are recruited from all walks of society (depending on the nature and quality of goods dealt in), but mostly they come from among people of respectable standing: sedate pensioners, for example, or adroit journalists, clever jurists, members of the creative professions like writers, actors, or other artists — in short, from people seeking decent living standards above those affordable on their paltry overt incomes. To sell their merchandise, they spend much of their time in lines in commission stores or in traveling to places where the goods they can offer may be in demand, if they cannot sell them profitably at their workplaces.

The black market boldly and deeply infiltrates state commerce and state services. There exists in the USSR a broad range of goods and services for which a "supplementary" payment is charged. The latter consists of a form of "surcharge" that may amount to 100 percent or more, and it is imposed on the bulk of goods in high demand, e.g. fashionable clothing, good-quality footwear, furniture, household appliances, jewelry, and much more. The same holds true for state services. Whoever seeks attentive and conscientious service from a physician, a jurist, a hospital orderly, a barber, a locksmith, or taxi driver has to pay more than the official price. Needless to say, the same goes for special services, such as receiving an apartment ahead of one's turn, for buying a burial place (that, too, is a "business" in the USSR), for being assigned a hard-to-get hospital bed, and for placing a small child in a desirable nursery or an older child in a prestigious school.

There is no opprobrium attached to black market involvement. On the contrary, the population gives its full support to the black market because it is the only institution that provides tasty food, good-looking clothing, and attractive home furnishings. However, Soviet citizens can also be drawn into covert forms of black marketeering against their will when in stores and workshops they receive short shrift in value, weight, or measure. The possibilities for "ripping off" the ordinary Soviet consumer abound. Both meat and milk products are sold in frozen form, which adds to their weight; many goods are misclassified, with second-best being sold as top quality, and downright defective ones as certified quality. Many products are adulterated, e.g. milk is added to sour cream, or water to milk.

The primary reason for such deceptive practices has to do less with the quality of Soviet manufactures or with constant commodity shortages and more with the ways Soviet commerce is structured and regulated. The latter rests on a maze of minute legal regulations. Without swindling and circumventing these laws, it would be impossible to maintain the whole Soviet system of "income padding." The system ties the seller to the store manager to the director of the supply base and onward to the head of the division, and to the bosses in the ministry, and Party leadership on local, district, urban, republic, and national levels. Trade employees in the Soviet Union are linchpins within the chain of such mutual interdependence and exchange of mutual favors. Otherwise they could not make up for numerous deficiencies or receive (even if in insufficient quantities) goods they require to meet the turnover targets set for them by the state plan. Their participation in the system of corruption also provides them with considerable income. Even according to purposely lowered figures that can be found in Soviet statistical publications, income of trade personnel exceeds their official salaries by 60 percent.[16]

The state trade network as a whole is deeply immersed in the "gray market," i.e. in rare goods for hard-to-obtain services exchanges. This mechanism relieves many hardships and helps solve many problems of ordinary people. Thus, a kilogram of sausage may be exchanged for a theater ticket, a set of imported furniture or a car for "facilitating" the admission of a child into some institute; special attention from a teacher, a physician, or a medical orderly for a placement in a rest-and-recuperation facility or a reservation in a good hotel. Favors are reciprocal in this market: the person who has nothing to offer will receive nothing.

The basic principle can be summed up as "If you do something for me, I'll do something for you." Only on this basis can one participate in yet another of the illegal markets, the "pink market," in which rare goods and services (or entitlement priorities) restricted to the privileged class of Soviet officials can, through appropriate "bending" of the regulations, be obtained by others. In other words, this provides unauthorized "rear-door" entry into the network of restricted supply establishments catering only to the *nomenklatura*.

The black market, including its gray and pink branches, undermines the reglamentation and strict hierarchy in allocation of goods according to one's social status in the USSR. This is what made the Party leadership determined to fight the black market. The question was *how*. Chernenko learned from Andropov's failure that putting on the screws would not bring results. Nor did means of moral suasion, which Chernenko initially espoused, work either.

The illegal market could be overcome only by eliminating the causes responsible for its rise and development. However, the causes are interwoven into the warp and woof of the Soviet economy, inseparably linked to the persistent shortages and supply disruptions. After Chernenko, Gorbachev would try to take some concrete steps toward suppression of the illegal market through restructuring (*perestroika*) of economic management. But Chernenko was not prepared for this. At that stage the perennial question "What is to be done?" remained without an answer.

As noted above, Chernenko preferred tinkering to radical changes. He did not propose much that was novel, but one thing that was new in his approach was his scale of economic priorities. After becoming general secretary, he hastened to distance himself from the ideas of his predecessor. The Soviet bureaucracy, quick to sense which way the winds were blowing, adapted itself with alacrity to Chernenko's style. In July *Pravda* printed an article by the academician A. Aganbegyan under the significant title "Spreading One's Wings." Only a short while earlier, under Andropov, its author had been an ardent advocate of reforms. In this article, however, one would look in vain for any call to reform society. Instead, in transparent adaptation to Chernenko's ideas, all needs of industry were supposed to be met by purely technical changes, such as speeding up the development of machine construction, the systematic absorption of new technological systems, and the integration of research with production.[17]

Starting with Lenin, all Soviet leaders called for the application of the most advanced ideas to production. However, the first radical document actually envisaging scientific-technical transformation was adopted by the Soviet government only on August 23, 1983 — sixty-five years after the Revolution. A half year later (after the death of Andropov) it was already possible to obtain some notion of the degree of the futility of these measures. In any case, in 1984 the plan targets for "scientific-technological progress' were not reached. The *nomenklatura* had immediately grasped the difference between Andropov and Chernenko and performed accordingly. Nevertheless, the problem did not go away. In the USSR there are 1.4 million scientific workers, one-fourth of the world's scientists, and 31 million, or one-ninth of the country's population, have received either higher education or middle-level vocational education. Yet, the country is still not able to make a rational use of the professional competence and expertise thus amassed.[18] Only a small fraction of Soviet manufactures is based on new inventions. This is why Chernenko decided not to reject the economic experiment advocated by Andropov but directed that it be carried out in several ministries. The purpose of the experiment was to free enterprises from petty supervision and permit them to make economic decisions autonomously. Moreover, the enterprises were, within specific limits, permitted to set their scale of wages. Salaries of highly skilled workers were increased by 24 percent, and those of technical personnel by up to 50 percent. To lower production costs, frugal use of raw materials, fuel, and energy was called for. The number of indicators in the plans was reduced, and industries were granted the right to determine how to allocate their development funds. Rebuilding workshops and constructing facilities for workers were cited as examples of legitimate allocations.[19]

Chernenko had serious doubts about the methods of introducing such changes. It should be stressed that the experiment was limited to a small fraction of enterprises operating under the authority of five ministries. Chernenko understood well that particularly favorable conditions would be created for the experimenting enterprises, which meant that the usual practice of *pokazukha* (showing off bogus achievements) would be in operation. This characteristic is shared by all limited or selective experiments conducted within the Soviet system. The findings obtained under such conditions are not valid predictors of the future performance of industry as a whole.

Chernenko was skeptical about the readiness and ability of the ministries to engage in anything more than token "laboratory-scale" experiments. He knew that the ministries feared that genuine experimentation could hamper their rights and authority. In fact, any display of initiative on the part of the enterprises was immediately resisted by the ministries, and Chernenko lacked the resolve to rein in the latter.

Nevertheless, Chernenko tried to exploit the experiment to his political advantage. Both within the country and abroad he sought the image of a good administrator willing and able to manage the economy in an efficient manner. At the same time he sincerely believed in the possibility of a fruitful coexistence between central planning and individual initiative. This is the context within which one has to interpret his words about the necessity of mending the economic machinery, and about creating conditions in production that would encourage initiative among the workers.

Chernenko's views on this subject were confused, but two salient themes stood out. One was the granting to productive units (brigades, teams) some rights of autonomous decision making within their sphere of activity. The other theme was the legalization of some segments of the "second" or black market economy.

The idea of expanding the rights of labor collectives had begun to attain currency in the early 1970s, long before Chernenko's rule. Chernenko tried to add something new to the idea by grounding it in brigade labor on either a contractual or piecework basis. Teams granted the right to cultivate allotted plots of land as they deemed fit were established in agriculture. This resembled the corvée system widespread in Russia prior to emancipation of the serfs: part of the harvest would go to the owner of the land, and the remainder was divided among those who farmed it. The difference was that now the landowner was not a nobleman but the collective farm.

In the industrial brigades the scope of autonomy was even more limited. Their productivity, calculated on the basis of output, affected only work assignments and salaries. This system was by no means new either. It had been a basis for contractual work in pre-Revolutionary Russia and existed in the Soviet period in the 1950s, albeit illegally, in the form of groups of nonorganized (*shabashniki*) workers who would engage to undertake various construction or agricultural work assignments.

Brigade work turned out to be less useful in industry than in agriculture because in the former the segmentation of the production process into "pieces" to be assigned to separate collectives clashed with the view of the modern production process as one and indivisible. Furthermore, given the disruptions inherent in the highly centralized planning system, brigades in industry could work independently only when they were guaranteed a timely supply of raw materials, which was hardly always the case.

Chernenko had not the slightest intention of establishing a private sector within the Soviet economy; he was not proposing anything as daring as that. All he did propose was to transfer some of the "cottage industry" (mainly in the rural areas) to private individuals and to organize family enterprises to draw on the experience of private plot farming. However, as long as the existing system of government administration was left intact, the potential achievements of such private individuals were limited, if not totally undermined by rigid controls from above and rigid prices.

Chernenko's supporters were leery even about the timid steps toward liberalization of the economy he did undertake. They were afraid of losing their power and influence. Consequently, their reaction was swift in coming and merciless. A pretext was provided by the appearance, in the April issue of the journal *Voprosy istorii*, of an article in which one of the advocates of Andropov's reforms, referring to the success of Lenin's New Economic Policy (NEP), called for the authorization of private enterprises. The article was subsequently fiercely attacked in the journal *Kommunist*, an organ of the conservative Party bureaucracy. In effect, the editorial board of *Voprosy istorii* had to produce a humble recantation of views "that Communist theory has proven mistaken"[20] and to express contribution for having published them.

In the USSR the centralization of the economy has long been a basic feature of the socioeconomic system. The individual has been reduced to the role of a cog in the state machine, and the workplace to the role of a mere link in the chain of other workplaces, none of them having any autonomy, and all of them strictly supervised by the pertinent sectorial ministry. Such a system of production is justified on the philosophical level by the theory of the rational division of labor, and on the practical level by the single-minded devotion to building communism and the subordination of all individual interests to this goal. It is obvious that such a system produces extreme alienation of individuals from the tools and the fruits of their labor. But because such alienation helps subordinate individuals to the state and deprive them of any autonomy, it may be a consciously chosen goal rather than an incidental by-product of the system.

With the accession of Andropov to power, the situation began to change. Experience had shown beyond any doubt that the situation was economically dysfunctional. The state, which had assumed the functions of an organizing master, found itself in no position to plan production rationally, to provide adequate supplies, whether of food and consumer goods to the population or of raw materials to plants and factories, or finally, to establish a reliable system of accountability. Hence the idea of transferring some of the responsibilities for supply to the citizens and enterprises themselves.

Under such circumstances the attitude of the authorities toward private initiative and supplementary farming changed radically. As an outcome of that change, not only collective farms and state farms but also plants, factories, and even military units were encouraged to establish collective and even private farming to provide food for themselves. And as is so often the case, the system went to the other extreme, with sometimes quite ludicrous consequences. For example, city dwellers wishing to obtain consumer goods in short supply were called on to provide the state with foodstuffs as groups of urbanites in cooperatives received small parcels of land outside the city on which to grow fruits and vegetables.

Various forms of providing for one's own needs were encouraged, even though this meant diversification of labor, in contrast to the previous emphasis on specialization. Under Chernenko the new tendency of plants and factories to provide for their own needs gained some currency. Although specialized enterprises were noticeably more efficient and productive, under Soviet conditions of permanent supply disruptions they were often unprofitable. Consequently, plants and factories tended to turn to production along the lines of self-sufficiency, which led to production that was poorer in quality and more expensive but was at least guaranteed some continuity. Thus, while professing the policies of encouraging advanced science and technology and of intensifying production, Chernenko was really moving the country back to a natural economy and primitive forms of labor organization.

The plan of Andropov to move from a system of centralized, primarily administrative, controls over the economy to reliance on "automatic" market regulators of production was shelved. His successor attempted to bury these reforms by putting the brakes on the process of their implementation.

It would be incorrect to say that the new general secretary had no economic program of his own. Convinced as he was that the only threat to the regime lay in dissatisfaction stemming from continued shortages of foodstuffs and consumer goods, Chernenko resolved to make ideological concessions, i.e. to allow, within definite limits, a revival of private enterprise and small-scale industry. It can be doubted whether in the long run such a policy would have yielded the expected results, but in any case Chernenko's perspective was short-run. He felt duty bound to satisfy partially the hunger of citizenry for consumer goods and very much wanted to create the impression that under his leadership the country was finally emerging from economic crisis and overcoming stagnation. Basically, Chernenko lacked the imagination (or courage) for anything more than a version of a program espoused already by Kosygin. However, the time for such palliative reforms had passed; by the second half of the 1980s things were already too bad to be remediable by patchwork. Nothing short of establishing a new system of managing the economy would do.

Of course, after he became general secretary, Chernenko still retained the personality traits prerequisite for reaching the top of Soviet hierarchy, such as will power and goal-centeredness. Yet, aging had its impact on him, especially when the configuration of forces in the Kremlin exacted compromises. Due to these circumstances, his other qualities, like rigidity, unimaginativeness, and conservatism, which in the past he had somewhat to subdue or suppress, now became more evident in his behavior. Still, at times he would again evince interest in novel ideas and try to assess events and information without relying on the advice or expertise of others. At such times the contradictions between his intentions and his performance were apparent.

Chernenko believed in the Soviet Union and in its ingrained way of life. But he essentially understood by the latter the way of life of the Communist elite, marked as it was by sudden career ascents and sudden falls, and in general by the tortuous process of career making through constant, relentless intrigue. He also professed commitment to a number of abstract values, such as communism. The commitment was by no means phony; the best proof of this was that his entire career was carried out under the auspices of these values and could be readily justified either by quotations from the classics of Marxism-Leninism or by Party doctrine, as espoused in its official pronouncements. Like all other Soviet leaders, he had no other intellectual background on which to draw. Thus, when he decided to make his own contribution to the Program of the Soviet Communist Party (which both Brezhnev and Andropov had intended to revise, but did not succeed in doing), he found nothing more original to justify the need for a new program than various dicta of Lenin. In fact, the new CPSU Program was a matter of necessity, and hence there is no reason to attribute its undertaking to vanity on the part of Chernenko.

It was necessary to resolve the contradictions between numerous formulas of the old Program and the actual development of Soviet society. In the 1960s Khrushchev had promised the Soviet people that within twenty years the USSR would succeed in attaining communism and would surpass the countries of the West in the level and quality of life. This promise was enshrined in the old Program. In the second half of the 1980s it was obvious that the Soviet Union not only had failed to create a classless society but had also fallen short of its more modest goal of establishing "real," "developed," or "mature" socialism. To avoid deceiving Soviet citizens with not-to-be-fulfilled promises of constructing a Communist paradise anymore, Chernenko preferred to refrain from specific promises and schedules for the emergence of a "new society," and replaced them in the new Program by vague generalities. The decision was that the new Program should be concise "so that every Communist Party member could easily learn it and understand it." It was intended to "reflect not only the life which we have transformed but also our transformed political language, a language that is businesslike and precise in its formulations."[21]

Like his predecessors, Chernenko was compelled to stress that the Kremlin leadership was unfaltering in marching toward communism, but he carefully avoided any indication of how long this march might take. Instead, he asserted that there was no doubt that socialism would in the end win in the competition with the West, even though he admitted that capitalism still possessed considerable resources that were far from exhausted.[22] The latter idea had not previously been voiced by any Soviet leader. All of Chernenko's predecessors asserted that imperialism had lost all its vitality and was doomed. The cliché "rotting capitalism" was one of the staples of Communist propaganda, and it was bold on Chernenko's part to challenge it.

Chernenko also departed from the norm in that he avoided excessive cruelty in the prosecution of dissidents. Dissidents were arrested, as they had been throughout Soviet history, and were usually given terms of five to seven years in prison. Under Chernenko, though, there was no hysteria regarding the supposed threat the dissidents posed and no calls for their exemplary punishment. Penalties remained severe but were administered routinely. Occasional acts of mercy were also possible. Some prosecutions, already prepared under Andropov, were called off. Among those thus pardoned was a Moscow resident, Lina Tumanova, freed because she was suffering from cancer.[23] In all probability Chernenko realized that almost all dissidents of note were already in jail, prison camp, or psychiatric hospital; the situation hardly warranted a witch-hunt atmosphere. It was preferable to frighten those few still remaining at large by petty police harassment and thereby avoid arousing concern and protests in the West.

The emigration of Jews from the Soviet Union continued to decline, but this was due less to any malice on the part of Chernenko than to a policy (initiated by Brezhnev and continued by Andropov) of keeping the Jew as hostages to trade with the United States. The Jews were treated as an asset, valued not for what they contributed to the USSR but for whatever modern technology and advantageous contracts and credits could be obtained in exchange for them from the United States and Europe.

The Jewish issue was the only area in which the Soviet Union was ready to make genuine concessions to the West. The USSR was not willing to compromise with the West by giving up its expansionist aspirations or by liberalizing its domestic regime. Hence, trading the Jews in return for Washington's halting deployment of the SDI in space seemed an alluring prospect. Like a wise merchant taking good care of his merchandise, the Soviet leadership saw to it that the Zionist movement in the Soviet Union was not totally annihilated, so that something would remain to offer the West. But at the same time severe limits were imposed upon the movement and precautions were taken so that it would not get out of control. It suited the Soviet leaders' interests to preserve the Jewish national movement in a semistifled state. Such was its condition when Chernenko came to power. He himself had no particular interest in the matter. The anti-Zionist committee established by Andropov continued out of inertia, alternatively increasing and decreasing its public performances with press conferences, meetings, and announcements in the press. In the phraseology that the committee used and in the style and nature of its work, chauvinism would often appear along with implacable hostility toward Israel. Even so, such views tended to be expressed without foaming at the mouth and even without particular enthusiasm. They were part and parcel of the run-of-the-mill propaganda at which Chernenko had long ago proved himself a master.

Hundreds of thousands of Jews could be expected to emigrate from the USSR if given the opportunity. Chernenko could have quite possibly provided them with this opportunity, as his mentor Brezhnev had done, if the struggle of Soviet Jews for the right to emigrate had not raised the danger of setting a precedent for other peoples. Nevertheless, a tentative step was undertaken by Chernenko. On a visit to Washington, Soviet representatives (including the chairman of the State Bank, Vladimir Alkhimov, who was quite close to Chernenko) promised that 50,000 Jews would be permitted to leave if the United States granted the Soviet Union better trade terms and lifted restrictions previously imposed upon U.S.-Soviet trade. This was the hope of Chernenko, who cautiously elicited the support of world public opinion for such a trade-off. In the course of this campaign Soviet diplomats intimated to the chief rabbi of France, Moshe Sirat, that he would be welcome to visit Moscow. This was the first instance in a decade of an official Soviet invitation's being extended to a Jewish religious leader in a Western country. Moreover, immediately afterward, the Soviet press published two articles symptomatic of ideological "readjustment" to the new course. The first was by the head of the Military Political Administration, General A. Epishev, and the second by the head of a Central Committee department, L. Zamyatin. Both abstained from the usual attacks on Zionism, which theretofore had been routine.[24]

The manifestations of political "softness" on the part of Chernenko apparently evoked dissatisfaction in the Politburo, and a provocation was staged to discredit him: The former president of Israel, Efraim Katzir, who was attending an international biochemistry congress in Moscow, was held for several hours in a Leningrad police station after meeting with some Jewish refuseniks. Nevertheless, Chernenko's ideological tolerance grew out of quite pragmatic concerns. He tried to explore a *modus vivendi* with various segments of the Soviet population, for example, with the intelligentsia. Surprisingly, he began with the writers. His ascent to power took place after an ideological "frost," when the humanistic aspirations of part of Soviet literature and its interest in historic national roots and universal human values collided with the ideological closed-mindedness of Andropov.

Authors of "village prose" had been blacklisted for their "idealization of the past," and writers of "city prose" for "besmirching the present." Denied the right of self-expression, many talented fiction writers preferred not to publish at all. In effect, the literary scene was dominated by opportunistic purveyors of the Party line, such as Aleksandr Prokhanov and Yury Trinov, whose novels stressed the revival of "national consciousness," were obsessed with "security," and reveled in the superpower status of the USSR.[25] Such writers expected the new general secretary to treat them royally because they viewed him as an upholder of Soviet nationalism, chauvinism, and militarism. They had grounds for their hopes. In fact, Chernenko had been one of the framers of the harsh 1982 government decree imposing measures against literature and he had played a major role in preparing the Central Committee Plenum of 1983 intended to impose ideological "steadfastness."

But Chernenko had taken the hard-line tack when he was aspiring to top leadership and for that purpose needed to earn the reputation of a conservative or even a reactionary. Once he attained power, he had greater room for maneuver and could — to a certain extent — follow his own inclinations or, alternatively, the prevailing fashion with the aim of leaving a mark in history, exactly as Brezhnev had done. Following in Brezhnev's footsteps, Chernenko bestowed his favors on middle-of-the-road writers, who although not liberals, were pragmatists rather than rabid nationalists. The signal to them was given by *Pravda*, which opened its pages to their mildly nonconformist commentary and critiques.[26]

Chernenko's reassessment resulted also in the reversal of the pre-Andropov attitude toward the "village" and "city" prose writers. The reversal soon gained momentum when, on the occasion of the fiftieth anniversary of the establishment of the Union of Soviet Writers, 296 medals were awarded quite evenhandedly among the writers representing the most diverse tendencies, from the right to liberal, without any preference-indicating policy statement. This helped establish a temporary balance of literary forces.[27] Chernenko appreciated an opportunity to address a jubilee plenum of the writers' executive. He made it clear that he intended to follow carefully future developments in literature. He professed to be well aware that "this matter, of course, is complex and does not allow a superficial, simplistic approach. A proverb immediately comes to mind: 'Wherever you go, send your mind ahead first.'"[28]

It appears that Chernenko prepared his speech with care. As a recipient of the Lenin Prize, he very much wanted to impress his audience. Courting its favor, he wished to demonstrate his understanding of the creative process. This explains why he went out of his way to express a number of quite unusual (certainly for a Party leader) views. Noting that humanistic values do not gain by being expressed in pompous rhetoric either in rhyme or in prose, he concluded that poor writing discredits whatever contents it conveys. He even quoted the satirist Saltykov-Shchedrin to the effect that a mindless recital of commonplace truths can be called "art" only in derision.[29]

Chernenko had another opportunity to display his literary bent when, already terminally ill, he again presented awards to selected writers. On this occasion, too, he extolled the high art of writing. More openly than ever (perhaps feeling death approaching) he called on writers to offer him their support. Yet, the form of his appeal remained faithful to Communist vocabulary and ideology, for Chernenko said that the writers should be "dependable auxiliaries of the Party."[30]

The clash between Andropov's and Chernenko's approaches persisted after the latter's death in the form of a philosophical dilemma that surfaced in various political, social, and ideological guises. It also cropped up in the area of aesthetics. Chernenko had stood for a compromise between the liberal and conservative tendencies in Soviet literature: the former represented by writers who favored democratic ideals, and the latter by believers in strong authority that would be capable of bringing the final victory of communism by any means necessary. By rehabilitating such previously shunned "liberals" as Yury Bondarev, Viktor Astafyev, and Leonid Leonov, Chernenko sought to present the system (and himself) as having a human face. Yet, at the same time he understood that the system could not do without a readiness to use the fist. Accordingly, the highest award—that of Hero of Socialist Labor—was granted to conservatives or neo-Stalinists. Four of these, A. Ananyev, A. Ivanov, S. Sartakov, and M. Khromchenko, who, not by coincidence, were all of either Russian or Ukrainian nationality, received their gold medals from Chernenko personally, while the others received theirs from the Central Committee secretary, M. Zimyanin.

With similar ambivalence, based on the logic of attempting to satisfy both the general public's wishes and those of the Party apparat, Chernenko related to other arts. In early 1984 the famous Soviet director and founder of the Taganka Theater, Yury Lyubimov, was forced to continue his artistic career outside the USSR. When in London to stage a dramatic version of Dostoyevsky's *Crime and Punishment*, Lyubimov made some incautious remarks to the press. To a reporter from *The Times* he said that at age sixty-five he no longer had enough time to wait until Soviet bureaucrats began to understand what sort of a culture would be worthy of their country. Several days later he repeated the same comment on the BBC in Russian, which was bound to reach listeners in the Soviet Union. In the eyes of the Soviet authorities, this was a crime. Punishment was swift: Lyubimov was ousted from directorship of the Taganka Theater. Chernenko could not allow himself (nor would his associates allow him) to pass over Lyubimov's impertinent words in silence. It was one thing to make such utterances privately in one's own country (as Lyubimov had done on many occasions), but it was another thing to pronounce them publicly in the West.

Chernenko was forced to act by standards set by his predecessors, from Lenin to Andropov. Still, he managed to distance himself from his predecessor's methods, to be sure indirectly, in his own way. The new appointee as artistic director of the Taganka Theater was not, as one might have expected, an artistic as well as a political conformist but Anatoly Efros, a director of passionate involvement and considerable talent, like Lyubimov himself.

On the eve of Andropov's ascent to power, hopes had been voiced by segments of Soviet opinion that in the 1980s the Soviet Union might revert to a period of experimentation and relative freedom resembling that of the 1920s. The hopes were soon dashed. Andropov obviously felt more comfortable with a mood like that of the 1930s: one of strict enforcement of order and of reliance on naked power and state coercion. When Chernenko succeeded Andropov, he did not dispel such hopes but also did nothing to encourage them. It looked as if society was stranded halfway between past and future while being bombarded by a barrage of sundry Party and government resolutions. There was no consistency or inner logic to these apart from Chernenko's ambition to show that his leadership meant action.

One of the first such resolutions, passed in April 1984, was a carryover from Andropov's brief rule, carried forward through sheer force of inertia. The resolution castigated industry for failures to meet targets, the poor quality of goods produced, and the lack of "scientific organization of work." However, the remedies suggested were already those of Chernenko: improved organization and socialist competition. After an earlier and futile attempt to spur productivity through activation of local soviets, Chernenko this time tried to achieve the same goal—again with no greater success—by resorting to the unpopular and obviously ineffectual method of "socialist competition."

The call in the same resolution for mass political organization work to help increase productivity and lower the costs of production was also a mere restatement of an approach advocated previously.[31] Attempts to reconstruct the national economy via slogans and exhortations were a constant (and futile) staple of Soviet history. Recent examples of this genre appeared in Soviet newspapers in May 1984, which was a busy month for Chernenko. One resolution he proposed dealt with improvement of education for labor; another with increasing teachers' salaries. A third supplemented the former two by dealing with upgrading the qualifications of educational personnel.[32] All three resolutions related to the same cluster of educational problems and were meant to concretize Chernenko's school-reform project.

Resolutions in the month of June also pertained to intellectual matters. One dealt with improving the quality of regional and urban newspapers. Chernenko apparently decided that it was time to do something about the Soviet press's lack of interest for its readers, failing to pay due attention to local events and problems, dealing too superficially and schematically with people's personal concerns, and ignoring letters from its readers.[33] After receiving a point-by-point castigation for its numerous lapses, the press was presented with a point-by-point enumeration of its duties for the next decade.

In terms of their scope and imagination, these initiatives of Chernenko's could be compared with the innovations of Andropov, but there was a difference. Both wanted to transform society: Andropov by reorganizing the economy; Chernenko by revising ideology. Both schemes were utopian (if their authors were sincere) because neither economic nor ideological change could possibly suffice to change the fundamental features of Soviet society.

To yield real results, reforms would have to begin with change in the social and, even more, political realms. Nothing less could possibly lead to stimulation of popular initiative and work motivation. Yet, the social and political status quo quite suited both Andropov and Chernenko. Neither could imagine himself operating under radically changed conditions, just as neither wished to contemplate new conditions that would make him superfluous. Such an attitude constrained Chernenko to tinkering rather than transforming, essentially to marking time in acquiescence to the protracted stagnation of the country.

In July Chernenko spearheaded a resolution concerning improving the work of young people.[34] Once again the familiar rhetoric appeared: "upgrade," "improve," "increase," "raise," and the like. This time, however, behind the rhetoric one could sense Chernenko's genuine concern for the young generation. A particular problem that troubled him, and the whole Soviet leadership as well, was how to attract young people to industry. In fact, the potential was enormous. There were 10 million pupils in the upper classes of high school, and more than 1 million college and university students who could join summer work detachments, in addition to 1 million who had completed their secondary schooling without continuing in institutes of higher education. What stood in the way of the exploitation of this huge pool of human resources was merely bureaucratic inefficiency and the lack of motivation of the young themselves, primarily their lack of motivation to work.

The resolution tactfully refrained from addressing this latter point. Nor did it mention the adverse impacts of official ideology and reigning social conditions on the young: cynicism, apathy, boredom, alcoholism, and antisocial behavior. Instead, the resolution focused on the difficulties encountered in Komsomol work, and criticized its methods and its inability to learn, to generate feedback and to react to it, and to carry out resolutions of its superordinate bodies.

What Chernenko was seeking were palliative solutions to real problems. Hence his bent for excoriation and exhortation. There was one partial exception, though, regarding the leisure activities of Soviet youth. There was considerable moralizing in his approach and he partly attributed their unacceptable behavior to "imitation of Western styles" and "apoliticality." However, his resolution also referred to the breakdown of Soviet values, to the prevailing careerism, and to lack of idealism and principle. He bitterly castigated the youth subculture that existed beyond the pale of officially endorsed values. Chernenko's resolution urged the inculcation in youth of class consciousness, albeit without acknowledging the fact that a certain form of class consciousness, even if different from the one officially recommended, had already existed in the young generation's ranks for some time.

The point is that social stratification had developed not only in adult Soviet society but among the youth as well. Quite contrasting groups emerged: a small privileged stratum and a very large mass of young people with a very restricted range of career and life-style options. The moral standards of the two groups were no less contrasting than their material conditions. Youths from elite Communist homes were pleasure seekers, determined to enjoy their considerable material resources, whereas youths from ordinary backgrounds had no choice but to replicate the gray, hopeless lives of their parents spent in unrewarding labor performed under coercion.

Chernenko understood that such stratification of youth posed a threat to the body as well as the spirit of the Party in which the under-forty membership had been growing rapidly and by 1984 constituted 30 percent.[35] The percentage was bound to increase. A generational change was inevitably taking place in the Soviet ruling class, with the effect that a reevaluation of the very foundations of both domestic and foreign Soviet policy could no longer be deferred.

Notes

1. "Reports of the Central Statistics Bureau," *Pravda*, January 29, July 22, 1984.
2. Ibid.
3. Ibid.
4. *Partiynaya zhizn*, no. 4 (1982): 7.
5. *Kommunist vooruzhennykh sil*, no. 12 (1984): 8.
6. "Once Again on the Right to Fly," *Izvestiya*, July 1, 1984; V. Minaev, "Obligations," *Pravda*, August 22, 1984.
7. "In the Politburo of the CC CPSU," *Izvestiya*, July 10, 1984.
8. "Millions with Any Return," *Pravda*, July 17, 1984.
9. V. Prokhorov, "Kilowatts from Vegetable Oil," *Pravda*, August 7, 1984, p. 3.
10. A. Aganbegyan, "Spreading One's Wings," *Pravda*, July 14, 1984, p. 2.
11. A. Roslyakov, "Someone Else's and One's Own," *Novy mir*, no. 1 (1984): 179.
12. "A Drama in Bechevinka," *Izvestiya*, July 12, 1984.
13. Iya Meskhi, "Attack on the Deficit," *Ogonek*, no. 33 (1984): 13.
14. See Galina Belenkova and Aleksandr Shokhin, "Cherni rynok: lyudi, veshchi, fakty" (Black market, the people, items, facts), *Ogonek*, no. 36 (September 1987): 6–9.
15. Ibid.
16. Ibid.
17. Aganbegyan, "Spreading One's Wings."
18. "Progress Begins with Science," *Izvestiya*, July 19, 1984; V. Vrublevsky, "The Labor Potential of the Society of Developed Socialism," *Pravda*, August 17, 1984, pp. 2–3.
19. *Planovoe khozyaystvo*, no. 11 (1984): 58.
20. *Voprosy istorii*, no. 4 (1984).
21. "In the CC of the CPSU," *Pravda*, April 26, 1984.
22. Ibid.
23. *Vesti iz SSSR* (1984): 22–23.
24. Army General A. Epishev, "Ideological Aggression of Imperialism," *Izvestiya*, July 10, 1984; "Dead Ends of Confrontation and the Horizons of Cooperation," *Literaturnaya gazeta*, November 28, 1984.
25. Aleksandr Prokhanov, *And Here Comes the Wind* (novel), *Znamya*, no. 10 (1984): 16; Yuriy Trinov, "Parade," *Radyank'ska Ukraina*, January 8–12, 1985.
26. Yevgeniy Sidorov, "Sharpness in View," *Pravda*, March 19, 1984.
27. See articles by Sergey Yuryenen in Radio "Svoboda," materialy issledovatel'skogo otdela (RFE-RL), April 30, November 30, 1984.
28. K. U. Chernenko, *Utverzhdat' pravdu zhizni, vysokie idealy sotsializma* (To

confirm the truth of life, the high ideals of socialism) (Moscow: Izd-vo politicheskoi literatury, 1984), p. 5.

29. Ibid., pp. 13–14.
30. "Awarding the Highest Honor of the Country. Speech of Comrade K. U. Chernenko," *Literaturnaya gazeta*, January 1, 1985.
31. "In the CC of the CPSU," *Pravda*, April 22, 1984.
32. "In the Central Committee of the CPSU and the Council of Ministers of the USSR," *Pravda*, May 4, 1984; "In the Central Committee of the CPSU and the Council of Ministers of the USSR," ibid., May 15, 1984; "In the Central Committee of the CPSU and the Council of Ministers of the USSR," ibid., May 23, 1984.
33. "In the CC of the CPSU," *Pravda*, June 21, 1984.
34. "In the CC of the CPSU. On Further Improving the Party Leadership of the Komsomol and Increasing Its Role in Communist Upbringing," *Pravda*, July 7, 1984.
35. "The Party and Youth: New Problems and Old Solutions," Byulleten' Radio "Svoboda," June 16, 1984. Also, *Partiynaya zhizn*, no. 14 (1984): 16; ibid., no. 15 (1984): 25.

8

The Future Can Be Known from the Past

The future is but one variation on the theme of the past.

It is not possible to trace precisely the influence of domestic conditions on Soviet foreign policy. Still, a plausible hypothesis can be formulated that the less stable a position of the leadership, the more openings it seeks for a detente with the West. Nonetheless, repair of the Soviet economy and the Kremlin's global aims remain variables to be considered in their own right. It can be observed that the two variables revolve around a constancy: the concept of hostile capitalist encirclement. This view, handy as a legitimizing device, serves also as the last line of defense resorted to by Soviet leaders when they find themselves in adversity. Like his predecessors, Chernenko invoked this concept as well.

In the first few months of the new general secretary's rule the Soviet press was gripped by a major war psychosis verging on hysteria. The mood was transmitted to television, which became even more hostile and threatening. Almost every evening the nation's screens showed fierce soldiers with machine guns across their chests, treading the burned earth of El Salvador, Nicaragua, and Angola or marching across NATO territory accompanied by the roar of planes and the noise of endless columns of tanks. The images were calculated to evoke associations with the fascist onslaught of World War II. The resemblance was usually hinted subtly and indirectly in the accompanying commentary, but sometimes was stated plainly and explicitly. In the press the analogy could, for example, be "hinted" by the following rhetorical question: "How much difference is there between Operation Barbarossa and the anti-Bolshevik crusades of the two statesmen overwhelmed by delusions of their grandeur?" Why *two* statesmen? The first was clearly the fiendish Hitler, and the second—

this point was left to be guessed — was Reagan. For the first time the Soviet press singled out the person of the U.S. president as its enemy number one.

Chernenko himself could not resist the temptation of comparing U.S. imperialism to fascism of bygone days. He once said: "The war of 1941 will not happen again. Any aggressor will immediately be handsomely recompensed by our deadly retaliation."[1] But in fact, Chernenko's attitude toward the United States was ambivalent. Like other Soviet leaders, he had mixed feelings of fear and respect. His fear had its source in Soviet propaganda itself, which defined the United States as the implacable enemy of his country. There is something truly amazing about the ways Communist concepts are formed. Propagandistic mendacity victimizes not only its audience but also its stage managers; not only the masses but also the authorities. No wonder that Chernenko believed in the U.S. military threat while at the same time respecting the industrial prowess of the United States and its strength. No wonder that at the same time he was anxious to reach a detente and feared its consequences, that he blamed the United States for everything conceivable, including a new cold war and the polarization between capitalism and socialism.

For all the disagreements between the Soviet masses and Soviet authorities, their respective attitudes toward the United States are essentially similar. The common people may not believe all biased and mendacious information of the Soviet press, but they tend to be swayed by visual propaganda: the photographs and photomontages. Press photographs of multitudes of homeless or unemployed on the streets of New York and Washington do have an impact upon the Soviet public, an impact that amounts to a popular critique of capitalist society. Manifestations of panic, such as the fright-seized children imploring, "Daddy, kill the Yankees!" (as revealed in letters to the editor) abound and grow in intensity. But adults are also vulnerable. When hail or floods destroy crops, there typically appear some who ask in all innocence whether the Americans were behind the calamity, whether a sort of meteorological warfare was involved.

Such manifestations are perfectly understandable. Soviet citizens have been trained to fear and hate the United States all their lives. If anything, more intriguing is the fact that so much common sense has yet prevailed. The question is often asked, signaling a danger for the authorities, How is it that a country that supposedly has been disintegrating for decades has produced the most advanced technology, the best satellites and airplanes? Soviet propaganda has not succeeded in distorting all the truth on this subject. In films and on television Soviet viewers see American slums, but they also see urban Americans appearing cheerful, elegantly dressed, enterprising, and full of vitality. Doubt grips the Soviet minds as attraction to and envy of the enigmatic but nevertheless appealing free world generate skepticism in regard to Soviet propaganda as a whole.

Of course, Chernenko was not inclined at all to pose any such embarrassing questions. He was mentally shielded from questioning his society by an ideology that promised him acceptable and satisfactory answers to all existing questions. But he was far from certain about the advisability and utility of encouraging anti-American sentiment. One should not overestimate Chernenko in this regard. He did not have a particular affinity for detente because he could not transcend the Soviet preconceptions about the bipolarity of the world and the inevitability of the ultimate victory of Communism. Nor could he be expected to respect the interests of other states or even take them into consideration. Consequently, like all other Kremlin leaders, he was deeply distrustful of the world beyond, which was different from the Soviet world and refused to bow to Soviet dictates. Yet, he tended to draw different conclusions from these preconceptions than did other Soviet leaders.

His predecessors, including Andropov, had been gripped by fear of the West to the point of being willing to go to the brink in confrontation with it. They approached the brink in the hope of jumping across it, by arming themselves to the teeth and thus becoming invulnerable. Yet, in trying to frighten the West, the Soviet leaders frightened themselves, particularly when they realized their potential vulnerability to the possible deployment of the U.S. Strategic Defense Initiative (SDI). This is why Chernenko felt compelled to change the Soviet stance: fear of the free world convinced him of the necessity to retreat. This was the source of the new direction of Soviet foreign policy that was immediately hailed in the West.

The Western pundits were quick to notice the verbal restraint of Chernenko, but failed to recognize that the change was less of substance than of style and tone. The West never viewed Chernenko as a "liberal," but it did perceive him as an energetic and pragmatic statesman, perhaps mainly because of the mere fact that he had won over other contestants for the top seat of power. And—this went without saying—a statesman with such qualities deserved to be shown goodwill; it was worth seeking mutual understanding with him. Hence, the U.S. president invited Chernenko for a summit.

The general secretary did not reject the president's invitation outright, but neither could he accept it. He was ailing and in no condition to undertake an exhausting trip, not to mention the fact that he felt ill-prepared for confronting Reagan. He had been barely initiated into the treacherous whirlpool of international politics with its intricate problematics and elaborate diplomatic etiquette, and Gromyko was in no hurry to come to his aid. Until the death of Andropov, the minister of foreign affairs had not allowed himself to reveal any views or sympathies of his own but would only unflaggingly execute the instructions of others — of the general secretary or the Politburo, as the case might have been. Gromyko respected only power, anyone's power. Chernenko, despite his top rank noticeably lacked power, so Gromyko began for the first time to seek power of his own. In effect, Soviet policy toward the United States pursued under Chernenko resembled an out-of-step waltz, the dancing partners being the general secretary and the foreign minister, each following a different beat.

Moscow announced the interest of the general secretary in meeting with the president, perhaps in Vienna or Helsinki, but then the proposal was retracted. Chernenko found himself inhibited by conflicting considerations. Ustinov warned that the class enemy was not to be trusted, and Gromyko urged that the summit meeting be postponed until after the American elections so as to avoid the danger of dealing with a lame-duck president. Chernenko vividly recalled the demise of the previous detente and had no desire for an armed East-West confrontation and consequent mutual destruction. However, he needed to reconcile the factional interests and positions competing in the Kremlin. In the absence of better solutions, he continued Andropov's "paper diplomacy," consisting of exchanging as many documents, letters, announcements, and press reports as possible.

Chernenko did not intend to revert to the customary Soviet siege mentality. Such an attitude appeared in his writings either unconsciously or as a sop to comfort his more militant Politburo colleagues. In many of his statements Chernenko professed his intention of defending peace, of reducing international tension and the danger of war. The statements had the air of conviction. The only problem with them was that they left unclear how they could be reconciled with well-known fundamentals of the official Soviet doctrine, primarily with the reliance of that doctrine on violence. Still, Chernenko avoided anything that could be interpreted as threats, was careful in his phrasing, and in effect sounded more moderate than his foreign minister.

A good example of Chernenko's moderation is a reply he gave to an American journalist. After the U.S. Congress refused to fund the testing of antisatellite weapons, Chernenko commented, "Either the militarization of space will be halted or it will be a terrible danger for the entire humanity."[2] Thereupon he proceeded to explain the Soviet position. The arguments he used were, of course, not new. They had often been heard from other Soviet leaders and were enshrined in official documents.

However, the tone Chernenko chose was strikingly mild. Without any righteous and indignant rhetoric, he stressed that the USSR had unilaterally undertaken not to introduce nuclear weapons into space. Of course, the moratorium announced by Chernenko did not solve the dilemmas posed at the Geneva Conference because he (and on this point he was in consensus with his Politburo colleagues) was not prepared to give up his bid to "catch up with and surpass" the United States in the arms race. Accordingly, Chernenko was willing to negotiate, with the strategy of conceding as little as possible and gaining as much as possible,[3] and he pursued the goal without resorting to threats and insults.

No less moderate (by Soviet standards) was the interview intended for domestic consumption that Chernenko gave to a correspondent of *Pravda*. Therein he commented on the meeting in London of the leaders of the major Western countries.[4] The irony to which Chernenko resorted was sharp, at times even biting ("One circumstance is quite clear, the American press is literally humming with it, that the whole thing was geared to the presidential elections in the United States"). But neither his sarcasm nor his occasional invective ("smoke screen . . . concealment . . . transformation of the territory . . . of the Western countries into a launching pad") exceeded the limits acceptable in diplomatic discourse.

The press reports of the Ministry of Foreign Affairs, Gromyko's fief, projected quite a different tone. There scorn prevailed, as in the following example: "Under the diktat of the United States the NATO countries are rejecting the principle of refraining from the use of force, are turning their backs on the anti-Nazi alliance as it existed during the War, and are elevating sabre rattling to the status of a norm governing international relations."[5]

Gromyko finally had the opportunity of a lifetime to speak with a voice of his own. His voice turned out to pretty much resemble Stalin's voice, one that was devoid of mollifying intonations and did not raise the concomitant hopes, or rather illusions, of peaceful coexistence that had been heard during the Khrushchev and Brezhnev periods. Scarcely had Chernenko begun speaking about the necessity of halting the arms race (in his encounters with Genscher and Mitterrand) when Gromyko interjected that calls for the renewal of negotiations on this matter could not be taken seriously, that there should be no illusions: the Cold War was back again.

At times one could almost suspect that the Kremlin was playing the good-cop, bad-cop game common in police interrogations: Chernenko as the peacemaker and Gromyko as the militarist, one of an extremist bent at that. But time proved that this was no game: the general secretary genuinely believed in the prospect of successful negotiations with the

West. He was desirous of continuing disarmament talks and did not object to an agreement providing for a ban on the production of chemical weapons. He was even prepared to make concessions on verification of already-signed agreements. He did not object to "exchanges of information and consultations . . . whenever clarification would be required." Furthermore, going beyond concessions already made, he promised "to find other forms of verification [to be applied] whenever necessary."[6]

The seriousness of Chernenko's proposals was not generally doubted. He was listened to with interest and treated with respect in the European capitals and Washington. Doubts about the merits of his ideas appeared only in Moscow, where criticism was voiced in the Politburo (perhaps by Ustinov and certainly by Gromyko).

On the pages of *Pravda* there appeared an article, evidently "inspired" by a highly placed opponent of Chernenko and signed by the Soviet armed forces' representative at the Geneva talks, Major General Lebedev. The article contained an attack on verification of arms control agreements. The objections cited were familiar: in the guise of verification the West intended to engage in espionage on Soviet territory.

In contrast to Chernenko, Gromyko declared that verification should be limited to devices "deployed on land, in the ocean, and in space and not include on-the-spot verification."[7] This was rather curious. The whole manner of conduct of the minister of foreign affairs was inexplicable. He was receiving visitors not in his own office but in the Kremlin, which was the prerogative of the general secretary, with rare exceptions being made for the hosting of the visitors by the chairman of the Council of Ministers, but never by a mere minister. To make matters more curious, the resplendent Yekaterininsky Hall (Hall of Catherine) was placed at Gromyko's disposal. And perhaps most surprising of all, when the short-of-breath Chernenko appeared in the Kremlin, Gromyko would show no restraint in unceremoniously interrupting him, as if to demonstrate that it was he rather than the general secretary who was the Soviet Union's boss.

Was Gromyko really the boss? The answer is by no means a simple no or yes but rather no and yes. No, Gromyko was not the boss; since the death of Stalin no single man has really been the boss because the Politburo has ruled collectively. The role of the general secretary is to set basic policy guidelines and occasionally to offer his own ideas, while the Party and diplomatic bureaucracies provide their rationales and elaborations. Furthermore, initiatives originate not with the general secretary but with aides, consultants, advisers, and the International Department of the Central Committee of the CPSU, which is staffed with professional political scientists and philosophers. Decision making and initiative taking in the Politburo have roughly followed this model. But idiosyncratic features of each successive general secretary, the way he was chosen, the circumstances surrounding his selection, the nature and scope of his power base, his age, and the state of his health, do make a difference and account for certain variations within this model's general assumptions.

With these qualifications, the general tendency is that as a rule a figure acceptable to all sides is raised to the top Party post. He is the one who suits best all or at least most of the Politburo members. Exceptions to this rule were the first Soviet leader, Lenin, and the present one, Gorbachev. Both came to power on the crest of a social change revolutionary in character; the former, at the Communist society's inception, the latter, at a point of its ebb and decline. Their respective ascents to the pinnacle of power were due to their personal qualities and surrounding circumstances, but not to the favor of others in the Party. This factor accounted for their comparatively greater say versus others in their entourage. All the other Party leaders — Stalin, Khrushchev, Brezhnev, Andropov, and Chernenko — owed their posts to the Politburo. Their incumbencies had unimpressive beginnings. Their initial role was to execute faithfully the will of the Party apparat. Only after a lapse of time could they begin to engage in political maneuvering of their own, and thus to try to alter the existing balance of forces.

The whole pattern was set by Stalin and since then it has been replicated by each general secretary. The pattern leaves no room for improvisation. It can be described in terms of several successive stages. As mentioned in chapter 4, first comes the period of transition, during which the Politburo dominates. The general secretary's options are then limited both by his supporters, who impose their will on him, and by his opponents, who push him toward decisions that are to their advantage. The general secretary therefore consolidates his position by playing off various factions in the Politburo against one another. The next stage arrives when the general secretary finds himself in a position to encourage some while curbing others. Then he begins to oust from the Politburo its most active and dynamic members. He first relies on his opponents to get rid of his supporters, who thereby become his first victims. He forms a temporary alliance with his enemies that enables him to co-opt into the Politburo new members totally dependent on him. The third stage follows: a balance of forces in the Politburo. It cannot last long because the new *co-optees* into the Politburo gradually begin to form a stable majority on the general secretary's side. They can then get rid of those who opposed his enthronement and thus establish a lasting consensus within the ruling clique. This is already the fourth stage: the clear primacy of the general secretary over others in the Politburo.

The general secretary tends to be busiest at the fourth stage, bringing his various plans and projects into realization. Nevertheless, tranquility in the Politburo is ephemeral as a new crisis gradually mounts. It breaks when the general secretary's hitherto subservient colleagues begin to feel they are his full-fledged partners. The Politburo does not tolerate equality. A new operation has then to be undertaken by the general secretary: reconstruction of the Politburo's membership. This happens again and again; inequality in the Politburo gives way to a temporary equality, which then proceeds to an even greater inequality. A general secretary who refuses to follow this pattern is bound to lose power.

Several Soviet rulers, e.g. Stalin, Khrushchev, and Brezhnev, went through all the ups and downs of this political teeter-totter. Andropov did not rule long enough to go through all its stages. Furthermore, he deviated from the rules somewhat: first, by his nonconventional ascent to power, over the head of the Party apparat and contrary to its will; second, by trying to skip the intermediate stages; and finally, by his failure to complete the cycle before his death. Because of the last point, he remained an enigma, a who-knows-what-he-might-have-become. Chernenko's incumbency was also somewhat unusual. At its very inception there appeared factors that had inhibited his predecessors only at the close of their careers: illness and physical incapacitation. From the outset it was clear that Chernenko had no chance to reach the consensus stage within the Politburo, that he did not have enough time. A number of ailments, including emphysema and heart disease, befell him and aggravated his problems. Consequently, his strategy became not so much how to play power games but rather how to survive until the next Politburo meeting.

Each effort Chernenko undertook was inimical to his health: he could not attend long meetings and yet convened a great many of them. He could not receive delegations from abroad and yet hosted numerous receptions. He could not deliver long speeches and public addresses and yet continued to deliver them. He had no strength to come to work day after day and yet stayed in his office until late in the evening. As a result, his health was deteriorating. He seemed to be wanting to challenge nature, to demonstrate to both himself and others his capacity for continued accomplishments, but he was thereby only straining himself more and more and losing whatever residual strength he had. His public appearances were pathetic. When he finally realized that his time for action had passed, the symbols of power became more important to him than power itself. At this point he no longer attempted to fight the Politburo but contented himself with what it agreed to give him in return: outward signs of respect.

For a while the members of the Politburo took delight in their independence and their privileges, of which they had never before had so many. They did not unduly concern themselves with Chernenko, openly mocking him and his weaknesses. But their satisfaction lasted only until they confronted the task of choosing a new leader. Thereupon it became clear that each Politburo member was trying to consolidate his power and increase his rights at the expense of the others. The consequence was that too much independence in effect meant very little independence. This circumstance forced them to seek means of restoring stability in the Politburo, which meant restoring the general secretary. He was weak and infirm, but his state of health offered certain advantages because he was not in a position to extend his power at the expense of their rights. Still, they could use him to mediate between the rival factions. The effect was that all of them were compelled to retreat to their initial positions.

In expectation of Chernenko's imminent demise, various political deals were made but the final carving up and distribution of political turfs was temporarily deferred. Chernenko discovered that in the Politburo attitudes toward him had changed. Various groups began to crystallize there: his supporters, interested in prolonging their political existence; and his recent rivals, interested in building their own power bases. Suddenly, Chernenko, aware that an imminent resumption of Party infighting could no longer pose any danger to him, was in the position to benefit from the temporary truce and even to carry out policies of his own.

In those domains in which Romanov and Gorbachev neutralized each other, Chernenko was able to maneuver in between them. This was his opportunity to pursue his own political ideas and interests. However, noting inconsistencies in Chernenko's foreign policy departures, Gromyko (who had no aspirations for the general secretaryship) took the liberty of violating the truce in the Politburo. Yet, in assessing Gromyko's role, one should keep in mind that communism cements the Soviet regime to a degree that reduces the role of individuals regardless of how much personal power they may have. This is because the system's functional imperatives always turn out to be decisive. Chernenko intuitively sensed this more than did Gromyko.

Certainly, it makes little sense to portray the Politburo as comprising hawks and doves. The truth is that the views of all members are determined by Communist ideology, in particular by the view that the world is divided into two hostile blocs pitted against each other in a terminal struggle that is inevitable and that cannot but end in capitalism's defeat, preferably to be achieved by ideological means, but if necessary, by military ones. Nevertheless, the Soviet power elite is split between two orientations in regard to foreign affairs. One tendency, which Chernenko supported, is more moderate, stemming from the belief that due to the natural laws of development time works in favor of the USSR, allowing it to concentrate its efforts on disarming the West psychologically and splitting it internally. The opposite tendency, adhered to among others by Gromyko, is more militant, espousing an aggressive and vigorous exploitation of all the weaknesses and errors of capitalism. In a nutshell, this tendency can be described as calling for no concessions to the free world and for building up tactical and strategic weaponry that, in all cases, will prevent the West from interfering in the internal affairs of the Soviet Union and, under fortunate circumstances, may facilitate the expansion of the Communist empire to the shores of the Indian Ocean and the Persian Gulf.[8] Each of the two views has its domestic policy implications: the former by commanding an effort to raise the population's standard of living; the latter by opposing any lifting of the iron curtain and any liberalizing change out of concern for the "weakness" that would inevitably accompany ideological relaxation or toleration of diversity.

Chernenko was hindered by the inertia of the system. The machinery of power in the USSR proved too resistant to his ideas to allow for their implementation. Nor did Chernenko any longer have the strength to direct the system toward the destinations he hoped to reach. His intentions and hopes remained unfulfilled. Future historians will probably judge Chernenko not by what he achieved but by what he avoided. He avoided encouraging domestic reaction and embroiling his country in risky foreign adventures.

Nevertheless, Chernenko did achieve something. He had the idea of promoting detente by increasingly involving both the East and the West in a nexus of mutually beneficial relationships. Acting on his instructions, the Soviet ambassador in Washington, Anatoly Dobrynin, in June 1984 contacted the State Department in order to convey Chernenko's offer to meet with President Reagan. Granted, this was a very modest step toward mutual understanding, stopping far short of a hoped-for resumption of the Geneva talks broken off by Andropov. Still, it was followed by cautious progress toward normalization of relations: an accord was concluded on the sale of U.S. grain to the Soviet Union; an agreement was signed to modernize the hot line between the Kremlin and the White House; the Americans rescinded their ban on access of Soviet fishing vessels to U.S. territorial waters; Moscow consented to an extension of consular relations; and scientific and cultural exchanges between the two superpowers increased.

Yet, despite Chernenko, the basic orientation of Soviet policy toward Washington remained unchanged. Efforts to isolate the United States by splitting the Western alliance via extensive use of propaganda and disinformation continued. After long debate a Politburo meeting in May 1984 decided that the USSR would not participate in the upcoming Olympic Games in Los Angeles. The decision was not coordinated with the other countries of the Soviet bloc. In the Politburo debate Romanov and Chebrikov argued that too many members of the Soviet delegation could defect. However, one can doubt whether defections were Romanov's and Chebrikov's real concern. Both knew all too well that Soviet athletes were unlikely to defect in any numbers. Once they became Western-style professionals, they would have nothing apart from their skills in athletics. In the West such skills are not in sufficient demand to ensure a comfortable standard of living. In contrast, in their own country they were privileged, having benefits unavailable to the majority of Soviet populace: cars, nice apartments, high salaries. Foreign travel would not be a motivating factor for defection because they already had the opportunity to travel abroad several times a year at Soviet government expense. Because of all this, Soviet athletes pose a lesser defection risk than do Soviet musicians, artists, or scholars permitted to travel to the West.

Nor could concern for the reputation of Soviet sports have motivated Romanov and Chebrikov to oppose, with the support by Ustinov and Gromyko, Soviet participation in the Olympics. Had the Soviet athletes been permitted to compete, they would undoubtedly have carried away a great many medals. The real motivation of the quartet was opposition to rapprochement with the West. Each of them had a different stake in the opposition, but their public support for Soviet negotiations with the United States had one single purpose: to create an image of Soviet intentions as being "peaceful." In this the USSR largely succeeded. European opposition to Reagan's planned Strategic Defense Initiative mounted. It seemed as if the West lacked the resolve to exploit its technological superiority to contain Communist expansion. The West was thus virtually aiding the Soviet Union to avoid the nightmarish prospect of an arms race in space where the Soviets could not compete with the United States. To forestall the nightmare, the USSR could only attempt to exert political pressure.

At the winter session of the Supreme Soviet on November 17, 1984, an increase in the military budget from 17 to 19 billion rubles was announced. To be sure, these figures cannot be taken at face value because a great many items of the Soviet military budget are concealed as civilian expenditures. What was significant was the very fact that the announcement was made. It was intended to serve as a warning to the West that it would not succeed in wringing concessions from the Soviet Union by applying economic pressure such as trade limitations.

Eventually Chernenko was forced to retreat by agreeing to reconvene the Geneva negotiations in January 1985. Even this concession, however, was qualified by a precondition, that the United States freeze its deployment of new missiles in Western Europe. Chernenko considered it imperative to cut the military-technological prowess of the West down to size and thereby lower the competitive strain on the Soviet economy. He conducted a worldwide campaign toward this end, as Brezhnev had done. The presentation of the Soviet case somewhat varied, depending on the region of the world to which the message was addressed. The methods also varied, depending on circumstances, ranging from diktat, blackmail, and bribery to exhortation.

Soviet foreign policy is not oriented toward pursuit of the national interest in the traditional sense. Rather, it is a function of Soviet domestic policy, projected internationally and determined ideologically. It is not oriented toward meeting national goals but merely the regime's goals, which may be disguised as efforts to foster "the world Communist movement," "international progress," "the preservation and establishment of peace throughout the world," or the like. *Raison d'état* is in Soviet foreign policy a secondary factor subordinate to the self-perpetuation of communism.

The decline of the appeal and prestige of Communist ideology throughout the world and its discreditation in the eyes of the Soviet citizenry in no way affected its role as a tool of Soviet political strategy. Under Chernenko also this strategy was aimed at the liquidation of non-totalitarian social systems, and it provided Soviet leaders with a rationale for their hegemonistic aspirations. The ancient impulse of Russian imperialism to extend the borders of the Russian state as far as possible was supplemented by the "scientific" concept of the inevitability of Communist revolution. This "science" was supposed to warrant the extension of Soviet influence to all corners of the earth. With the help of slogans calling for the defense of "revolutionary" and "national liberation" movements, Moscow attempted to ensure that developments in every nation on every continent correspond to its interests.

"Peaceful coexistence," far from being a Soviet goal, is rather a means to facilitate the growth of Soviet military power. Soviet leaders from Lenin to Chernenko have never equated improvement of relations with capitalist countries with accepting the political pluralism reigning there. They have always exhorted Communists to be at all times ready for an intensification of the struggle between the opposing social systems. It follows that Soviet militarism is intended to perpetuate the regime. The motive-pattern behind Soviet foreign policy somewhat resembles the traditional Russian *matreshka* toy, i.e. a doll-shell enclosing a number of increasingly diminutive dolls. The outer shell, in this case ideology, is readily visible and ornate, but it merely provides an outer cast for something more essential that is being concealed: Soviet expansionism and militarism.

These features of Soviet foreign policy strategy are dictated primarily by two fears, namely, fear of the Soviet popular masses and fear of the democratic states beyond the USSR's borders. The former are feared because neither spiritually, morally, nor psychologically are they in tune with the leadership; the latter, because they are not only freer but also more highly developed than the USSR.

The Soviet regime had no way of meeting the democratic states' challenge. Its promise to build a Communist society that will in all aspects, but primarily in organizational efficiency and quality of life, catch up with and surpass the West had remained unfulfilled. For one thing, ethnic antagonisms within the multinational Soviet empire tend with time to become aggravated. Prior to Chernenko the Soviet leaders had been compelled to devote increasing effort to propping up their own power and to maintaining the domestic stability of their regime by means of foreign ventures. This meant that the Soviet Union kept pulling into the Communist orbit one nation after another, with the aim of showing the world, and especially its own people, the strength and vitality of its system and hence the hopelessness of resisting or even opposing it. In this sense Soviet expansionism is a profoundly determined rather than freely chosen venture. It is why the beefing up of Soviet military power goes beyond what is rationally needed for defense. Nevertheless, Chernenko did try to soften Soviet policies toward those regions of the world where Brezhnev had, quite successfully, used brute force.

The changes in Chernenko's approach in foreign policy stopped short of being far-reaching or decisive. One of their strategic focuses remained, as previously, Western Europe. Soviet hopes were attached to liberal segments of Western European public opinion, to their possible tilting of the electoral balance in their countries in favor of left-socialist governments.

But the Soviets also retained a keen interest in Latin America, where after the unsuccessful attempt to foster the "creeping" spread of Communism from Nicaragua to El Salvador, they switched to a defensive posture, advancing only when chances for success were good and risk was minimal. Although the Soviets maintained their interest in the Middle East, under Chernenko Moscow did not have any special plans for further activity there. Without investing anything much, the USSR harvested the fruits of the work of others. For example, it successfully exploited the fact that Israel had become mired in the swamp of the war in Lebanon. But in the Far East and Southeast Asia, the USSR had a broad range of options, including distancing China from the United States, embroiling China with Vietnam, and neutralizing Japan.

The facts indicate that despite all the problems cropping up in both public and private life, Chernenko did not mean to put a halt to Soviet expansionism around the world. Persistent Western expectations that Soviet domestic crises would lead to an imposition of brakes upon Soviet hegemonism proved unfounded. The opposite was the case, at least in the sense that some Politburo members sought to counterbalance domestic decline and stagnation by major foreign policy successes. They believed such successes would be capable of distracting the populace's attention from shortages of bread and butter. Likewise, they thought of guns and missiles produced in plenty as compensating the masses for the lack of freedom, democracy, or equality. True, such expectations were not fated to materialize, despite the best hopes of Romanov and Ustinov. This was because Brezhnev's policy of expansion eventually produced a major backlash, as a result of which the Soviet Union found itself isolated in the international arena and virtually encircled by hostile forces. The backlash, however, far from being a result of some sinister plot of the imperialists, was in large degree the Soviets' own doing.

To the southeast of the Soviet Union, China actively opposed the hegemonistic aspirations of the Kremlin. To its east, Japan preferred a pro-Western orientation and a certain disinterest in rapprochement with her western neighbor. To the south, Afghanistan continued to resist Soviet aggression and Iran was not reluctant to reveal its hatred of the Soviet "atheist" regime. Finally, in the countries of Eastern Europe hostility toward the USSR was, if anything, growing. The Soviet invasion of Afghanistan undermined Soviet prestige in the Third World. Only Cuba continued to coordinate its "revolutionary" ventures with the Soviets. In Africa and Latin America the leaders of many states appeared to be in no great hurry to exchange their autocracies for the Soviet type of Party oligarchy.

The culmination of Moscow's international crisis came with the U.S. Strategic Defense Initiative and the resolve of the Reagan administration to contain Soviet expansionism. As if that were not enough, the ground began to quake and slip from under Chernenko's feet in his own country. The cracks in the social fabric resulting from economic stagnation, disunity among the political elite, and ideological erosion were becoming increasingly difficult to conceal. The Soviet Union was proving incapable of offering its own people (much less the world) any appealing ideas or goals worth striving for. Only the armed forces symbolized the Soviet strength and purposiveness. Naked military force was the only political argument that could "persuade" anyone to accept Soviet values. The hopes of Chernenko to improve the reputation of his country in the world by means other than military were dashed. Because of political weakness, the stress on military means was inevitable and, predictably, it continued throughout Chernenko's term of office.

On a number of occasions Chernenko professed his desire to renew detente and to reduce international tensions, adding that the Soviet Union did not aspire to military superiority. Moreover, he was well aware that international stability, including the possibilities for detente, depended on the shape Soviet-U.S. relations assumed. He therefore persisted in his efforts to renew direct contacts with Washington. Pursuing this end, he decided to invite to Moscow the well-known and influential industrialist Armand Hammer, via whom he hoped to bypass Gromyko and establish direct contacts with the U.S. president. Hammer, who had known Lenin, had journeyed to Moscow many times before, most notably in 1962 during the Cuban missile crisis. Then he had been the envoy of President Kennedy, who wanted to use as his messenger a person well known in Moscow. However, Chernenko's reliance on a U.S. citizen was not easy to explain and amazed many in Moscow. To some in the West and perhaps also in the East, it presumably indicated how strong and apparently sincere was his desire to have direct intercourse with the president. Chernenko's idea of "conducting negotiations about the possibility of conducting negotiations," which was the hypercautious formula for the possible renewal of the Geneva disarmament talks, pointed in the same direction.

Chernenko's proposal stemmed from his belief that his overtures could complicate the U.S. administration's attempts to convince U.S. allies to become involved in various aspects of the SDI. But this does not mean that his offer was insincere, or that it was a mere diplomatic maneuver. It reflected Chernenko's understanding that the growth of Soviet armed power has limits beyond which it becomes self-defeating. Chernenko understood that the United States was perfectly capable of meeting the Soviet military challenge on the basis of its more advanced economy and technology and even of finally winning the arms race through a cosmic leap that would leave the Soviets hopelessly behind, bereft of any hope of ever catching up with the West. The alternative for the Soviet Union was to allocate all its resources to the military and thus destroy its civilian economy.

Calling for the preservation of the existing military balance, Chernenko appealed to the White House:

We are turning to the U.S.A. and to its allies with an unambiguous appeal. The time has come to affirm our share of responsibility for the fate of the world with concrete deeds, which means to recognize that policies based on force, an arms race, have reached a dead end. We are anxious to demonstrate our real, not at all feigned, readiness for dialogue, for negotiations to reach mutually acceptable solutions to issues which will determine the future destiny of mankind.[9]

Chernenko proposed a fundamental, free-of-preconditions review and comparison of the military potentials of the two sides. However, his own estimates were far from being either fundamental or free of preconditions; they were in fact quite biased. Speaking of strategic nuclear weapons, for example, he noted an "approximate equality," and in discussing conventional weaponry, he said that although in some types of weaponry the USSR had a degree of superiority, in others the West did. This was the first admission by any Soviet leader that in certain types of weaponry the USSR indeed had quantitative superiority over the West. But the sole purpose of this admission was to attract the West to the idea of "preventing the militarization of space."[10]

For all the effort he made to present himself as an experienced and insightful statesman, Chernenko hardly sounded credible when he insisted that the source of tension in the world was the arms race itself rather than the mutually irreconcilable policies of the great powers. His claim stood in direct contradiction to the official Soviet ideology, which attributes the threat of war to the "imperialist nature of the capitalist countries." Yet, he needed to insist on this point in order to persuade the West to join him in the struggle against the "threat of war."

The most important of Chernenko's proposals was his agreement to review the second Strategic Arms Limitation Treaty (SALT 2). This was a clear retreat from the USSR's previous all-or-nothing position about its ratification.

Chernenko expressed readiness to negotiate with the United States on a number of other issues: limiting the deployment of new submarines, banning the modernization of ballistic missiles already deployed, and construction of new such missiles. Moreover, he refrained from responding to President Reagan's vituperation about the amorality of the Soviet leadership. The intention was clear: by refusing to trade invective for invective, and by concentrating instead on substance, he made his proposals for normalization of relations with the United States sound all the more serious and genuine.

Chernenko's proposals for convening a conference to discuss issues related to the SDI and control of strategic weaponry were targeted at three audiences: the U.S. government, the opposition Democratic party in the United States (presidential elections were in the offing, and Moscow was not averse to the idea of influencing their outcome), and European leaders. With an eye on the latter, in *Pravda* of May 1984, there appeared remarks by Minister of Defense Ustinov expressed in the harsh language of the cold war. The intention was to convey the impression that the Politburo was divided into hawks like Ustinov and doves like Chernenko. Judging from Western European reactions, this impression was conveyed and given credence.

The impression was not entirely false. For the first time in many years contradictions indeed appeared in the Kremlin's foreign policy doctrines. Chernenko advocated detente while Ustinov feared that in the event of Western rejection of Soviet peace overtures no alternative would be left apart from an arms race. Due to this duality in Moscow's approach, Washington was compelled to adapt itself hurriedly to a more complex response pattern than the one it had followed previously. A hard line of the United States on El Salvador and international terrorism was presented, together with U.S. readiness in principle for negotiations with the USSR without the delay that would have been warranted by the need to coordinate strategy and elaborate a common position with U.S. allies.

Moscow's political gambit consisted of pitting Western Europe against the United States. Western Europe was the prize that the Soviet Union was hoping to win without war. Chernenko expressed Soviet willingness to make concessions in that region that would be unthinkable elsewhere, such as halting deployment of new intermediate-range missiles in the entire European part of the USSR, on condition that Western Europe enter upon a parallel commitment.

Chernenko proposed that all European countries undertake not to be the first to use either nuclear or conventional weapons, that existing military blocs not be expanded and new ones not be established. He noted that in its effort to achieve progress in negotiations on the reduction of military forces in Central Europe the Soviet Union had already "gone more than halfway." Because Soviet superiority over Western Europe had become more marked, Chernenko could safely afford to be generous in his offers.

Soviet policy in relation to the Third World had for many years consisted of variant combinations of the following strategies: diplomatic penetration, and the supply of military equipment, followed by intervention (either directly or by proxies) or coups. Conflict-torn nationalist regimes were ready prey for Communist subversion. However, as an outcome of many of its successes, Moscow found itself quite isolated, both politically and ideologically, for Soviet victories often tended to produce backlash in the form of resistance movements or new anti-Soviet coalitions. This paradox of Soviet expansion was not sufficiently understood either by Brezhnev or by Andropov. Chernenko, however, linked his desire for cooperation with the West with the resolution of regional conflicts in Asia and Africa. He also declared the willingness of the Soviet Union to withdraw its troops from Afghanistan, but on condition of the preservation of communism there.

Confidence-building measures were also proposed by Chernenko for the Middle East. He sought to convince the United States that the security of the Persian Gulf countries should be treated separately from other issues. This had been a long-standing Soviet view. However, he did not object to the Western and Muslim countries' demand that the problems of Afghanistan be discussed jointly with the Persian Gulf security issue.

The Soviet Union supposed that it would gain from the Iraq-Iran war no matter what the outcome. The victory of the former could be seen as a victory for Soviet arms; the defeat of the latter could be expected to activate pro-Soviet forces and in the optimal case lead to a Communist takeover that even if it ended in failure, would cause trouble for the Khomeini regime and halt the spread of pan-Islamic ideas into the southern Soviet republics. Conversely, an Iranian victory would enable the USSR to entrench itself in Iraq, which in recent years showed signs of independence. Furthermore, the hostilities could potentially result in the destruction of the pipelines or disruption of the oil routes via which Western Europe and Japan receive huge quantities of petroleum, with the effect of crippling the Western European and Japanese economies to Soviet advantage. What Moscow did not expect, however, and what did not suit its interests was the ensuing prolonged stalemate without a clear outcome. As a consequence, both Iran and Iraq became hostile toward the USSR. This is why Chernenko referred to the war as senseless and offering no hope for a reasonable outcome, in contrast to Moscow's earlier view that the war was "justified."

Chernenko's new evaluation of the Iraq-Iran war was reflected in a change in his expressed views about Islam and the Islamic revolution. Khomeini's victory had at the time been hailed by the Soviets as an "anti-imperialistic revolution" because it freed Iran from the U.S. hold. At the same time the resurgence of Islam in Iran raised concerns in the Politburo that a religious fanaticism as vigorous as the Iranian one might "infect" the Muslim population of close-by Soviet republics. Nevertheless, under Brezhnev any Soviet critique of Islam was hushed up and replaced by a wary wooing of the Muslims. Chernenko viewed Islam with more discrimination. He saw that both liberation (i.e. suiting Soviet interests) or counterrevolutionary (i.e. defined by the Soviets as such) movements could develop under the banner of Islam. The Afghan resistance to Soviet troops was naturally an example of the latter category.

In the Middle East Soviet policy measures reflected the Soviet capacity to adapt itself to the vagaries of the almost-forty-year-long Arab-Israeli conflict. Under Chernenko, as under his predecessors, the Soviet Union did not want a new war, but neither did it want a stable peace that could only make further Soviet presence in the region unneeded and unjustifiable. The goal of Chernenko, as of previous general secretaries, was the consolidation of the highly unstable (and widely varying in degree) Soviet influence in Syria, Jordan, and Lebanon. Chernenko realized that this goal could not be achieved by friendship and cooperation treaties, which the Arab states kept annulling as readily as they had signed them. He concluded that the Soviet Union could really rely only on regimes bearing similarity to the Soviet one because only there could Soviet interests be defended by Communist ideology and hosts of Party bureaucrats dependent on Moscow for support and training. Such regimes existed in Ethiopia, Angola, South Yemen, and at least for the meanwhile, Afghanistan. And in order to "socially reconstruct" the region to some extent, a Palestinian state that would be completely dependent on Moscow was considered an enticing prospect. Such was the traditional Soviet view, from which Chernenko departed slightly. But his departure should be viewed as merely tactical. It is in this context that one should interpret his calling for an "honest search for a comprehensive settlement in the Middle East on a just and realistic basis."[11]

To anyone not familiar with Soviet vocabulary, words like *honest, just,* and *realistic* must suggest a change in Chernenko's approach in the Middle East. In fact, these words veil ideas that are not new at all. Chernenko was merely restating that without an end to the Israeli occupation of all Arab territory captured in 1967 and establishment of Palestinian statehood no real peace could ever be reached. The only thing new was that Chernenko did not reiterate standard Soviet invective, like "the aggression of Tel Aviv," and refrained from heaping abuse on the leaders of Israel. However, this was merely a change in the form of the discourse, not its contents.

Only in regard to Eurocommunism was Chernenko unwavering and constant in his opposition. He refused to recognize it as a legitimate point of view in that it undermined Moscow's status as the center of international Communism because its doctrine had originated from the periphery, Spain and Italy, instead of the center, the Politburo in Moscow. He considered a reconciliation with Eurocommunism impossible because it would perforce contradict the Leninist teaching about revisionism as an imperialist ideological subversion in the ranks of the working-class movement.

Eurocommunism was indeed a serious and dangerous alternative to orthodox Marxism, not only in the countries where it originated and subsequently declined in strength but also in the countries of Eastern

Europe, where it gained overt supporters (in Poland and Hungary) and more covert ones (in Bulgaria and Romania). This gave Chernenko additional reason for refusing to recognize Eurocommunism's existence or granting it legitimacy. If he could have, he would have terminated the Polish drama revolving around the Solidarity Union as the Czech spring had been ended, and thus bury Eurocommunism once and forever. However, he was not free to act in Poland as he would have wished, albeit for no fault of his own. In the end the Polish situation was bound to affect the views of Chernenko and even influence Politburo debate. Thus, Ustinov believed that it was both possible and necessary to keep a tight rein on Eastern Europe and to suppress any popular stirrings not to Moscow's liking and any governments deviating from Moscow's line. In contrast to Ustinov, Gorbachev's remarks were less ideologically dogmatic and left room for political compromise. It appeared that the youngest Central Committee secretary cherished hopes that the Poles might succeed in liberalizing their regime without changing its essence. He proposed allowing the Communist parties of the "fraternal" socialist countries a degree of latitude, noting that the USSR should refrain from petty interference in domestic affairs.

Chernenko preferred to rely on tested means of controlling "the socialist camp." Following the pattern set by Brezhnev, he held periodic meetings with Eastern European leaders. The meetings, both multilateral and bilateral, were not confined to ideological, economic, and political issues; Party organization, control over production, and Party work issues were also discussed.

Chernenko was kind and generous to submissive Eastern European leaders. He received them lavishly in the Kremlin with elaborate pomp and circumstance, and — an innovation of his — showered awards of the highest honors upon not only Party and government heads but also their most zealous second-echelon associates. Thus, the highest Soviet award, Hero of the Soviet Union, was granted to the president of Czechoslovakia, Gustav Husak, and the head of the Czech labor unions received the Order of the October Revolution. The Polish leader General Jaruzelski received a lesser honor, the Order of Lenin, than did his Czech counterpart, which is understandable in that the Kremlin found it easier to install Jaruzelski as head of state than to keep him under its thumb. Unlike Husak, Jaruzelski on occasion was stubborn and independent, but he could not be bypassed when it came to awards; after all he was still the ruler of the most populous Eastern European country. The solution resorted to was to grant the same award to him and to his minister of defense, Florian Siwicki. As a military man, Jaruzelski could be expected to welcome with satisfaction the award granted to his fellow military man. Hungarian Party head Janos Kadar was honored indirectly by the award of the Order of Lenin to his minister of defense, Lajos Sinyei. Romanian President Nicolae Ceausescu was slighted by being awarded the Order of the October Revolution, an honor obviously unbefitting his rank and notorious vanity.[12]

Chernenko attached high hopes to economic cooperation of the Eastern bloc within the Council for Mutual Economic Assistance (CMEA, or COMECON) framework. He advocated an extension of the powers of the plenipotentiary committee of ministers of these countries, hoping that it would succeed in coordinating the respective economies of the member countries. At the same time the nature of the relations of these countries with the USSR aroused his concern. For example, at an economic meeting of the CMEA states on June 13, 1984, it was publicly admitted that it would not be correct to depict the situation in the socialist world as too rosy. Chernenko himself admitted that problems and difficulties in the development of Communist countries had recurrently arisen. Apparently, he had in mind the differences between the USSR and Romania, and Soviet opposition to changes taking place in Poland. These "problems and difficulties" in the development of the socialist countries were attributed by Chernenko to the transition to intensive development of the economy, to the realization of major social programs, and to failures in molding the Communist consciousness.[13]

Compared to Brezhnev's pronouncements on Eastern European issues, Chernenko's were less aggressive and more forbearing by virtue of his professed desire to solve problems "in a friendly manner." Yet, when he exhorted the Communist parties to "learn from each other," there was no question that either social developments in Poland or the nationalistic self-assertiveness of Romania could be possible models to emulate. In fact, "learning from each other" basically meant learning from the Soviet Union, and in some respects from the German Democratic Republic, which in Chernenko's view had gained valuable experience in rationalizing production and in saving energy and raw materials. Chernenko also pointed to Hungarian successes with agricultural cooperatives and enterprises, and Bulgarian successes in agroindustrial cooperation.

Problems of economic cooperation between socialist countries were too serious for Chernenko to pass over in silence. Although clichéd praise of the successes of CMEA, in particular of its long-range achievements in economic integration, abounded in his pronouncements, he repeatedly called attention to the organization's serious problems, which he held to be remediable by intensified efforts at standardization, coordination, and improving the mutual exchange of information about scientific-technological developments.[14]

Chernenko thought it possible to overcome the problems of economic development of the CMEA countries through close coordination of their national economic plans over a fifteen-to-twenty-year period. This was not the first time such an idea had been voiced by a Soviet leader, but it was the first time that a rather radical economic reform (which included creation of joint industrial firms) was proposed with the aim of bringing the CMEA countries into closer alignment. Still, the proposed measures could not guarantee real progress in economic development of the socialist countries. The economic decline of Eastern European countries was predetermined by the nature of their economic agreements with Moscow. The Soviet Union annually received from them many billions of rubles' worth of consumer goods and foodstuffs that were in short supply in these countries in exchange for much-needed expensive industrial equipment. The Soviets have a positive balance of trade with other CMEA members, but this is in a large part to be accounted for by high world market prices for petroleum, natural gas, and other raw materials, which are primary Soviet exports.

Understandably, the countries of Eastern Europe were increasingly reluctant to keep to the pace set by the Kremlin despite the urgings of the coachman, Chernenko. None of their leaders, not even Kadar and Ceausescu, who otherwise have given proofs of their relative independence, would ever contemplate severing their ties to Moscow because they owe their power in their countries to Moscow's fiat. However, while enjoying Soviet protection, these pragmatic leaders had dared to offer some criticism of the Kremlin. And the Kremlin listened, knowing that silent majorities in the Eastern European countries would support the leaders in any challenges to Soviet domination. But under Chernenko, instead of requesting, they were demanding economic aid from Moscow. And when the aid was tardy in coming or was in insufficient quantities, they looked westward, seeking and gaining there most-favored trading status.

To everyone's surprise, East Germany was also becoming self-assertive, this for the first time. Despite its submissiveness to Moscow, the German Democratic Republic was interested in establishing closer ties with the Federal Republic of Germany. Other Soviet satellites had pursued this goal, but the case of East Germany was special as the USSR's most important World War II prize, as the most economically advanced Communist country, and as a springboard for a possible attack against Western Europe. The Soviet design was to keep the German Democratic Republic totally subordinate. When GDR leader Erich Honecker indicated an interest in visiting the FDR in late 1984, the Kremlin got upset because it opposed in principle any detente between the two Germanys. The Soviets were concerned, first of all, by the prospect of ideological contamination, but economic considerations played a role as well. Honecker could have expected to be received with highest honors in the West German capital, and the Soviets were worried about his responding too warmly to the hospitality extended to him and about his enticement by his encounter with West German successes in industrial development and in social welfare. A possible rapprochement was a specter. Moscow also had second thoughts about Bonn's granting East Germany $350 million in credits. Paradoxically, these second thoughts were expressed in the form of an "altruistic" concern about the impact of such generosity on a socialist country's economy.

Honecker hoped for support from both Chernenko and Tikhonov for his venture because both of them had been known as advocates of relaxation in East-West relations. This is why he was inclined to accept Bonn's invitation. But the Politburo conservatives of various stripes and orientations — Gromyko, Ustinov, Romanov, Grishin, Shcherbitsky, and Chebrikov — resolved to frustrate Honecker's plan and succeeded in closing ranks on the issue. Disagreements and clashes in the Politburo in working out a policy in regard to Eastern Europe had taken place previously; this at least is what the official reports, when read between the lines, and various leaks of information would suggest. This time, however, the clash found public expression in the form of mutually contradictory views appearing in *Pravda* and *Izvestiya*.

The government organ *Izvestiya* (which, as noted earlier, Chernenko had under his control) expressed a view opposed to that of the Party organ *Pravda* (where Gorbachev's views predominated). The former supported Honecker's desire to visit West Germany on the ground that the states of the socialist community supported normal trade relations with all countries. *Izvestiya* also argued that capital borrowing was a normal practice; that this was precisely what the European banks had been established for.[15] *Pravda* presented the matter differently, much more laconically and categorically, arguing that economic leverage was bound to be exploited by Bonn to ideologically disarm East Germany.[16]

The exact role of Gorbachev in this episode is unclear. Did his opposition to the rapprochement of the two Germanys stem from his relative inexperience in international affairs or did it already manifest a redirection of his concern from foreign to domestic policy? Or alternatively, was he perhaps impressed by historical examples that seem to show that stagnant and decadent empires begin to fall apart at their peripheries? Certain clues on how to answer this question would become apparent after Gorbachev became general secretary. Meanwhile, under considerable pressure from Moscow, Honecker was forced to call off his visit to the Federal Republic of Germany. (A visit finally took place three years later, in September 1987, when Gorbachev was general secretary.)

The postponement of Honecker's visit may have reminded the Soviet leaders about other matters that had been postponed. Ties linking the Eastern European states to the Soviet Union were tightened. One by one the leaders of these states began to be invited to Moscow for "rest," which actually meant for some arm-twisting; the meaning became transparent as official newspapers defined the purpose of the visits as "relaxation and work." Chernenko's *modus operandi* with them was simple: he exposed his guests to a combination of threats and comforts at luxurious Black Sea coast villas.

It was more difficult for the Soviet Union to deal with specters. One specter that had haunted Europe for a number of years was pacifism. Moscow had hoped it could enlist pacifism to manipulate world opinion in its favor, but the peace movement unexpectedly began to target the Soviets as well as the Americans. In Eastern Europe hundreds of thousands of people protested U.S. *and* Soviet missiles. In Poland, Czechoslovakia, and Hungary pacifist and antinuclear literature was printed and distributed in *samizdat*, and newspapers published numerous letters to the editors against the buildup and deployment of nuclear weapons. Even in Bulgaria, the most conformist Communist country, head of state Zhivkov found it advisable to propose the creation of a nuclear-free zone in the Balkans.

For quite some time the Kremlin leaders were off balance and could not decide how to react. The official Soviet tenet of the "struggle for peace" could not be easily opposed directly. Yet, in the end this was precisely what Gromyko did: in April 1984 in Budapest he attacked the advocates of disarmament for their "lack of a class approach" to the problem. This was the first time that the peace movement in Eastern Europe was authoritatively referred to as the enemy. The covert target of Gromyko's attack, however, was Romania, as became clear two months later when Chernenko met Ceausescu in Moscow.

The official TASS communique described the Soviet-Romanian talks as having been conducted in a *"businesslike* comradely spirit and an atmosphere of friendship and *frankness."* In Soviet esoteric language such phrasing indicates that there were differences of opinion between the two sides. Behind the formulas there loomed an unpleasant reality. Ceausescu had raised an issue that for the Kremlin leaders was particularly sensitive, namely, Soviet missiles in Eastern Europe. For the Soviets, the topic was a taboo, which Ceausescu violated in expressing his concern about missile deployment close to his country's borders.[17]

The Soviet leaders were quite put out. However, the lack of unity in the

Soviet camp (including the insubordination of Romania, the aborted self-assertiveness of East Germany, and the preference of Hungary for its own way to "socialism") did not prevent Chernenko from attacking the United States in the name of the Warsaw Pact and CMEA bloc as a whole. Chernenko was anxious to present himself as a defender of peace. If he succeeded in obtaining world public opinion's support for his proposals, so much the better. But even if he failed, he would still reap advantages from the sheer rejection of these proposals by the U.S. president, who would thereby earn the stigma of a warmonger.

What concerned Chernenko most, though, was the nature of relations with China. He realized that dealing with Beijing required sophistication, that a simple dichotomy of China's being either "on our side" or "on the side of the United States—against us" would not do. Chernenko recognized that errors of both Khrushchev and Brezhnev in regard to China had been predicated on precisely such dichotomization. In contrast to his predecessors, Chernenko discriminated. He reasoned that ideologically China had always been closer to the Soviet Union, but politically it recently, and possibly only temporarily, had leaned toward the United States. He anticipated that in time China might be attracted to the Japanese market, but that this should not necessarily preclude its eventual rapprochement with the USSR. In a complex gamble, the Soviet Union had the option of encouraging Beijing's expansion southward and southwestward against smaller countries like Malaysia, Burma, and Thailand, which were plagued by ethnic and religious strife and in which China could rely on the support of millions of ethnic Chinese with considerable political and economic influence. Such a direction might be more tempting to Beijing than trying to expand northward into the Soviet Union, with possibly fatal effect for the very existence of the Chinese state, not to speak of the lives of the millions of its citizens.

Chinese expansion southward and southwestward would open the possibility of the Chinese requesting Soviet help or, alternatively, of a Chinese confrontation with the United States. Under either circumstance Moscow stood to reap advantages. Chernenko desisted from following the Soviet tradition of extolling the Chinese people while attacking the Chinese government. After all, the same distinction between "people" and "government" could be applied to the USSR. Chernenko had reason to believe that the Chinese government lacked popular support and appeal. He refrained from the customary clichés of Soviet propaganda about the rule of bureaucracy in China and about the hegemonistic aspirations of the Chinese leaders. His restraint in this respect could have a twofold explanation: either he hoped for a reduction of tensions with China and was determined to act accordingly, or he merely wanted to score some points in the Politburo by leaving the advocacy of a hard-line "ostracize-China" position to others. The latter hypothesis has the advantage of cogently explaining the Politburo decision to postpone the planned (for May 1984) visit of Ivan Arkhipov, deputy chairman of the Council of Ministers, on the flimsy excuse of "lack of required preparation." Almost certainly, Chernenko was outvoted on this issue by the hard-liners.

Despite all the limitations imposed by his age and by the existence of a vocal opposition to his authority, Chernenko retained considerable room for strategic maneuvering. He preferred ideological subversion and psychological warfare to gunboat diplomacy, believing that the age of territorial conquests was over, superseded by the era of a battle for hearts and minds. It follows that real peace between the Soviet Union and the United States was not possible, even with a weak leader at the former's helm, that the maximum that could be achieved would be an armed truce, a state of no peace and no war.

But before the West realized it, the KGB seized its opportunity and moved to make a contribution of its own to international politics. The KGB acted crudely but effectively: it spread rumors incriminating top U.S. statesmen. The rumors were eagerly taken up by left-wing publications. Supporters of the deployment of U.S. missiles in Europe received threatening telegrams. The KGB also forged State Department documents with the aim of subverting U.S. influence in the Third World.

Such methods had been resorted to by the KGB in the past. This time, however, the initiative was Chebrikov's. He wished to emerge from the late Andropov's shadow and remind his colleagues of the full Politburo membership that he had been promised. He also devised the innovative idea of attempting to attract Soviet emigrants back to the USSR. To some extent he succeeded. Nikolay Rozhkov, a former Soviet soldier who had defected to the Afghan partisans, returned to the Soviet Union and to considerable publicity, a homecoming that attracted little attention in the West. Likewise, there was scarcely a ripple in the West when several other former Soviet soldiers in Afghanistan returned to the Soviet Union from London and Washington. They could not get used to the West, could not adapt to its alien ways, and could not learn English. They may have been subject to psychological pressure from Soviet agents or may simply have given in to homesickness, which after a year or two more on foreign soil they could possibly have overcome.

Still, in some cases nostalgia for one's country cannot be overcome with passing time. This seems to have occurred to Svetlana Allilueva, Stalin's daughter, who decided to return to the USSR after spending close to twenty years in the West. Her flight from the Soviet Union in 1967 had excited the world greatly, but her (in fact short-lived) return to the USSR was met with general indifference. This is why Chebrikov persisted in seeking a greater sensation. This was the origin of the meticulously planned "operation Bitov."

Oleg Bitov, the deputy editor of the international department of the newspaper *Literaturnaya gazeta*, suddenly disappeared while touring Italy. Who could have abducted him? The answer: no one.

Bitov was a journalist with close KGB ties. To put it differently, he was a professional chekist (a KGB man) with a second career as a journalist. He came to the attention of the West as the author of articles in *Literaturnaya gazeta* detailing the involvement of U.S. intelligence in planning the attempt to assassinate the pope. In the first half of 1983 the series could still be dismissed as intended only for domestic Soviet audience, as a sort of warning to listeners to Western radio stations not to believe and not to pass on to others Western reports about how two KGB agents, the Turkish terrorist Mehmet Ali Agca, and the head of the Rome office of the Balkanturist agency, Sergey Antonov, had plotted the May 13, 1981, attempt on the life of the pontiff. The investigation was still under way when in the second half of 1983 the news suddenly spread (in the USSR via the grapevine) that the KGB was deeply involved in the crime, and that its head, Yuriy Andropov, bore personal responsibility as planner of the whole operation. If true, this would mean the collective responsibility of the Soviet government for giving its approval to the attempted killing in Rome.

Despite a number of damaging international scandals revolving around the deeds of the KGB in the 1960s, the Kremlin had not renounced murder as a means of foreign policy conduct but merely put curbs on its frequency by requiring prior authorization of each single case by the Politburo.

The thrust of Soviet propaganda was simple, but for the Soviet reader it had certain plausibility. Because the KGB and the CIA were respectively accused by the West and the Soviets of plotting the pope's assassination, the Soviet reader was all too likely to conclude that the truth lay somewhere in between, i.e. that either both sides or neither side had been involved. The latter conclusion seemed particularly plausible: after all, John Paul II could have been attacked by a madman or someone seeking fame via ignominy, like the ancient Herostratus.

In September 1983 Bitov visited Italy, ostensibly for the purpose of attending the Venice international film festival, about which he was going to inform the Soviet readers. In the opinion of Western observers, however, his mission was more likely the collection (or fabrication) of material substantiating his (and the KGB's) claim of U.S. involvement in the attempted assassination of the pope. The Western observers' assumption was by no means farfetched, especially because in September 1983 even the Soviet press contained hints to the same effect. Moreover, indications of Bitov's KGB ties were not lacking; what else could explain his being entrusted to write about so sensitive a subject. Furthermore, the evidence he cited bore clear marks of being "inspired" by the Soviet security organs.

However, in the fall of 1983 not even the boldest imagination could foresee the shape of things to come. By then Bitov had already assumed his role as the main protagonist of a complex and multistage KGB intelligence operation. Had Western intelligence analysts been more attentive, they could have noted certain curious circumstances of Bitov's undertaking.

On September 8, 1983, Bitov disappeared from Venice. The Soviet press immediately reported that he had been kidnapped to halt the investigations he had been pursuing, and asserted that the CIA was responsible for the abduction. There was no shadow of a doubt about it; Bitov could be nowhere but in the hands of a Western intelligence service.

Several weeks later Bitov appeared in London at a press conference to say that he had chosen to stay in the West voluntarily. Curiously, the Soviet press then refrained from its customary abuse of a "turncoat" who sunk to the level of "moral degradation" and "treason" to his country. On the contrary, its tone was compassionate rather than wrathful. The journalist's mother called on the pages of *Literaturnaya gazeta* for sympathy for her son who at that very time was protesting the persecution of dissenters in the Soviet Union and denouncing the Soviet system with all possible vigor.

The Soviet forbearance was hardly explicable. It should have alerted the West, but it did not. Ten months later, on August 18, 1984, everything became quite explicable, even obvious. On that day Bitov disappeared for the second time, this time from London, but not before managing to travel around England, visit the United States for several months before returning to England, and amass a bank account of 40,000 pounds. This money was left behind in the bank, and his new automobile was abandoned near the Soviet embassy in London. Bitov himself turned up in Moscow. At a press conference there he recounted a fantastic tale resembling a Soviet detective story: he claimed to have been kidnapped by the British secret service, furtively shipped from Vienna to London, incarcerated, and tortured. He pronounced his previous denunciations of the Soviet Union to have been fabrications made by someone else.

What in fact did take place between Bitov's two disappearances on September 8, 1983, and August 18, 1984? The Soviet leadership had been deeply disturbed by the findings of the Italian government's investigation of the attempt to assassinate the pope. The Soviets tried to ascertain the extent of the Western intelligence services' knowledge of KGB involvement in the affair but evidently without success. Consequently, KGB headquarters on Dzerzhinsky Square in Moscow came up with an idea of planting its man in one of the Western intelligence services. The KGB choice fell on the British. Bitov's articles in *Literaturnaya gazeta* were but the first stage of the operation. He probably compiled or edited them himself in order to prepare to act out his subsequent role; their purpose was to make it clear to Western intelligence analysts that Bitov had access to KGB secrets. Drawing on KGB sources enabled him to insert a certain amount of detail and offer some interesting interpretations. The latter were slanted to cast strong suspicion on the CIA as the real culprit behind the shooting in Rome.

With time, the Western intelligence services became firmly convinced that Bitov—then in Italy—had ties with Soviet intelligence. Conditions were ripe for the KGB to instruct him to start with his "defection."

The KGB expected, rightly it appears, that during his interrogations by British intelligence officers, Bitov would succeed in learning quite a lot from the nature of the questions asked and of the topics raised about how much evidence of KGB involvement in the affair the West had and what the limits of its knowledge were. The Kremlin also had no doubt, and in this it was right on target, that in England Bitov would be welcomed generously precisely because of his access to evidence linking the KGB to the assault on the pope's life. While subject to investigation by British intelligence, Bitov would be conducting an investigation of his own.

Soon the leading pieces of the game were back in place: Bitov was in Moscow, and British intelligence was now disabused of the notion that it could have obtained any information from him. The only thing that remained unclear was how many secrets, and which, Western intelligence had inadvertently divulged to Bitov and whether Chebrikov would obtain a full Politburo membership as his reward. (In fact, Chebrikov did eventually become a full Politburo member, only not under Chernenko, who was not in the position to make any changes whatsoever in the configuration of forces in this body.)

In July 1984 Chernenko again fell seriously ill; so seriously that the Party considered it advisable to offer a public explanation of his protracted disappearance from sight. To pass over it in silence would have been risky so shortly after the recent deaths of Chernenko's two predecessors. The people needed to be reminded that they were being ruled, especially when the signs of a strong authority were not visible. Hence, a laconic announcement was made: "On the 15th of July the General Secretary of the CC of the CPSU, Chairman of the Presidium of the Supreme Soviet of the USSR Comrade K. U. Chernenko left Moscow for a rest."[18]

The announcement evoked neither surprise nor alarm; the public had been prepared for it. Less than six months from the day of Chernenko's ascent to power, his figure on photographs and films already resembled those of Brezhnev and Andropov in their last days: he was shown supported by bodyguards, and with trembling hands barely able to hold the text of his speech. The shadow of death was stalking yet another Soviet dictator who for fifty-four days had not appeared in public. Taking turns, Gorbachev, Romanov, Tikhonov, Grishin, Ustinov, and Gromyko all ruled in his name. This meant that nobody was in charge. Each of these Politburo members had one topmost concern: to present himself as a worthy successor. As previously, the seat of the general secretary was empty at Politburo meetings. This empty seat suggested a symbolic warning that mortality catches up with even the mighty and shuffles them on to oblivion.

Chernenko's time had not yet come, however. He unexpectedly e-merged from seclusion, not surprisingly looking even older and sicker than before. His first appearance was as if from off stage, via an interview in *Pravda*. There was no indication who the interviewer was nor when the interview was given, but Chernenko's replies were symptomatic of a loss of touch with reality. The impression conveyed was that the Soviet leader and his government were incapable of responding to the U.S. government's announcement of June 26 declaring its readiness to negotiate a ban on the arms race in space. Chernenko attempted to show that the willingness of the U.S. president to begin negotiations was in fact its opposite. In a ploy intended for foreign consumption, Chernenko also expressed distress at Washington's supposed intention of linking "the narrow problem of the militarization of space" to a total ban on nuclear weapons.[19]

Chernenko's position boiled down to the proposal that if the United States would renounce deployment of missiles in space, the Soviet Union would be ready to resume the negotiations it had broken off and to discuss the issue of limiting strategic weapons. While Communist newspapers around the world were busily hailing the "brilliant new initiative" of the general secretary (whose whereabouts and condition were in fact unknown), the Soviet people were wondering about their future after Chernenko.

The expectation of Chernenko's death was still somewhat premature, for in the meantime the general secretary moved back onto the political stage for a public appearance in the Kremlin to award decorations to three Soviet cosmonauts, two men and one woman, who had been waiting several months (since July) for the ceremony. Either Chernenko himself or his Central Committee colleagues so anticipated the reappearance of the general secretary in public that the ceremony was announced to Western correspondents well ahead of time. In the end, however, the correspondents were not permitted to attend, probably because somebody in the Kremlin decided that the world should be spared the sight of a haggard-looking and decrepit ruler of the Soviet empire.[20]

Holding the supreme authority failed to provide the incapacitated Chernenko with the once eagerly sought and relished satisfaction. Now it was difficult for him even to grasp the sense of communications and react, especially because the messages intended for him were blocked, jammed, or tampered with by Party bureaucrats. Yet, they still needed him to ensure the preservation of the status quo. Soon before his death they arranged for one final triumphal occasion for him: he was to be awarded his third gold star of Hero of Socialist Labor. This was quite unusual. Soviet rulers are awarded orders and medals on anniversaries, such as their fiftieth, sixtieth, or seventieth birthdays, or in special cases, their seventy-fifth. September 24 marked Chernenko's birthday, but that year, 1984, it was his seventy-third. Normally, such a birthday would not be noted officially or hailed with congratulations in the press but merely celebrated by intimates. Instead, on September 24 newspapers carried the decree about the awarding of the Hero of Socialist Labor to Chernenko.

On September 27 his closest associates assembled in the Kremlin to confer the award and hail him as an "outstanding political figure, a loyal and unwavering continuer of the cause of the great Lenin."[21] This effusive praise was expressed by Ustinov, who normally steered clear of high-flown rhetoric. On this occasion, however, the minister of defense apparently expressed his genuine feeling. This could be noticed not so much in the wording of the eulogy, which was pretentious (he spoke of the great contribution of the general secretary to Soviet domestic and foreign policy and his personal role in developing the country's economy, culture, and defense), as in the general warm tone of his remarks, which fit the mood that pervaded the Kremlin on this occasion. Surrounding Chernenko stood the members of the Politburo smiling as if no fierce rivalries and no intrigues had ever divided them.

In the crowd of full and candidate members of the Politburo, Central Committee secretaries, and ministers, one man was conspicuously absent: Romanov. What had happened to him, and why did Ustinov look so pleased when, for the first time, he introduced Chernenko as chairman of the Defense Council and commander in chief of the armed forces? And why did Gorbachev look so pleased? Gorbachev was chatting affably with Chernenko as he supported him by the arm. The reason for this rejoicing in the Kremlin was obvious: the struggle for succession had already begun, with one contender, Romanov, already out of the race.

Only a month before the festive party in the Kremlin Romanov had been very much in the race. He had traveled to Ethiopia, spoken at and sometimes even chaired meetings of the Politburo until the general secretary recovered, and fulfilled his responsibility of supervising the armed forces with dynamism. It turned out that he had done so with too much dynamism. He had been anxious to retire the decrepit Ustinov and have him replaced by the chief of the general staff, Ogarkov. Such a step could have altered the balance of forces in the Kremlin. Romanov and Ogarkov had close work ties and were also close in views and personality. Both were authoritarian, despotic characters. With Ogarkov as defense minister, Romanov not only would have had a powerful and trusty ally but also would have gained a power base for his leap to the very top, which the support of the armed forces could make possible.

Such a prospect was bound to engender the almost unanimous opposition of the Politburo. Chernenko understood that once Romanov had his man as minister of defense, he would have had sufficient power to threaten not only Gorbachev but also him. He feared that unlike Gorbachev, Romanov would not patiently await his death but might seize the first opportunity to topple him from power. Thus, against Romanov's ambitions Chernenko mobilized all his associates: Tikhonov, Grishin, Kunaev, and Shcherbitsky, to whom Gorbachev also lent his support. All of them were unwilling to part with their privileges voluntarily, all the more so because Romanov posed a threat not just to their Party status but also to their continued presence in the political arena, and possibly even to their lives! Ustinov certainly had no desire to be relegated to oblivion; nor did Gromyko feel any more affection for the "upstart" from Leningrad.

Aliev, Grishin, and Vorotnikov supported Chernenko against Romanov for a different reason: they feared a military coup whose whiff they could detect in the air. Over the years, Ogarkov had gained considerable political influence by skillfully exploiting frequent changes in the Politburo and the poor health of the minister of defense. There was even speculation that he might later push Romanov aside and grab power for himself. His authority in the army was sufficient for such a risk, and he scarcely concealed his ambition.

In recent years the Party had lost some of its control over the army. While Party leaders retained their right to comment on political implications of Soviet military doctrine, they were capable of articulating their viewpoints only in generalities. The military chiefs, on the other hand, emboldened by the example of Ogarkov, more and more allowed themselves to address military aspects of Party politics. The head of the general staff sought to involve generals in various government activities, such as negotiations with the leaders of other countries, press conferences, and drafting articles to be printed in the central press.[22]

Increasing public visibility of the Soviet military leadership reflected the objective growth of its influence on policy decision making. The armed forces had become a key tool of the Kremlin's geopolitical policy based either on actual force or on the threat of using it. In a nutshell, Soviet history of the preceding years can be described as militarization of society on the one hand, and political extremization of the military on the other. Furthermore, military construction had expanded so vastly that it affected all walks of civilian life.

Ogarkov demanded and won a great deal of decision-making power for the armed forces in matters of international politics. Within the body of *spetsnaz* (special task) forces, groups were established to assassinate Western statesmen and other renowned figures in wartime. Other planned tasks of the groups would be destruction of the enemy's nuclear installations, targeting for aerial attacks, and subversion deep in the enemy rear.

The party leadership was disturbed by the growing numbers of the *spetsnaz* forces. The size of these units was first planned not to exceed 30,000 men in peacetime. In fact, their planned size was soon exceeded, with at least sixty to seventy select soldiers and officers attached to each military district and quartered close to Moscow and the republic capitals. Such a potential threat did not please the Politburo.

The powers and responsibilities of the head of the general staff changed. For a long time the post ranked third in the military hierarchy after the minister of defense and the head of the GlavPUpr (Main Political Administration), who had a status equal to the head of a Central Committee department and was responsible to the Party leadership for political and ideological instruction in the armed forces. With the ascent of Ogarkov the situation changed; the head of GlavPUpr no longer had operational control over the armed forces and was replaced as number two in the ranking order of top army officials. When Ustinov was absent, Ogarkov served as acting minister. In this capacity he issued the instruction that every operation-related document needed to be submitted for his approval before being passed to the minister for his signature. This should, however, not be taken as an indication that Ogarkov had gained more power than the minister. Ustinov was a member of the Politburo and by virtue of this had incomparably greater room for action than his head of general staff. But, being old and often ill for long periods, he tended to delegate an increasing amount of his responsibilities to his first deputy. This is why Romanov, while supervising the armed forces and military industry for the Politburo, could rely on dealing primarily with

Ogarkov. Their relationship was one of mutual trust and cooperation. Romanov represented the interests of Ogarkov vis-à-vis the Party leadership, and Ogarkov ensured that Romanov's control over the armed forces yielded effective results.

At Romanov's urging, Ogarkov began to be frequently invited to attend meetings of the Defense Council, even though formally he was not a member of this prestigious body that comprised only the chairman of the Council of Ministers, the minister of defense, the foreign minister, the head of the KGB, and CC secretaries who were simultaneously members of the Politburo. This entree gave Ogarkov significant opportunities to expand his knowledge of politics. He became extremely powerful, with a dual function of participating in Soviet military policy decision making by raising military-technical implications for consideration and, jointly with Politburo members, of advising on political and social implications of military policy.

Ogarkov won an immense authority among the military brass by virtue of his unique position, but he simultaneously evoked considerable alarm among the Party elite, for whom he conjured the image of a commander riding into the Kremlin on a white horse. The issue was no longer that of power or of succession at Chernenko's death but of the perceived danger of a military coup that could put to an end the very existence of the partocratic regime.

The Politburo dealt with Ogarkov just as it had dealt with Marshal Zhukov twenty-seven years earlier. It accused him of Bonapartist tendencies and removed him from office. And yet, like Zhukov, Ogarkov had not even dreamed of launching a military plot. His guilt merely consisted in letting himself be used by Romanov. For his own purposes and apparently without seeking Ogarkov's assent, Romanov had been capitalizing on his ties with Ogarkov so that the army could tip the scales in his favor if the Party leadership were split. Romanov hoped to bring matters to the point of a political crisis wherein Chernenko would fail to act strongly against him. Under these circumstances, the Politburo members had no alternative but to remove Ogarkov from politics. Ogarkov's ouster was therefore a side effect of Romanov's intrigues. Because Ogarkov's innocence was recognized, his punishment was relatively mild. He soon reappeared as operational commander of the Western theater of the Soviet strategic forces, i.e. of the forces directly posed against NATO forces. Meanwhile Romanov withdrew to lick his wounds, but not for long. He soon began weaving the web of a new plot into which he would eventually entice Grishin, Kunaev, and Shcherbitsky.

Gorbachev took a different tack. Realizing that Chernenko would not live much longer, he decided to refrain from any further attempts to discredit Chernenko. He offered this peace for a price, however, and Chernenko agreed to it. Thus, Gorbachev was anointed heir designate and gradually responsibilities began to be transferred to him.

The decision to make the upcoming trip of Gorbachev to England an official state visit was the first direct result of this deal. The purpose was to give Gorbachev the opportunity to gain experience in international affairs. In the Politburo there ensued a period of relative quiet marked by unanimous glorification of Chernenko. The honeymoon, however, turned out to be quite brief.

During the short truce in the Politburo Chernenko could to a certain extent free himself from intrigues in the Party apparat and devote himself to theoretical problems that commanded his interest. Apparently, he felt more at ease when alone with just pen and paper than when coping with external realities. In a number of articles published at that time his attitude was mildly critical of existing conditions. The topics varied, ranging from superficial but nevertheless real problems to cautious disclosures of some systemic faults.[23] Among the latter, the one that concerned him particularly was the inability of Soviet society to change in a gradual and smooth manner, without sharp leaps upward and perilous falls downward.

Chernenko defended and explained his advocacy of continuity by referring to the needs to maintain stability, constancy of purpose, and faithfulness to the ideals of the past. Plainly, Chernenko's purpose here was an indirect polemic against Andropov and Gorbachev, both known as advocates of rapid and radical change. His conclusion sounded paradoxical but there was historical evidence to support it: the moments of greatest peril in development of a society come when it embarks on the road of self-correction. Chernenko believed that the USSR could successfully survive such moments only with the help of ideology (Marxist-Leninist by definition), for ideology was the foundation of Soviet statehood. In other words, for Chernenko, the cultivation of ideology was no less important than the growth of the Soviet economy.

While thinking about the distinctive features of the October Revolution, Chernenko came to the conclusion that the building of communism was bound to take much more time than had been expected, that it would still take many more years, and that prerequisite for reaching the stage of communism was the prior time-consuming passage through the stage of developed socialism. The latter by necessity entailed ideological tensions. One of these related to the lack of knowledge of the properties and of the necessary duration of the various stages toward communism. Challenging customary Soviet doublethink, Chernenko urged that life be studied in all its complexity and contradictions. The first precondition for this was the recognition of these contradictions as a social phenomenon. He rejected the view that Soviet society was free of conflict. He noted that socialist development affects the interests of various segments of the population differentially, and concluded that solving the needs of each was the key to resolving the contradictions.[24]

The idea that lay behind Chernenko's conviction was that there had appeared in Soviet society specifically socialist kinds of conflict. Various modes of analysis suggested to him various ways of resolving them. Although Chernenko downplayed the potential explosiveness of these conflicts, he understood that "developed socialism" generated forces that could destroy it.

Andropov had endeavored to remedy the ills afflicting Soviet society by improving its economic structure and raising productivity. In other words, he sought to strengthen the state by developing its infrastructure. In contrast, Chernenko searched for remedies in the realm of superstructure, particularly in changing the style and methods of ideological work. He hoped that by paying due attention to such matters as upbringing and life-style formation, he would find ways to alter the country's social structure in a positive manner.

Both methods of transforming the USSR proved ineffectual. Under Andropov industry continued to fluctuate wildly from satisfactory to quite unsatisfactory performance, and Chernenko's ideological solutions did not vindicate his hopes for shaping new attitudes and new behavior on the part of the masses. A new Soviet man failed to materialize. The only thing new in Chernenko's approach was his realization of the explosive potential of Marxist theory as a body of doctrine that might still engender a revolutionary transformation of Soviet society. Previous Kremlin leaders, accustomed to Marxist clichés, had not suspected this possibility.

Chernenko was too ill to wield much real power. His rulership was basically symbolic in nature, but his yen for public appearance persisted. In early October he gave a major speech at a meeting of people's inspectors. The speech was of major significance in that he attempted to present a balance sheet of his successes and failures as a ruler, attempting to evaluate realistically what had been achieved without exaggeration or bias. Successes in economic and political development of the country were mostly projected for the future, whereas the present abounded in faults of production, management, and supplies. He stated that social development could do no more than bring society to the brink of envisaged changes. To effect truly watershed transformations, Chernenko proposed a surprising measure: to subject people to even more comprehensive surveillance than already existed. Of course, the idea was not phrased quite so bluntly. He said, "It is urgently necessary that all Soviet people take a conscious interest in the quality of their work."[25] Moreover, he did say explicitly that he meant an "all-embracing and all-penetrating control." He was not referring to the 10-million-strong ranks of professional "controllers" already operating in the Soviet Union; they were not sufficient. He wanted everyone, not just the professionals, to be involved in control. "One should strive for precisely this goal. It is imperative that everyone behave like a supervisor. Take note: every Soviet person should be a rule enforcer, so as to think and act in accord with his supreme civic duty."[26] And Chernenko made crystal clear what would be the tasks of the new "popular overseers." The first task would be to note who were living beyond their means. The goal was defined succinctly: to put an end to bribery, speculation, embezzlement in money or in kind, and abuse of office. This detection of unearned income of citizens was to be carried out by citizens. Such volunteer supervisors and informers were supposed to supplement the police, the prosecutor's office, and the KGB.

Citizen-supervisors were also supposed to assume the duties of administrators in detecting and even apprehending alcoholics and violators of labor discipline, and also seeing to it that production was orderly, material resources not wasted, and plan targets met. In brief, each person was supposed to watch over every other person and to inform on wrongdoers. Chernenko believed this approach was convenient and feasible, and capable of preventing major disasters by timely reporting of negligence and misperformance. He justified such universal surveillance by the best interests of those being kept watch over, without of course realizing that such a justification bore the characteristics of the Orwellian newspeak.

Such were the theoretical concerns and discoveries of Chernenko during the period of his truce with Gorbachev. Truces in general rarely last long, and in Soviet politics particularly they are most often doomed to a speedy expiration. Chernenko did not have long to live. Knowing that he therefore had little time to move, Romanov attempted to disrupt the "misalliance" of his enemies in the Politburo.

While his other passions were fading, Chernenko's passion for power never abated. The more desperately he clung to it, the more its vestiges eluded him, to the point that even the stability of his position was no longer to be taken for granted. This is why he appreciated the idea suggested to him by Romanov to publish in the London-based *New Statesman* a summary of one of his speeches in the form of a paid announcement. Chernenko viewed this as a way of winning attention and approval.[27]

But Romanov had his own interests in mind. Gorbachev's trip to England was scheduled for December. Romanov wanted to minimize the significance of this visit by diverting the interest of the Western public from the person of the rising young Kremlin star and reminding that public that Gorbachev was not yet in charge in Moscow. It was not clear how data concerning the growth of productivity in Soviet agriculture achieved under and cited by Chernenko could interest a British reader. The *New Statesman* announcement did present a favorable image of the old general secretary as a wise and well-meaning statesman sincerely working for peace and concerned with the welfare of his people, frankly admitting the existence of problems in the USSR; otherwise his keen concern about the price of grain and consumer goods would be inexplicable.[28] The reader was supposed to be persuaded that Chernenko was just the Soviet leader that Europe needed, reasonable, restrained, one to whom adventurism or brinkmanship and an appetite for foreign conquests or bellicosity were quite alien. Consequently, the Western public was supposed to refrain from anticipating any new Soviet leader, because no one would offer better prospects than he for resolving world conflicts peacefully and smoothly.

The Chernenko announcement was intended to lower Gorbachev's prestige indirectly by downgrading the expectations that might be attached to his age and image. The intrigue misfired. Chernenko's "article" was in the usual Soviet style, awkward, dull, with the customary Communist exhortations and promises, and hence unreadable. It hardly attracted attention, and hence hardly added to Chernenko's popularity or the public's respect for his views. Romanov thereupon shifted his attention to the home front, where he could better anticipate reactions to his own doings and foresee their consequences.

Romanov began to spread rumors that Gorbachev, impatient that Chernenko's illness had not yet proved terminal, was at the point of "encouraging" his being pensioned off. For this reason Gorbachev ostensibly wanted to postpone the Central Committee plenum session from October until November. The rumor was apparently so effective that the editor of *Pravda* had to issue an official denial: "It is impossible that Chernenko leave his post: I believe that *the time for this has not yet come*" (emphasis added).[29] The denial was so awkward and inept that instead of undermining the rumor's credibility, it conferred on it an aura of plausibility, especially in view of the phrase "not yet." Evidently, Chernenko himself did not remain indifferent to this matter. In any event, whether due to this or other reasons (Chernenko might have feared becoming Gorbachev's hostage, or Chernenko's long-standing hostility to his successful, young rival may have rekindled), Romanov's comeback was assured. Beginning with the second half of October the return of Romanov to active political life was evident, as can be amply documented.[30]

Romanov went on an official visit to Finland, where he displayed his usual self-confidence and assertiveness. Together with Tikhonov, he welcomed a Mongolian government delegation at Sheremetevo airport, and a day later hosted it with Chernenko but without Gorbachev. Then, despite Chernenko's apprehensions, the CC Plenum was convened on schedule. At the Plenum Romanov appeared to be at the center of things, remaining close to Chernenko at the festive Kremlin reception for the Plenum participants while Gorbachev remained on the sidelines.

Gorbachev found himself on the sidelines also at the Plenum itself, in spite of its being devoted to agriculture, his long-standing field of expertise. Despite his background, he was silenced: a major speech about melioration of the soil was delivered by Tikhonov, whose competence in the subject was minimal. Worse still, Chernenko's speech that called for increasing the grain harvest by farming new lands and by irrigation directly contradicted the views of Gorbachev, who assigned priority to increasing labor productivity.[31]

But the Kremlin ranking order at that time was subject to rapid change. When Gromyko was awarded the order of Lenin on the occasion of his seventy-fifth birthday, Soviet television showed Gorbachev next to Chernenko, and the following day's newspapers showed Romanov to the general secretary's right. The two rivals were alternating in second rank, which meant that neither could feel himself the secure, unchallengeable successor. This situation continued until Chernenko's preference began to incline toward Romanov. However, no one in the Kremlin could be sure whether this was the general secretary's momentary whim or was based on a deeper calculation.

Gorbachev's visit to England received broad coverage in the world press. Exalted compliments were lavished not only on him but also on his attractive wife, Raisa. In sharp contrast, the Soviet newspapers did not publish a single photograph of the visit. There were only dry, laconic reports on the inside pages.

The jockeying for succession continued when the death of Ustinov suddenly provided Romanov with a short-lived triumph. Yet, this was a moment of both the peak of his career and of the beginning of his slide downward. Romanov was appointed chairman of the funeral commission, thereby gaining the opportunity to rehearse the role of top leader while heading the funeral ceremony on Red Square. To the strains of Chopin's funeral march and in the glare of spotlights, triumphantly heading the cortege in the absence of Chernenko, Romanov marched through the square and delivered the eulogy from the tribune atop Lenin's mausoleum. Gorbachev did not speak at all during this ceremony. Romanov, however, was overreaching himself. The death of Minister of Defense

Ustinov destroyed the fragile balance of forces in the Kremlin. The members of the Politburo now placed their final bets on the outcome of the succession struggle: Tikhonov, Gromyko, and Vorotnikov flocked to Gorbachev, both to safeguard their own futures and to preserve the regime from the arbitrariness that was Romanov's forte. They were soon joined by Shevardnadze, who encouraged Aliev to support Gorbachev, and by Demichev, Chebrikov, Ponomarev, and Dolgikh. Romanov found himself almost totally isolated. The only tentative exception was Kunaev, who was reluctant to switch sides and had an oriental respect for power, which Romanov radiated.

Still vacillating was Shcherbitsky. He knew that in the event of Gorbachev's becoming general secretary he would inevitably share the fate of all other Brezhnev holdovers in having an end put to his career. But Shcherbitsky was also reluctant to support Romanov because the latter was too abrasive and too quick to get rid of people who stood in his way.

At this point Romanov made his final move, using Grishin as his stalking horse. Grishin was the most veteran member of the Politburo; he headed and hence was supported by the most influential Party organization in the country, that of the capital, which he had controlled for eighteen years. Romanov calculated that he could thus count on the support of the Kremlin's old guard, which was likely to see in Grishin's candidacy for general secretaryship its last chance of staying put in power and blocking the younger men from advancing at its expense. Romanov could also count on support of the press and on Grishin's shrewdness, perseverance, and skills at manipulating the system.

Romanov encouraged Grishin to run for general secretary against Gorbachev. Romanov's hope was that Grishin would be a compromise choice, capable of winning a majority in the Central Committee Plenum if not in the Politburo. Naturally, he perceived Grishin's incumbency as temporary, as a period of respite that would allow him to gather strength to himself and jump at the first opportunity to the top. In point of fact, Grishin received the eager support of Shcherbitsky and Kunaev in the Politburo and that of Zimyanin from among the Central Committee secretaries. Thus, in the Politburo the count was four votes in favor of Grishin and six against. That was not enough. Everything depended on Chernenko, whom Romanov planned to activate at any price, even if it meant straining him to the point of accelerating his death.

In fact, Romanov's scheme was but a replay of an old Kremlin drama with a new cast. The precedent had occurred at the deathbed of Brezhnev; Brezhnev's role was now assigned to Chernenko.[32] This was to be Chernenko's swan song, one of short duration at that. On two brief occasions he appeared to make a farewell from the Soviet political stage. One of these was in his office, the other at a polling station. Chernenko was incapacitated to the point of barely being able to take more than a few faltering steps. Soviet medicine had performed a temporary "miracle": it resuscitated the chief of the nation so that he could mumble the word "khorosho" (fine) and put his ballot tremulously into the box. The elections were to the Supreme Soviet of the RSFSR, the Russian republic. Two days previously, on February 22, 1985, a press announcement had appeared about the general secretary's illness. Soviet citizens understood the meaning of the announcement: the Politburo was now ready to allow Chernenko to die. However, the time to detach Chernenko from the life-support care he was provided with had not yet come.

Romanov needed Chernenko alive; otherwise he could not use the latter's name and authority to solicit votes for himself in the Central Committee. Gorbachev meanwhile did not intervene in the course of the events. For him, the sight of the scarcely alive general secretary was satisfactory enough; it prepared everyone concerned for the impending change. Because Romanov had lost support in the Party apparat, Gorbachev saw no reason to protest when Chernenko was taken out of his oxygen tent and briefly set on his feet again to receive congratulations on the occasion of his strictly symbolic election to the Supreme Soviet. The one chosen to hand Chernenko his certificate of election was Grishin. This was another of Romanov's theatrical gestures intended to project the image of the two leaders, one descending from the Party Olympus and the other ascending it. However, Romanov miscalculated badly, for although several days intervened between the two final appearances of Chernenko staged by Romanov, the set was unchanged. Instead of being on location, e.g. at the polling place, it was obvious that both times Chernenko was being shown against the same pale pink walls of the hospital ward, with the same rug with its bright oriental Persian patterns and the same white blinds gently filtering the light from outside. His last performance was a flop.

There had been no mercy for Chernenko. Only after attempting, unsuccessfully, to squeeze the last advantage out of him, did Romanov let Chernenko die. During his lifetime Chernenko had succeeded in planning and arranging much, but he was not free to plan or arrange his own death. He died in pain and agony. With him the generation of Bolsheviks who were contemporaries of the Revolution departed from the Soviet political scene.

Chernenko died on March 10 at 7:20 P.M. On the next day his successor was proclaimed. The election of Gorbachev proceeded smoothly and quickly. Old age and the successive deaths of his predecessors were the best arguments in his favor. The country bade farewell to its past without nostalgia.

The death of the top Soviet leader is always a dramatic event. When it occurs, it stirs mingled feelings of uncertainty, fear, and hope, both in the Soviet Union and in the world at large. When people learned of the death of Chernenko, however, there was neither fear nor uncertainty. There was only hope.

Notes

1. "Meeting of K. U. Chernenko with the workers of the Moscow Metallurgical plant 'Hammer and Sickle.' Speech of Comrade K. U. Chernenko," *Pravda*, April 30, 1984.
2. "Answers of K. U. Chernenko to questions of the American journalist J. Kingsberry-Smith," *Pravda*, June 12, 1984.
3. Ibid.
4. "Answers of K. U. Chernenko to questions posed by the newspaper *Pravda*," *Izvestiya*, June 1, 1984.
5. TASS communiqué, *Pravda*, June 3, 1984.
6. See note 2, above.
7. See note 5, above.
8. See *Gorbachev: The Man and the System*, by Ilya Zemtsov and John Farrar (New Brunswick, N.J.: Transaction Books, 1989).
9. See note 4, above.
10. Ibid.
11. K. U. Chernenko, *Izbrannye rechi i statyi* (Selected speeches and articles) (Moskva: Izd-vo politicheskoy literatury, 1984), pp. 545-55; Report at the Plenum of the CC, CPSU of June 14, 1983, *Pravda*, June 15, 1983.
12. *Izvestiya*, April 20, 1984; *Krasnaya zvezda*, May 8, 1984; *Pravda*, May 5, June 5, 15, 1984.
13. *Pravda*, June 14, 17, 1984.
14. "Report on the Basic Direction of Future Development and Strengthening of Economic, Scientific and Technological Cooperation of the COMECON Member Countries," *Izvestiya*, June 16, 1984.
15. *Izvestiya*, July 24-30, August 3-8, 1984.
16. *Pravda*, July 21-29, August 2-11, 1984.
17. "Talks in the Kremlin," *Pravda*, July 5, 1984.
18. "Departure of Comrade K. U. Chernenko for Vacation," *Izvestiya*, July 16, 1984.
19. "Answers of K. U. Chernenko to Questions of the Newspaper *Pravda*," *Pravda*, September 2, 1984.
20. "For Courage and Heroism in Conquering Space," *Pravda*, September 6, 1984.
21. "Presentation of the Country's High Award," *Pravda*, September 28, 1984.
22. "Report on press conference in Moscow," *Pravda*, December 6, 1984; Marshal of the Soviet Union N. V. Ogarkov, "For the World—A Reliable Defense," *Krasnaya zvezda*, October 23, 1983; N. V. Ogarkov, *Istoriya uchit bditel'nosti* (History teaches vigilance) (Moscow: Voenizdat, 1985).

23. K. U. Chernenko, *Narod i partiya ediny* (The people and the party are one) (Moscow: Izd-vo politicheskoy literatury, 1984), pp. 450–60.
24. K. U. Chernenko, "On the Level of the Requirements of Developed Socialism," *Kommunist*, no. 18 (1984): 4–21.
25. "'The High Civil Calling of the People's Inspector,' Speech of Comrade K. U. Chernenko," *Partiynaya zhizn*, no. 20 (1984): 15.
26. Ibid., p. 16
27. *New Statesman*, November 9, 1984, p. 21.
28. Ibid.
29. *Ashai Shimabun*, November 10, 1984.
30. One can practically pinpoint the time when Romanov returned to active political life; it was between October 7 and 24, because he did not participate in the October 5 presidium of the All-Union Conference of People's Inspectors but did take part in the greeting at Sheremetyevo airport of a government delegation from Mongolia on October 25.
31. "Speech of Comrade K. U. Chernenko at the Plenum of the CC, CPSU," *Kommunist*, no. 16 (1984): 3–11.
32. Vladimir Solovyev and Elena Klepikova, *Bor'ba v Kremle* (*Struggle in the Kremlin*) (*Vremya i my* Publishers, 1986), pp. 185–90.

Bibliography

Adams, Jan S. *Citizen Inspectors in the Soviet Union.* New York: Praeger, 1977.

Adelman, Jonathan R. "The Soviet Use of Force: Four Cases of Soviet Crisis Decisionmaking." *Crossroads* 19 (1985): 47–81.

Adomeit, Hannes. "Soviet Crisis Prevention and Management: Why and When Do the Soviet Leaders Take Risks?" *Orbis* 30 (Spring 1986): 42–64.

"Agrarian-Industrial Integration in the Soviet Union." *Radio Liberty Research Bulletin*, 351/76. New York: Radio Liberty, July 14, 1976.

Alexandrov, Victor. *Krushchev of the Ukraine.* New York: Philosophical Library, 1957.

Alexeyeva, Ludmilla. *Soviet Dissent: Contemporary Movement for National, Religious and Human Rights.* Middletown, Conn: Wesleyan University Press, 1985.

Alexiev, Alex R. "Soviet Strategy and the Mujahidin." *Orbis* 29 (Spring 1985): 31–40.

———. "The Soviet Campaign against INF: Strategy, Tactics and Means." *Orbis* 29 (Summer 1985): 319–50.

Alford, Jonathan, ed. *The Soviet Union: Security Policies and Constraints.* New York: St. Martin's Press, 1985.

Anderson, Lisa. "Qaddafi and the Kremlin." *Problems of Communism* 34 (September–October 1985): 29–44.

Atherton, Alfred L., Jr. "The Soviet Role in the Middle East: An American View." *Middle East Journal* 39 (Autumn 1985): 688–715.

Azrael, Jeremy. "Varieties of De-Stalinization." In *Change in Communist Systems*, ed. Chalmers Johnson. Stanford: Stanford University Press, 1970.

Barghoorn, Frederick C. *Politics USSR.* 2d ed. Boston: Little, Brown, 1972.

Barron, John. *KGB: The Secret Work of Soviet Secret Agents*. New York: Reader's Digest Press, 1974.

Baxter, William P. *Soviet Air-Land Battle Tactics*. Novato, Calif.: Presidio Press, 1985.

Becker, Abraham. *Soviet Military Outlays since 1955*. Santa Monica, Calif.: RAND Corporation 1964.

Beissinger, Mark R. "In Search of Generations in Soviet Politics." *World Politics* 38 (January 1986): 288–314.

Bennett, Alexander J. "Arms Transfers as an Instrument of Soviet Policy in the Middle East." *Middle East Journal* 39 (Autumn 1985): 745–74.

Bennigsen, Alexandre. "Islam in the Soviet Union." *Journal of South Asian and Middle Eastern Studies* 8 (Summer 1985): 115–33.

Berliner, Joseph. "Prospects for Technological Progress." In *Soviet Economy in a New Perspective*, comp. U.S. Congress, Joint Economic Committee. Washington, D.C.: Government Printing Office, 1976.

———. *The Innovation Decision in Soviet Industry*. Cambridge: MIT Press, 1978.

Bialer, Seweryn. "The Soviet Political Elite and Internal Developments in the USSR." In *The Soviet Empire: Expansion and Detente*, ed. William Griffith. Lexington, Mass.: Lexington Books, 1976.

———. "The Harsh Decade: Soviet Policies in the 1980's." *Foreign Affairs* 59 (Summer 1981): 999–1020.

———. *The Soviet Paradox: External Expansion, Internal Decline*. New York: Knopf, 1986.

Bittman, Ladislav. *The KGB and Soviet Disinformation: An Insider's View*. New York: Pergamon-Brassey's, 1985.

Bloomfield, Lincoln P.; Clemens, Walter C., Jr.; and Griffiths, Franklyn. *Khrushchev and the Arms Race*. Cambridge: MIT Press, 1966.

Bodansky, Yossef. "The Initial Period of War: Surprise and Special Operations." *Global Affairs* 1 (Spring 1986): 123–35.

Bond, Daniel L., and Levine, Herbert S. "The 11th Five-Year Plan, 1981–1985." In *Russia at the Crossroads: The 26th Congress of the CPSU*, ed. Seweryn Bialer and Thane Gustafson. London: Allen & Unwin, 1982.

Braker, Heinz. "Soviet Domestic Policy 1977–1979." In *The Soviet Union 1978–1979*, vol. 5. New York and London: Holmes & Meier, 1980.

Breslauer, George. "Khrushchev Reconsidered." *Problems of Communism* (September–October 1976).

———. "The Twenty-Fifth Party Congress: Domestic Issues." In *The Twenty-Fifth Congress of the CPSU*, ed. Alexander Dallin. Stanford: Hoover Institution Press, 1977.

———. *Five Images of the Soviet Future*. Berkeley: University of California, Institute of International Studies, 1978.

———. "Political Succession and the Soviet Policy Agenda." 29 *Problems of Communism* (May–June 1980): 34–52.

_____. "Research Note." *Soviet Studies* (July 1981).

_____. *Khrushchev and Brezhnev as Leaders: Building Authority in Soviet Politics*. London: Allen & Unwin, 1982.

Brinkley, George. "Khrushchev Remembered: On the Theory of Soviet Statehood." *Soviet Studies* 24 (January 1973): 387–401.

Brown, Archie. "The Power of the General Secretary." In *Authority, Power and Policy in the USSR*, T. H. Rigby, Archie Brown, and Peter Reddaway. London: Macmillan, 1980.

_____. "Andropov: Discipline and Reform." *Problems of Communism* 32 (January–February 1983): 18–31.

_____. "Gorbachev: New Man in the Kremlin." *Problems of Communism* 34 (May–June 1985): 1–23.

Brown, Archie, and Kaser, Michael, eds. *The Soviet Union since the Fall of Khrushchev*. New York: Free Press, 1975.

_____, eds. *Soviet Policy for the 1980s*. Bloomington: Indiana University Press, 1982.

Brzezinski, Zbigniew. "The Soviet System: Transformation or Degeneration?" *Problems of Communism* 15 (January–February 1966): 1–15.

_____. *Game Plan: How to Conduct the US-Soviet Contest*. Boston: Atlantic Monthly Press, 1986.

Brzezinski, Zbigniew, and Huntington, Samuel. *Political Power: USA/USSR*. New York: Viking Press, 1963.

Bunce, Valerie. *Do New Leaders Make a Difference? Executive Succession and Public Policy under Capitalism and Socialism*. Princeton: Princeton University Press, 1981.

Bush, Keith. "Soviet Capital Investment since Khrushchev: A Note." *Soviet Studies* 24 (July 1972): 91–96.

_____. "Resource Allocation Policy: Capital Investment." In *Soviet Economic Prospects for the Seventies*, comp. U.S. Congress, Joint Economic Committee. Washington, D.C.: Government Printing Office, 1973.

_____. *Soviet Agriculture: Ten Years under New Management*. Radio Liberty Research Paper, 21. New York: Radio Liberty, August 1974.

_____. "Major Decree on Private Plots and Livestock Holdings." *Radio Liberty Research Bulletin*, 38/81. New York: Radio Liberty, January 26, 1981.

Butson, Thomas G. *Gorbachev: A Biography*. New York: Stein & Day, 1985.

Caldwell, Lawrence T. *Soviet Attitudes to SALT*. Adelphi Papers no. 75. London: Institute of Strategic Studies, 1971.

Chadwick, Michael Lloyd. "The Strategic Defense Initiative: Meeting the Soviet Military Challenge in the 21st Century." *Global Affairs* 1 (Spring 1986): 136–48.

Chapman, Janet. *Wage Variation in Soviet Industry: The Impact of the 1956-1960 Wage Reform*. Santa Monica, Calif.: RAND Corporation, 1970.

Cigar, Norman. "South Yemen and the USSR: Prospects for the Relationship." *Middle East Journal* 39 (Autumn 1985): 775–95.

Clement, Peter. "Moscow and Southern Africa." *Problems of Communism* 34 (March–April 1985): 29–50.

Cocks, Paul. "Science Policy and Soviet Development Strategy." In *The Twenty-Fifth Congress of the CPSU*, ed. Alexander Dallin. Stanford: Hoover Institution Press, 1977.

———. "Rethinking the Organizational Weapon: The Soviet System in a Systems Age. *World Politics* 32 (January 1980): 228–257.

Cohen, Stephen F. "Foreword." In *Khrushchev: The Years in Power*, ed. Roy Medvedev and Zhores Medvedev. New York: Norton, 1979.

———. "The Friends and Foes of Change: Reformism and Conservatism in the Soviet Union." *Slavic Review* 38, no. 2 (1979): 187–202.

———. *Sovieticus: American Perceptions and Soviet Realities*. New York: Norton, 1985.

Coker, Christopher. *NATO, the Warsaw Pact and Africa*. New York: St. Martin's Press, 1985.

Colton, Timothy J. *Commissars, Commanders and Civilian Authority: The Structure of Soviet Military Politics*. Cambridge: Harvard University Press, 1979.

———. *The Dilemmas of Reform in the Soviet Union*. New York: Council on Foreign Relations, 1984.

Connor, Walter D. "Looking Backward, Looking Forward: Lessons of the Brezhnev Era." *Studies in Comparative Communism* 18 (Winter 1985): 261–69.

———. "Social Policy under Gorbachev." *Problems of Communism* 35 (July–August 1986): 31–46.

Conquest, Robert. *Power and Policy in the USSR*. New York: Harper & Row, 1961.

———. *Russia after Khrushchev*. New York: Praeger, 1965.

Conyngham, William J. *Industrial Management in the Soviet Union*. Stanford: Hoover Institution Press, 1973.

Crankshaw, Edward. *Khrushchev: A Career*. New York: Viking Press, 1966.

Csaba, Laszlo. *Problems of Intra-CMEA Cooperation after the Moscow Summit*. Köln: Berichte das Bundesinstituts für ostwissenschaftliche und internationale Studien, 34, 1986.

Davis, M. Scott, and Sloss, Leon, eds. *A Game for High Stakes: Lessons Learned in Negotiating with the Soviet Union*. Cambridge, Mass.: Ballinger, 1986.

Diamond, Douglas B. "Soviet Agricultural Plans for 1981–1985." In *Russia at the Crossroads: The 26th Congress of the CPSU*, ed. Seweryn Bialer and Thane Gustafson. London: Allen & Unwin, 1982.

Donaldson, Robert H. "The Soviet Union in South Asia: A Friend to Rely Upon?" *Journal of International Affairs* 34 (Fall/Winter 1980–81): 235–58.

_____, ed. *The Soviet Union and the Third World: Successes and Failures.* Boulder, Colo.: Westview Press, 1981.

Dornberg, John. *Brezhnev: The Masks of Power.* New York: Basic Books, 1974.

Dunmore, Timothy. "Local Party Organs in Industrial Administrations: The Case of the *Ob'edinenie* Reform." *Soviet Studies* 32 (April 1980): 195–217.

Elad, Shlomi, and Merari, Ariel. *The Soviet Bloc and World Terrorism.* Tel Aviv: Tel Aviv University, Jaffee Center for Strategic Studies, 1984.

Elliot, Ianin. "And Now Chernenko." *Survey* 28 (Spring 1984): 5–8.

Ellison, Herbert J. "United Front Strategy and Soviet Foreign Policy." *Problems of Communism* 34 (September–October 1985): 45–64.

Ellison, Herbert J., and Valenta, Jiri, eds. *Grenada and Soviet Cuban Policy.* Boulder, Colo.: Westview Press, 1986.

Erisman, H. Michael. *Cuba's International Relations: The Anatomy of a Nationalistic Foreign Policy.* Boulder, Colo.: Westview Press, 1985.

Fainsod, Merle. "Khrushchevism." In *Marxism in the Modern World*, ed. Milorad M. Drachkovitch. Stanford: Stanford University Press, 1965.

Falk, Pamela. *Cuban Foreign Policy: Caribbean Tempest.* Lexington, Mass.: Lexington Books, 1985.

Farrar, John H. "Soviet Strategic Nuclear Thought." *Crossroads* 21 (1987): 31–57.

Feher, Ferenc; Heller, Agnes; and Markus, Gyorgyi. *Dictatorship over Needs.* Oxford: Basil Blackwell, 1983.

Feiwel, George R. "Economic Performance and Reforms in the Soviet Union." In *Soviet Politics in the Brezhnev Era*, ed. Donald R. Kelley. New York: Praeger, 1980.

"Financial Aid for the Construction of Private Homes in Rural Areas." *Radio Liberty Research Bulletin*, 124/77. New York: Radio Liberty, May 25, 1977.

Fitzgerald, Mary C. "Marshal Ogarkov on the Modern Theater Operation." *Navel War College Review* 39 (Autumn 1986): 6–25.

Frankland, Mark. *Khrushchev.* New York: Stein & Day, 1967.

Freedman, Robert O. "Moscow and a Middle East Peace Settlement." *Washington Quarterly* (Summer 1985): 143–160.

Fremeauz, Philippe, and Durand, Christine. *Comprendre l'Economie Sovietique* (Understanding the Soviet economy). Paris: Syros, 1985.

Friedgut, Theodore. *Political Participation in the USSR.* Princeton: Princeton University Press, 1979.

"Further Aid to Private Farms." *Radio Liberty Research Bulletin*, 125/77. New York: Radio Liberty, May 25, 1977.

Gaddis, John Lewis. "The Long Peace: Elements of Stability in the Postwar International System." *International Security* 10 (Spring 1986): 99–142.

Garfinkle, Adam M. "Obstacles and Optimism at Geneva." *Orbis* 29 (Summer 1985): 268–80.

Garthoff, Raymond L. "Mutual Deterrence and Strategic Arms Limitations in Soviet Policy." *International Security* 3 (Summer 1978): 112–147.

Gati, Charles. "The Soviet Empire: Alive but Not Well." *Problems of Communism* 34 (March–April 1985): 73–86.

Gelman, Harry. "Rise and Fall of Detente." *Problems of Communism* 34 (March–April 1985): 51–72.

Gilison, Jerome. "New Factors of Stability in Soviet Collective Leadership." *World Politics* 19 (July 1967): 563–581.

Golan, Galia. "The Soviet Union and the PLO since the War in Lebanon." *Middle East Journal* 40 (Spring 1986): 285–305.

Gonzalez, Edward. "The Cuban and Soviet Challenge in the Caribbean Basin." *Orbis* 29 (Spring 1985): 73–74.

Green, Donald. "Capital Formation in the USSR: An Econometric Investigation of Bureaucratic Intervention in the Process of Capital Construction." *Review of Economics and Statistics* 60 (February 1978): 39–46.

Greenberg, Linda Lubrano. "Soviet Science Policy and the Scientific Establishment." *Survey* 17 (Autumn 1971): 51–63.

Griffith, William E. "Superpower Problems in Europe: A Comparative Assessment." *Orbis* 29 (Winter 1986): 735–52.

Griffith, William E. "Superpower Relations after Afghanistan." *Survival* 22 (July–August 1980): 146–51.

Grossman, Gregory. "Notes for a Theory of the Command Economy." *Soviet Studies* 15 (October 1963): 101–123.

Gustafson, Thane. *Reform in Soviet Politics.* New York: Cambridge University Press, 1981.

_____. "Soviet Energy Policy: From Big Coal to Big Gas." In *Russia at the Crossroads: The 26th Congress of the CPSU*, ed. Seweryn Bialer and Thane Gustafson. London: Allen & Unwin, 1982.

Ha, Joseph M. "The Soviet Policy toward East Asia: Its Perception on the Korean Unification." *Asian Perspective* 10 (Spring–Summer 1986): 133–46.

Hammer, Darrell. *USSR: The Politics of Oligarchy.* Hinsdale, Ill.: Dryden Press, 1974.

Hardenbergh, Chalmers. "The Other Negotiations." *Bulletin of the Atomic Scientists* (March 1987): 48–49.

Harris, William R. "Arms Control Treaties: How Do They Restrain Soviet Strategic Defense Programs?" *Orbis* 29 (Winter 1986): 701–8.

Haselkorn, Avigdor. "The Soviet Union and the Radical Entente." *Global Affairs* 1 (Spring 1986): 100–122.

Hasewega, Tsuyoshi. "Soviets on Nuclear War Fighting." *Problems of Communism* 35 (July–August 1986): 68–79.

Hauner, Milan. "Seizing the Third Parallel: Geopolitics and the Soviet Advance into Central Asia." *Orbis* 29 (Spring 1985): 5-31.

Hewett, Ed A. "Gorbachev's Economic Strategy: A Preliminary Assessment." *Soviet Economy* 1 (October-December 1985): 285-305.

Hill, Ronald J. *Soviet Politics, Political Science and Reform*. White Plains, N.Y.: M. E. Sharpe, 1980.

Hodnett, Grey. "Succession Contingencies in the Soviet Union." *Problems of Communism* 24 (March-April 1975): 1-21.

_____. "The Pattern of Leadership Politics." In *The Domestic Context of Soviet Foreign Policy*, ed. Seweryn Bialer. Boulder, Colo.: Westview Press, 1980.

Hoffman, Erik P., and Laird, Robin F. *The Politics of Economic Modernization in the Soviet Union*. Ithaca: Cornell University Press, 1984.

_____. *Technocratic Socialism: The Soviet Union in the Advanced Industrial Era*. Durham, N.C.: Duke University Press, 1985.

Hohman, Hans Hermann. *Strukturen, Probleme und Perspektiven sowjetischer Wirtschaftspolitik nach dem XXVII Parteitag der KPdSU* (Structures, problems and prospects of Soviet economic policy following the XXVII Party Congress of the CPSU). Köln: Berichte des Bundesinstituts für ostwissenschaftliche und internationale Studien, 22, 1986.

Holloway, David. *The Soviet Union and the Arms Race*. 2d ed. New Haven: Yale University Press, 1984.

Holzman, Franklyn. *Financial Checks on Soviet Defense Expenditure*. Lexington, Mass.: Lexington Books, 1975.

Hough, Jerry F. "A Bare-brained Scheme in Retrospect." *Problems of Communism* 14 (July-August 1965): 26-32.

_____. "Enter N. S. Khrushchev." *Problems of Communism* 13 (July-August 1964): 28-33.

_____. *The Soviet Prefects*. Cambridge: Harvard University Press, 1968.

_____. "The Party Apparatchiki." In *Interest Groups in Soviet Politics*, ed. H. Gordon Skilling and Franklyn Griffiths. Princeton: Princeton University Press, 1971.

_____. "The Brezhnev Era: The Man and the System." *Problems of Communism* 25 (March-April 1976): 1-17.

_____. *The Soviet Union and Social Science Theory*. Cambridge: Harvard University Press, 1977.

_____. *Soviet Leadership in Transition*. Washington, D.C.: Brookings Institution, 1980.

_____. "The World as Viewed from Moscow." *International Journal* 32 (Spring 1982): 183-97.

_____. "Soviet Succession: Issues and Personalities." *Problems of Communism* 31 (September-October 1982): 20-40.

_____. *The Struggle for the Third World: Soviet Debates and American Options*. Washington, D.C.: Brookings Institution, 1986.

Hough, Jerry F., and Fainsod, Merle. *How the Soviet Union Is Governed?* Cambridge: Harvard University Press, 1979.

Hutchings, Raymond. *The Soviet Budget*. Albany: State University of New York Press, 1983.

Hyland, William G. "Kto Kogo in the Kremlin." *Problems of Communism* 31 (January–February 1982): 17–26.

Ioffe, Olimpiad S. *Soviet Law and Soviet Reality*. Dordrecht: Martinus N. Nijhoff, 1985.

Jamgotch, Nish, Jr., ed. *Sectors of Mutual Benefit in U.S.-Soviet Relations*. Durham, N.C.: Duke University Press, 1985.

Johnson, D. Gale, and Brooks, Karen McConnell. *Prospects for Soviet Agriculture in the 1980s*. Bloomington: Indiana University Press, 1983.

Jones, Ellen. *Red Army and Society*. London: Allen & Unwin, 1985.

Jones, Ellen, and Woodbury, Benjamin L. "Chernobyl and 'Glasnost.'" *Problems of Communism* 35 (November–December 1986): 28–39.

Jowitt, Kenneth. *Revolutionary Breakthroughs and National Development*. Berkeley: University of California Press, 1971.

———. "An Organizational Approach to the Study of Political Culture in Marxist-Leninist Systems." *American Political Science Review* (September 1974).

———. "Inclusion and Mobilization in European Leninist Regimes." *World Politics* (October 1975).

Juviler, Peter. *Revolutionary Law and Order*. New York: Free Press, 1976.

Kanet, Roger. "The Rise and Fall of the 'All-Peoples State': Recent Changes in the Soviet Theory of the State." *Soviet Studies* 20 (July 1968): 81–93.

Kanet, Roger, and Ganguly, Sumit. "Soviet Strategy in Southwest Asia and the Persian Gulf Region." *Crossroads* 20 (1986): 1–20.

Kass, Ilana, and Burger, Ethan A. "Soviet Responses to the U.S. Strategic Defense Initiative: The ABM Gambit Revisited." *Air University Review* (March–April 1985): 55–64.

Katseneilinbogen, Aron. *Studies in Soviet Economic Planning*. White Plains, N.Y.: M. E. Sharpe, 1978.

———. *Soviet Economic Thought and Political Power in the USSR*. New York: Pergamon Press, 1980.

Katz, Abraham. *The Politics of Economic Reform in the Soviet Union*. London: Pall Mall Press, 1973.

Katz, Mark N. *Russia and Arabia: Soviet Foreign Policy toward the Arabian Peninsula*. Baltimore: Johns Hopkins University Press, 1986.

Kelley, Donald R., ed. *Soviet Politics in the Brezhnev Era*. New York: Praeger, 1980.

Kerblay, Basile. *Modern Soviet Society*. Trans. Rupert Swyer. London: Methuen, 1985.

Kerst, Kenneth. "CPSU History Revisited." *Problems of Communism* 26 (May–June 1977): 17–32.

Khalidi, Rashid. "Arab Views of the Soviet Role in the Middle East." *Middle East Journal* 39 (Autumn 1985): 716–32.

Khalilzad, Zalmay. "Moscow's Afghan War." *Problems of Communism* 35 (January–February 1986): 1–20.

Kirsch, Leonard. *Soviet Wages: Changes in Structure and Administration since 1956.* Cambridge: MIT Press, 1972.

Kitrinos, Robert W. "International Department of the CPSU." *Problems of Communism* 33 (September–October 1984): 47–75.

Kolkowicz, Roman. "The Military and Soviet Foreign Policy." *Journal of Strategic Studies* 4 (December 1981): 337–55.

Kontorovich, Vladimir. "Discipline and Growth in the Soviet Economy." *Problems of Communism* 34 (November–December 1985): 18–31.

Kushnirsky, Fyodor I. "The Limits of Soviet Economic Reform." *Problems of Communism* 33 (July–August 1984): 33–43.

Kusin, Vladimir V. "Gorbachev and East Europe." *Problems of Communism* 35 (January–February 1986): 39–53.

Labedz, Leopold. "Chernenko: The Future of the Past." *Survey* 28 (Spring 1984): 1–4.

Lee, William. *The Estimation of Soviet Defense Expenditures for 1955–1975.* New York: Praeger, 1977.

Leonhard, Wolfgang. *The Kremlin and the West: A Realistic Approach.* New York: Norton, 1986.

Levi, Arrigo. "The Evolution of the Soviet System." In *The Dilemmas of Change in Soviet Politics,* ed. Zbigniew Brzezinski. New York: Columbia University Press, 1969.

Levine, Herbert. "Pressure and Planning in the Soviet Economy." In *Industrialization in Two Systems: Essays in Honor of Alexander Gerschenkron,* ed. Henry Rosovsky. New York: Wiley, 1966.

Lewin, Moshe. *Political Undercurrents in Soviet Economic Debates.* London: Pluto Press, 1975.

Linde, Gerd. *Libyen: Terroristenbasis und sowjetischer Klient* (Libya: A base for terrorists and Soviet client). Köln: Berichte des Bundesinstituts für ostwissenschaftliche und internationale Studien, 25, 1980.

Linden, Carl. *Khrushchev and the Soviet Leadership, 1957–1964.* Baltimore: Johns Hopkins University Press, 1966.

Litwack, Robert S., and MacFarlane, S. Neil. "Soviet Activism in the Third World." *Survival* 29 (January–February 1987): 21–39.

Lowenthal, Richard. "The Soviet Union in the Post-revolutionary Era: An Overview." In *Soviet Politics since Khrushchev,* ed. Alexander Dallin and Thomas B. Larson. Englewood Cliffs, N.J.: Prentice-Hall, 1968.

_____. "Development versus Utopia in Communist Policy." In *Change in Communist Systems,* ed. Chalmers Johnson. Stanford: Stanford University Press, 1970.

Luttwack, Edward W. "Delusions of Soviet Weakness." *Commentary* (January 1985): 32–38.

MacFarlane, S. Neil. "The Soviet Conception of National Security." *World Politics* 37 (April 1985): 235–316.

_____. *Superpower Rivalry and Third World Radicalism: The Idea of National Liberation.* Baltimore: Johns Hopkins University Press, 1985.

Mackintosh, Malcolm. "The Russian Attitude to Defense and Disarmament." *International Affairs* 61 (Summer 1985): 385–94.

Mastanduno, Michael. "Strategies of Economic Containment: U.S. Trade Relations with the Soviet Union." *World Politics* 37 (July 1985): 503–31.

May, Michael M. "The U.S.-Soviet Approach to Nuclear Weapons." *International Security* (Spring 1985): 140–53.

McCauley, Martin. *Khrushchev and the Development of Soviet Agriculture.* London: Macmillan, 1976.

_____. *The Soviet Union after Brezhnev.* London: Heinemann, 1983.

McConnell, James M. "Shifts in Soviet Views on the Proper Focus of Military Development." *World Politics* 37 (April 1985): 317–43.

Medvedev, Roy. *All Stalin's Men.* Trans. Harold Shukman. Oxford: Basil Blackwell, 1983.

Medvedev, Roy, and Medvedev, Zhores. *Khrushchev: The Years in Power.* New York: Norton, 1977.

Medvedev, Zhores A. *Gorbachev.* New York: Norton, 1986.

Meissner, Boris. "The 26th Party Congress and Soviet Domestic Politics." *Problems of Communism* 30 (May–June 1981): 1–23.

_____. "Transition in the Kremlin." *Problems of Communism* 32 (January–February 1983): 8–17.

Meyer, Alfred G. "Authority in Communist Political Systems." In *Political Leadership in Industrial Societies,* ed. J. Edinger. New York: Wiley, 1967.

Mickiewicz, Ellen. *Soviet Political Schools.* New Haven: Yale University Press, 1969.

Miller, Robert F. "Continuity and Change in the Administration of Soviet Agriculture since Stalin." In *The Soviet Rural Community,* ed. James R. Millar. Urbana: University of Illinois Press, 1971.

_____. "The Policy of Implementation in the USSR: Soviet Policies on Agricultural Integration under Brezhnev." *Soviet Studies* 32 (April 1980): 171–194.

Mills, Richard M. "The Soviet Leadership Problem." *World Politics* 30 (July 1981): 590–613.

Mitchell, R. Judson. "The Soviet Succession: Who and What Will Follow Brezhnev?" *Orbis* 23 (Spring 1979): 9–34.

_____. "The CPSU Politburo in 1990: A Projection." *Crossroads* 19 (1986): 21–44.

Mitchell, R. Judson, and Gee, Teresa. "The Soviet Succession Crisis and Its Aftermath." *Orbis* 29 (Summer 1985): 293-317.

Moreton, Edwina, and Segal, Gerald, eds. *Soviet Strategy toward Western Europe.* London: Allen & Unwin, 1984.

Murphy, Patrick. "Soviet Shabashniki: Material Incentives at Work." *Problems of Communism* 34 (November-December 1985): 48-57.

Myagkov, Alexei. *Inside the KGB.* New York: Ballantine Books, 1976.

Napper, Larry C. "The Arab Autumn of 1984: A Case Study of Soviet Middle East Policy." *Middle East Journal* 39 (Autumn 1985): 733-44.

Nation, R. Craig, and Kauppi, Mark V., eds. *The Soviet Impact on Africa.* Lexington, Mass.: Lexington Books, 1984.

Nicolaevsky, Boris. *Power and the Soviet Elite.* New York: Praeger, 1965.

Nimitz, Nancy. "Reform and Technological Innovation in the Eleventh Five-Year Plan." In *Russia at the Crossroads: The 26th Congress of the CPSU,* ed. Seweryn Bialer and Thane Gustafson. London: Allen & Unwin 1982.

Nove, Alec. *An Economic History of the USSR.* London: Allen Lane, 1969.

————. *The Soviet Economic System.* London: Allen & Unwin, 1977.

————. *The Economics of Feasible Socialism.* London: Allen & Unwin, 1983.

Odom, William E. "Soviet Force Posture: Dilemmas and Directions." *Problems of Communism* 34 (July-August 1985): 1-14.

Olgin, Constantin. *Socialist Competition under Brezhnev: An Interim Report.* Radio Liberty Research Supplement. New York: Radio Liberty, May 16, 1975.

Osborn, Robert. *The Evolution of Soviet Politics.* Homewood, Ill.: Dorsey Press, 1974.

Paarlberg, R. L. *Food Trade and Foreign Policy.* Ithaca: Cornell University Press, 1985.

Page, Stephen. *The Soviet Union and the Yemens: Influence in Asymmetrical Relationships.* New York: Praeger, 1985.

Paltiel, Jeremy. "De-Stalinization and De-Maoization." Paper presented at the Annual Meeting of the Canadian Political Science Association, Universite du Quebec a Montreal, June 2-4, 1980.

Pankhurst, Jerry G., and Sacks, Michael Paul, eds. *Contemporary Soviet Society: Sociological Perspectives.* New York: Praeger, 1980.

Papp, Daniel B. *Soviet Perceptions of the Developing World in the 1980s: The Ideological Basis.* Lexington, Mass.: D. C. Heath, 1985.

Parrott, Bruce. "Politics and Economics in the USSR." *Problems of Communism* 26 (May-June 1977): 54-59.

Payne, Keith B. *Strategic Defense: "Star Wars" in Perspective.* Lanham, Md.: Hamilton Press, 1986.

Pipes, Richard. "Why the Soviet Union Thinks It Could Fight and Win a Nuclear War." *Commentary* (July, 1977): 21–34.

_____. *Survival Is Not Enough: Soviet Realities and America's Future.* New York: Simon & Schuster, 1984.

Platt, Alan. *Soviet-West European Relations.* Santa Monica, Calif.: RAND Corporation, March 1986.

Ploss, Sidney J. "Soviet Succession: Signs of Struggle." *Problems of Communism* 31 (September–October 1982): 41–52.

_____, ed. *The Soviet Political Process.* Waltham, Mass.: Ginn, 1970.

Poljanski, Nikolai, and Rahr, Alexander. *Gorbatschjow: der neue Mann* (Gorbachev: The new man). Munich: Verlag Universitas, 1986.

Pollack, David. "Moscow and Aden: Coping with a Coup." *Problems of Communism* 35 (May–June 1986): 50–70.

Porket, J. L. "Unemployment in the Midst of Labor Waste." *Survey* 29 (Spring 1985): 19–28.

Prybyla, Jan S. "The Dawn of Real Communism: Problems of COMECON." Orbis 29 (Summer 1985): 387–402.

Ramet, Pedro. "The Soviet Syrian Relationship." *Problems of Communism* 35 (September–October 1986): 35–46.

Rigby, T. H. "A Conceptual Approach to Authority, Power, and Policy in the Soviet Union." In *Authority, Power and Policy in the USSR*, ed. T. H. Rigby, Archie Brown, and Peter Reddaway. New York: St. Martin's Press, 1980.

Rigby, T. H., and Miller, R. F. *Political and Administrative Aspects of the Scientific and Technological Revolution in the USSR.* Canberra: Australian National University, 1976.

Rivkin, David B., Jr. "What Does Moscow Think?" *Foreign Policy* 59 (Summer 1985): 85–105.

Rosefielde, Steven. *Underestimating the Soviet Military Threat.* New Brunswick, N.J.: Transaction Books, 1981.

Ross, Dennis. "Coalition Maintenance in the Soviet Union." *World Politics* 32 (January 1980): 258–280.

Rothberg, Abraham. *The Heirs of Stalin.* Ithaca: Cornell University Press, 1972.

Rubinstein, Alvin Z. "The Changing Strategic Balance and Soviet Third World Risk Taking." *Naval War College Review* 38 (March–April 1985): 5–17.

Rubinstein, Joshua. *Soviet Dissidents: Their Struggle for Human Rights.* 2d ed. Boston: Beacon Press, 1985.

Rumer, Boris. "Structural Imbalance in the Soviet Economy." *Problems of Communism*, 33, 4 (July–August 1984): 24–32.

_____. "Realities of Gorbachev's Economic Program." *Problems of Communism* 35 (May–June 1986): 20–31.

Rush, Myron. "Understanding Brezhnev's Political Strength." *Wall Street Journal*, August 20, 1981.

_____. "Succeeding Brezhnev." *Problems of Communism* 32 (January–February 1983): 2–7.
Ryavec, Karl. *Implementation of Soviet Economic Reforms*. New York: Praeger, 1976.
Schlesinger, James. "The Eagle and the Bear: Ruminations on Forty Years of Superpower Relations." *Foreign Affairs* 63 (Summer 1985): 937–61.
Schmidt-Hauer, Christian. *Gorbachev: The Path to Power*. London: I. B. Tauris, 1986.
Schroeder, Gertrude E. "Recent Developments in Soviet Planning and Incentives." In *Soviet Economic Prospects for the Seventies*, comp. U.S. Congress, Joint Economic Committee. Washington, D.C.: Government Printing Office, 1973.
_____. "The Slowdown in Soviet Industry 1976–1982." *Soviet Economy* 1 (January–March 1985): 42–74.
Schwartz, Donald V. "Decisionmaking, Administrative Decentralization and Feedback Mechanisms: Comparison of Soviet and Western Models." *Studies in Comparative Communism* 7 (Spring–Summer 1974): 146–183.
Scott, Harriet Fast, and Scott, William J. *The Armed Forces of the USSR*. Boulder, Colo.: Westview Press, 1979.
Sharlet, Robert. *The New Constitution of 1977: Analysis and Text*. Brunswick, Ohio: King's Court Communications, 1978.
Sheetz, Elizabeth C. "Stepped-up Efforts to Curb Dissent in the USSR." *Radio Liberty Research Bulletin*, 164/77. New York: Radio Liberty, July 12, 1977.
Shevchenko, Arkady N. *Breaking with Moscow*. New York: Knopf, 1985.
Shultz, Richard H., and Godson, Roy. *Dezinformatsia: Active Measures in Soviet Strategy*. Washington, D.C.: Pergamon-Brassey's, 1984.
Simes, Dimitri K. "The Military and Militarism in Soviet Society." *International Security* 6 (Winter 1981–82): 123–43.
_____. "National Security under Andropov." *Problems of Communism* 32 (January–February 1983): 32–39.
_____. "Are the Soviets Interested in Arms Control?" *Washington Quarterly* 8 (Spring 1985): 147–56.
Smith, Gordon B., ed. *Public Policy and Administration in the Soviet Union*. New York: Praeger, 1980.
Smits, William H., Jr. "Significance of the Question of High-Technology Transfer to the Soviet Union and Soviet Bloc States." *Technology in Society* 8, no. 3 (1986): 157–70.
Solomon, Peter, Jr. *Soviet Criminologists and Criminal Policy: Specialists in Policy Making*. New York: Columbia University Press, 1978.
Spaulding, Wallace. "Communist Fronts in 1985." *Problems of Communism* 35 (March–April 1986): 72–78.

_____. "Shifts in CPSU ID." *Problems of Communism* 35 (July–August 1986): 80–86.

Spechler, Dina. "Permitted Dissent in the Decade after Stalin." In *The Dynamics of Soviet Politics*, ed. Paul Cooks, Robert Daniels, and Nancy Heer. Cambridge: Harvard University Press, 1976.

Steinbrunner, John. "Arms Control: Crisis or Compromise." *Foreign Affairs* 63 (Summer 1985): 1036–47.

Stent, Angela E., ed. *Economic Relations with the Soviet Union: American and West German Perspectives*. Boulder, Colo.: Westview Press, 1985.

Stevens, Sayre. "The Soviet Factor in SDI." *Orbis* 29 (Winter 1986): 689–700.

Strauss, Erich. *Soviet Agriculture in Perspective*. New York: Praeger, 1969.

Strode, Rebecca. "The Soviet Armed Forces: Adaptation to Resource Scarcity." *Washington Quarterly* 9 (Spring 1986): 55–69.

Stubbs, Eric. "Soviet Strategic Defense Technology." *Bulletin of the Atomic Scientists* (April 1987): 14–19.

Sturman, Dora. "Chernenko and Andropov: Ideological Perspectives." *Survey* 28 (Spring 1984): 9–21.

Tatu, Michel. *Power in the Kremlin: From Khrushchev to Kosygin*. New York: Viking Press, 1969.

Taubman, William. *Governing Soviet Cities*. New York: Praeger, 1973.

Teague, Elizabeth. "Signs of Rivalry between Andropov and Chernenko." *Radio Liberty Research Bulletin*, 214/82. New York: Radio Liberty, May 25, 1982.

Thomas, John R. *Natural Resources in Soviet Foreign Policy*. New York: National Strategy Information Center, 1985.

Thornton, Judith. "Chernobyl and Soviet Energy." *Problems of Communism* 35 (November–December 1986): 1–16.

Thornton, Richard C. "Is Detente Inevitable?" East Asia Forum Series. Washington, D.C.: Washington Institute for Values in Public Policy, 1985.

Ulam, Adam B. *Expansion and Coexistence*. 2d ed. New York: Praeger, 1974.

_____. *A History of Soviet Russia*. New York: Praeger, 1976.

Unger, Aryeh. "Politinformator as Agitator: A Decision Blocked." *Problems of Communism* 19 (September–October 1970): 30–43.

United States. Central Intelligence Agency. *Estimated Soviet Defense Spending in Rubles, 1970–1975*. Washington, D.C., May 1976.

United States. Department of Agriculture. "Grains: USSR Grain Situation and Outlook." Foreign Agricultural Circular. Washington, D.C., May 1985.

United States. Department of Defense. *Soviet Military Power 1986*. Washington, D.C.: Government Printing Office, 1986.

Valenta, Jiri, and Potter, William, eds. *Soviet Decisionmaking for National Security.* London: Allen & Unwin, 1984.

Valenta, Jiri, and Valenta, Virginia. "Soviet Strategy and Politics in the Caribbean Basin." In *Rift and Revolution: The Central American Imbroglio,* ed. Howard J. Wiarda. Washington, D.C.: American Enterprise Institute, 1984.

_____. "Sandinistas in Power." *Problems of Communism* 34 (September–October 1985): 1–28.

Valkenier, Elizabeth K. "Revolutionary Change in the Third World: Recent Soviet Reassessments." *World Politics* 38 (April 1986): 415–34.

Van der Kroef, Justus M. "The East-West Conflict and the Cambodian Problem." *Crossroads* 18 (1985): 1–21.

Vigor, Peter. "The Soviet View of Geopolitics." In *On Geopolitics: Classical and Nuclear,* ed. C. E. Zappo and C. Zorgibe. Dordrecht: Martinus N. Nijhoff, 1985.

Volten, Peter M. E. *The Soviet 'Peace Program' and Its Implementation towards the West.* Amsterdam: Foundation for the Promotion of East-West Contacts, Free University, 1977.

Waedekin, Karl-Eugen. *The Private Sector in Soviet Agriculture.* Berkeley: University of California Press, 1973.

Weinstein, John M. "Non-military Threats to the Soviet National Security." *Naval War College Review* 38 (July–August 1985): 28–40.

Wells, Samuel F. "Sounding the Tocsin: NCS 68 and the Soviet Threat." *International Security* 4 (Fall 1979): 116–58.

Wettig, Gerhard. *A New Soviet Approach to Arms Control.* Köln: Berichte des Bundesinstituts für ostwissenschaftliche und internationale Studien, 2, 1987.

White, Stephen. "Propagating Communist Values in the USSR." *Problems of Communism* 34 (November–December 1985): 1–17.

Willis, David K. *Klass: How the Russians Really Live.* New York: St. Martin's Press, 1985.

Wohlstetter, Alfred. "Between the Unfree World and None: Increasing Our Choice." *Foreign Affairs* 63 (Summer 1985): 962–94.

Wolfe, Thomas. *Soviet Strategy at the Crossroads.* Cambridge: Harvard University Press, 1965.

Yanov, Alexander. *Detente after Brezhnev.* Berkeley: University of California, Institute of International Studies, 1977.

_____. *The Russian New Right.* Berkeley: University of California, Institute of International Studies, 1978.

Yanowitch, Murray, and Fisher, Wesley A., eds. *Social Stratification and Mobility in the USSR.* White Plains, N.Y.: International Arts and Sciences Press, 1973.

Zamostny, Thomas J. "Moscow and the Third World: Recent Trends in Soviet Thinking." *Soviet Studies* 36 (April 1984): 223–35.

Zemtsov, Ilya. *Lexicon of Soviet Political Terms*. Fairfax, Va.: Hero Books, 1985.

————. *Policy Dilemmas and the Struggle for Power in the Kremlin. The Andropov Period*. Fairfax, Va.: Hero Books, 1985.

Zlotnik, Marc D. "Chernenko's Platform." *Problems of Communism* 31 (November–December 1982): 70–75.

————. "Chernenko Succeeds." *Problems of Communism* 33 (March–April 1984): 17–31.

Glossary

ACCELERATION (*Uskorenie*). One of the methods of improving the socialist system. The ideology of acceleration derives from the belief that a "better" socialism is possible and feasible. It envisages a transition of Soviet society to a new era marked by such achievements as the doubling of national income and of industrial production by the year 2000 and the attainment by then of economic development no less than that attained by the USSR in its first seventy years. The policy of acceleration, however, requires much more social order and discipline than now exists and a much more advanced level of organization and production.

ANTIALCOHOL CAMPAIGN (*Antialkogol'naya kampaniya*). The totality of measures, legal enactments, and practical steps undertaken by the authorities to counter widespread alcohol abuse. Such campaigns take place periodically, usually shortly after a new leader ascends to power.

CEMA, CMEA, or COMECON, Council of Economic Mutual Aid (*Sev; Sovet ekonomicheskoy vzaimopomoshchi*). The international economic organization of the socialist countries established in 1949. It now includes the countries of the Eastern bloc – the USSR, Bulgaria, Hungary, the GDR, Poland, Romania, and Czechoslovakia – plus Vietnam, Cuba, and Mongolia. Other Communist countries have observer status in the organization.

CENTRAL COMMITTEE OF THE COMMUNIST PARTY OF THE SOVIET UNION (CC, CPSU) (*Tsentral'ny Komitet Kommunisticheskoy Partij Sovetskogo Soyuza [TsK KPSU]*). The CC, CPSU, is selected at the Party Congress. The most recent Congress, the 27th, was convened in 1986 and was attended by 5,000 delegates. They represented over 19 million members of the CPSU and elected 307 full and 170 candidate members to the Central Committee.

Most of those selected as either full or candidate members of the CC, CPSU, are high Party officials: heads of republic, territorial, provincial, and city Party organizations. But a significant number of slots are reserved for the highest echelon of the government bureaucracy: ministers, chairmen of state committees, and army and state security officers. Also represented in the membership are various other Soviet elites, including the artistic and scientific. In other words, membership is firmly pegged to standing in the Party and state bureaucracies. Consequently, representation of the authentic intelligentsia, authentic workers, and authentic peasants, who make up a majority in the Party, is reduced to barely several dozen slots. Their token presence amounts to a façade of democracy because they have no real voice in CC decision making. As stipulated by the CPSU statutes, during the intervals between Party Congresses, the CC, CPSU, is charged with directing all activities of the Party and supervising both central and local Party organizations. In fact, this task is carried out by the Politburo and Central Committee Secretariat, which are chosen at the CC, CPSU, Plenum. The CC, CPSU, also selects the members of the Party Control Committee.

CENTRAL INSPECTION COMMISSION (*Tsentral'naya Revizionnaya Komissiya [TsRK]*). The body whose membership is formally elected at a Party Congress but is in fact determined by the Politburo. Its function is to oversee the speed and correctness of the operations of the central Party bodies, and to exercise supervision over the finances and institutions of the CC, CPSU. At the 27th Congress of the CPSU (in 1986) eighty-eight members were appointed to the Central Inspection Commission.

CHEKA (*Ch.K.*, *Chrezvychaynaya Komissiya*) (Extraordinary Commission). State security service. By derivation, *chekist* means an employee of this service. The CHEKA was established in December 1917, right after the Bolshevik coup, as a body to combat counterrevolution.

The Soviet security service has changed its name several times. In the 1920s its name was GPU (Gosudarstvennoe politupravlenie), the State Political Administration, and the *O[b'edinennoe]GPU*, the United State Political Administration. After World War II it became the *MGB* (*Ministerstvo Gosudarstvennoy Bezopasnosti*), the Ministry of State Security. Since 1954 it has been known as the *KGB* (*Komitet Gosudarstvennoy Bezopasnosti*), the Committee on State Security. Throughout this succession of names, its function has remained the same: repression, unfettered by legal restraint, its targets depending solely on the will and interests of the Party bureaucracy and its leaders.

CPSU, Communist Party of the Soviet Union (*KPSS*; *Kommunisticheskaya Partiya Sovetskogo Soyuza*). Both in abbreviation and in its full form the term appears mostly in official documents. In oral discourse it is replaced by the more laconic "the Party," as the CPSU came to be known ca. 1920 when all other parties in the USSR were liquidated.

The CPSU presently has a membership of over 19 million. Although it is hailed as the guiding or ruling power, in actuality it is not the Party as a whole that rules over the country but, rather, the apparat or bureaucracy of several hundreds of thousands of professional Party workers who impose their authority and will on the state and social institutions and organizations.

According to the Party statutes, anyone can resign from the Party at will. The voluntary character of Party membership is nevertheless a fiction. Withdrawal from the Party always ends up as expulsion from its ranks, and the status of an expellee is tantamount to the status of a criminal offender in that it entails social and political ostracization.

CONGRESS OF THE COMMUNIST PARTY OF THE SOVIET UNION (*S'ezd KPSS*). A Congress of the CPSU is convened at least every five years by the Central Committee of the CPSU after a resolution of the Politburo and a recommendation of the Secretariat of the Central Committee. In violation of the statutory stipulation to this effect, however, not a single Party Congress was held in the years 1939–53. There was no need to convene one because the Party apparat under Stalin arrogated to itself the authority and functions of the Congress as the highest Party body, together with all its prerogatives in determining the strategy and tactics of the Party and approving its policies and activities. From the time that regular convocation of the Congresses resumed, proceedings have assumed the character of spectacles, of mere forums for speeches of the Party leaders rather than genuinely deliberative sessions. The Congress of the CPSU also rubber-stamps the recommendations of the Politburo for membership in the Central Committee and its Party Control Committee.

COUNCIL OF MINISTERS OF THE USSR (*Sovet ministrov SSSR*). Formally the highest executive body of government but actually an appendage to the Party bureaucracy acting under the supervision of the Politburo and of the Secretariat of the Central Committee, the Council of Ministers. It deals mainly with economic and, to a lesser extent, social affairs.

The members of the Council of Ministers, its chairman, his deputies, the various ministers, and chairmen of state committees are formally selected by the Supreme Soviet at a joint meeting of its two chambers, the Soviet of the Union and the Soviet of Nationalities. In fact, the Supreme Soviet merely rubber-stamps the personnel decisions of the Politburo and Central Committee Secretariat passed on in the form of the supposed "recommendations" of the two latter bodies to the former.

Formally, the Council of Ministers is subordinate to the Supreme Soviet and its Presidium, but in fact it is supervised by the Central Committee of the CPSU acting through its Secretariat and the Politburo.

The Presidium of the Council of Ministers, consisting of the chairman and his deputies, operates as a permanent body in charge of issues of government administration and the economy. For specific purposes, a minister or several ministers may be co-opted to the Presidium.

One of the oddities of the Soviet government structure is the fact that it has not one but several *first* deputies of the Council's chairman. The total number of deputies of the chairman of the Council varies between twelve and sixteen, and the number of ministers and chairmen of state committees in the Council of Ministers fluctuates around one hundred. The chairmen of the councils of ministers of the union republics are *ex officio* members of the Council of Ministers of the USSR.

CULT OF PERSONALITY (*Kul't lichnosti*). Phrase used in the USSR from 1956 on to describe Stalin's rule. The concept covers virtually everything Stalin and his accomplices did: mass reprisals and convictions, policy errors, economic disasters, and so on.

DEMOCRATIZATION (*Demokratizatsiya*). The process of limited liberalization begun in the Soviet Union in the second half of the 1980s. Democratization is a travesty of democracy. It does not offer all Soviet citizens equal rights and freedoms but rather seeks more effective ways to impose socialism on them. Subjectively, the Soviet leadership has been and remains in favor of authoritarian methods of control. But such methods have proved to be rather ineffective as means of organizing and mobilizing the masses. It would be dangerous to resort to terror of the type used in the 1930s because it might boomerang on the Soviet elite itself. These considerations compelled the Soviet leaders to opt for some measures of political liberalization, first of all in economics, where they were designed to effect a transition from administrative forms of management to reliance on economic incentives. Democratization also entails granting some, even if limited, independence to enterprises, making their operations economically accountable and effecting their transition to self-financing status.

FIVE-YEAR PLAN (*Pyatiletka*). Five-year plan for the economic development of the country. Since 1928 the centralized command of the economy has directed Soviet development through the medium of five-year segments, each with set objectives to be met no later than at the end of that period.

GENERAL SECRETARY (*General'ny Sekretar'* or *Gensek*). Head of the Communist Party, and hence the most powerful official in the Soviet Union. His power has no basis in the constitution or any other Soviet legislation. He is elected by the Plenum of the Central Committee on the recommendation of the Politburo. However, there have been instances when the Central Committee refused to accept the Politburo recommendation. In 1957 it ignored the call of the Politburo (then known as the Presidium) to oust Khrushchev, and in 1984 it chose Chernenko as *gensek*, even though in the Politburo he did not have a majority.

GLASNOST. Openness within limits, or criticism to the extent allowed by the present Soviet leadership to its citizens. Glasnost completely fits within the framework of Communist control over society because it stops short of permitting genuine freedom of expression; its scope is restricted to suit the authorities' interests.
    Gorbachev's espousal of glasnost had several causes. Among them were the intention to revitalize the Soviet economy via increased involvement of the masses in the management of production, and the desire of the new Soviet leadership to put an end to the struggle for power in the Kremlin. Glasnost, in the form of broad popular criticism of the failures of recent rulers, aids Gorbachev and his associates in struggles with their rivals and opponents. Thus, the limits and scope of glasnost in the Soviet Union are determined by Communist authorities. As long as glasnost serves the latter, it will be pursued and encouraged, but as soon as it collides with the ends or means of Communist policy, it will be quashed.

GORKOM (*Gorodskoy Komitet*). City Party committee.

KOLKHOZ (abbreviation for *kollektivnoe khozyaystvo*, literally collective farm). The first kolkhozes were established in the USSR soon after the Bolshevik coup. In the 1930s the kolkhozes were established by force, in the end almost completely replacing private farms. The word *kolkhoznik*, member of a collective farm in its literal meaning, is also used figuratively to refer to a disorganized, sluggish, uncultured person.

KOMSOMOL (*Kommunistichesky Soyuz Molodezhi*). Abbreviated version of full name, *Vsesoyuzny Leninsky Kommunistichesky Soyuz Molodezhi* (VLKSM). The Komsomol is the youth branch of the Party. Founded in 1918, in the second half of the 1980s its membership is over 40 million. Its structure replicates that of the Party, and its functions reflect those of the Party as defined in the Party statutes.

KRAYKOM (*Kraevoy komitet*). Territorial Party committee.

KULAK. Term employed during the early years of Soviet history to refer to rich peasants.

MILITIA (*Militsiya*). Government police force charged with enforcing public order, established in 1917. It is formally subordinated to the local soviets, but is actually subordinate to the Ministry of Internal Affairs (the MVD).

MVD (*Ministerstvo Vnutrennikh Del*). Ministry of Internal Affairs. Police Department, the Penal Institutions (corrective camps and colonies) Department, and the Political Department are its most important departments. During World War II the same institution was known under the name *Narodny Kommissariat Vnutrennikh Del* (NKVD), or People's Commissariat of Internal Affairs, and in the early 1960s under the name *Ministerstvo Okhrany Obshchestvennogo Poryadka* (MOOP), the Ministry for the Preservation of Social Order.

NEW ECONOMIC POLICY (NEP; *Novaya ekonomicheskaya politika*). The complex of agricultural and industrial reforms carried out in the Soviet Union in the 1920s. NEP marked the Soviet authorities' rejection of their policy of building communism instantly and led to the revival within the Communist system of some elements of capitalism, e.g. of the market mechanism, private property, and so on.

NEW POLITICAL THINKING (*Novoe politicheskoe myshlenie*). Foreign policy concept of the Soviet leadership involving a rejection of some of the ideological postulates of Marxism in regard to other countries. It is defined as aiming at basing foreign policy on humanistic rather than class foundations, at putting the interests of other states on a level equal to one's own state, at supporting global aid programs to underdeveloped countries, at renouncing war, in particular nuclear war, as a means of resolving international conflicts, and so on. The new political thinking reflects the evident inability of the Communists to impose their political will on the rest of the world—at least at the present time.

OBKOM (*Oblastnoy komitet*). Provincial Party committee.

PARTY CONTROL COMMITTEE (*Komitet Partiynogo Kontrolya* [KPK]). Agency of the Central Committee in charge of assessing the responsibility of Party members for infractions of the Party program, statutes, or discipline, as well as civil law. The KPK also reviews appeals of the decisions of republic and local Party organizations to expel members from the Party or otherwise punish them. Basically, however, the KPK and its republic branches function as a kind of closed-access court to protect Party members guilty of crimes or discipline infractions from criminal prosecution. No prosecution of a high-ranking Party member by judicial bodies can begin without the approval of the KPK.

PARTY MEMBER (*Partiets*). Literally refers to a member of the Communist Party. But the term has connotations that are narrower in scope and more specific in content because it often denotes not just any rank-and-file member of the Party but only a Party bureaucrat who is a member of the privileged, elite stratum of professional Party functionaries.

PERESTROIKA. The social and economic policy aimed at improving the government and social structure of the USSR. In Soviet propaganda perestroika is often presented as a kind of social revolution. In actuality, it merely refers to gradual change within socialist society to be carried out through piecemeal reforms, mainly in the sector of the economy where the policy intention is to effect a change from methods of highly centralized control to granting the enterprises a margin of decision-making freedom in planning and management.

PLENUM OF THE CENTRAL COMMITTEE. Meeting of the members of the Central Committee. According to the statutes of the Communist Party of the Soviet Union, plenary meetings (Plenums) of the Central Committee should be convened at least once every six months. In contrast to full members, candidate members attend Plenums in an advisory capacity, with the right to express their views but without the right to vote. At Plenum sessions, as a rule, the members of the Central Inspection Commission are present. The Plenums discuss topical political issues and the work of the Party apparat and the government bodies.

POLITBURO (*Politbyuro*) (referred to from 1952 to 1966 as the Presidium). The highest body of the Central Committee of the Party, selected at the Plenum of the committee to direct the activity of the Party and the government. The Politburo concentrates its attention on key issues of domestic and foreign affairs. The range of issues discussed at Politburo meetings (which take place weekly, on Thursdays, and are chaired by the general secretary) is broad and diversified. Issues that exceed Politburo members' scope of competence may be referred to special commissions for problem analysis and submission of reports. Full Politburo membership fluctuates from eleven to sixteen.

The Politburo was established as a permanent body in 1919 at the 8th Congress of the Party. Its initial task was to make decisions about problems too urgent to be deferred until the next session of the Central Committee. Gradually, however, the Politburo usurped the latter's role and became an oligarchy monopolizing the highest authority in the country. Under Stalin the composition of the Politburo was totally arbitrary, determined only by the despot's whim. After Stalin certain objective criteria began to be applied in selecting Politburo members. Slots came to be reserved for the chairman of the Council of Ministers of the USSR and the chairman of the Presidium of the

Supreme Soviet of the USSR. Slots as either full or candidate members also go to first deputy chairmen of the Supreme Soviet (one or two slots); first secretaries of the most important Party committees, e.g., of the Ukraine (always), of Belorussia, Kazakhstan, Moscow, and Leningrad (usually), and also, alternatively, to heads of the Party organizations of the Transcaucasus and the Baltic republics. Incumbents of the office of minister of defense, minister of foreign affairs, and chairman of the KGB also stand a good chance of becoming Politburo members.

PRESIDIUM *See* Politburo.

RAYKOM (*Rayonny komitet*). Regional Party committee.

RSFSR (*Russkaya Sovestskaya Federativnaya Sotsialisticheskaya Respublika*). Russian Soviet Federal Socialist Republic, one of the fifteen Soviet Union republics.

SECRETARIAT OF THE CENTRAL COMMITTEE (*Sekretariat TsK*). Ruling organ of the Central Committee for conducting routine business of the Party and the government. Its membership is selected at the committee plenum. The Secretariat selects and assigns personnel, directs the activity of central Party and government institutions, and oversees the implementation of resolutions passed by the Politburo and plenum.

The Secretariat was established as a permanent Party body in 1920, after the 9th Party Congress. Initially, it had three members but with time its membership increased; recently it has had ten or eleven members. The secretaries fall into three categories: senior secretaries, those who are full Politburo members; regular secretaries, those who are candidate Politburo members; and junior secretaries, those who are members of the Central Committee only. Each secretary has his own area/s of responsibility and, accordingly, department/s of the Central Committee under his authority.

Political oversight of the work of the Secretariat is exercised by the general secretary. Its operational oversight is the responsibility of the (unofficial) second Central Committee secretary. The general secretary, as a rule, conducts the meetings of the Secretariat, which are generally held once a week.

SEREDNYAK. Term employed during the early years of Soviet history to refer to well-off peasants.

SOVIETS (*Sovety*), or councils. In theory legislative bodies of government. The Soviets, from the Supreme Soviet to local soviets, are elected by direct ballot. The elections are neither universal, because the population by and large boycotts them, nor democratic, because all candidates have to be recommended by the Party organizations. Until recently, with the exception of a brief period just after the Revolution, there was only one candidate for each position, but in 1987 two or more candidates were allowed to run. This innovation was introduced on an experimental basis. However, because competing candidates were all selected by Party committees, the choice was hardly a free one.

The terms of Soviets range from five years for the Supreme Soviets of the union and republics to two and a half years for the territorial, provincial, regional, city, and rural Soviets. At the opening meeting of each new term the local Soviets select, from a list provided by the Party, the members of their own executive committees and of the Supreme Soviets, or their Presidiums. Neither the executive committees nor the Presidiums have any real political influence; they deal only with day-to-day social affairs.

SOVKHOZ (abbreviation for *Sovetskoe khozyaystvo*, literally Soviet farm). In contrast to a *kolkhoz*, which is formally a cooperative, the *sovkhoz* is a state enterprise.

SUPREME SOVIET OF THE USSR. According to the Soviet constitution, the highest body of power. In fact, it is a façade for the nonexistent Soviet democracy. It has no political power and no real influence or executive authority. It consists of two chambers: the Soviet of the Union, elected proportionally by electoral districts, and the Soviet of Nationalities, elected according to the following key: thirty-two delegates from each union republic, eleven from each autonomous republic, five from each autonomous province, and one from each autonomous district.

Annotated Index

Adzhubey, V. (journalist; Khrushchev's son-in-law; editor in chief, *Izvestiya*, early 1960s; after Khrushchev's fall removed from CC and Supreme Soviet), 176.

Afanasev, V. G. (philosopher; member of the Academy of Sciences; member, CC; editor in chief, *Pravda*, 1976–present (pres.); expert on "scientific Communism" and social control), 125, 167, 195, 196.

Aganbekyan, A. G. (economist; member, Academy of Sciences; expert on labor productivity, wages, living standards, economic modeling; academic secretary, Department of Economics, Academy of Sciences; adviser to Gorbachev), 213.

Agca, Ali (Turkish terrorist imprisoned for assassination attempt on Pope John Paul II), 255.

Aleksandrov-Agentov, A. M. (aide to Brezhnev, 1965–82; expertise in international relations), 63, 85.

Aliev, G. A. (first deputy chairman, Council of Ministers; member, Politburo; career due to patronage of Brezhnev and Andropov; chairman, KGB of Azerbaijan, 1967–69; first secretary, CC, CP of Azerbaidzhan), 1969–82), 121, 125, 133, 148, 154, 155, 158, 161, 180, 184, 188–90, 260, 268.

Allilueva, S. (Stalin's daughter, now living in England), 254.

Altman, S. (Moldavian writer criticized by Chernenko for "infiltrating bourgeois ideals into Soviet literature"), 27.

Ananyev, A. A. (writer; editor in chief, journal *Oktyabr*, 1973–pres.), 222.

Andropov, I. Yu. (diplomat; special ambassador, Foreign Ministry; son, Yu. V. Andropov), 155.

Andropov, Yu. V. (general secretary, CC, 1982–84; from 1983, simultaneously chairman, Presidium of the Supreme Soviet; before becoming member of Politburo, KGB head for more than 15 years), xi, 2, 39, 67, 100, 103, 104, 117, 123–50, 153–79, 182–84, 186, 188, 189, 191–95, 198, 204–6, 213, 214, 216–24, 231, 232, 235, 238, 245, 254, 255, 258, 263, 264.

Antonov, S. (head, Bulgarian Balkanturist office in Rome; accused of planning assassination attempt on Pope John Paul II), 255.

Aristov, A. B. (secretary, CC, 1952–53, 1955–60), 41, 60.

Arkhipov, I. V. (deputy chairman, 1974–80, and first deputy chairman, 1980–86, Council of Ministers), 254.

Barghoorn, F. (Yale University Sovietologist held by Soviets until intercession of President Kennedy), 74.

Belyaev, N. I. (member, CC Presidium, 1957–60; supported Khrushchev against opposition, 1957; subsequently fell into Khrushchev's disfavor), 54, 61.

Beria, L. P. (associate of Stalin's; for many years head of security services; shot in 1953 for attempt to organize coup), 12, 39.

Bitov, O. (staff member, *Literaturnaya gazeta*; on KGB assignment in 1983 staged defection to West), 255–57.